INTRODUCTION TO COMPUTER MUSIC

INTRODUCTION TO
COMPUTER MUSIC

Wayne Bateman

A WILEY-INTERSCIENCE PUBLICATION

JOHN WILEY & SONS
NEW YORK CHICHESTER BRISBANE TORONTO

Library of Congress Cataloging in Publication Data:

Bateman, Wayne, 1951–
Introduction to computer music.

"A Wiley-Interscience publication."
Includes index.
1. Computer composition. 2. Computer sound processing. I. Title.

MT41,B37 781.6′1′02854 79-26361
ISBN 0-471-05266-3

Printed in the United States of America

10 9 8 7 6 5 4 3 2 1

PREFACE

Can a computer create music? It can as much as a violin or a piano can create music. A computer is a tool; it is not a musician. If a computer, like a conventional musical instrument, is used to make music, it requires an operator who is a musician.

This book is for musicians. It is intended for composers and students of contemporary music who are interested in the application of electronic technology to the arts. In the 30 years since the invention of the tape recorder, many modern composers have begun to realize the tremendous possibilities that electronic devices offer them. Electronic music composition is probably one of the fastest growing trends in the arts in the last decade. It is widely utilized from the concert hall to the television commercial studio. Consequently, contemporary composers have a great reason to be interested and fluent in the use of electronic musical instruments.

The digital computer is the most recent and most powerful electronic device to be introduced to the music scene. Although computers have had scientific and technical uses for 30 years, it is only in the last few years that their capabilities for sound synthesis have been developed and explored. Computers that talk are just now reaching the market. Technicians interested in electronic music are demonstrating that computers can synthesize speech, and can be programmed to create musical tones of unlimited variety and versatility. Thus, to the contemporary musician, the computer is the most recent and provocative of musical instruments.

The artistic and technological development of computer music is still in its infancy. It is an outgrowth of the electronic music movement, which itself has had only 20 years of development. The current explosion of computer technology indicates that computer music will proliferate in the next decade, extending even beyond the conventional nondigital electronic medium from which it was born. It is impossible for any book to define what computer music actually is. Art defines itself as it evolves, and the artistic definition and analysis of computer music will have to be done by future musicologists only after major computer compositions have had time to be written and establish themselves.

This book describes what a computer is, how it operates, and how it can be made to produce music. Most musicians are not electrical engineers, but computer music composition requires a fair understanding of basic mathematics, computer science, acoustics, and several other related fields. Fortunately, in spite of their complexity, computers can now be programmed by people with a minimal background in simple algebra and electronics. Although the reader is expected to have a general understanding of music theory, he or she need not be a mathematics or engineering student. The material is presented in mostly nontechnical explanations.

This book discusses computer music in terms of its theoretical possibilities. It does not attempt to report on the actual hardware, devices, programs, and systems that have been developed at various institutions. Such a presentation would serve only the few people who have access to a particular system, and would very soon become obsolete. This book also avoids a cumbersome technical description of how digital electronic equipment is designed and built. Hence it would help the reader to actually build a system for computer music synthesis. Nevertheless, this depth of technical knowledge is not needed by composers and students who use computer facilities as they are operating.

To use a computer artistically to create interesting musical sounds, a composer must know more than basic music theory and computer programming. He or she must understand what sound is, how it is naturally produced and transmitted, and how a computer can be programmed to simulate the behavior of natural sound sources. The composer must know what a musical tone is, and what distinguishes it from noise. He or she must be capable of analyzing a musical sound acoustically and mathematically to determine its properties, just as a musicologist analyzes the score of a symphony for its style. With the knowledge gained from such acoustical analysis, a composer can use the computer to invent new, interesting, and original musical sounds to be used in a new family of compositions. This book is therefore addressed to the analysis and synthesis of complex musical tones.

When the reader becomes familiar with the techniques of computer sound synthesis, he or she is ready to mathematically compose original tones from their fundamental acoustical building blocks just as melodic phrases are composed from the notes of the scale. The composer of computer music is a pioneer, because the ability to create original sounds purely from scratch has not been available to past generations. The variety of sounds that a computer can create is limited only by the composer's imagination, and every aspect of the generated sound is under his or her explicit control. The infinite flexibility of the computer thus demands even more knowledge, creativity, and skill than traditional music.

Wayne Bateman

Salt Lake City, Utah
February 1980

CONTENTS

INTRODUCTION TO COMPUTER MUSIC

1

THE COMPUTER AND THE MUSICIAN

Can a digital computer compose music? Can it be considered a musical instrument? It is possible for a computer to produce patterns of musical sounds with a loudspeaker and other audio electronic equipment. In fact, unlike other musical instruments, the variety of the sounds that a computer can produce is without limit. It is interesting to compare a computer and a piano. Each of the piano's 88 keys makes a nearly unique sound when struck. The sequence of notes played on the piano is determined by the composer and the performing pianist. The tonal quality, or timbre, of a note is always similar if the key is depressed with the same force. An accomplished pianist can use the keys of the piano to create beautiful lyrical music, and the piano has long been recognized as the most versatile and universal of musical instruments. But only a player piano can perform by itself, and then only according to a preset note sequence inscribed on a paper roll. No piano can be made to sound like a clarinet or a violin, regardless of how accomplished the performing pianist is. A computer, however, can generate data patterns that can be converted into musical structures. It also has the theoretical capability of emulating any instrument or ensemble of instruments. It can, at least in theory, be programmed to imitate the sound of a cymbal crash, a harp, a human voice, a bell, a tuba, a belching frog, a touch-tone telephone, the London Symphony Orchestra, or the Mormon Tabernacle Choir.

This comparison is not to undermine the capabilities of pianos or other conventional musical instruments. Its purpose is to create a perspective whereby the computer may be compared with the musical instruments long familiar to people. To understand what one can accomplish with a computer, we may contrast it with other instruments. The claim that a computing machine can compose or synthesize any possible sound is very bold indeed, but there is a catch. The catch is that the computer is void of any creative intelligence. To make any sound at all, it must be given explicit instructions that detail exactly how the sound is to be created. Although one may easily say that a computer can create a melody for or imitate the sound of a violin, it is much more difficult to mathematically define a sequential procedure that a nonthinking machine can follow to perform such a feat.

It is understandably difficult to imagine a computer composing music. A human artist generally composes according to his or her intuitive impulses. But a computer is a deterministic machine that does not have creative impulses or artistic intuition. It can only act according to explicitly defined procedures. The procedures that the computer is to follow in generating sound patterns must therefore be defined in advance by a human programmer. Consequently, an assertion that a computer can *spontaneously* compose music would be highly questionable if not altogether inaccurate.

Although it takes one years of training and practice to perform on the piano, to play a single note requires no more than the trivial act of depressing a key. The performer certainly does not need to explain to the piano *how* to make the sound. The piano does that automatically like other conventional instruments, and the quality of its tone is determined by its mechanical properties. A piano note will always sound the same as long as the piano is not damaged or mechanically modified.

With a computer the situation is the exact opposite. The computer can do nothing until it is programmed *how* to do it. When the computer finally does generate a sound, the nature of that sound is a direct outcome of the instructions input into the machine. This raises an interesting question: how does one explain in precise logical terms what makes an oboe sound like an oboe? It is easy to say that the instrument's low B sounds like a duck, but a computer does not know what a duck sounds like. It is also useless to describe a tone as being "bright" or "dark," because the computer is not poetic enough to comprehend those terms. The computer must be told everything in explicit mathematical logic. Suppose that we want a computer to generate a tone having the timbre of a flute, but the onset of a plucked string. Although this description of the sound requires less than a single sentence, its understanding demands cognitive intelligence. It also requires recollection of past sensory experience with sounds created by flutes and plucked strings. The computer lacks both the intelligence and the experience. So how would one *logically* explain to the computer or even to another human being how to compute the sequence of voltages to drive a loudspeaker for it to sound like a plucked string with the tone color of a flute? This is the challenge facing one who wishes to program a computer to synthesize musical sounds.

Another important distinction arises between the computer and conventional musical instruments. Traditionally the production of musical events has always been shared by the composers, the performers, and the instruments. No performer can make a cheap violin sound like a Stradivarius, and the best quality instrument cannot compensate for a poor performance. But in the case of computers, a composition will sound no different on a Honeywell machine than it will on a DEC or IBM. More importantly, the composition of computer music and tape-recorded electronic music is its own performance—they are the same event. This does not dehumanize the composition because it is still entirely the creation of a human being. What does happen, nevertheless, that is disconcerting to listeners, is that the human appearance becomes more remote from the audience. The prearranged mechanical performance creates the false impression that the artistic role has been assumed by a machine. Actually the human integrity of a computer composition should seem no further removed than an orchestra recorded on a stereo LP phonograph.

Although it is generally true that the performance of computer music is comprised in the composition, the statement should be qualified. In some cases a computer can perform "live" if it is operating in *real time*. This implies that the computer is performing computation fast enough to produce sound continously without delay. A computer interfaced with a keyboard can do this and function similar to an electric organ. But while modern computer music systems can generally accommodate real-time performance, this is not always done in practice. The greatest limitation to real-time operation is the tremendous amount of information required for a computer to synthesize complex and interesting musical sounds. It is difficult, if not impossible, for a person to input the entirety of this information fast enough to accomplish this. Even a large computer may require minutes of computing time to perform all the necessary calculations to generate a few seconds of sound if the tones are varied and complex.

To illustrate how a computer may be employed to generate musical sounds, the following procedure outlines some of the steps necessary in preparing a composition for computer performance:

1. **Write a sequence of instructions to the computer.** Indicate how to synthesize the desired sounds as well as the starting times, durations, envelopes, and dynamic levels of each tone.
2. **Start the computer to run the program.** As mentioned before, the computer will ordinarily require much more time than the tone's actual duration to perform the necessary computation for its synthesis. If the computer is performing in real time, however, much of the required information will have been input in advance of the performance.
3. **Instruct the computer to store the results in memory.** This step is only necessary if the computer is not working in real time. The computation will result in a long table of numbers representing electrical voltages. Such a table may have 30,000 numbers to comprise one full second of sound. These numbers represent a sequence of voltages that will drive a loudspeaker. The computer stores this list of numbers in its memory as it performs the computations.
4. **Convert the computed results into actual sound.** This is accomplished by an electronic device called a *digital-to-analog converter* (DAC). It functions by reading a number from the computer's memory

> and generating a voltage whose level is equal to that number. Let us suppose that the computer has finished running a program for 10 seconds of a composition. It has stored a table of 300,000 numbers in its memory representing the voltage levels of the desired electrical signal at 1/30,000-second intervals. The DAC has a clock that will be set to 30,000 samples per second. It will proceed then to output the voltages corresponding to the numbers in the table once every 1/30,000 second. Thus the 300,000 tabulated numbers in the computer's memory will result in a 10-second sequence of voltages at the output of the DAC. The discrete voltages are smoothed by a low-pass filter into a continuous fluctuating electrical signal. This signal can then be tape-recorded or amplified and converted to sound by a loudspeaker.

The procedure just described is quite complex and will be elaborated in the remainder of this book. It is important to realize at the outset what the computer is *not* doing as much as what it actually *is* doing. The reader has undoubtedly noticed from the mention of DAC that the computer itself does not make the sounds in a composition directly. The sounds are made by the apparatus attached to the outside of the computer. The only noise I know of that a computer makes by itself is the whir of its cooling fans and disk drive units. Neither does the computer originate any of the musical ideas of a composition. That is the responsibility of the composer-programmer. What the computer does do is process data. It does not accomplish anything that cannot also be done by a person with a pencil, paper, and hand calculator. The difference is that the computer can perform an amount of arithmetic in a millisecond, which would take a person several minutes by hand calculation. Although the computer promises to be a marvelously versatile new musical instrument, it will never replace the musician any more than did the electric organ, the piano, harpsicord, flute, or lyre at the time of their invention.

At the time of this writing, a full-sized digital computer is both physically and conceptually a formidable piece of machinery. For a computer to have the memory capacity and the processing speed necessary to be useful in synthesizing a musical composition in a realistic amount of time, it must be too large to be portable and too expensive to be within the means of the average consumer. However, the technology of computer manufacture is advancing with such incredible speed that in a few years this will no longer be true.

A brief examination of how rapidly the computer industry has advanced in the past 25 years dramatizes what one may expect of it in the near future. In 1950 a computer was built that was the grandfather of today's modern commercial computing systems. It was called the UNIVAC 1, was made out of vacuum tubes and filled a large room. Some of the computers built in the 1950s were so horrendous that they required full-time electrical engineers just to continually replace the vacuum tubes as they burned out. Obviously, such machines consumed megawatts of power and cost a king's ransom to manufacture, operate, and maintain. Yet those dinosour computers had less capability than a modern $300, battery-operated microprocessor.

A single vacuum tube occupies about 4 cubic inches of space, consumes several watts of power, and costs about $5. One tube can function as a single logical element, that is, a gate or a flip-flop, of a computer circuit. It is necessary for even a small computer to contain thousands of such logical elements. Hence the reason why vacuum tube computers were so colossally large and expensive. In the 1060s the transistor revolution made the vacuum tube virtually obsolete. While a transistor performs the same duty as a vacuum tube, it is only the size of a pencil eraser, consumes only a few milliwatts of power, and does not wear out, requiring periodic replacement.

The 1970s have marked another revolution in electronic circuitry. Semiconductor integrated circuits can contain more than 100,000 transistors etched on a silicon chip the size of a thumbtack head. A connecting path in such a circuit has a width narrower than the diameter of a red blood cell. The circuitry for the entire processing unit of a microcomputer is often comprised in a single such integrated circuit chip, circuitry that 20 years ago would have filled a large cabinet. Whereas a single logical device cost several dollars in 1958, in 1978 its cost is comparable to the expense of printing a word on the page of a book. Integrated circuits usually require trivial amounts of electric current to operate, and some of them are so voltage-sensitive that if they are handled, shipped, or stored improperly, they can be damaged by the static electricity in dry air.

This situation projects what the world of computers is destined to become in the next decade as further advances are made in digital technology and the cost and size of electronic components continues to plummet. From this one can confidently predict that musicians interested in computer compositions will soon be able to afford and accommodate their own personal computer facilities as easily as one can own and play a piano.

This book is aimed at the composer who is interested in synthesizing musical tones with a computer. Its objective is to outline some of the basic concepts necessary to do this without extensive training in engineering or mathematics. This presentation introduces some ideas and theories in computing, acoustics, and signal processing that are fundamental to computer music synthesis. This information is normally presented in physics, engineering, and computing textbooks in a format that requires training in advanced calculus. However, the following chapters will try to discuss these topics without relying on much esoteric mathematical terminology.

The introduction of this chapter juxtaposed the computer with the piano and other conventional musical instruments. It should also appropriately discuss electronic music in context with the computer. The age of electronics in music was introduced in America in 1952 when a large loudspeaker in a cabinet was placed on stage to "perform" during a concert led by Leopold Stokowsky at the New York Museum of Modern Art. Since that time tape-recorded and live electronic music has penetrated the musical scene with a spectacular impact. Computer music has been an outgrowth of electronic music and is very often confused with its predecessor. Nevertheless, the two are fundamentally different from each other. All the computer's operations are performed digitally, and its output consists of discrete numbers as opposed to live electric signals.

The equipment in an electronic music studio consists of analog devices that directly generate and process continuous voltages. Its output is generated in real time and can be monitored as it is working. It is not programmed on a teletype or with punched cards as is a computer, but is controlled with patch cords, dials, and switches. An electronic synthesizer is a network of various modules, each having a specialized function in signal processing or generation. A typical synthesizer contains several oscillators, filters, voltage-controlled amplifiers, mixers, voltage processors, trigger generators, ring modulators, envelope generators, and a sequencer. These units of the synthesizer are connected with patch cords like a telephone operator's switching panel. They may be patched together for control and modification of their outputs, which in turn may regulate still other modules. One operates a synthesizer by patching its modules and setting volume, duration time, pitch, and other controls on its front panel. The variety of possible configurations and settings on the synthesizer is nearly infinite. Consequently, the sound that emanates from a synthesizer is very unpredictable, and the composer typically reaches results by experimentation and repeated trial and error. He or she will repatch, reset, and readjust the controls until an interesting sound is heard and then tape-record it.

By contrast, the computer programmer-composer is often not working within the limitations of real time. If this is the case, he is not able to hear what he is composing immediately. This would be like a pianist having to play on a silent keyboard and then wait until after he has finished the selection before hearing what he has played. Like a composer on the synthesizer, a computer composer will have to experiment and modify the programs several times before obtaining desirable results. This may become tedious, but the product of a computer music program will always remain consistent and controllable. A synthesizer patch, on the other hand, could probably never be exactly duplicated or repeated with all its control settings.

One might incorrectly infer from this discussion that computers and synthesizers must operate exclusively from each other. But the example of digital sound synthesis involving D-to-A conversion is not the only way a computer can be used to make music. A digital computer and an analog synthesizer may be coordinated so that the computer is programmed to control the modules of the synthesizer. In this way the synthesizer still produces the sounds, but its controls are set and changed automatically by the computer rather than by hand. This can relieve the composer of a tremendous burden since he or she only has two hands to manipulate nearly a hundred controls. A computer-controlled synthesizer consequently has much more flexibility than a manually controlled instrument.

The introduction of electronics to music has in a very short time opened tremendous possibilities in the expansion of the art. While its influence is felt across the whole musical spectrum from television commercials to the concert hall, it has done nothing and can do nothing to detract from the heritage established by Bach, Mozart, Beethoven, Brahms, and the other great geniuses of musical tradition. Although the patterns and norms they set are generally no longer followed in modern compositions (in or out of the electronic studio), their place in our musical heritage is indelibly engraved, and will never disappear. The developments of modern music, be it electronic, computerized, instrumental, or vocal, are only additions to the culture that has already been established. They can substract nothing from it, and have no intention of doing so. The innovators in the electronic medium have no less appreciation for Beethoven than Beethoven had for Mozart. But like Beethoven, today's creative, experimenting composers realize that the established musical traditions are not the end of the art's evolution but are part of its continuous development.

The aesthetic merits of various computer and electronic compositions will be properly evaluated only by the next century's musicologists. For the time being, we will have to sit back and allow the failures and the mediocrity to fade away while the great works will remain, becoming the established patterns of the future. This is a general statement that applies to the evolution of the arts, sciences, technology, and even organic life itself. The direction that this evolution will take in the arts is determined by the artist and not by the medium of the art. The medium, the inventions, and the art itself follow the creative human intellect.

REFERENCES

Alles, H. G., "*A Portable Digital Sound Synthesis System*," *Computer Music Journal* 1(4), 5–9 (1977).

Alonso, S., J. Appleton, & C. Jones, "*A Special Purpose Digital System for Musical Instruction, Composition, and Performance*," *CHUM* **10**, 209–215 (1976).

Appleton, J., & R. C. Perera, Eds., *The Development and Practice of Electronic Music*, Prentice-Hall, 1975.

Buxton, W., E. A. Fogels, G. Fedorkow, L. Sasaki, & K. C. Smith, "An Introduction on the SSSP Digital Synthesizer," *Computer Music Journal* 1(4), 16–21 (1977).

Byrd, Donald, "An Integrated Computer Music Software System," *Computer Music Journal* **1**(2), 55–60 (1977).

Divilbliss, J. L. "The Real-Time Generation of Music with a Digital Computer," *Journal of Music Theory* **8,** 99–111 (1964).

Fedorkow, G., W. Buxton, & K. C. Smith, "A Computer-Controlled Sound Distribution System for the Performance of Electroacoustic Music," *Computer Music Journal* **2**(3), 33–42 (1978).

Ferretti, Ercolino, "The Computer as a Tool for the Creative Musician," *Computers for the Humanities?* A Record of the Conference Sponsored by Yale University, Jan. 22–23, 1965, 107–112, Yale University Press.

Ferretti, Ercolino, "Some Research Notes on Music with the Computer," *American Society of University Composers: Proceedings* **1,** 38–41 (1966).

Franco, S., *Hardware Design of a Real-Time Musical System*, PhD thesis, University of Illinois, Urbana, 1974.

Freedman, David M., "A Digital Computer for the Electronic Music Studio," *Journal of the Audio Engineering Society* **15,** 43–50 (1967).

Gabura, J. & G. Ciamaga, "Digital Computer Control of Sound-Generating Apparatus for the Production of Electronic Music," *Electronic Music Review* **1,** 54–57 (1967).

Gabura, J. & G. Ciamaga, "Computer Control of Sound Apparatus for Electronic Music," *Journal of the Audio Engineering Society* **16** (1968).

Howe, Hubert, *Electronic Music Synthesis: Concepts, Facilities, Techniques*, Norton, 1975.

Howe, Hubert, "Composing by Computer," CHUM **9**(6), 281–290 (1975).

Howe, Hubert, "Electronic Music and Microcomputers," Perspectives of New Music, **16**(1), 70–84 (1977).

Koenig, Gottfried, "The Use of Computer Programmes in Creating Music," *Music and Technology*, Stockholm Meeting, organized by UNESCO Jan. 1970.

Koenig, Gottfried, "Notes on the Computer in Music," *American Society of University Composers: Proceedings* **5,** p. 111 (1972).

Lawson, J. & M. Mathews, "Computer Programs to Control a Digital Real-Time Sound Synthesizer," *Computer Music Journal*, **1**(4), 16–21 (1977).

LeBrun, Marc, "Notes on Microcomputer Music," *Computer Music Journal* **1**(2), 30–35 (1977).

Lincoln, H. B., Ed., *The Computer and Music*, Cornell University Press, 1970.

Manthey, Michael, "The Egg: A Purely Digital Real-Time Polyphonic Sound Synthesizer," *Computer Music Journal* **2**(2), 32–37 (1978).

Mathews, Max, *The Technology of Computer Music*, MIT Press, 1969.

Mathews, M. et al., "Computers and Future Music," *Science* **183,** 263–268, 25 Jan. (1974).

Melby, J. B. Jr., "Some Recent Developments in Computer-Synthesized Music," *American Society of University Composers: Proceedings* **5,** p. 111 (1972).

Moorer, James A., "Music and Computer Composition," *Communications of the Association for Computing Machinery* **15,** 104–113 (1972).

Moorer, James A., "How Does a Computer Make Music?" *Computer Music Journal* **2**(1), 32–37 (1978).

Pierce, J. R., "The Computer as a Musical Instrument," *Journal of the Audio Engineering Society* **8,** p. 139 (1960).

Pierce, J. R., "Computers and Music," *New Scientist* **25,** p. 423 (1965).

Russcol, Herbert, *The Liberation of Sound*, Prentice-Hall, 1972.

Seay, Albert, "The Composer of Music and the Computer," *Computers and Automation* **13,** p. 16 (1964).

Slawson, A. Wayne, "A Speech-Oriented Synthesizer of Computer Music," *Journal of Music Theory* **13,** 94–127 (1969).

Smoliar, Stephen W., "Basic Research in Computer Music Studies," *Interface* **2,** 121–125 (1973).

Strang, Gerald, "The Computer in Musical Composition," *Computers and Automation* **15,** p. 16, 1966.

Tenney, James C. "Sound Generation by Means of a Digital Computer," *Journal of Music Theory* **7,** 24–70 (1963).

Truax, Barry, "Computer Music in Canada," *NUMUS-W* **8,** 17–26 (1975).

von Forster, H. and J. Beauchamp, Eds., *Music by Computer*, Wiley, 1969.

Wiggen, Knut, "The Musical Background of Computer Music," *Fylkingen International Bulletin* **2** (1969).

2

TONES AND HARMONICS

The elementary unit of a musical composition is the note. Its position on the staff indicates a pitch to be played at a particular time. The tonal quality of the note is not generally indicated in a musical score, since that is already determined by the instrument assigned to play the note. A composer seeking a particular tone color obtains it by selection of the proper instrument or combination of instruments.

To program a computer to synthesize a tone, the composer must specify much more than the tone's pitch. He or she must be able to define the desired tone color and articulation and must also provide all the acoustical information needed to produce that particular sound. To supply such information to the computer, the programmer must describe the characteristics of the tone in mathematical terms. Although this may seem difficult to do, it is quite feasable. In the same way that a musical chord is a combination of notes having different pitches, a musical tone is an aggregate of many separate pure tones having different frequencies. Although this is not obvious to the ear, it is a fundamental fact of acoustics. The following discussion aims to demonstrate this principle in terms of mathematically formulated tones.

A pure tone is the fundamental element of a complex tone and in the terminology of physics and mathematics, it is a sine tone. It is defined this way because its sound pressure level can be represented mathematically by a sine function. The understanding of a sine tone does not require mastery of trigonometry, however. An easy way to describe a sine tone is to visualize a simple, hypothetical, machine that can mechanically produce one. In fact, we may take extraordinary liberties in designing such an imaginary instrument, since we will never actually have to physically build one. God is kinder to dreamers than to mechanical engineers, and as a result, one can endow an imaginary motor with such marvelous properties as no inertia and no friction. Nothing like this exists in real life, but for this discussion that does not matter!

Suppose that such an imaginary ideal motor is turning a crankshaft to drive an imaginary ideal piston back and forth as shown in Fig. 2.1. This

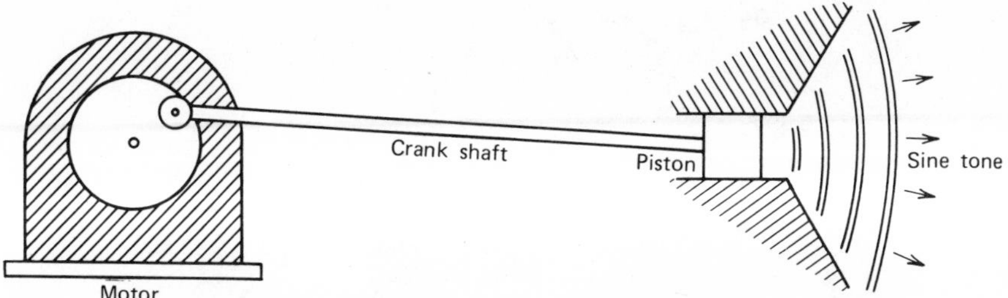

Figure 2.1 An imaginary tone-producing instrument.

ideal piston, like the ideal motor, has no inertia and no friction. Assume that the motor is turning at 440 cycles per second. The back-and-forth motion of the piston will cause the air in front of it to compress and expand, emitting a pure sine tone with the pitch of A_{440}.

The sound wave created by the piston will be a pure sine tone, which can be shown pictorially. Imagine that the crank shaft no longer drives a piston, but instead activates an attached ideal pencil and turns much more slowly. The pencil then traces a curve on a roll of ideal paper that moves underneath it. (An ideal pencil is defined as one that never needs to be sharpened and ideal paper has no grease spots or pieces of wood floating in it.) The curve that the pencil records as it moves back and forth will be identical to the graph of a sine function. Figure 2.2 illustrates this. Here the equivalent of the sound pressure level at the site of the piston is graphed as a function of time. Since the frequency of the periodic motion is 440 cycles per second, the time period of one complete cycle will be $1/440$ seond. (For some mysterious reason, physicists and engineers loathe the term "cycles per second" and insist upon the term "hertz." It is with apologies to my professional colleagues that I use the term "cycles per second" here.)

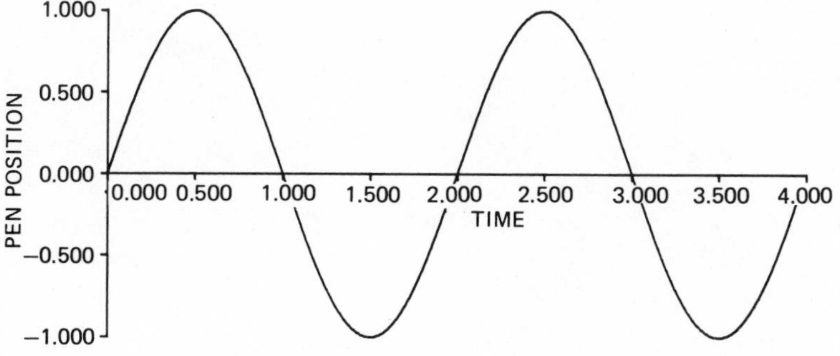

Figure 2.2 Curve traced by pencil.

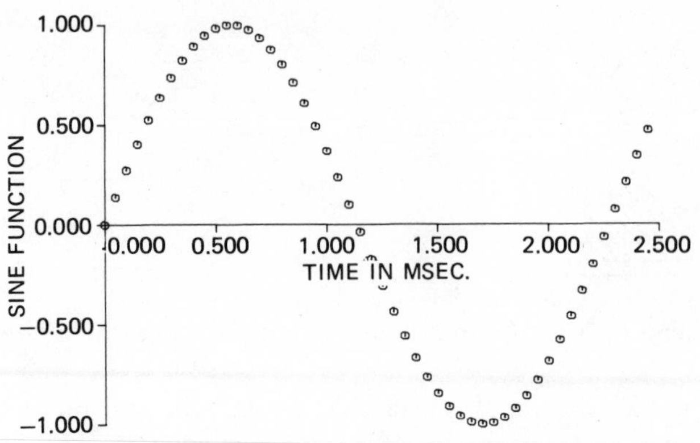

Figure 2.3 Sine function graphed in discrete steps.

Time		Sine Function
Seconds	Milliseconds	
0	0	0
1/20000	0.05	0.138
2/20000	0.10	0.273
3/20000	0.15	0.403
. . .	. . .	. . .
¼ cycle (approximately)	0.60	0.996
. . .	. . .	. . .
½ cycle	1.15	−0.038
. . .	. . .	. . .
¾ cycle	1.70	−0.999
. . .	. . .	. . .
Full cycle	2.25	−0.063

Figure 2.4 Tabular representation of sine function.

The actual construction of a loudspeaker with a motor and a piston would obviously be a ridiculous idea. The purpose of fictitiously imagining it here is to visualize a sine wave without rigorous, abstract, mathematical description. An actual sine tone may be generated much more practically with an electronic oscillator and a loudspeaker. An oscillator generates a voltage whose variation is sinusoidal. When this voltage drives a loudspeaker electromagnetically, the cone of the loudspeaker is forced to vibrate. The motion of the cone and the sound it emits are identical to the motion and sound of the imaginary piston depicted earlier.

Suppose that we want a computer to synthesize a sine tone. Our most immediate problem is that the computer is a digital rather than an analog instrument and cannot accommodate a continuous function. A function in a computer must instead be represented by discrete numbers. For example, if a computer's memory is to store a sine function, the function must be listed in discrete steps of time. In order to reasonably approximate the function, the time interval must be much shorter than the function's period. Recall that in our case the period is $\frac{1}{440}$ second = 2.273 milliseconds. We then choose as our sampling interval 1/20000 second = 0.05 milliseconds. The discrete function can be graphed as in Fig. 2.3. A computer would actually represent this in a table such as Fig. 2.4. Note that the values of the function near the ¼ cycle points are close to the extremal values +1 and −1, and near the midpoint at ½ cycle it is near 0. The values at the ¼, ½, ¾, and full cycle points are not in the table because they do not coincide with the sampling interval of 1/20000 second.

Instructing the computer to store such a table in its memory is a simple procedure. We wish to program the computer to calculate a sine tone that will last for 1 second. Our sampling rate will again be 20,000 samples per second and the tone's frequency will be 440 cycles per second. The computer has a built-in function that calculates the sine of a number. The sine function has a full cycle length of 2π (approximately 6.283), so this number is multiplied by the frequency (440) for use in calculating the function.

Now we can formulate a set of instructions for the computer to follow. For now the program is not written in an actual computer programming language, but is outlined in a logical format that models the usual syntax of a computer language. In the program below, the variables and parameters are given all-capital-letter names, and the "*" symbol is used to indicate multiplication:

1. Reserve 20,000 locations in a memory file.
2. Let SAMPLING INTERVAL = 1/20000.
3. Let FREQUENCY = 440.
4. Let RADIAN FREQUENCY = 6.283 * TIME.
5. Let TIME = 0.

6. Let FUNCTION = Sine of RADIAN FREQUENCY * TIME.
7. Write the value of FUNCTION into next location in memory file.
8. If TIME is equal to 1, stop; otherwise continue.
9. Increase TIME by the value of SAMPLING INTERVAL.
10. Go to step 6 and repeat.

—END OF PROGRAM—

This program will follow the instructions #1–#3 in consecutive order. It begins by setting the variable TIME equal to 0. Then it calculates the sine of 0 for the variable FUNCTION and places this value in the first memory location. When it reaches step 8, it tests the value of TIME. Since it is initially less than 1, the program will increase it by 0.00005 and return to step 6 for calculation of a new value for FUNCTION. Then it stores the new value in the next memory location. The program continues to repeat steps 6 through 10, calculating new values for FUNCTION, storing them in consecutive memory locations, and incrementing TIME until it has performed this sequence 20,000 times and TIME reaches 1. As soon as TIME is equal to 1, step 8 stops the program and the computation is finished.

There are now 20,000 numbers in the memory file. The numbers must next be converted to voltages. As mentioned in Chapter 1, this is done by a DAC with its clock set to 20,000 samples per second. The output of the DAC is shown graphically in Fig. 2.5. The jagged, staircase shape occurs because the computer stored a discrete rather than a continuous function. So the output must be smoothed out by a low-pass filter to obtain the appearance of a true sine wave. When this is done, it can be amplified and sent to a loudspeaker. The entire process takes place in five stages as represented in the block diagram of Fig. 2.6. The sound that comes from the loudspeaker will be a pure sine tone at the pitch A_{440}.

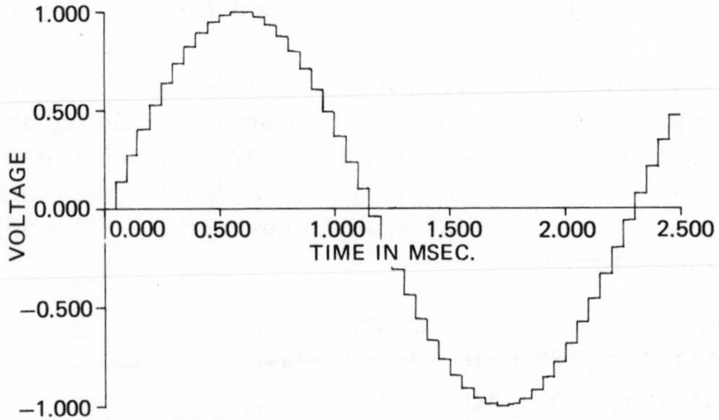

Figure 2.5 Output of DAC.

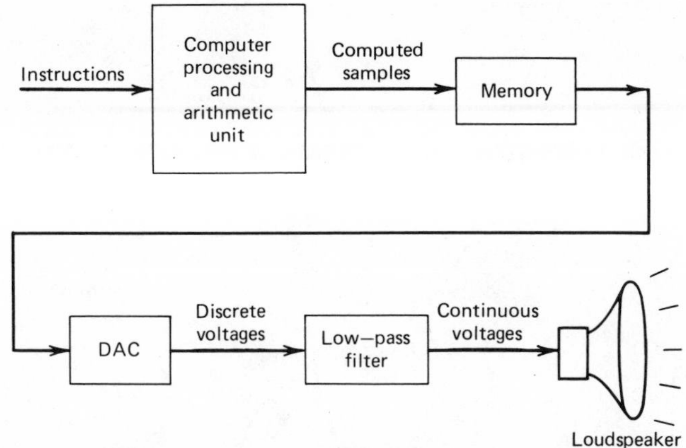

Figure 2.6 Digital production of computer-synthesized sound.

Fortunately, the potentialities of computer music go far beyond the production of simple sine tones. A sine tone is very uninteresting, and listening to one for more than a few seconds can be downright nerveracking. Its importance to this discussion is its role as the starting point for the generation of complex tones. A musical instrument does not make a pure sine tone, but the tone that it does make can be acoustically broken down into the sum of several pure tones having different frequencies. As a rule, the frequencies of the higher components, the overtones, are harmonics of the fundamental pitch. One can understand why this is so by studying the example of a vibrating string. If a string is stretched between two points, it

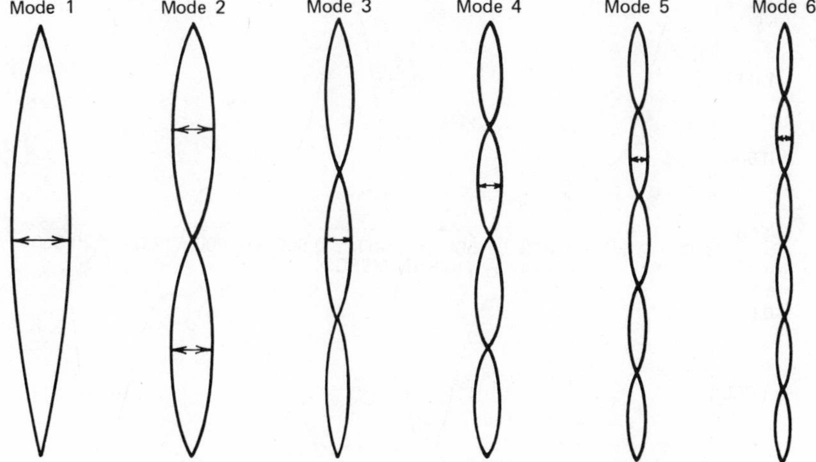

Figure 2.7 Vibration of string in first six modes.

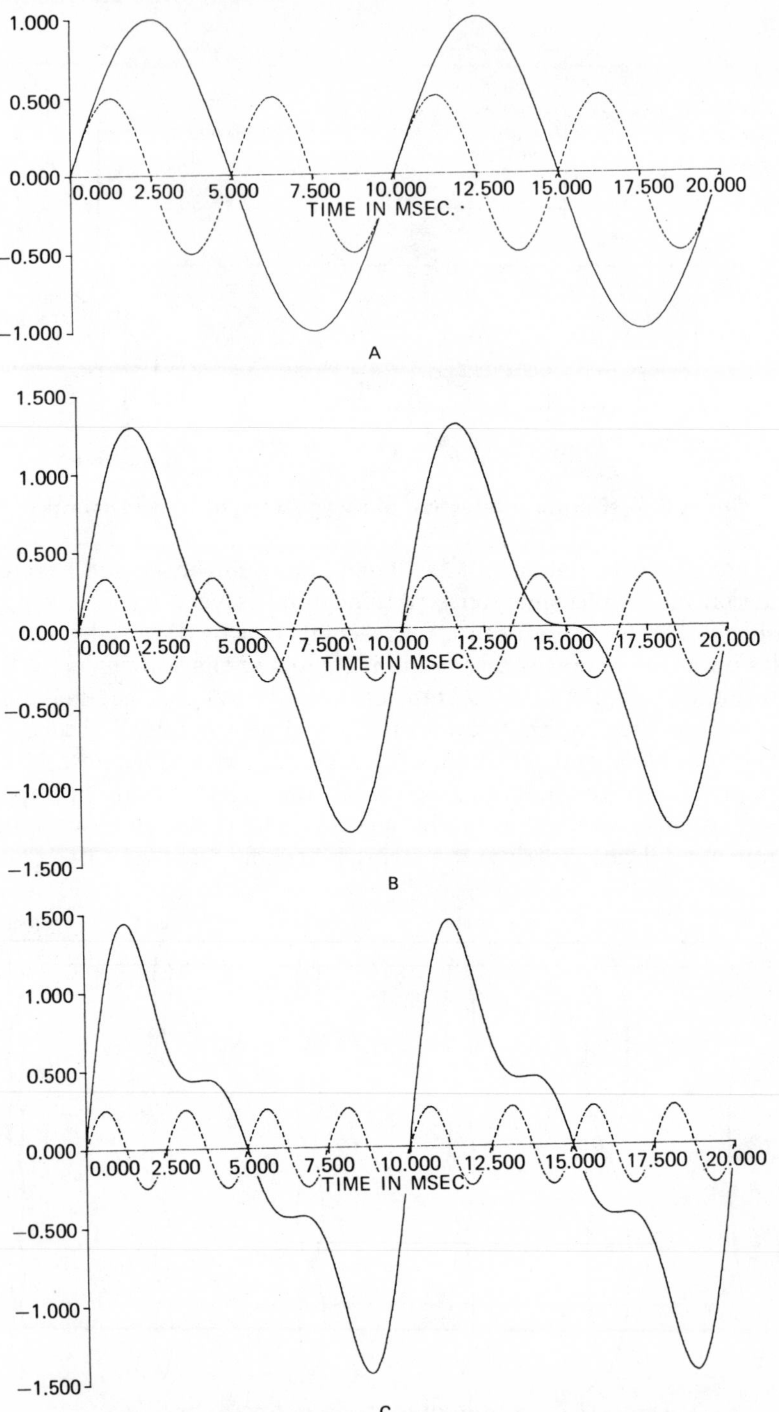

Figure 2.8 Production of sawtooth wave by additive synthesis.

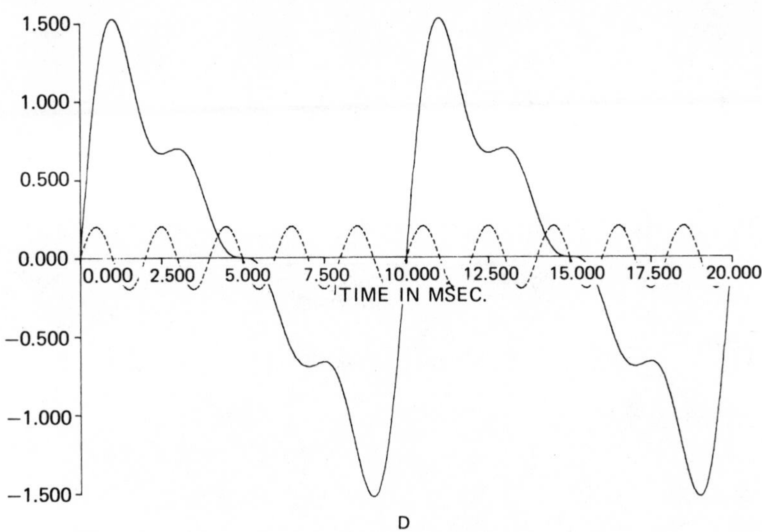
1.500
1.000
0.500
0.000
−0.500
−1.000
−1.500
0.000 2.500 5.000 7.500 10.000 12.500 15.000 17.500 20.000
TIME IN MSEC.

D

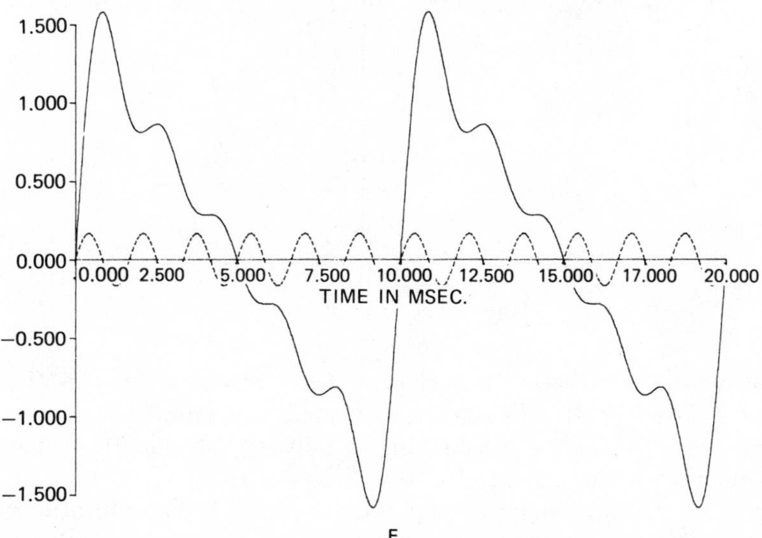
1.500
1.000
0.500
0.000
−0.500
−1.000
−1.500
0.000 2.500 5.000 7.500 10.000 12.500 15.000 17.000 20.000
TIME IN MSEC.

E

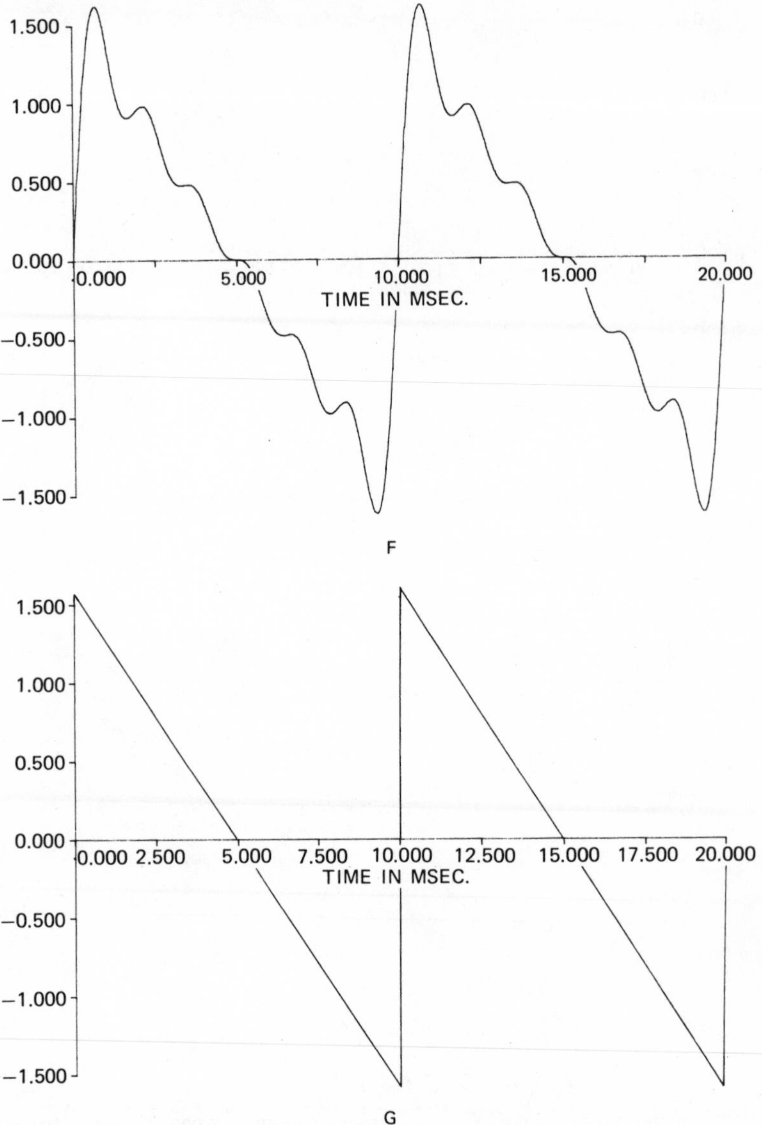

Figure 2.8 (***Continued***).

may be excited to vibrate in a variety of different ways or modes. The diagram of Fig. 2.7 illustrates the first six modes of vibration. One can see that the string in mode 2 is vibrating at half the wavelength, hence twice the frequency as mode 1. Modes 3, 4, 5, and 6 similarly vibrate at those multiples of the fundamental frequency of mode 1. The vibrations of an ideal (perfectly elastic) string produce pure sine waves at each of these frequencies.

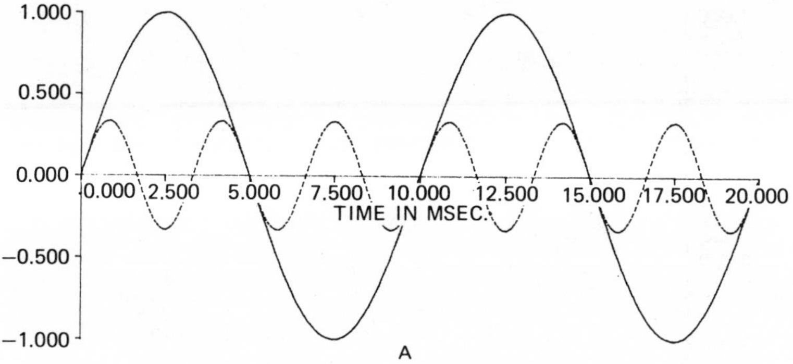

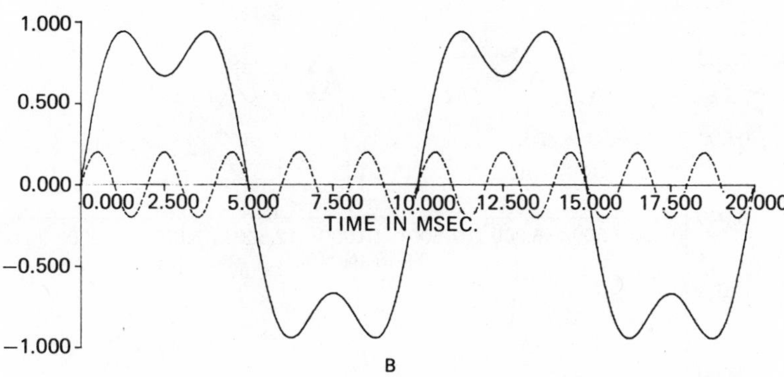

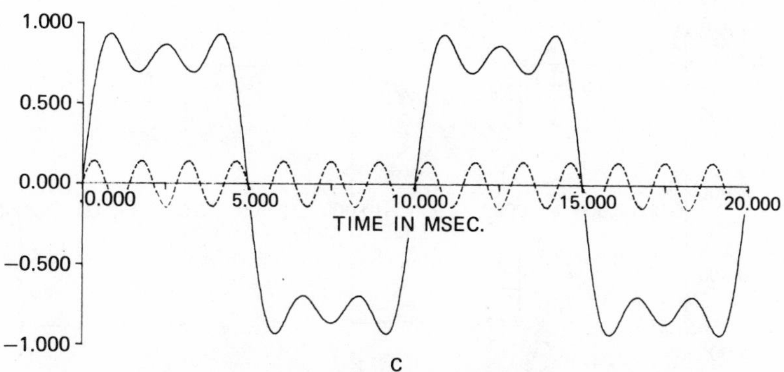

Figure 2.9 Production of square wave by additive synthesis.

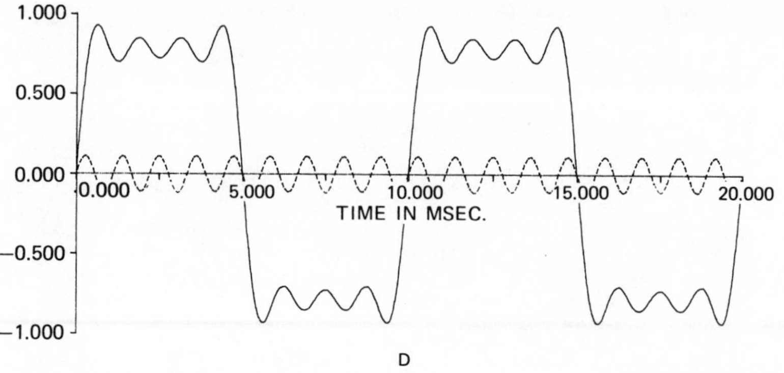

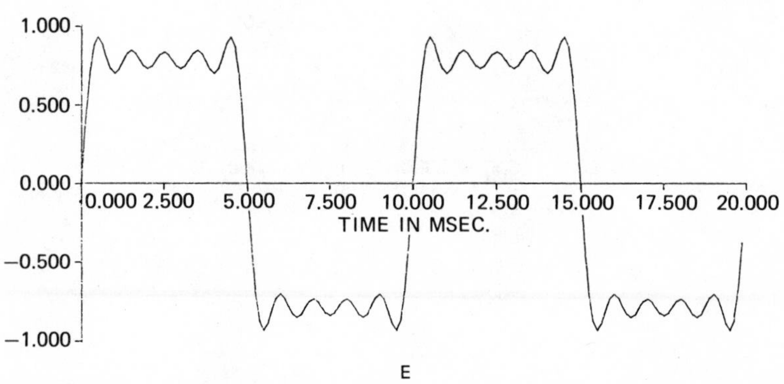

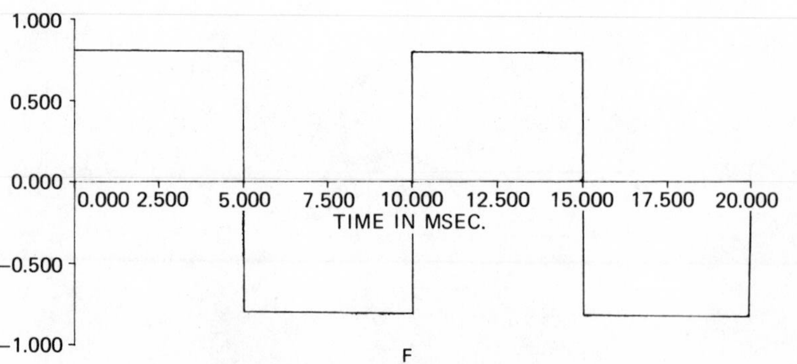

Figure 2.9 (***Continued***).

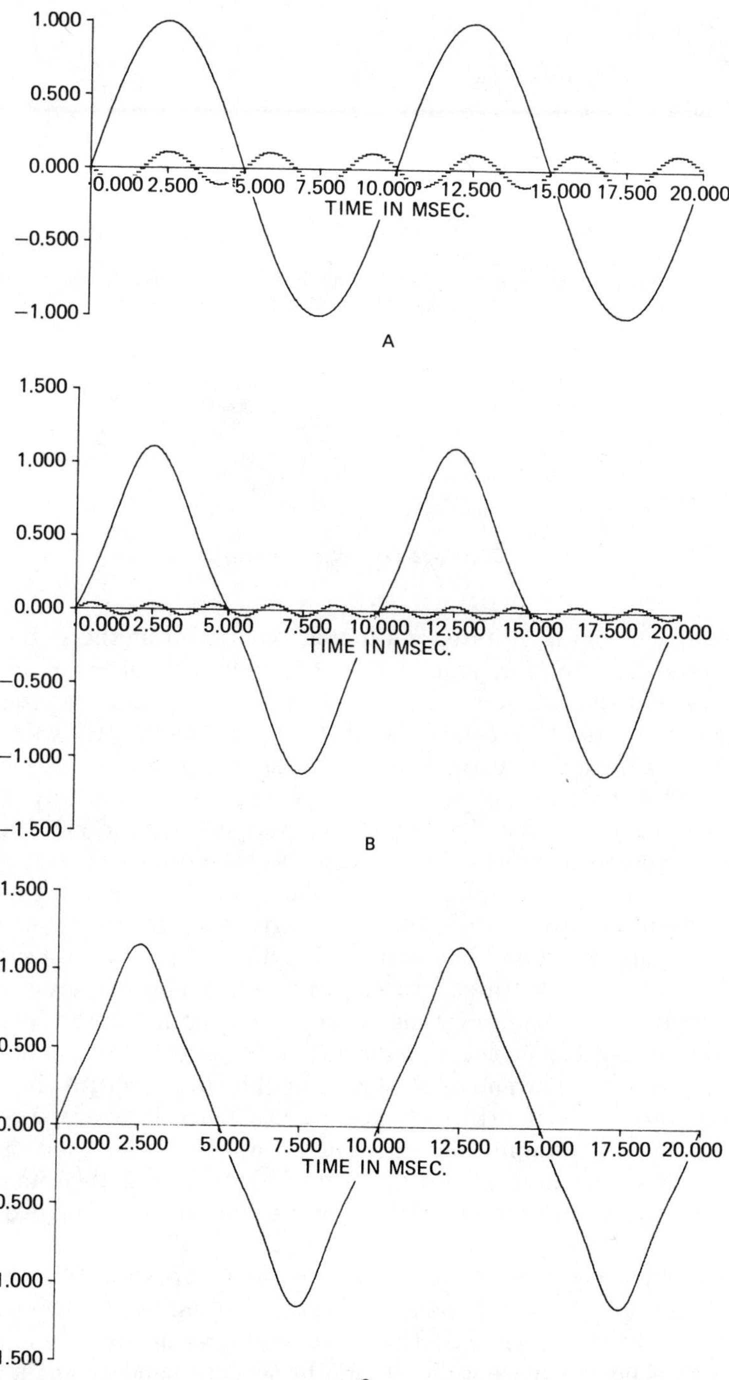

Figure 2.10 Production of triangle wave by additive synthesis.

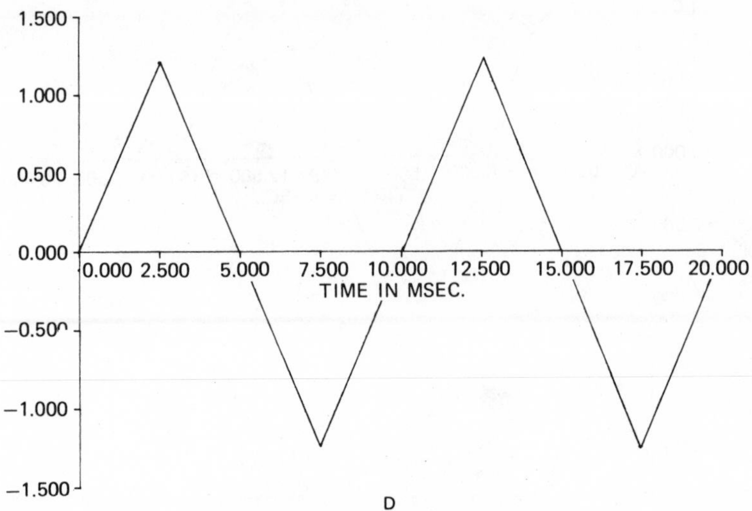

Figure 2.10 (*Continued*).

In reality, a string vibrates in different modes all at the same time. It thus produces a complex tone that is a combination of the fundamental pure tone and the harmonic tones produced by the higher modes. This is what gives the tone its color. The different modes vibrate with varying intensities, depending on the way the string is excited and several other factors. This behavior of a string is analogous to the way sound is produced in air columns. To more completely understand how a complex tone is composed of different pure tones, we may perform an experiment with graphs. The first graph in Fig. 2.8 shows a sine wave of 100 cycles per second. Another sine wave is superimposed on it, having a frequency of 200 cycles per second and one-half the amplitude of the first wave. In the second graph, we add these two curves together and display their sum. The third harmonic shown by the dashed line is added to the sum at one-third the amplitude of the fundamental. The sum of the fundamental, second, and third harmonics is shown in the third picture. In the subsequent graphs, the fourth, fifth, and sixth harmonics are successively added with their amplitudes in inverse proportion to their harmonic number. If we continue to add the higher harmonics in this manner, the waveform representing their sum approaches the sawtooth-shaped wave of Fig. 2.8*g*.

In the next experiment we follow the same procedure as above, but instead only add the fundamental and its odd-numbered harmonics. The results are shown in Fig. 2.9. This time as the harmonics are added, the sum approaches a square wave. In another experiment, we again add just the odd-numbered harmonics, but in inverse proportion to the square of their harmonic number and with the phase of the harmonics alternately inverted. The sum in Fig. 2.10 quickly approaches a triangle wave.

Although this text does not undertake its rigorous proof, one can show mathematically that *any* waveshape can be decomposed into simple sine waves of different frequencies. This leads to an alternative way of representing tones on a graph. So far, we have represented them in the *time domain*, that is, the amplitude of the wave is represented as a function of time. The function may also be represented in the *frequency domain*. Here the graph is a spectrum indicating amplitude as a function of frequency. The graphs in Fig. 2.11 show sine, sawtooth, square, and triangle waves in both the time and frequency domains.

The graphs in the frequency domain only represent one dimension of the function. Although the amplitudes of the frequency components are clearly represented, their phase is not indicated unless it is shown on a separate graph. The phase of a wave is its relative position along the horizontal time axis. For example, all the sinusoidal waveforms of Fig. 2.12 have the same amplitude and frequency, but have a different phase. When

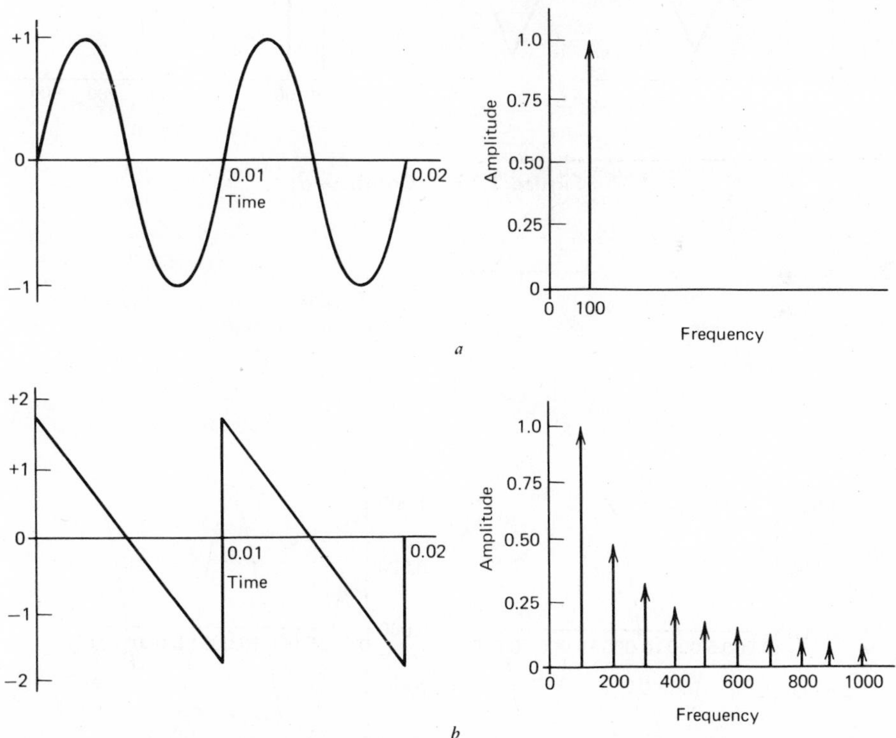

Figure 2.11 Time and frequency domain representations of sine, sawtooth, square, and triangle waves.

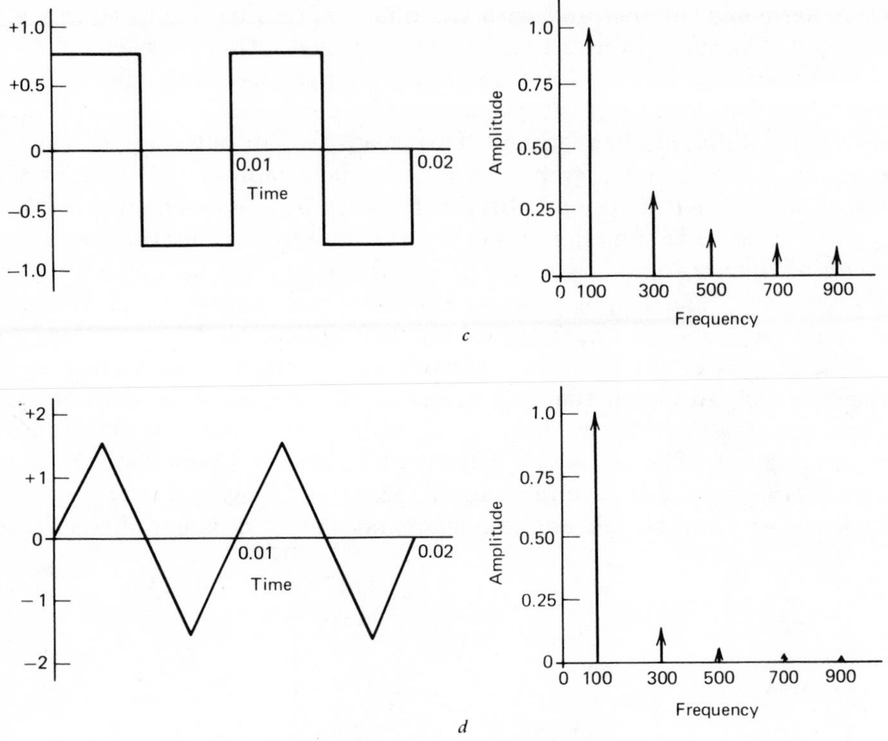

Figure 2.11 (*Continued*).

A B

Figure 2.12 Sinusoidal waveforms having different phase.

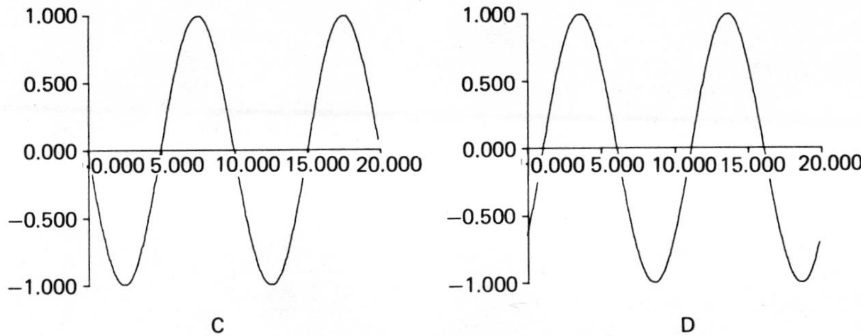

Figure 2.12 (*Continued*).

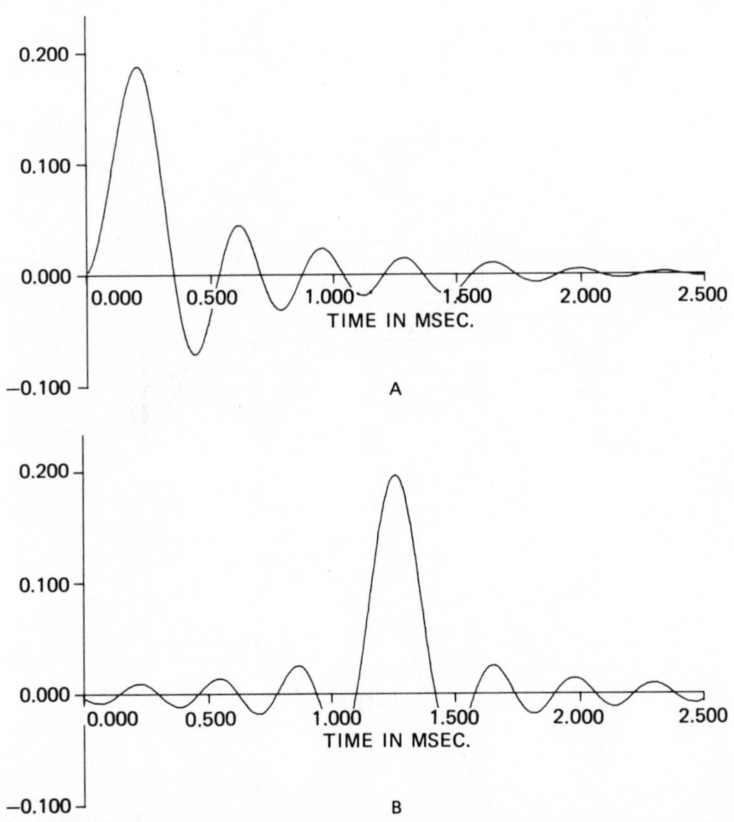

Figure 2.13 ***a*** **minimum phase,** ***b*** **linear phase, and** ***c*** **maximum phase.**

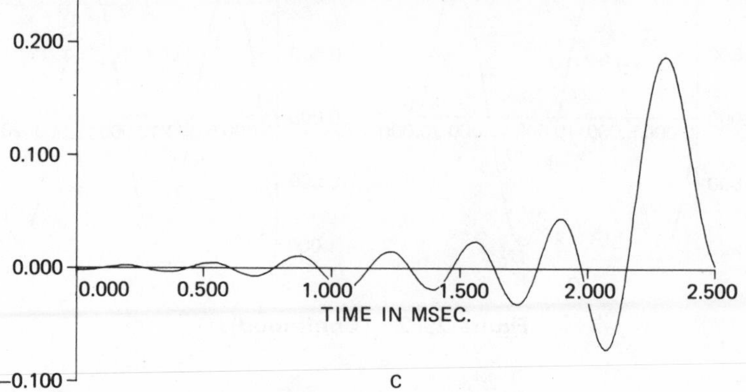

Figure 2.13 (*Continued*).

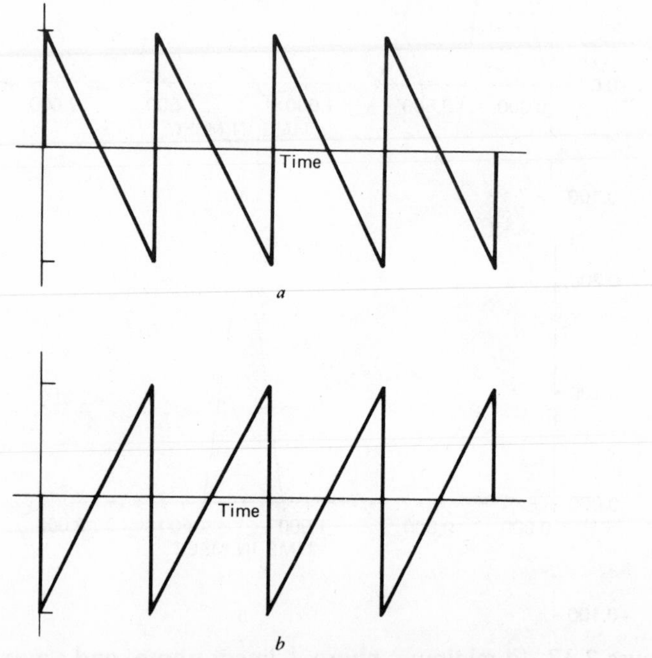

Figure 2.14 Inversion of sawtooth wave.

we added harmonics together to form a sawtooth wave, all of them were added in the same phase. With the triangle wave, the harmonic components were added in alternate phase. If we had not added the sine waves together with their phase arranged this way, the resulting wave shapes would not have been perfect sawtooth, square, and triangle waves. Nevertheless, an important point needs to be emphasized: no matter how the phase of the component sine waves is arranged to form a complex wave, to the human ear the resulting wave will sound almost the same even though its shape is different. This is because the ear has been shown experimentally to be extremely pitch sensitive, but not very phase sensitive. When interpreting a sound, the hearing process perceives the sound in terms of its component frequencies and practically ignores the phase differences.

The graphs of Fig. 2.13 display three complex waveforms that all have identical frequency spectra. They only differ by the phase of their harmonic components. The first waveform is referred to as "minimum phase" because most of its energy is concentrated in the beginning of the wave pulse. The second is called "linear phase" and is symetrical around its midpoint. The last waveshape is termed "maximum phase" because most of its energy is delayed toward the end of the wave pulse. If these wave pulses are cycled repetitiously, they will sound virtually the same as when heard. In the same way, a sawtooth wave such as Fig. 2.14*a* sounds identical to its mirror image shown in Fig. 2.14*b*. Its frequency spectrum is the same, but its phase is reversed.

The preceding discussion implies one of the most fundamental concepts of waveform analysis and synthesis. Just as it is possible to decompose a complex wave into its component pure sine waves, it is also possible to synthesize a complex wave by adding various sine waves. To demonstrate this, we will formulate two procedures, both of which will generate sawtooth waves. The first will use a direct, time-domain method and the second will use the indirect, component sine-wave method in the frequency domain. Let us say that the sawtooth wave has a frequency of 1000 cycles per second. The time period of one complete cycle will therefore be 1 millisecond.

Computation of the values of a sawtooth function is very straightforward. An example of a discrete sawtooth function is shown in Figs. 2.15 and 2.16. The function used to generate this table is $f(n) = 1 - 2n$, where the value of n must lie in the interval from 0.05 to 0.95 millisecond. For $n = 0$, $f(n) = 0$. Consequently, when the total time reaches 1 millisecond, n must be reset to 0 to begin the second cycle. n will also be reset to 0 again at the beginning of each subsequent cycle. Figure 2.17 shows a flowchart of a procedure that will calculate the sawtooth function for the duration of 1 second.

Computer programming will be presented in greater detail later in the text, but the diagram shown here is simple and traces the logic of an

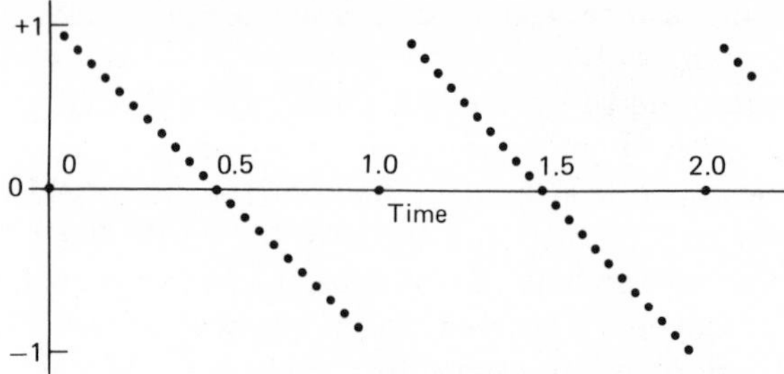

Figure 2.15 Discrete sawtooth wave.

algorithm that a computer can follow. As with the sine wave program presented earlier in this chapter, the control path goes into an iterative loop. This loop causes the same sequence of instructions, including calculation of the function and storage of its value in memory, to be repeated over and over again. With each repetition it will test n to make sure it is in the required interval of 0 to 0.95, and it will also test t to determine if it is less than the total time of 1000 milliseconds. It also increments n and t each time in preparation for the next calculation. When t reaches 1000, the program stops.

Now we move into the frequency domain and formulate F by adding together a sine wave and its harmonics. Recall that the amplitude of each harmonic is inversely proportional to its frequency. The fundamental frequency of our sawtooth wave is 1000 cycles per second. The frequencies of the harmonics will consequently be 2000, 3000, 4000, and so forth. For the sum of these to be a perfect sawtooth wave, an infinite number of these harmonics would have to be calculated and added in phase to the total. However, the human ear cannot normally hear frequencies higher than 15,000 cycles per second. Therefore the highest harmonic requiring calculation for the sake of human hearing is 15,000 cycles per second. The function we need to calculate is

$$f(t) = \sin 2\pi ft + \tfrac{1}{2}\sin 2\pi(2f)t + \tfrac{1}{3}\sin 2\pi(3f)t + \cdots + \tfrac{1}{15}\sin 2\pi(15f)t$$

where $f = 1000$. It is not necessary here to annotate another computer program because its logic would be the same as the earlier example of the simple sine wave. We need only to modify instruction #6, which calculates the function. The modified instruction will compute the sum of the fundamental sine wave and its harmonics rather than just the original simple sine wave. The frequency variable is also set to 1000. Otherwise the steps of the program are the same.

At this point in the discussion a reader who is familiar with computers and programming may justifiably recoil at the inefficiency of the examples presented in this chapter. However, these programs were written to be conceptually simple. Other programs could also be designed that would accomplish the same task, but require much less computation. Computing time is expensive, and in actual practice one designs programs to eliminate redundant calculations and minimize computing time. But introducing the shortcuts into a program that increase its efficiency often

n	Time milliseconds	$f(n)$
0.00	0.00	0
0.05	0.05	0.9
0.10	0.10	0.8
0.15	0.15	0.7
.	.	.
.	.	.
.	.	.
0.50	0.50	0
.	.	
.	.	
.	.	
0.90	0.90	−0.8
0.95	0.95	−0.9
0.00	1.00	0
0.05	1.05	0.9
0.10	1.10	0.8
.	.	.
.	.	.
.	.	.
0.95	1.95	−.9
0.00	2.00	0
.	.	
.	.	
.	.	

Figure 2.16 Tabular representation of discrete sawtooth wave.

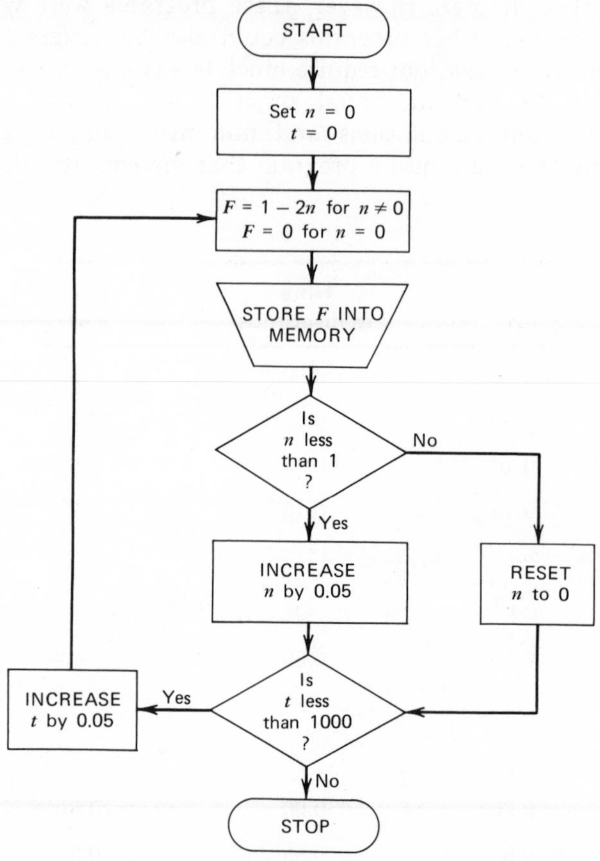

Figure 2.17 Flowchart of program to generate sawtooth wave.

complicate its logic. This is why the programs presented in this book are formulated to be easily understood, and to illustrate fundamental concepts rather than to be practical for actual use. The reader who wishes to undertake computer composition must use ingenuity to create programs that are economic and practical after gaining some actual programming experience.

The art of composition can be described as the ability to gather fundamental elements into a meaningful whole. A composer writing an orchestral score combines the separate tones of each instrument and the notes of the chromatic scale into an artistically meaningful phrase. A composer who uses the computer as a muscial instrument is operating in a new domain that is not present in conventional composition. Since the timbre of the tones that a computer is programmed to synthesize are not predetermined in advance as they are on most other instruments, the responsibility of formulating these tones out of their basic components is left to the composer. Consequently, in accepting this responsibility, the computer composer must diligently familiarize himself with the concepts of waveform analysis. As with the arts of orchestration and choral arranging, the challenge of composing interesting and aesthetic musical sounds from scratch using mathematical logic will become an art requiring tremendous study, experimentation, ingenuity, experience, and creativity. To be artistic at all, the sounds will have to be much more interesting and complex than square or sawtooth waves.

Naturally, in using the computer as an instrument, one may create prefabricated subprograms that generate certain prescribed sounds. These subroutines can reside in the computer system for immediate access and general use. The composer then may easily and conveniently employ these canned subprograms in formulating his compositions, sparing much time and energy. However, taking such shortcuts generally proves to be quite self-defeating. When the computer's process becomes automatic and self-contained to the extent that it can be activated by simply depressing a button on a console, it has lost the flexibity and versatility that were its original paragon. For example, a computer could easily be programmed to be played by a keyboard with a set of stops attached to it like an electric organ. But then the computer would be no more advantageous than a grossly expensive electric organ.

I suggest that the essence of computer music composition will be the full exploitation of the computer's uncommitted flexibility. A serious artist will not profit by trying too hard to circumvent the complexities and additional skills that the computer's utilization entails. Future composers will not necessarily have to become highly trained mathematicians who can prove existence theorems in sets of measure zero, but much of the language, practice, and logic of mathematics and computing will have to be added to their repetoire of skills and knowledge.

REFERENCES

Backus, John, *The Acoustical Foundations of Music*, Norton, 1969.

Benade, A., *Fundamentals of Musical Acoustics*, Oxford University Press, 1976.

Dashow, James, "Three Methods for the Digital Synthesis of Chordal Structures with Non-harmonic Partials," *Interface* **7**, 67–94 (1978).

Helmholtz, Hermann, *On the Sensations of Tone*, Dover, 1954.

Hutchins, Carleen Maley (Comp), *Musical Acoustics*, Halsted Press, 1975.

Josephs, Jesse J., *The Physics of Musical Sound*, D. Van Nostrand, 1967.

Levarie, Siegmund, & Ernst Levy, *Tone, a Study in Musical Acoustics*, Kent State University Press, 1968.

Olson, Harry F., *Music, Physics, and Engineering*, Dover, 1967.

Roederer, Juan G. *Introduction to the Physics and Psychophysics of Music*, Springer-Verlag, 1973.

Rosenstein, Milton, "Computer-Generated Pure Tones and Noise in its Application to Psychoacoustics," *Journal of the Audio Engineering Society* **21,** 121–127 (1973).

Taylor, Charles Alfred, *The Physics of Musical Sounds*, American Elsevier, 1965.

Winckel, Fritz, *Music, Sound, and Sensation*, Dover, 1967.

3

HOW THE COMPUTER OPERATES

Composers do not need to be virtuoso performers on the piano or any instruments of the orchestra to compose successfully. Nor do they need to possess an in-depth knowledge of the construction of the instruments. Similarly, it is unnecessary for computer-music composers to have a detailed, technical understanding of the circuitry and electromechanical operation of a computer. A computer is far more complicated than any other musical instrument, including the most sophisticated organ or even electronic synthesizer. Computer manufacturers realize this, and take great pains to design computer systems that can be used to maximum capacity by people who have very little technical training. As a result, an acquaintance with the BASIC, FORTRAN, or PASCAL programming languages is actually sufficient for a person who is not an engineer, mathematician, or technician to program a computer.

Nevertheless, it is prudent for one who undertakes any use of the computer to become acquainted with the overall design and operation of computer systems. Even though composers do not necessarily play, design, or build the instruments for which they compose, a skillful composer is very familiar with the ranges and capabilities of these instruments. The composer of computer music need not be able to operate and maintain a computer facility. He or she does not need to be capable of designing its hardware or system software, but should have a basic understanding of how computers are programmed and operated.

We now introduce some of the general principles of computer science and explain basically how a computer functions. The computer can interpret and follow simple, logical instructions to perform complicated and lengthy tasks. Understanding how it does this enables one to more easily learn the logic of a programming language and become fluent in its use. Even though the circuitry of a computer is a mass of microscopic elements and connections numbering in the millions, it is possible to present its overall structure in a relatively simple exposition. The digital computer must receive and execute all of its instructions in a numerical code designed to accommodate the logic of its circuitry. The universal code of digital computing is the binary number system. This system is chosen because each digit of a binary number is either a 0 or a 1. A computer is actually an enormous array of on/off switches; hence the state of any switch that is on can be assigned the number 1 whereas a switch that is off is assigned 0. If the ordinary decimal numbering system were used for computing, the switches would require 10 separate positions—something that would be extremely impractical to design.

This presents one of the basic dilemmas of computer programming. For a computer to be able to carry out the instructions of a program, the program must be presented to the computer in a code that reflects this "on/off" logic and incorporates the binary number system. This is the way computers are programmed at the machine level. Consequently, the engineers who compose machine-level programs are required to be familiar with the binary code. Unfortunately, the binary machine language is tedious to learn and difficult to use. To make matters worse, machine languages are not universal—each machine has its own peculiar code. As a result, one can readily see that it would be grossly impractical to expect everyday programmers to struggle with machine code.

In actuality, computer systems are designed so that their users are not required to program at the machine level. Programmers instead use a number of high-level languages that are much easier to learn and use than machine code and reflect their particular programming needs. FORTRAN is the longest-established of these languages for use in scientific and engineering applications. More recently, a simpler language called BASIC has been introduced. Although easier to learn and use, BASIC lacks much of FORTRAN's power and flexibility. In the academic community, a popular language called ALGOL has been in use for many years. Lately, a new language named PASCAL has been developed as a refinement of ALGOL and is currently enjoying widespread acceptance in most college computer science curricula. Although FORTRAN and BASIC are commonly used in industry for engineering problems, ALGOL and PASCAL are emphasized for academic use in communicating algorithms and programming concepts. Hence they are often preferred in teaching computer science and communicating operating system procedures. In the business community the standard language is COBOL, which was specially designed for financial record keeping.

Other specialties also have given rise to different high-level programming languages. These include APL, PL/I, LISP, SNOBOL, and even one called SPITBOL. Each language is designed to meet the needs of a particular application. In the field of computer music a number of specialized languages such as MUSICOMP, MUSIC 4BF, SCORE, and MUSIC 360 have been developed and implemented at some universities. These languages greatly facilitate programming for the students of computer composition at the locations where they are available. Naturally, it is not necessary for a typical programmer, whether an engineer, a bookkeeper, or a computer music student, to learn all of these languages any more than to learn machine language. He or she may simply select the language that is available and best suits the needs.

It would be highly presumptuous to assert that any one of the languages mentioned above should be used by composers in preference to another language. Programmers with an engineering background will probably prefer FORTRAN. A hobbyist with a popular "home computer" might be limited to BASIC. The students of systems software are generally more familiar with PASCAL. The current music composition languages are highly specialized and only exist on certain facilities where they are sponsored. Many of them may be prone to rapid obsolescence as newer languages are developed and implemented on other systems. Consequently, rather than focus on any one language in specific detail, this book will concentrate on general concepts and assume that the reader will apply them to the language he or she personally chooses.

The important idea to be introduced here is that all of these high-level languages are designed to be easily understood and used by human programmers, but they are not capable of direct implementation by computer hardware. This means that a computer program written in a language such as FORTRAN or PASCAL cannot be run on a machine until it is first translated into the machine's own binary code. The translation of a program from high-level code to binary machine language does not have to be done by a programmer or operator. Each computer facility contains a built-in program in its software system that performs this translation for each language. These translator programs are called *compilers* and *interpreters*. The difference between a compiler and an interpreter is that a compiler translates the entire program in one operation whereas an interpreter translates each statement of a program individually as it is written.

To introduce the operation of computers, we may describe the execution of a program in a typical operating environment. Suppose that a programmer has written a simple FORTRAN or PASCAL program and is ready to run it on the computer. The programmer may enter the statements of the program, line by line, into a teletype or graphics display terminal. This would, by itself, present difficulties if the programmer accidentally typed the wrong symbol and had to make corrections as he went along. But most computer facilities provide built-in programs called editors to assist the programmer in entering the code. The editors allow a programmer to enter lines of code and recall them for display in the order they are entered. Then lines can be corrected, added, inserted, deleted, or rearranged. When the entire program is written and entered into the system by the editor, it is stored in a section of the computer's memory. At this point, the programmer may have the computer print the program on a line printer or display it on the terminal screen. Alternatively, it can be stored on a magnetic tape, punched paper tape, or diskette so that later the same program can be entered without having to retype the whole thing.

At this point we assume that the program is entered and ready to run from the programmer's point of view. Although the computer is storing the alpha-numeric symbols of the program in its memory, the statements in their FORTRAN or PASCAL form have no meaning yet to the actual computer. This is where the compiler comes in. The user must issue a command to the computer (via the terminal) to invoke the FORTRAN or PASCAL compiler program. Then the computer system accesses the FORTRAN or PASCAL code sitting in its memory, and automatically translates it into binary machine code. There are now two versions of the program in memory: the original high-level version and the translated machine-language version. Like the original, the translated version, called the *object* code, can also be printed, displayed, or stored on tape or disk. The object code version is meaningless to a programmer who is not a software expert. But the original version is also meaningless to the computer. It is the object program that the computer must actually run. This is why both versions of the program are necessary.

If the original program contains syntactical errors (as do nearly all first-run programs), the compiler detects them and displays messages to the programmer informing him of the nature and location of these errors. Such errors generally consist of omitted or misplaced punctuation symbols or misspelled words. The programmer can then use the editor to correct the mistakes, and then try again to have the program compiled. As soon as the compiler runs successfully and does not detect any more errors, it produces the object code version of the program. We assume that the program is intended to be run repeatedly at various future times as well as immediately. It would be a waste of time to recompile the original program each time it is to be run. This is why the programmer should retain both versions of the program. He or she will want the high-level version for personal reference and the object version to run on the machine. The computer system cannot afford to retain all of the programs of all its users in its main memory all of the time. The programmer must be responsible for keeping track of the programs when not "on the system." He may retain copies of his own programs—both original and compiled versions—on storage media such as cassette tapes or floppy disk or keep them on file in the computer's secondary disk memory system. When he wants to run the program again at a future time, he can reenter the object version from the tape or disk into main memory and issue the command for the computer to run the program.

The foregoing description of a computer operating environment is necessarily very general but not very comprehensive. This is because operating environments vary widely from one system to another and whereas one person may be programming a small, inexpensive, hobby microcomputer that has only a BASIC interpreter, another programmer will be one of several hundred users on a large time-sharing complex. To accurately and completely describe the protocol for every system would be impossible. The principle of writing a program in a high-level language and subsequently compiling or interpreting it into a machine-level code for execution by the machine's hardware is, however, virtually universal.

This procedure for entering and running a program is typical for problems that involve implementing algorithms. Languages like FORTRAN and PASCAL are designed mainly for mathematical problem solving. If a programmer-composer defines a method of generating a musical tone with a particular harmonic spectrum, it is not uncommon to program in a language like FORTRAN. However, computer music is not limited to digital sound synthesis. More commonly, computer music students experiment with sophisticated programs that have been engineered and are resident on the systems they are using. Rather than writing original programs to generate sounds, they utilize the existing programs to formulate their compositions. As such, they actually specify the notes, key and time signatures, instruments, dynamics, and other parameters of their composition as data to these programs. The data is entered into the system through a terminal in a manner similar to the way programs are entered. But the notes and other details of a musical composition are specified much more conveniently with specialized input devices. One example of such a device is a touch-sensitive keyboard. A computer monitoring the keyboard can "remember" the notes that are played as well as their durations and the force used to strike the key at that particular instant. Specification concerning the note's timbre may be entered with dials, switches, or other hardware attached to the input device. Here the composer may be "programming" or "performing" depending on one's point of view. Alternatively, a composer may enter the notes and specifications of a composition by literally scoring it on manuscript paper and entering it on a score-reading device. There are a variety of other sophisticated machines on the market designed especially for computer music composition, and one must consult the available periodical literature to keep abreast of their state of the art and availability.

Having introduced the procedure for entering and running a program, we turn to the topic of how the computer functions at the machine level. Actually, this level of operation is only of indirect concern to the average user. Indeed, a user can easily run the programs on the computer without knowing what it is actually doing with the object program, in the same way that one can drive an automobile without knowing how the engine, transmission, and carburator work. Nevertheless, this author believes it is wise of a computer programmer to be informed about the basic principles of a computer system's physical operation.

The physical computer is a complex system of on/off switches. A switch in a computer circuit is called a flip-flop. It is activated electrically and delivers an output voltage that reveals whether it is in a 1 state or a 0 state. A typical flip-flop usually has two input connections: one to set its state to 1 and another to reset it to 0. If a flip-flop is in the 1 state, it is said to be "high," whereas the 0 state is referred to as "low." The voltage that a flip-flop delivers at its output is typically a positive 10 volts if it is high and 0 volts if it is low. At any point in an operating computer circuit at a particular instant, the voltage will either be high at 10 volts or low at 0 volts.

In the original monster computers of the early 1950s, flip-flops were made of mechanical relays. These switches were approximately a cubic inch in size, weighed several ounces, used large amounts of electric current to set and reset them, took several milliseconds to switch on and off, were noisy and subject to mechanical failure, and cost several dollars apiece. Today they are electrical rather than mechanical and can switch back and forth in less than 1/10,000,000 second. A tiny, durable, and inexpensive integrated circuit chip may contain thousands of them.

In a computer a binary digit is called a bit. One bit of information may comprise either a 1 or a 0, which can be stored in a single flip-flop. Consequently, a full-length binary number can be represented by a register of several bits placed in tandem the same way a decimal number is composed of several single digits. The relationship between binary numbers and decimal numbers can be seen by studying Fig. 3.1.

A full-length binary number in a computer is called a word. In a large computer, a word is 32 to 64 bits long, whereas most minicomputers have word lengths of 12 or 16 bits. Microprocessors normally use 8-bit words, but recently several companies have begun to manufacture and sell 16-bit microcomputers. In the same way that a single bit of information is stored in a single flip-flop, a full word is stored in a register. A 16-bit register, therefore, is a row of 16 flip-flops that store the bits of a word. All the information that a computer processes, be it numbers, instructions, or alphabet characters, is coded into binary words that are "written" into its registers. The contents of any register can be changed, transferred to another register, incremented, tested, added to numbers from other registers, and have other logical operations performed upon them.

The central register of a computer processor is called the accumulator. A sophisticated computer will actually contain more than one accumulator in the central processor, but for the purposes of this study, we will describe a simplified model. The accumulator contains the word that is currently being operated upon. In a typical computer operation, a number will be loaded into the accumulator from a register in the memory. Then the logic circuitry of the processor will electronically perform some operation such as addition, negation, or multiplication on the number while it is sitting in the accumulator. Then the modified number can be transferred to another register for use in a different operation or stored in a memory register.

Binary	Decimal	Binary	Decimal
0	0	1101	13
1	1	1110	14
10	2	1111	15
11	3	10000	16
100	4	10001	17
101	5	.	
		.	
		.	
110	6	11111	31
111	7	100000	32
1000	8	100001	33
1001	9	.	
		.	
		.	
1010	10	111111	63
1011	11	1000000	64
1100	12	1000001	65

Figure 3.1 Binary number system.

The central processor of the computer has other registers besides the accumulator that enable it to carry out the steps of a program. Recall that a computer program is a sequential list of instructions that are coded into binary words. The processor must therefore have a register, called the instruction register, which contains the coded instruction word currently being executed. Suppose that the instruction in this register is COMPLIMENT ACCUMULATOR. This means that each bit of the word in the accumulator is to be complimented. For example, the zeros are exchanged for ones and the ones for zeros. The logic circuitry will read the word in the instruction register that is currently the binary code for the instruction COMPLIMENT ACCUMULATOR. The instruction activates the logic circuitry to take each bit (that is each flip-flop) of the accumulator and set it to 1 if it is 0 or reset it to 0 if it is already 1. Then the instruction register is ready to receive a new instruction.

At this point one may wonder where the instructions come from and how they get into the instruction register. The primary memory of the computer consists of several thousand registers containing the coded instruction words of the program and the data for the program. The registers of the primary memory differ from the registers in the central processing unit in that they are not directly connected to logic circuitry and their contents are not tampered with while they are in the memory. The numbers are simply stored in the memory registers until they are transferred to a register in the processing unit to be acted upon.

The most essential feature of the primary memory is that each of its registers has a unique address. This makes it possible for the processing unit to access any one of the memory registers directly simply by specifying its address. The memory addresses are numbered sequentially. The steps of a program can then reside inside the primary memory in sequential order. A companion to the instruction register in the central processing unit is called the program counter. The program counter contains the address number of the instruction being executed. Each time an instruction in the instruction register is performed, the address in the program counter is incremented. Then a new instruction is loaded into the instruction register from the memory location whose address is now in the program counter. As an example, suppose that the computer is midway in the execution of a program and the primary memory contains the contents as shown in Fig. 3.2. In this hypothetical program, the instructions in locations 110–112 direct the processor to add the numbers 39 and 24. Note that the memory addresses 1001 and 1002 do not contain instructions, but

Address	Contents of Register
.	.
.	.
.	.
0110	LOAD INTO ACCUMULATOR CONTENTS OF ADDRESS 1001
0111	ADD INTO ACCUMULATOR CONTENTS OF ADDRESS 1002
0112	STORE ACCUMULATOR INTO ADDRESS 1003
.	.
.	.
.	.
1001	39
1002	24
1003	63 (after execution of program)

Figure 3.2 Memory contents during typical program execution.

contain data—that is the two numbers to be added. Memory address 1003 is an empty register reserved to store the results of the addition after it is performed. It is important to remember that in the actual computer words, these instructions and data numbers are not represented as seen in Fig. 3.2, but in their coded binary form. The reader may note that these instructions each have two parts; the first indicates the actual operation, that is, LOAD, STORE, or ADD; and the second part gives the address of the word to be operated upon. Consequently, the coded instruction word will be divided into separate fields for the different parts of the instruction. For example, in a 16-bit computer, the STORE instruction may use the 6 bits on the left side for a short binary-code number meaning STORE and the remaining 10 bits on the right side to specify the address of the memory register where the number in the accumulator is to be stored.

Not all instructions, however, make reference to the memory. Some instructions change the number in the program counter, thus affecting the order in which the rest of the instructions are executed. One can readily see the purpose of this by recalling the programs described in the preceding chapter. In each of them the control of the program was sent into a loop where the same set of instructions was repeated many times. Consider a situation where a programmer desires to add a list of 100 numbers. The direct way to accomplish this would be the program listed in Fig. 3.3. This kind of programming, however, is obviously very inefficient. To alleviate the redundancy, one can incorporate other instructions that will enable a shorter version to be written. The instructions SKIP and JUMP may be employed as in Fig. 3.4. This program is much shorter and more efficient than the one of Fig. 3.3, but some steps need explanation. The indirect ADD instruction in location 0002 differs from the direct ADD instruction on the previous program in the following way: the instruction ADD 1101 means "add to accumulator the contents of register 1101," but ADD (INDIRECT) 1101 means "add to accumulator the contents of the register whose address is in location 1101." This form of indirect addressing has a very important advantage in that it gives the programmer much more flexibility in designing programs that does direct addressing. Recall that in the original redundant program, 100 separate ADD instructions were necessary, each of which had to specify a separate address of the number to be added. In the improved program, the ADD instruction appears in the program only once, but is repeated 100 times as the program iterates through a loop. The problem here is that each time the ADD instruction is executed, the address it specifies must be changed. It must pointed to 1000 the first cycle, 1001 the second cycle, 1002 the third cycle, and so forth until it has repeated the loop 100 times. This is accomplished by using another register (register #1101) as the target address of the indirect ADD instruction. The first time the processor encounters ADD (INDIRECT), it will go one step further and find the number in the register whose address is in location 1101. Initially, this number is 1000,

Address	Contents
0000	START
0001	CLEAR ACCUMULATOR
0002	ADD CONTENTS OF 1000 TO ACCUMULATOR
0003	ADD CONTENTS OF 1001 TO ACCUMULATOR
0004	ADD CONTENTS OF 1002 TO ACCUMULATOR
.	.
.	.
.	.
0102	ADD CONTENTS OF 1099 TO ACCUMULATOR
0103	STORE ACCUMULATOR IN 1100
0104	STOP
.	.
.	.
.	.
1000	(first number to be added)
1001	(2nd number)
1002	(3rd number)
.	.
.	.
.	.
1099	(100th number)
1100	(location reserved for sum)

Figure 3.3 Direct addition of 100 numbers

the address of the first data number to be added. But then the instruction INCREMENT 1101 increases it by one each time the program cycles through the loop, so that all of the 100 data numbers in locations 1000–1099 will each be added once.

The loop in the program is implemented by the JUMP instruction. This instruction simply resets the program counter to 0002 where it is incremented, causing the instructions starting in location 0002 to be repeated. Notice, though, that if this instruction were used without any additional provision, the program would cycle indefinitely and never stop. For this reason, another memory register is selected for use as a counter and initialized at -100. Each time the program cycles, the instruction INCREMENT AND SKIP IF ZERO will change it by $+1$ until it reaches 0. By then, all 100 numbers have been added into the accumulator, and the program is ready to exit from the loop. On the 100th cycle, the contents of register 1002 will be 0. Consequently, this time the processor will skip the JUMP instruction and go to the next instruction which stores the result of the addition in location 1100. Then the program is finished.

This chapter is not purported to elaborate upon machine-level programming in great detail. The foregoing examples were presented and explained to illustrate one of the most important fundamental concepts of computing—enormous flexibility and versatility in programming may be realized by exploitation of conditional branching instructions (statements containing an "IF") and loops. Another essential concept needs introduction as well. The use of subroutines is a procedure that is at the heart of programming pedagogy. To exemplify the use of a subroutine in a program, we may recall the example in Chapter 2 where a sine function was repeatedly calculated. A computer processor does not normally comprise logic circuitry to directly calculate such functions. (Actually, many processors contain built-in sine-wave generators, but they are not an essential part of a computing system.) This presents the problem of how to instruct the machine to calculate the sine function. In the first program

Address	Contents
0000	START
0001	CLEAR ACCUMULATOR
0002	ADD (INDIRECT) 1101
0003	INCREMENT 1101
0004	INCREMENT 1002 and SKIP IF ZERO
0005	JUMP TO 0002
0006	STORE ACCUMULATOR IN 1100
0007	STOP
.	.
.	.
.	.
1000–1099	(100 numbers to be added)
1100	(location reserved for sum)
1101	(address of number to be added; initially set to 1000)
1102	(counter; initially set to −100)

Figure 3.4 Indirect method of addition.

outlined in Chapter 2, instruction #6 directed the computer to find the sine function at various values of a variable t. On each iteration through the loop, the same sine function was called on to compute its different values as t changed from cycle to cycle.

There are different ways of finding the values of a sine function, and the computer usually employs a numerical method involving a complete subprogram. The procedure employed in such a subprogram is irrelevant to this discussion and need not be outlined here, but we may take it for granted that it already has been formulated and exists as a resident of any computer's software system. As an example of how a sine subroutine may be used in a machine-level program, consider the instructions of Fig. 3.5, which may be part of a larger program.

In this hypothetical example, the first 500 memory locations are used for the main program. We assume that the sine subroutine contains 100 instructions and thus occupies locations 0501–0600. Instructions 0051–0053 are part of a loop that will calculate the sine function of 100 different numbers stored as data in memory registers 1001–1100. After they have been calculated, the results will be stored in the same locations 1001–1100 where they replace the original data. To enable the program to repeatedly calculate different values of the sine function using the same set of instructions, the indirect mode is used. The instruction LOAD (INDIRECT) 1000 causes the accumulator to be loaded not with the *number* in address 1000, but instead with the number whose *address* is in location 1000. We assume that this address will initially be 1001 and then incremented each time the program iterates through the loop as was the case in the addition program of Fig. 3.4.

As the processor executes the JUMP TO SUBROUTINE instruction, it uses register #0500 as a reference location to store the address of the next instruction of the main program to be executed after the subroutine has finished. The program counter is then reset to 0501, which contains the first instruction of the subroutine. It will take the number in the accumulator, calculate the sine of it, and leave the result in the accumulator. The control must now return to location 0053 where it left off. Since the number 0053 was left in location #0500 by the JUMP TO SUBROUTINE instruction, it can be found and control returned to it by the JUMP (INDIRECT) 0500 instruction. Obviously, if the entire sine routine had to be rewritten into a program every time it were used, programming would be intolerably tedious. Consequently, a typical computer library contains hundreds of subroutines that are commonly called on and used repetitively as in the example above.

To gain further insight into the operation of computers, we will examine a direct, though extremely impractical, method of loading and executing a program. We may choose for our example the addition program of Fig. 3.4. We have the written outline of the program, which lists the memory locations and their initial contents. Our objective is to load this program into

Address		Contents
	.	.
	.	.
	.	.
(main program)	0051	LOAD ACCUMULATOR (INDIRECT) 1000
	0052	JUMP TO SUBROUTINE 0500 AND SAVE PROGRAM COUNTER
	0053	STORE (INDIRECT) 1000
	.	.
	.	.
	.	.
(reference location for return address)	0500	(this address will contain 0053 after the JUMP instruction is executed)
(sine subroutine)	0501	(first instruction of sine routine)
	.	.
	.	.
	.	.
	0600	JUMP (INDIRECT) 0500
(reference location to data addresses)	1000	(address of argument to sine function)
(data and results)	1001–1100	(list of 100 arguments to sine before execution—calculated values of sine after execution)

Figure 3.5 Memory contents for program with subroutine.

the computer so that it is actually sitting in the memory waiting to be performed. As mentioned earlier, this is a machine-level program, and cannot be entered into the computer with English words, decimal numbers, or even alphabet characters. The example program as written is readable to a human operator, but for the computer it must be translated into a binary code, containing only zeros and ones. We assume, therefore, that we have a dictionary to use in translating the instructions of our program into binary computer words.

A typical 16-bit computer has a front panel with a row of 16 lights and 16 switches called the switch register. The lights indicate the status of each of the 16 bits of the accumulator in the processing unit. If a light is on, it indicates the bit in that position is high whereas a low bit is indicated if it is unlit. By watching these lights, the operator can observe the number in the accumulator at any instant. In addition to these lights and switches of the switch register, the front panel contains a LOAD ADDRESS button, an EXAMINE button, and a DEPOSIT button. By using the EXAMINE button, the operator may inspect the contents of any address in the primary memory. To do this, the switches in the switch register are set to high or low positions, which correspond to the binary form of the memory address, and then the LOAD ADDRESS button is depressed. The switch register and light panel now reference that location. Depressing the EXAMINE button causes its contents to be displayed by the lights. Then if the operator wishes to change the contents of that memory location, the switches can be set to correspond to the bits of the word he or she wants to load and then the DEPOSIT button is depressed. The memory register will then be modified accordingly.

Thus, to load our hypothetical program after it has been translated into binary machine code, we can start with memory address 0 and load the code word for START. Address #1 will be loaded with the code for CLEAR, #2 will be the code for ADD (INDIRECT), which includes the address that the instruction specifies, and so forth. Since this program occupies only addresses 0000–0007, the addresses 0008–1000 may be left blank and ignored. We then load addresses 1000–1099 with the 100 numbers (in binary form) that we want to be added. Address 1100 is reserved for the sum, so it is left blank until the program loads the answer into it on execution of the program. Addresses 1101 and 1102 are loaded with the initial values 1000 and −100, respectively.

After the program is loaded, the operator can start the processor. The program counter will be set to zero and the processor will fetch the contents of memory address #0 and load them into the instruction register. The logic circuitry senses the states of its 16 flip-flops and responds electronically to the instruction. Then the program counter is incremented, and the next instructions are fetched and executed until the STOP instruction is encountered. After the computer finishes the program, the operator can find the answer by inspecting the contents of address 1100 using the front-panel LOAD ADDRESS and EXAMINE buttons.

This procedure is obviously highly inconvenient. Fortunately, computing systems do all of this work automatically. In practice, programs are loaded into the computer via teletype, cassette cartridges, floppy disk, punched paper tape, magnetic tape, or consoles with keyboard and display. The programs may be written in forms that are much more comprehensible and manageable than machine languages, as described in the beginning of this chapter. The results are automatically output on the line printers, teletypes, and terminal display screens, and done so in a large variety of forms easily readable by the user. The method of manually loading and running machine-level programs and inspecting their results is only actually used in installation, repair, and diagnostic procedures. Our purpose in describing it here is to develop an intuitive grasp of how the computing system operates.

To facilitate the entry of a source program into the computing system, every computer has a code whereby a letter of the alphabet, punctuation symbol, or a decimal number is represented by a binary number. One alphanumeric or control character commonly uses 8 bits. Figure 3.6 shows a few characters and their corresponding ASCII codes, which are in widespread use. Since one character occupies 8 bits, a 16-bit machine may store two characters in one memory word. Thus the FORTRAN statement, "GO TO 100" could sit in a primary memory as shown in Fig. 3.7. The ASCII code enables symbols to be stored in memory, but an important point must be emphasized. The ASCII characters *are not machine-level instructions* and they mean nothing to the computer processor. As one recalls the discussion of compilers and interpreters, their duty is to start with the source language program statements (such as GO TO 100) in their ASCII code and then translate them into an entirely different machine-language program. the ASCII characters' only purpose is to occupy the memory while they are waiting to be translated by the compiler.

One point should presently become obvious to the reader. A computing system must have an enormous amount of memory space to accommodate all the various software it must commonly use. The FORTRAN and PASCAL compilers, the BASIC interpreter, the editor, and the sine function are examples of the hundreds of built-in programs that must reside permanently in the computer system. It would be far too inconvenient for programmers to have to write and load sine functions and other mathematical subroutines every time they were to be used. therefore, such standard subroutines must also have their residence in the software system. Moreover, a user will likely want to have several subroutines that he or she wishes to use repeatedly, even though other users are not interested in them. The computing system must also contain programs that enable it to receive information from input devices, transmit data to output devices, organize and keep track of the programs in memory, do bookkeeping, inform the operator of process errors or other contingencies, save the memory contents in case of power failure, and automatically control its overall operation.

This represents a horrendous amount of programming whose instructions number in the thousands. It would be very nice if a primary memory could economically be built that contained enough registers to accommodate all this resident programming and still have room for the user's program and data. Unfortunately, unlike some people, computers do not have unlimited memory capacity. Consequently, one of the computer's first imperatives is its process of memory management. Actually, a computer can store as much information as it ever needs on various external devices, but it does not have room for all of it in the registers of its primary memory. Programs, and data that are not in immediate demand by the processor are stored in these devices outside the main memory. Thus the computer has two entirely separate memory systems. The secondary memory system has a major advantage over the primary memory in that it can store many times more information. Its major disadvantage is that it requires much more time to access that information.

The characteristic difference between primary and secondary memory is that in primary memory any memory word may be accessed directly by specifying its address. The time that it takes to fetch the contents of any one location is approximately 1 microsecond, and it takes no longer to access one word than it does any other. Thus this type of memory is called *random-access-memory* (RAM). Until recently most RAMs were constructed out of tiny, doughnut-shaped iron rings with wires threaded crosswise through their holes. Each ring, or core, represents 1 bit of

Character	ASCII code	Character	ASCII code
A	11000001	!	10100001
B	11000010	"	10100010
C	11000011	#	10100011
D	11000100	$	10100100
E	11000101	%	10100101
F	11000110	&	10100110
G	11000111	'	10100111
H	11001000	(	10101000
I	11001001	)	10101001
J	11001010	*	10101010
K	11001011	+	10101011
L	11001100	,	10101100
M	11001101	–	10101101
N	11001110	.	10101110
O	11001111	/	10101111
P	11010000	:	10111010
Q	11010001	;	10111011

Figure 3.6 8-bit ASCII Code.

Character	ASCII code	Character	ASCII code
R	11010010	<	10111100
S	11010011	=	10111101
T	11010100	>	10111110
U	11010101	?	10111111
V	11010110	@	11000000
W	11010111	[	11011011
X	11011000	\	11011100
Y	11011001	]	11011101
Z	11011010	↑	11011110
0	10110000	←	11011111
1	10110001	Leader/Trailer	10000000
2	10110010	LINE FEED	10001010
3	10110011	Carriage RETURN	10001101
4	10110100	SPACE	10100000
5	10110101	RUBOUT	11111111
6	10110110	Blank	00000000
7	10110111	BELL	10000111
8	10111000	TAB	10001001
9	10111001	FORM	10001100

Figure 3.6 (***Continued***)

information. As electric current passes through the wires, the core is magnetized in either a clockwise or counterclockwise direction depending on the polarity of the electric current. The direction that the core is magnetized determines whether the bit represents a 0 or a 1. Most computers built before 1975 use core memory, but the semiconductor revolution is making it obsolete. Today RAMs are made almost exclusively of integrated circuit flip-flops that are smaller, faster, and cheaper than core. In fact, some V-Moss transistors are currently being developed that measure 1/1000 millimeter and can switch on and off in a billionth of a second.

Even with this incredible progress in RAM technology, a computer's primary memory cannot have enough room for all of the system's software and user's programs. The computer's library must be located in its sec-

Symbols	Memory Address	Memory Contents
.	.	.
.	.	.
.	.	.
GO	0400	11000111 11001111
(space) T	0401	10100000 11010100
0 (space)	0402	11001111 10100000
10	0403	10110001 10110000
0 (Car. Ret.)	0404	10110000 10001101
.	.	.
.	.	.
.	.	.

Figure 3.7 Memory contents of text GO TO 100.

ondary memory that consists of magnetic storage devices such as disk and tapes. As the disk rotates past a set of pickup heads, information can be read off or written onto the magnetic surface. Consequently, the time it takes to access a bit of information can be any duration up to the period of one revolution of the disk. On the average this time is approximately 10 milliseconds—very slow when compared with RAMs that cycle in less than a microsecond!

However, the computer can afford the longer access time when the secondary memory is just used for auxiliary storage. It means, though, that the major preoccupation of a computing system is memory management. It must constantly monitor what programs and data are immediately needed by the central processing unit and move them in and out of the primary memory accordingly. Since a large computer has several external, secondary memory devices attached to it, careful track must be kept of where each bit is located at all times. This kind of management requires complicated programming that would take several textbooks to describe. Fortunately, the user need not be burdened with the details of such management. Nevertheless, in writing the programs, instructions must be included that relate to the transfer of information between primary and secondary memory. A programmer is therefore wise to develop a fundamental understanding of the memory system.

To aid in further developing this understanding, we may suppose that a composer has written a lengthy, detailed program to synthesize 30 seconds of a composition. This program calls several subroutines, some of which the programmer has previously written and has saved on file, some belonging to colleagues, and others that are part of the system. When the program is run, the results will be input to a DAC. Let us examine a typical procedure to be used in running this program. We assume that the programmer has a personal file in the computer's secondary memory. Physically, this file is a space reserved on the disk. The computer's memory management system is programmed to automatically keep track of where every file is and where each record is located in that file.

Once the fully corrected and loaded program has been compiled, the interpreted machine-code version of it is written on the user's file space in secondary memory. Beyond this point, the original program is ignored. As mentioned earlier, this hypothetical program calls a number of subroutines. Each of the subroutines as well as the main program will have a name and some sort of identification code or number. To prepare the program for execution, the user gives the computer a LOAD command. This command is followed by a list of the names and identification tags of the main program references. The computer will then look them up in its files on disk and transfer them into the primary memory. The loading system has the ability to economically organize the main memory addresses so that the program statements can be expeditiously carried out.

A typical computer program contains several PRINT statements that tell the computer to directly output the results on the scope, teletype, or line printer. However, our music program calls for computation and storage of enough waveform samples to produce 30 seconds of sound. If the sampling rate is 30,000 samples per second, then we are considering 900,000 numbers. Clearly, to print these numbers would be ridiculous and serve no purpose. Moreover, 900,000 numbers is far too many to be stored in the limited space of the primary memory. This is why the main program must periodically contain instructions to compute a few (perhaps 1000) of the samples, using a block of space in the primary memory. Then a WRITE statement or subroutine can cause this block of 1000 samples to be transfered and stored in the user's file on disk. Following this, the program can continue to compute 1000 more samples at a time, repeatedly using the same block in main memory and writing it on file until the program is finished and the file has written into it the full 900,000 samples. When this is accomplished, the user's file contains the samples, a copy of the programs and subroutines in machine-code for future use, and if desired, another copy of them in their original source-language form. Retention of these is generally desirable so that they can be referenced and modified. At any later time, the samples on file may be input to a DAC and tape-recorded.

This chapter has attempted to provide a composer who wishes to undertake computer music composition with some information and explanation of what computing systems are and how they operate. This basic knowledge, though far from comprehensive, is important to acquire for anyone who is to interact in the world of digital computers. The concepts presented here should be sufficient to enable a novice in computer music synthesis to begin dealing with equipment he or she must use, and develop the skills required of a computer programmer.

REFERENCES

Alonso, Appleton, & Jones, "A Special Purpose Digital System for Musical Instruction, Composition, and Performance," *CHUM* **10,** 209–215 (1976).

Buxton, William, E. A. Fogels, Guy Fedorkow, Lawrence Sasaki, & K. C. Smith, "Introduction to the SSSP Digital Synthesizer," *Computer Music Journal* **2** (4), 28–38 (1978).

Forsythe, A. I., Keenan, E. I. Organick, & Stenberg, *Computer Science: A First Course*, Wiley, 1978.

Gear, C. W., *Introduction to Computer Science*, Science Research Associates, Chicago, 1973.

Gschwind, Hans W., & Edward McCluskey, *Design of Digital Computers*, Springer-Verlag, 1975.

Hilburn, John, & Paul Julich, *Microcomputers/Microprocessors Hardware, Software, and Applications*, Prentice-Hall, 1976.

Howe, Hubert, "Electronic Music & Microcomputers," *Perspectives of New Music* **16**(1), 70–84 (1977).

Korn, Granino A., *Minicomputers for Engineers and Scientists*, McGraw-Hill, 1973.

Nolan, R. L., *FORTRAN IV Computing and Applications*, Addison-Wesley, 1971.

Oppenheim, David, "Microcomputer to Synthesizer Interface for a Low-Cost System," *Computer Music Journal* **2**(1), 6–11 (1978).

Organick, E. I., A. I. Forsythe, & R. P. Plummer, *Programming Language Structures*, Academic Press, 1978.

Organick, E. I., & L. P. Meissner: *FORTRAN IV*, 2nd ed., Addison-Wesley, 1974.

Osborne, Adam, *An Introduction to Microcomputers*, Berkeley, Adam Osborne, 1975.

Perlis, A. J., *Introduction to Computer Science*, Harper & Row, 1975.

Petersen, W. W., *Introduction to Programming Languages*, Prentice-Hall, 1975.

Pratt, T. W. *Programming Langauges: Design & Implementation*, Prentice-Hall, 1975.

Souček, Branko, *Minicomputers in Data Processing and Simultation*, Wiley, 1969.

Sutherland, I. E., "SKETCHPAD: A Man-Machine Graphical Communication System," MIT Lincoln Laboratory, Report No. TR 296, Lexington, MA, 1963.

Ullman, J. D., *Fundamental Concepts of Programming Systems*, Addison-Wesley, 1976.

Wirth, N., *Systematic Programming: An Introduction*, Prentice-Hall, 1973.

Wirth, N., & K. Jensen, *PASCAL User Manual and Report*, Springer-Verlag, 1975.

4

COMPUTER PROGRAMMING IN TONE GENERATION

In the early days of computing systems it was impossible for anyone to program a computer who was not an expert technician. The computer was programmed by the way it was electrically wired. Subsequently, programming was greatly simplified when processors were developed that could decode machine-language instructions. The preceding chapter touched on the way a computer is programmed at this level. Its capabilities notwithstanding, programming in machine language is nevertheless difficult and tedious and requires the sophisticated technique of an expert programmer. The purpose of introducing a computer's machine-level operation and programming was to illustrate the basic concepts of programming theory. The presentation here introduces computer programming in a practical context as it can be applied to musical composition and tone generation. The examples in this study are presented in FORTRAN and PASCAL. In addition, the programs are listed in an English-like pseudolanguage for the benefit of readers who are not familiar with FORTRAN or PASCAL.

We may begin our discussion of computer programming by writing a short routine that will synthesize a sequence of notes. In Chapter 2, we outlined a simple procedure for generating the samples of a sine wave on a computer. Now we are prepared to formulate it as an actual program. We assume that the waveform of the tones will be a simple sine function. Each note will be represented in a data record that specified the note's pitch in cycles per second. It will also specify the note's intensity and duration. The program will read the data records sequentially and compute the samples to generate a tone for each note. Hence, the number of notes to be played will be determined by the number of records. The program thus terminates through an attempt to read through the end of the file. Before writing the actual code, we plan the procedure with a flowchart shown in Fig. 4.1. Figure 4.2 then lists the FORTRAN, PASCAL, and "English" codes for the procedure.

This program is very simple and is presented as a starting point for this discussion that follows. Because of its extreme simplicity, it does not have enough flexibility to allow for a very interesting composition. The purpose

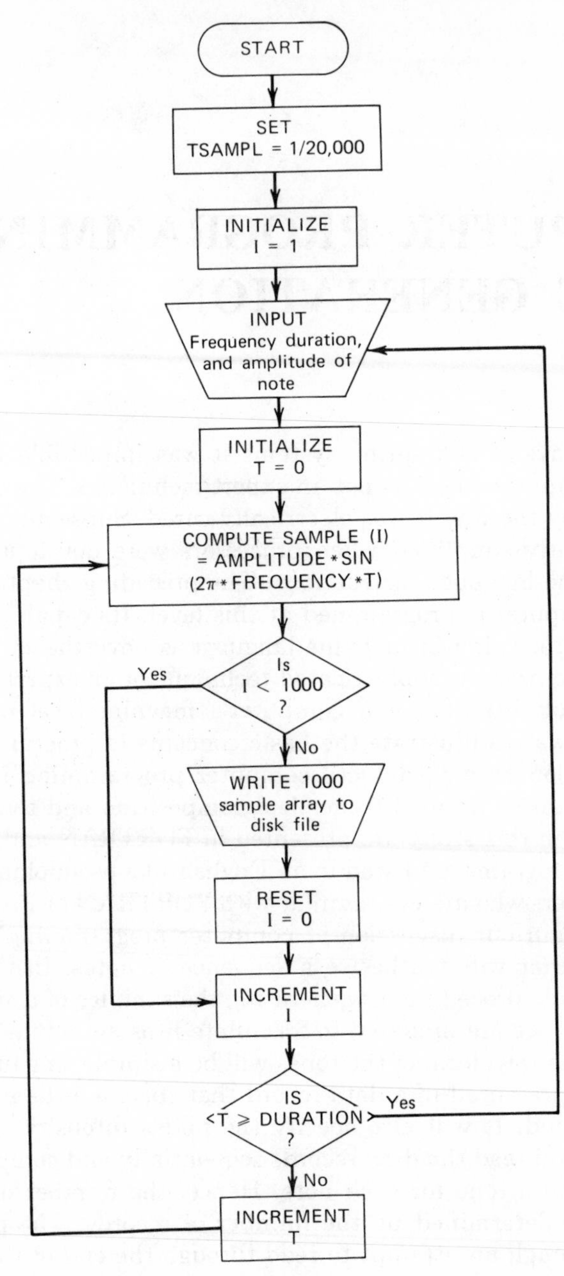

Figure 4.1 Flowchart for sample-generation program.

of this chapter is to begin with this example and modify it to enhance its capabilities. In making these modifications and additions one step at a time, we may study and examine some of the basic challenges inherent in computer programming as it applies to music synthesis. Some of the features of this introductory program should be clarified. The sampling interval was chosen here to be 1/20000 second. The choice of sampling fre-

```
C—PROGRAM TO SYNTHESIZE A SEQUENCE OF NOTES OF
C—VARIOUS PITCHES
      DIMENSION SAMPLE(1000)
      TSAMPL = 1.0/20000.0
      I = 1
1     READ 100, FREQ, DUR, AMPLTD
100   FORMAT (3F10.4)
      T = 0.0
C—PI2F IS THE RADIAN FREQUENCY TO BE USED IN
C—COMPUTING THE SINE FUNCTION
      PI2F = 6.2831583 * FREQ
2     SAMPLE(I) = AMPLTD * SIN(PI2F*T)
      IF (I.LT.1000) GO TO 3
C—WRITF IS A LIBRARY SUBROUTINE TO STORE AN ARRAY
C—ON TO A FILE IN DISK MEMORY
      CALL WRITF(. . . argument list . . .)
      I = 0
3     I = I + 1
      IF (T.GE.DUR) GO TO 1
      T = T + TSAMPL
C—PROGRAM WILL TERMINATE WHEN NO MORE DATA CARDS
C—ARE LEFT TO BE READ
      GO TO 2
      END
```

Figure 4.2a FORTRAN.

```
program notesynthesis;
  const tsample = 0.00005
  type sampleblock array [1..1000] of real;
    note = record   frequency: real;
                    duration: real;
                    amplitude: real
          end;
  var i: integer; sample: sampleblock;
    t, pi2f: real;
    begin i: = 1
    while not eof do
      begin
        read(note);
        t: = 0.0;
        while t <note_duration do
          begin
            pi2f: = 6.2831585*note.frequency;
            sample[i]: = note_amplitude * sin(pi2f*t)
            if i ≥ 1000 then
              begin
                WRITEFILE(sample);
                i: = 0
              end;
            i: = i+1;
            t: = t + sample
          end;
      end;
  end;
```

Figure 4.2*b* PASCAL.

PROGRAM NOTESYNTHESIS

Variables SAMPLE: Array of 1000 numbers

TSAMPLE: Sampling interval = 1/20000 second

I: counting index in program loop

T: time variable

FREQUENCY, DURATION, AMPLITUDE: specifications for each note

2πf: radian frequency

Procedure
1. Initialize I to 1
2. Read one record from data file
   a. assign 1st number to FREQUENCY
   b. assign 2nd number to DURATION
   c. assign 3rd number to AMPLITUDE
3. Initialize T to 0
4. Set 2πf to 6.2831585 * FREQUENCY
5. Set SAMPLE(I) to AMPLITUDE * sin(2πf*T)
6. If I is less than 1000, skip to instruction #7, otherwise, do the following:
   a. Call subroutine WRITEFILE
   b. Reset I to 0
7. Increment I by 1
8. If T is greater than DURATION, return to instruction #1
9. Increment T by TSAMPLE
10. Return to instruction #5

Figure 4.2c English.

quency required a compromise between computer economy and high-frequency content in the output waveform. Naturally, the higher one chooses the sampling frequency, the greater will be the number of computations that must be performed. This increases the cost in computer time. On the other hand, the sampling frequency must be at least double the frequency of the highest component in the computed or sampled signal for it to reproduce that component.

We have previously discussed how a complex waveform is a composite of various pure tones that have different frequencies. If, then, the sampling frequency is set to 20,000 samples per second, the highest component frequency of any waveform sampled at this rate is limited to 10,000 cycles per second. The average human ear is not sensitive to frequencies much higher than 15,000 cycles per second. Therefore, a sampling rate of 30,000 samples per second is the highest one necessary to reproduce any sound within the average range of human hearing. But since the waveforms generated for musical compositions do not necessarily always contain frequency components in the extreme upper range, we may achieve some economy by using sampling rates lower than 30,000 cycles per second. The program presented here, for example, merely calculates one simple sine wave. Therefore, in this case, we could use a sampling rate even much lower than 20,000 per second with acceptable results.

When 20,000 numbers are to be saved in memory for a single second of sound, the program must be designed to arrange for their storage. The previous chapter discussed how the primary memory of a computer is inadequate for storing information in this volume. For this reason, we construct our program to perform the computation of the output samples in blocks of 1000 samples at a time. 1000 samples represents 1/20 second at our chosen sampling rate. When this 1000 sample array is computed, the program calls a subroutine that transfers the block of data from the array SAMPLE to a file in secondary memory. It is not pertinent in this text to discuss the details of such a subroutine or present its documentation. We assume in our example that a FORTRAN subroutine called WRITF or a PASCAL procedure WRITEFILE already exists for this purpose. Most computer facilities should have similar routines for storing large blocks of data on disk memory. After our program writes the array on file, it continues to calculate samples for a new array. It increments the index I by one and the time variable T by the sampling interval TSAMPL each time until T reaches the value of the note's duration. Then it reads a new record for the next note. Since the duration of each note is chosen arbitrarily, one may expect that the time variable T will reach its final value when the index I is somewhere between 1 and 1000. When this happens, the program must input the pitch, loudness, and duration of the next note. But the index I is not reset until 1000 samples are computed, even though a new note may be input and T reset to 0. This program may also accommodate rests in the composition. If a record is to indicate a rest rather than a note, its amplitude may be specified at 0. Then the program will compute the value of the samples to be 0 for the duration of the rest.

The next improvement to be made in our program is to substitute a complex tone for the pure sine wave. We write it so that the first record read by the program establishes the harmonic content of the tones to be generated. Let us say that the tone consists of the first 10 harmonics added in varying proportions determined by the composer. The first record then contains 10 numbers corresponding to the amplitudes of each harmonic. To accomplish this, we insert the following statements in the beginning of our program:

FORTRAN

```
        DIMENSION HARMNC(10)
        READ 200, (HARMNC(J) J=1,10)
    200 FORMAT (10F8.3)
```

PASCAL

```
type harm_amp array [1..10] of real;
var harmonic: harm_amp;
begin read (harmonic) end;
```

English

Variables: HARMONIC: Array of 10 numbers
Procedure: 1. read 10 numbers from data file and assign them to array HARMONIC

Next, in Fig. 4.3 we write a function subprogram to calculate the waveform. With the inclusion of this function we substitute it for the sine function in the original program. It allows the composer to experimentally create different tones by separately adjusting the amplitudes of the harmonics. The tone color of the computed waveform is determined by the values of the array HARMONIC.

Although the waveform computed by this function is a considerable improvement over the original sine wave, it still suffers a major limitation. Thus far the composer has no control over the tone's onset or dynamics other than its mere intensity. The topic of loudness and envelope control is examined in some detail in the Chapter 5, but we may present an example of a simple envelope generator here in a computational framework.

```
      FUNCTION WAVFRM(T,PI2F,HARMNC)
      DIMENSION HARMNC(10)
      HRM = 0.0
      DO 1 J = 1,10
C—THE VARIABLE FLTJ IS USED TO AVOID MIXING MODES
      FLTJ = FLOAT(J)
    1 HRM = HRM + HARMNC(J) * SIN(FLTJ*PI2F*T)
      WAVFRM = HRM
      RETURN
      END
```

Figure 4.3a FORTRAN.

```
function waveform(t,pi2f:real;
            harmonic: harm_amp): real;
   var hrm: real; j: integer;
   begin hrm:=0.0;
     for j:=1 to 10 do
       hrm:=hrm+harmonic[j]*sin(j*pi2f*t);
     waveform:=hrm
   end;
```

Figure 4.3b PASCAL.

FUNCTION WAVEFORM

Variables	T: time variable
	$2\pi f$: radian frequency
	HARMONIC: array of 10 harmonic amplitudes
	HRM: temporary storage variable
	J: counting index for program loop
Procedure	1. Set HRM to 0
	2. Initialize J to 1
	3. Reset HRM to its current value plus HARMONIC(J) * sin(2π f*J*T)
	4. Increment J by 1
	5. If J is less than 10, return to instruction #3
	6. Set the function WAVEFORM to the final value of HRM
	7. Return to main program

Figure 4.3c English.

There are a great variety of different envelope shapes that can be employed by a program like the one we are using, and it would be possible to specify the envelope characteristics individually for each separate note. But for the purposes of this discussion, we merely devise the simplest of envelope generators to demonstrate its implementation. Beyond this introduction, the reader is left to construct more interesting and versatile envelopes as his or her skills and familiarity with computer programming increases.

Let us assume that each note input to our program has a minimum duration of ⅛-second or 125 milliseconds. The amplitude of the note rises linearly from 0 to the maximum value specified on the third number of its data record. After the amplitude of the waveform rises to this value, it is sustained for a length of time 125 milliseconds less than the total duration of the note. Then it decays linearly back to 0 amplitude in the final 100 milliseconds. Seen graphically, the amplitude of the note is a function of time having three distinct intervals: the rise attack time of 25 millisecond, the sustain time that may be any length, and the decay time of 100 milliseconds. Figure 4.4 illustrates this. To incorporate this envelope into our program, we write another function subprogram for the envelope. Figure 4.5 is its flowchart, and the subprogram is listed in Fig. 4.6. In the program of Fig. 4.4, the statement that calculates the value of SAMPLE(I) will now read:

```
SAMPLE(I)
    = ENVELOPE(AMPLITUDE, DURATION, T)*WAVEFORM(T,PI2F,HARMONIC)
```

We can also add another improvement to our tone-generation program. Although we now have more flexibility in defining waveforms having any number of different timbres, the note's exact pitch is still static. The tone would sound much warmer and musically interesting with a slight vibrato. To add vibrato to the tone, we modulate the frequency variable PI2F with a low-frequency sine wave. A natural vibrato has a period of

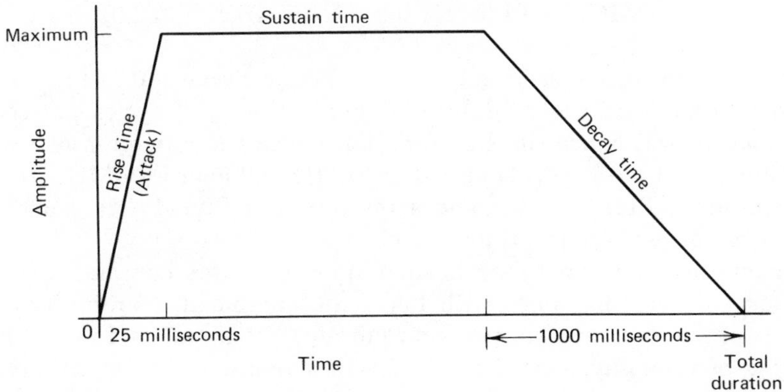

Attack time: envelope function = maximum amplitude (t/0.025)
Sustain time: envelope function = maximum amplitude (t = time)
Decay time: envelope function = maximum amplitude * 1/0.100 (duration − t)

Figure 4.4 A typical single envelope.

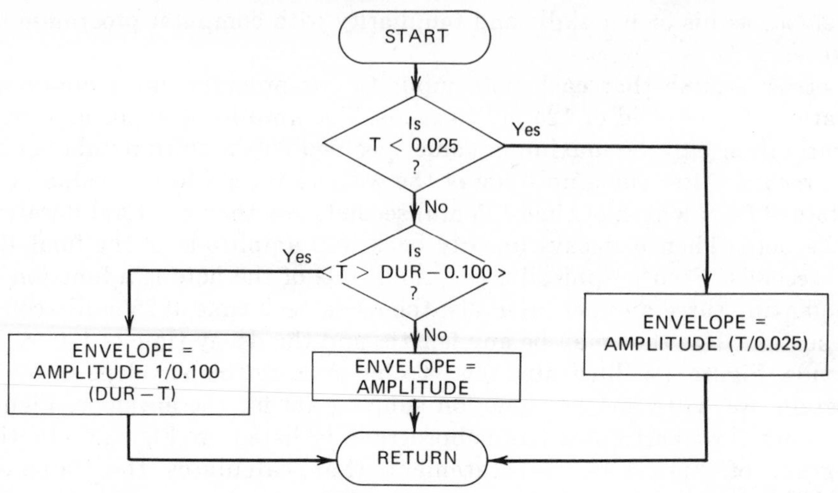

Figure 4.5 Flowchart for envelope-generation subprogram.

approximately ⅛ second and causes the pitch to vary about ¼ step in either direction. ¼ Step corresponds to a fractional variation of approximately $1/32$. The pitch will thus rise and fall within the interval of its specified value plus or minus $1/32$ that value. Consequently, the sine wave that we use to modulate the frequency variable will have an amplitude of $1/32$ and a frequency of 8 cycles per second. Let FRQMOD be the modulated frequency. It is defined in the WAVEFORM function and substituted for the static frequency variable PI2F. The statement defining FRQMOD may read,

```
FRQMOD = PI2F * (1.0 + SIN(50.2655*T)/32.0)
```

The number 50.2655 is used in the sine function because it is equal to the radian frequency of the modulating signal—that is 8 cycles per second multiplied by 2π. Since the sine function reaches a maximum of 1 and a minimum of -1 with a cycle period or 2π, the value of FRQMOD reaches a maximum of PI2F$(1 + 1/32)$ and a minimum of PI2F$(1 - 1/32)$ and fluctuates 8 times per second, which is what we want.

The methodology that has been employed so far contains the logic necessary to generate tones with harmonic complexity, simple envelope control, simple dynamic control, and vibrato. Yet it suffers a major defect in terms of economy. One second of sound requires the computation of 20,000 samples. Each individual sample requires the computation of 10 sine functions plus the envelope function and vibrato control. Each sine function requires the order of 100 multiplications, and a single multiplication requires several additions. One sine calculation can therefore require

```
      FUNCTION ENVLP(AMPLTD, DUR, T)
      IF (T.GE.0.025) GO TO 1
C—CALCULATION FOR RISE TIME
      ENVLP = AMPLTD * T/0.025
      RETURN
    1 IF (DUR-0.100-T) 2,3,3
C—CALCULATION FOR DECAY TIME
    2 ENVLP = AMPLTD * (DUR - T)/0.100
      RETURN
C—SETS TO MAXIMUM AMPLITUDE DURING SUSTAIN TIME
    3 ENVLP = AMPLTD
      RETURN
      END
```

Figure 4.6a FORTRAN.

```
function envelope(amplitude,duration,t: real): real;
  begin
    if t < 0.025 then
    envelope: = amplitude*t/0.025;
      else begin
              if t > duration-0.100 then
                envelope: = amplitude+(duration-t)/0.100;
                else envelope: = amplitude
            end
  end;
```

Figure 4.6b PASCAL.

	FUNCTION ENVELOPE
Variables	AMPLITUDE: peak amplitude of onset
	DURATION: total duration of note
	T: time variable
Procedure	1. If T is greater than .025, skip to #2, otherwise set ENVELOPE to AMPLITUDE * T/0.025 and return to main program
	2. If T is greater than DURATION - 0.100, then set ENVELOPE to AMPLITUDE * DURATION - T)/0.100; otherwise set ENVELOPE to AMPLITUDE
	3. Return to main program

Figure 4.6c English.

several milliseconds to complete. So an entire second may be required to compute a few mere samples, and this is only for a monophonic composition.

Clearly, if the waveforms are generated by this method of additive synthesis for each cycle, the demands made on the computer processor present a major problem, unless a shorter method is found. As mentioned earlier, some computer systems overcome this difficulty by installing hardware that is designed to calculate the sine function without calling a lengthy subprogram. Another alternative to the waveform generation method described thus far is one that employs a table-lookup procedure. One may note that in the program we have formulated thus far, each cycle of the tone being generated requires the same set of identical calculations. In a table-lookup procedure, the calculations used to synthesize a waveform are performed once to produce a table of numbers long enough to represent one cycle of the wave. Then that table is used as a prototype to generate copies of itself. To synthesize a tone consisting of repetitive cycles of that prototype waveform, we use the table rather than the sine subprogram. Suppose that the pitch of a particular note is 500 cycles per second. (500 cycles is chosen because it is a round number, even though it does not actually correspond to a note on the standard tempered scale.) One cycle of this waveform will then have a period of $\frac{1}{500}$ second or 2 milliseconds. Since the sampling interval is 1/20000 second = 0.05 millisecond, each waveform cycle will contain 2/0.05 = 40 samples. Suppose, now, that the duration of this note is $\frac{1}{2}$ second. When the computation for this note is performed, the same set of 40 samples would ordinarily be computed 250 times. This redundancy is quite unnecessary and can be greatly reduced. We may now develop a method of obtaining our waveform for 250 cycles or as many repetitions as we like, but do it without requiring all the unnecessary, repetitive calculation. In upgrading the simple program presented in the first example of this chapter, our objective has been to increase its flexibility and versatility. By doing this, the compositions obtainable from this program become potentially more interesting and artistically satisfactory. But in the modification we are currently pursuing, our aim is not directed at any of the characteristics of the composition per se. Our concern here is with the efficiency of the method being used to generate the composition. It has no artistic significance, but must be given due consideration in view of the expense of computer time. Whenever possible, a competent computer programmer should be thrifty and economical in designing his programs. Avoiding redundant computation often requires increased length and complexity in the computer programs themselves. The reduction of repetitious calculation in our tone-generating program will correspondingly require some further complication. But the complication and additional programming will be worthwhile in view of the computer processing time that it will save.

The formation of the prototype array is quite simple. We use the same WAVEFORM function that we employed previously. But for flexibility the prototype array should have many more samples than the actual tone array will have. The reason for this will become apparent later as we see how the prototype is used. Let us load it with 2000 samples. The frequency variable in its computation will then be the sampling frequency of 20,000 per second divided by the number of samples (2000) which is 10 cycles per second. We need not write another program to compute this 2000 prototype waveform array, because it will be almost identical to the WAVEFORM function if it is called 2000 times with the frequency variable equal to 10 cycles per second.

Assume that the array has been computed and is sitting in a block of memory. Suppose, also, that the samples of this array are represented as shown in Fig. 4.7. At this point, the array is fixed in memory and for our purposes, the waveform's frequency is unspecified. Our goal is to obtain a

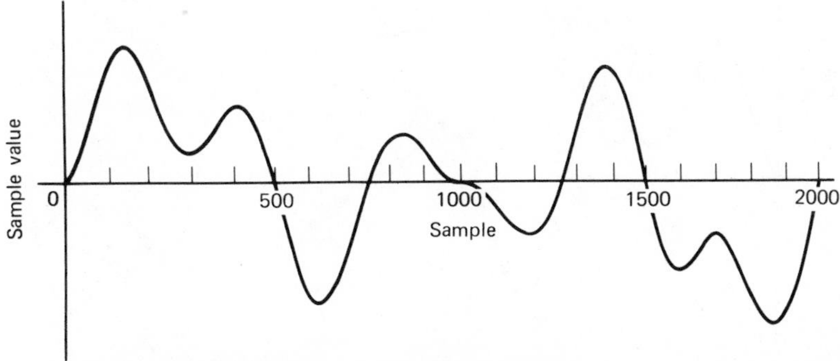

Figure 4.7 A prototype waveform.

waveform that looks similar to the one in Fig. 4.7, but has a number of samples that set it to a particular frequency. In our example the frequency is 500 cycles per second. The sampling rate is 20,000/second so the number of samples in one cycle of the waveform is still 20,000/500 = 40. The prototype waveform of Fig. 4.7 contrains 2000 samples; and even though the waveform we want to extract from it is to have only 40 samples, it still must have the same shape. To obtain this, we simply need to take 40 samples out of the original array at equally spaced intervals. This calls for selection of every fiftieth sample as shown in Fig. 4.8.

The forty samples represented by the points in the graph correspond to a duration of 40/20000 = 0.002 second or 2 milliseconds. Although this example coincidentally chooses a desired waveform interval that divides evenly into the number of samples in the prototype array, this will not typically be the case. In Fig. 4.8, we conveniently took one sample for every 50 in the array. But if the frequency had been 501 cycles per second instead to 500, the intervals between the chosen points would be 50.1. This is impossible to realize because the array does not contain values for fractional intervals. If Fig. 4.8 were a continuous function, its value at intervals of 50.1 would be defined. For example, the value of such a continuous function at sample 50.1 would be just slightly greater than the value at sample 50. But the array, being a discrete set of numbers, does not have a value defined for sample 50.1 or for any sample that is not an integer.

Consequently, to obtain samples for frequencies that are not integrally divisible by 10, we must find some form of compromise. The simplest and most direct compromise available in this situation is to use the value of the sample nearest to the point desired. For example, let S be a discrete variable representing the index of the prototype waveform array. S must be an integer between 0 and 2000. Now let $\overline{S}$ be a continuous variable that is a time index for our desired function. We will also let $W(S)$ be the value of the waveform magnitude as in Fig. 4.8. If the frequency of the desired waveform is 501 cycles per second, the first sample point will occur at $\overline{S}$ =

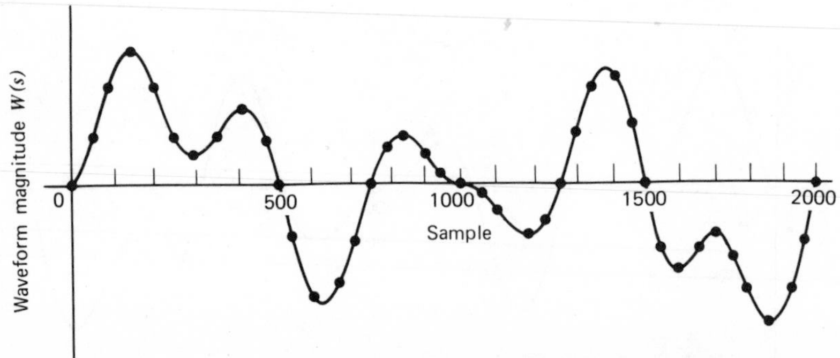

Figure 4.8 Sampled array of prototype waveform.

50.1 sampling intervals. The second will occur at $\bar{S}$ = 100.2, and the third at $\bar{S}$ = 150.3, and so forth. Since these points do not exist in the array, we round $\bar{S}$ off to the nearest integer. The first point in the waveform to be generated is therefore $W(S)$ where S = 50. Similarly, the second and third points are W(100) and W(150). Where $\bar{S}$ = 400.8 and 450.9 at the eighth and ninth points, the values of W(401) and W(451) are called for.

One can readily see that use of the rounding-off method just described will result in some jitter in the output. For some applications where the prototype waveform is not too complex, this distortion will not be too significant. However, if the waveform does have strong high-frequency components or if greater precision is desired, we can improve its accuracy. One way is to increase the number of samples in the prototype array, thus effectively shortening the intervals between successive values of S. This naturally makes greater demands on the computer's available memory space. Another method is that of interpolation. To illustrate an example of linear interpolation, let us assume that we are seeking a value of the waveform magnitude at $\bar{S}$ = 100.2. Assume also that in the array the values W(100) = 2.10 and W(101) = 2.30 as shown in Fig. 4.9. To find the interpolated value for $\bar{S}$ = 100.2, we first calculate the difference between it and the nearest lower value of S which is 100.2 − 100 = 0.2. This simply tells us that $\bar{S}$ is 0.2 times the distance from S = 100 to S = 101. We therefore want the interpolated value to lie 0.2 times the interval between W(100) and W(101) away from W(100). Since W(100) = 2.10 and W(101) = 2.30, this interval length is 2.30 − 210 = 0.20. 0.2 Times that is 0.04, so the interpolated value we are looking for is consequently 2.10 + 0.04 = 2.14. Needless to say, the price to be paid for the increased precision gained by interpolation in table-lookup procedures is the increase in the number of computations required to carry them out.

This chapter has concentrated on the description of a method of tone generation called *additive synthesis*. The procedure is so titled because it comprises the addition of a fundamental tone and its separate harmonics. The harmonics are derived from sine waves of different frequencies that are computed before their sum is taken. The method of additive synthesis described here is the most basic approach because all of the component tones are sinusoidal and are harmonics of the fundamental tone. Moreover, the partials are all summed into a complex, but strictly periodic waveform before any modulation takes place. Only the presynthesized, output waveform is enveloped or frequency-modulated. Although this basic form of additive synthesis is relatively easy to implement on the computer, it suffers some serious limitations. It can be used to generate tones with an infinite variety of timbres, but the quality of these tones is very static. To the ear, they sound sterile and mechanical, and lack the mellow richness of tones played by musicians on natural instruments.

It is possible, though, to use additive synthesis to produce tones that are acoustically much more interesting than can be derived from the method

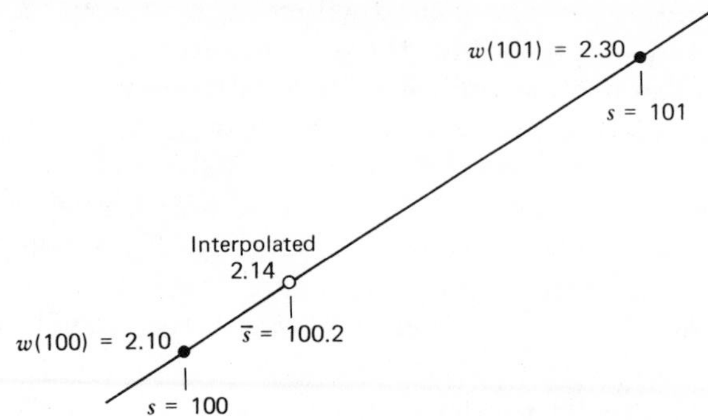

Figure 4.9 Example of linear interpolation.

described thus far. Their production usually involves the inclusion of partials that are not harmonic to the fundamental frequency. It also entails separate dynamic control of the individual partials. Once again, the increased complexity pays its price in computation time. Because the computation of many sine tones required by additive synthesis techniques demands much more time of the computer processor than is the duration of the actual sound to be generated, the computed samples must be temporarily stored in secondary memory before they can be converted to sound by the DAC. However, it is possible to use alternative methods of tone generation that are much less demanding on the processor. If the method chosen is computationally simple enough to allow the processor to calculate samples faster than the sampling rate, the tone-generation can be done in real time. This allows the processor to send computed samples directly to the DAC interface without writing files or involving the disk or drum memory units. The composer or performer then hears the music directly as it is being produced.

Earlier in the chapter, we noted how our basic additive synthesis procedure could be used to generate a prototype waveform. A stored waveform such as this could actually be formulated in any one of several ways, including the sampling and digitization of an actual tape-recorded sound. When the prototype waveform is used in a table-lookup procedure such as the one previously described in this chapter, the savings in computation time render it a candidate for real-time application. A computer program that generates tones for on-line use in real time does not need to store blocks of samples in arrays and write them on file as does the tone-generation programs heretofore discussed. An on-line program merely needs to compute one sample at a time and send it directly to the DAC at the required sampling rate. However, this introduces a problem that we have not encountered so far in our memory-oriented programs. In those programs, it did not matter what rate the samples were computed and sent to disk, as long as the job got done. But now in real time, the DAC is involved directly with the central processor. It takes its samples from the processor rather than from the secondary memory, and the secondary memory is not even involved. This situation is analogous to a secretary who must type the pages of a long report and submit each page to his or her boss at exact 5 minute intervals rather than be allowed to type the report and submit it as a whole after it is completed. The secretary has no trouble typing fast enough, but is being constantly interrupted by telephone calls and people coming into the office. Let us assume that even with the interruptions, the secretary can alternate between typing, answering the telephone, and other duties, yet still finish at least one page every 5 minutes. But while he or she is able to do this fast enough, she cannot submit the pages at the required exact intervals of 5 minutes because of her interruptions.

To overcome this difficulty, the secretary buys a machine that contains a stack of 16 slots. The slots each hold one sheet of paper, and they rotate in such a way that each time one of the slots moves past a certain position, a mechanical arm pulls the paper from it and places the paper in a dispenser. The slots pass the dispenser exactly once every 5 minutes. For example, he or she could type four or five pages in a 5-minute interval, and then not type for 20 minutes. As long as the machine remains loaded with between 1 and 16 pages, it will dispense a page exactly every 5 minutes as required.

Like this fictitious secretary, a computer processor does not execute a program at a constant, steady rate, but is continually interrupted by other procedures that relate to system management. Although in real-time operation, the processor can send samples to the DAC fast enough, it cannot normally send them at the exact sampling intervals. This makes it necessary to build special hardware to interface the DAC to the central processing unit. Such a device works analogously to the secretary's machine. It accepts computer words at an intermittant rate, holds them in a small buffer of a few registers, then outputs them to the DAC at the clocked sampling rate. Fortunately, once this hardware is built into the computer, it is invisible to the programmer or composer. It is mentioned here in conjunction with on-line tone generation because this situation is encountered whenever a computer is to be used in real time. Thus, it is pertinant for one to be aware of this aspect of computer architecture for the sake of understanding how the system operates even if it does not directly affect his programming procedure.

This chapter has described one possible method of deriving musical tones by means of computation. It aimed to illustrate the logical principle involved in simple tone-generation rather than to attempt an exhaustive survey of the wide range of compositional techniques. The procedure that was illustrated was useful for synthesis of a plain, monophonic sequence of notes, but would be highly impractical for an actual musical composition. However, with nearly trivial modifications in its logic, the program could be further revised to play chords, place several voices in counterpoint, exercise increased dynamic control, and be adapted to various musical styles. The application of computer programming techniques to musical composition requires the ingenuity of the composer and cannot be supplied as a recipe from a textbook. The techniques described in this chapter are offered as a starting point for the development of advanced skills and practice required to synthesize music of artistic value. As mentioned earlier, the technique of simple, additive synthesis described here is very restrictive in the kinds of tones it can produce. But they are fundamental to the understanding of more sophisticated techniques that will be explored later in this book. The reader is therefore recommended to become familiar with these basic concepts of sound synthesis and gain practical experience in implementing them on the computer.

REFERENCES

Alles, H. G., "A Portable Digital Sound Synthesis System," *Computer Music Journal* **1**(4), 5–15 (1977).

Baker, R. A., "Musicomp," Technical Report No. 9, University of Illinois, Experimental Music Studio, July 1963.

Bischoff, J. R. Gold, & J. Horton, "Music for an Interactive Network of Microcomputers," *Computer Music Journal* **2**(3), 24–29 (1978).

Buxton, Reeves, Baecker, & Mezei, "The Use of Hierarchy and Instance in a Data Structure for Computer Music," *Computer Music Journal* **2**(4), 10–20 (1978).

Byrd, Donald, "An Integrated Computer Music Software System," *Computer Music Journal* **1**(2), 55–60 (1977).

Dashow, James, "Three Methods for the Digital Synthesis of Chordal Structures with Non-Harmonic Partials," *Interface* **7** 67–94 (1978).

Howe, Hubert, *Electronic Music Synthesis*, Norton, 1975.

Manthey, Michael W., "The Egg: A Purely Digital Real-Time Sound Synthesizer," CHUM **11,** 353–365 (1977).

Mathews, M. V., *The Technology of Computer Music*, MIT Press, 1969.

Nolan, R. L., *FORTRAN IV Computing and Applications*, Addison-Wesley, 1971.

Organick, E. I., & L. P. Meissner, **FORTRAN IV,** 2nd ed, Addison-Wesley, 1974.

Powell, R., "Synthesizer Techniques: Computers and Synthesis," *Cont. Keyboard*, **3,** 54 (Sept. 1977).

Risset, J., *An Introductory Catalog of Computer Synthesized Sound*, Murray Hill, New Jersey Bell Telephone Laboratories, 1969.

Rolnick, N. B., "A Composer's Notes on the Development and Implementation of Software for a Digital Synthesizer," *Computer Music Journal* **2**(2), 13–22 (1978).

Smith, L. "Score: A Musician's Approach to Computer Music," *NUMUS-W* 4, 21–28 (1973).

Smoliar, Stephen W., "A data Structure for an Interactive Music System," *Interface* **2,** 122–140 (1973).

Truax, Barry, "The Computer Composition-Sound Synthesis Programs POD4, POD5, & POD6," *Sonological Reports*, No. 2, Institution of Sonology, Utrecht, 1973.

Truax, Barry, "Some Programs for Real-Time Computer Synthesis and Composition," *Interface* **2,** 159–167 (1973).

Truax, Barry, "General Techniques of Computer Composition Programming," *NUMUS-W* no. 4 17–20 (1973).

Vercoe, Barry, "The Music 360 Language for Sound Synthesis," Proceedings of the American Society of University Composers **6,** 16–21 (1971).

Wirth, N., & K. Jensen, *PASCAL User Manual and Report*, Springer-Verlag, 1975.

5

MODULATION AND DYNAMICS

The introductory portion of this text has pursued two main objectives: to introduce the reader to the operation and use of a digital computer, and to relate this operation to the synthesis of musical sounds. Thus far, it has mostly concentrated on generating static tones with fixed harmonic characteristics. Although such static tones are convenient to study mathematically and simple to produce electronically, they are not plentiful in nature. Moreover, static sounds are aesthetically uninteresting. If a computer were only capable of synthesizing dry, sterile, mechanical-sounding waveforms, it would prove entirely unacceptable as a musical instrument. The conventional musical instruments that have been invented, developed, and perfected in past generations survive as permanent fixtures of the musical repertoire because they model the sounds of nature. A natural sound is pleasing and interesting to the human ear according to its complexity and the modulation of its structure. Music is an admixture of structured elements modulated by quasi-random processes. Consequently, the analysis and synthesis of a complex sound involve its decomposition into these static and dynamic elements.

The topic of musical analysis as an interrelationship of static and dynamic constituents is essential to the development of a theoretical foundation for the study of computer music composition. The basis of any art is variety and repetition. A tone such as an organ note sustained without any modulation very quickly becomes uninteresting. On the other hand, if a listener hears a sequence that follows no recognizable logical pattern and occurs unpredictably, it will also be uninteresting because no musical idea is communicated by it. But a musical composition that is unpredictable noise to one listener may have elements that are recognizably meaningful to another person who is familiar with the medium of the composition. This medium is analogous to a spoken language. A language is familiar to one group of people who speak it, but unintelligible to those to whom it is unfamiliar. By this analogy, a sound that is considered unintelligible noise may be termed an unpredictable or randomly modulated sound.

The degree of randomness or unpredictability of a signal is termed "entropy" in the literature of information theory. Since a musical composition synthesized by a computer becomes a voltage signal whose parameters are strictly defined and controlled by a programmed set of instructions, its information content is the primary interest of the composer. Just as randomly modulated noise has no aesthetic value, a static or predictably modulated sound is equally uninteresting. A random signal having maximum entropy is defined as noise. Its information content is unintelligible, hence uncommunicative. By contrast, a purely static tone such as a sustained sine tone is totally predictable, having zero entropy. Such a signal is maximally redundant, containing no new information. Thus a signal's redundancy may be considered as the inverse of its entropy, that is, the more new information it contains, the greater is its entropy and the less its redundancy. As already mentioned, a signal must sacrifice some entropy to be communicative; otherwise it is random noise.

A sine tone with minimal entropy is boring and even offensive to a listener who must hear it for more than a few seconds. Much less obnoxious is a sustained tone of an electric organ that contains not only the fundamental frequency, but some of its higher harmonics, adding tone color. A triangle wave sounds very much like the sustained tone of an oboe, but the oboe's tone is much warmer and more interesting because of the minute fluctuations in intensity, intonation, and tone color caused by the person playing the instrument. Tones produced by a violin or human voice possess the greatest latitude for modulation of amplitude, pitch, and timbre; consequently, they are the most expressive of musical instruments. They are also the most difficult to simulate mechanically or electronically.

One can surmise from this argument that the potential for aesthetic interest of a musical tone varies in relation to the manner and degree of its modulation. Similarly, a sequence of eight tones that have changing rhythmic patterns is much more interesting and artistically communicative than a single, sustained tone. But after three or four exact repetitions of the sequence, it too becomes boring. To be musically viable, the sequence itself must be modulated, and the modulation in turn be modulated, and so forth.

One may define music as sound that conveys a meaningful emotional message to its listener, and noise as a random signal that conveys no such message. According to this definition, musical sounds can be represented on a scale with unmodulated or predictably modulated signals at one pole and random noise at the other. Music, then, falls in the middle of this scale where it represents the interposition of both recognizable and unpredictable elements. One can readily observe that the location of any particular composition on such a scale will depend substantially on the mental and emotional disposition of the listener. Moreover, for any particular listener, the effects of a composition will depend on his or her frame of mind while listening to it as well as the number of times the piece has previously been heard.

The duty of a composer is to arrange notes into a pattern that forms a matrix of logically structured elements interwoven with special, original elements. The structure and originality of these elements define the style of the composition. The composer of computer music assumes the additional responsibility of stylistically defining and formulating the tonal characteristics of each particular sound of the composition as well as its overall contour. It is as if a composer of symphonic music were required to design and construct each of the instruments of the orchestra in addition to writing the score.

One fundamental way in which a tone is modulated is by change of its amplitude. Amplitude is the property of a sound that the ear perceives as loudness. However, the measure of a tone's amplitude and the estimation of its loudness are very different from each other. If the signal is electronic, the amplitude is the amount of variation in its instantaneous voltage or current. If the signal is acoustical, the amplitude is the variation of the air pressure constituting the sound. Loudness, on the other hand, is one's subjective aural response to the intensity of a sound. The relationship between amplitude and loudness is not linear—the ear does not respond to changes in amplitude with exactly corresponding changes in loudness perception. This concept is essential for the understanding of basic acoustics, and it can be demonstrated by an experiment involving a signal generator and a loudspeaker. Let us suppose that the generator is producing a sine wave at a midrange audible frequency such as 1000 cycles per second and its amplitude may be varied with a volume control. Its output is graphed in Fig. 5.1. Suppose also that the generator is feeding its signal to a loudspeaker which has 100% efficiency, namely, it loses no energy in transforming the electric current into sound.

We begin by setting the amplitude control to zero and then steadily increase it at the rate of 10 millivolts per second. The increase in amplitude is plotted in Fig. 5.2.

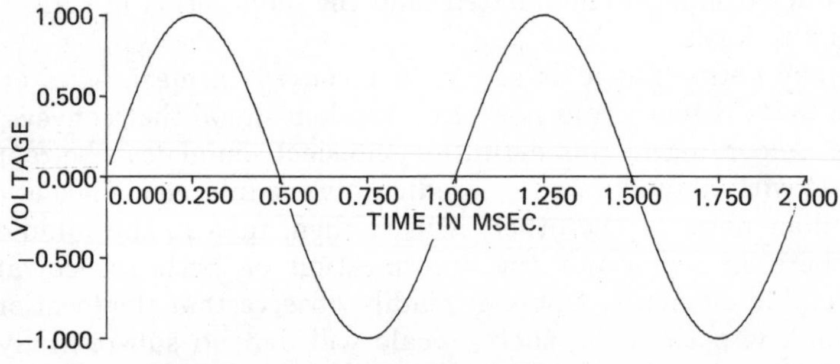

Figure 5.1 A sine wave.

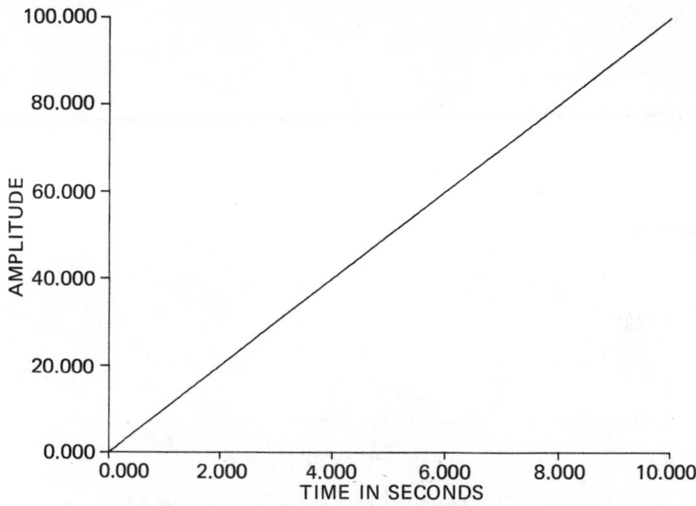

Figure 5.2 Linear increase of amplitude.

The next step is to graph the increase in the loudness of the tone coming out of the loudspeaker. This is not so easy, since loudness is a subjective quality and consequently is not directly measurable. Harvey Fletcher and other scientists have made extensive measurements of the psochoacoustical characteristics of different sounds and their intensity levels. In investigating the ear's response to acoustic intensity, scales have been devised to approximate the loudness of sound as perceived by the ear. The loudness is generally measured (albeit inexactly) in units of "sones," or "phons." These units were scaled so as to divide loudness levels into equal increments according to the hearing mechanism. As one listens to the loudspeaker of our experiment while the tone's amplitude increases linearly with time as in Fig. 5.2, he or she may plot its increase in loudness as in Fig. 5.3. We immediately notice from this graph that the ear does not respond immediately to the applied sound. Rather, the sound is not heard until its amplitude reaches the threshold of hearing. Although the amplitude is below that threshold, it is too faint to be heard at all. Then, even though the rate of increase in amplitude is constant, the rate of increase in loudness tapers. Figure 5.3 shows how the slope of the loudness curve gradually decreases as the actual amplitude increases.

It is found mathematically that the logarithmic function is a good approximation of this amplitude-loudness relationship. In fact, the graph of a log function closely resembles the curve of Fig. 5.3. Consequently, physicists have chosen a logarithmic scale for use in measuring sound intensity. The unit for this measurement is the decibel. The absolute decibel scale is defined so that its zero point corresponds to the threshold

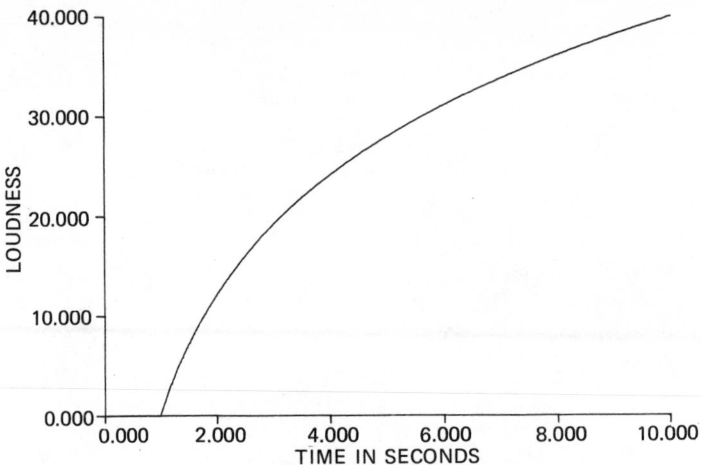

Figure 5.3 Logarithmic increase of loudness.

of hearing. Normally, the decibel scale is used comparatively to measure the intensity of a signal in relation to an arbitrary standard. Its mathematical definition is:

$$\text{intensity (decibels)} = 10 \log_{10} \frac{P_1}{P_0}$$

Here, P_1 is the power of the sound being measured and P_0 is the power of the reference to which it is being compared. If one is comparing amplitudes rather than power, the equation is

$$\text{intensity} = 20 \log_{10} \frac{A_1}{A_0}$$

In this alternate equation, A_0 and A_1 are the relative amplitudes. If P_0 is the threshold of hearing, it is found that an intensity of 120 decibels is loud enough to cause physical pain. It is also found experimentally that a change of approximately 1 decibel is necessary to be perceptible to the human ear. The mathematical consequence of this is that each time the power of a signal is doubled, its intensity increases by approximately 3 decibels. This is because 10 $\log_{10}$ 2/1 approximately equals 3. Consequently, if a loudspeaker is being driven with 1 watt of power and putting out 60 decibels of sound intensity, 2 watts will produce 63 decibels, 4 watts will increase it to 66 decibels, 10 watts will deliver 70 decibels, and 100 watts would theoretically increase it to 80 decibels except that so much power would actually destroy the loudspeaker first.

If a composer wishes to write a crescendo into a passage of composition on the computer, he or she will probably be tempted to increase the amplitude of the computed waveform in uniform increments similar to Fig. 5.2. But doing this would lead to the undesirable auditory results of Fig. 5.3 as has been demonstrated. If one is to form a crescendo that actually increases in loudness uniformly the amplitude must be increased by a relation that is the inverse of the logarithmic function. Such a relation is the exponential function. Since the decibel scale is defined with the common base 10 logarithm, one may correspondingly use the base 10 for an exponent, although another base such as 2 or the constant *e* could be used with essentially the same results. One may write the increase in amplitude as a function of time with the equation

$$\text{amplitude}\ (t) = \text{intensity} * 10^{(rate\ *\ t)}$$

where intensity is the amplitude level at time $t = 0$ and rate is the rate of increase of the crescendo. Figure 5.4 is a graph of this function for intensity = 10 and rate = 0.1. If the amplitude of a tone increases according to this relationship, its loudness will increase uniformly as in Fig. 5.5.

When one plays an electric organ, he or she controls the loudness of the tone with the organ's stops and a foot pedal. But as each note is played, its articulation is static. The organ key acts as an on/off switch so that the onset of the tone is immediate as the key is depressed. Its decay is also immediate as the key is released, unless it has a built-in envelope generator. Natural instruments, however, do not behave this way. The timbre of a tone is determined by its harmonic content, but two tones having

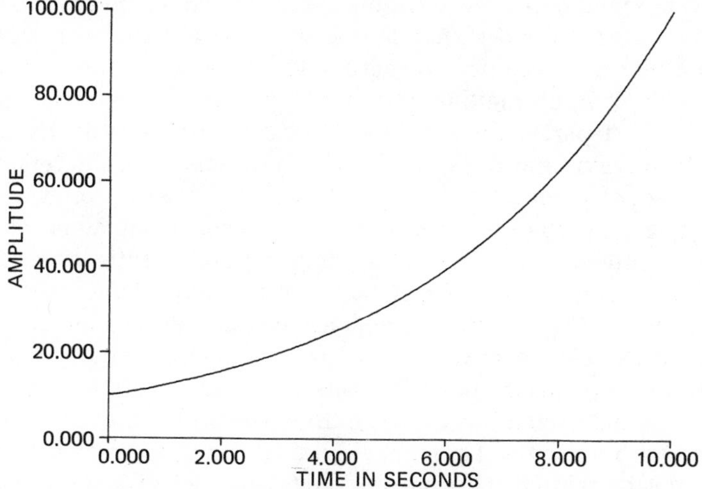

Figure 5.4 Exponential increase of amplitude.

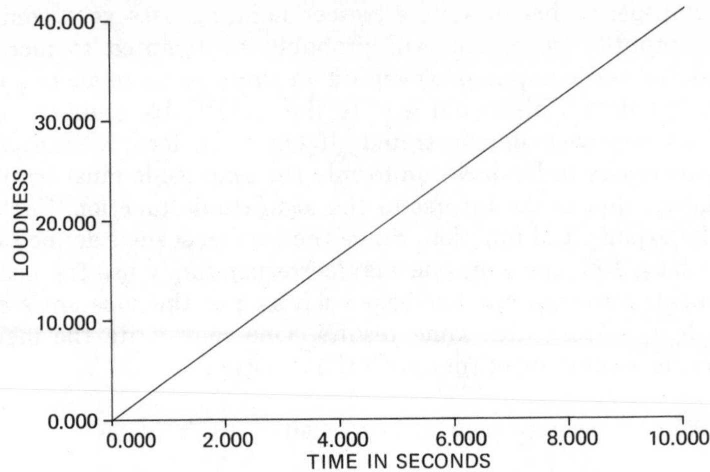

Figure 5.5 Linear increase of loudness.

identical harmonic content may sound radically different from each other depending on their articulations. This fact can be fully appreciated if one plays a recording of piano music backward. The resulting tones have no resemblance to piano notes!

It is possible to analyze the articulation of various sounds by plotting their amplitudes as they vary with time. The onset period as the amplitude increases is called the rise time or attack time. Then as the tone dies out, the decrease in amplitude is referred to as the decay time. The overall contour of the sound is called the envelope. Figure 4.4 of the preceding chapter depicted a simple, artificial envelope with linear rise and decay times. Suppose that a sine wave of 120 cycles per second is modulated by this envelope. The actual waveform will appear as in Figure 5.6. Writing a computer subprogram that takes an arbitrary waveform and shapes it with a particular envelope is a fairly simple task. By assigning the attack, sustain, and decay periods with different parameters, the tone can be made to sound mellow, twangy, percussive, or whistle-like. Obviously, a tone that is given a carefully shaped envelope will sound much more interesting and natural than a purely static tone. But how natural does even a well-enveloped tone sound? One can listen to electronically synthesized tones, which have complex envelopes that are nearly identical to the envelopes of natural instruments, yet they still sound sterile and electronic. Why this is so is an interesting question. Actually, this discussion has oversimplified the problem of dynamic sound synthesis. With apologies to Henry David Thoreau, one may say that simplicity is not correlated with nature. The dynamics of a sound cannot be modeled by one envelope alone. The reader may recall the discussion in Chapter 2 about the harmonic properties of tones. A string was shown to vibrate in different modes, producing harmonics as well as its fundamental frequency. A column of air behaves similarly. If an instrument produced a purely static tone, having no amplitude modulation, it could be simulated electronically or with the computer directly by adding sine tones of its fundamental frequency, the higher harmonics, and whatever subharmonics are present in their correct proportions. But as soon as the resulting waveform, which is the sum of several tones, is shaped by a single envelope, the trouble begins. This is because when a string is actually plucked or bowed, when a wind instrument is played, or when a tonal percussive instrument is struck, the constituent frequency components of the tone it makes each have separate envelopes that are different from each other. This means that the amplitude is not the only property of a waveform to be modulated as the tone is sounded. The timbre is also modulated.

To illustrate how timbre modulation is affected by separately enveloping the component frequencies of a tone, we may view an overall envelope for a typical note played on the trumpet. The envelopes of Figs. 5.7 and 5.8 similar to those obtained by Meyer and Buchmann's experiments cannot be interpreted strictly because the actual articulations of different trumpet notes exhibit a large variation. But one may interpret them as general characteristics of trumpet and violin tones. Their analysis reveals that the lower harmonics have envelopes that are remarkably dissimilar to their upper harmonics.

There is another interesting phenomenon that results from modulating the amplitude of a tone. We recall that any static tone having a strictly periodic waveform can be decomposed into a discrete set of sine tones having different frequencies. Chapter 2 showed how these components could be graphed as impulses or singularities in the frequency domain. This was possible because the tones were considered to have infinite duration and

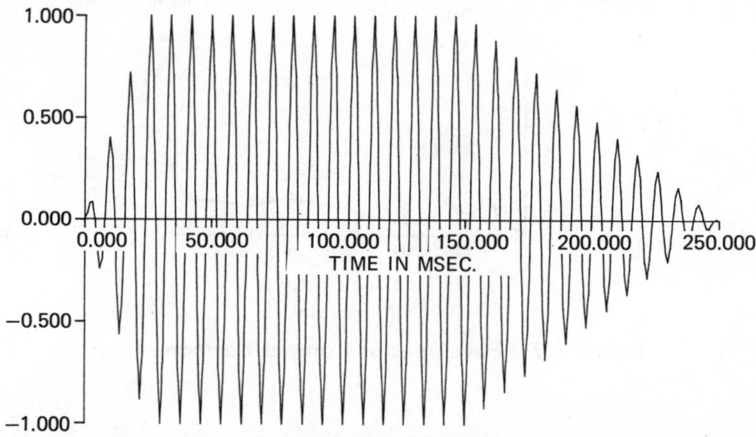

Figure 5.6 Sine wave modulated by envelope.

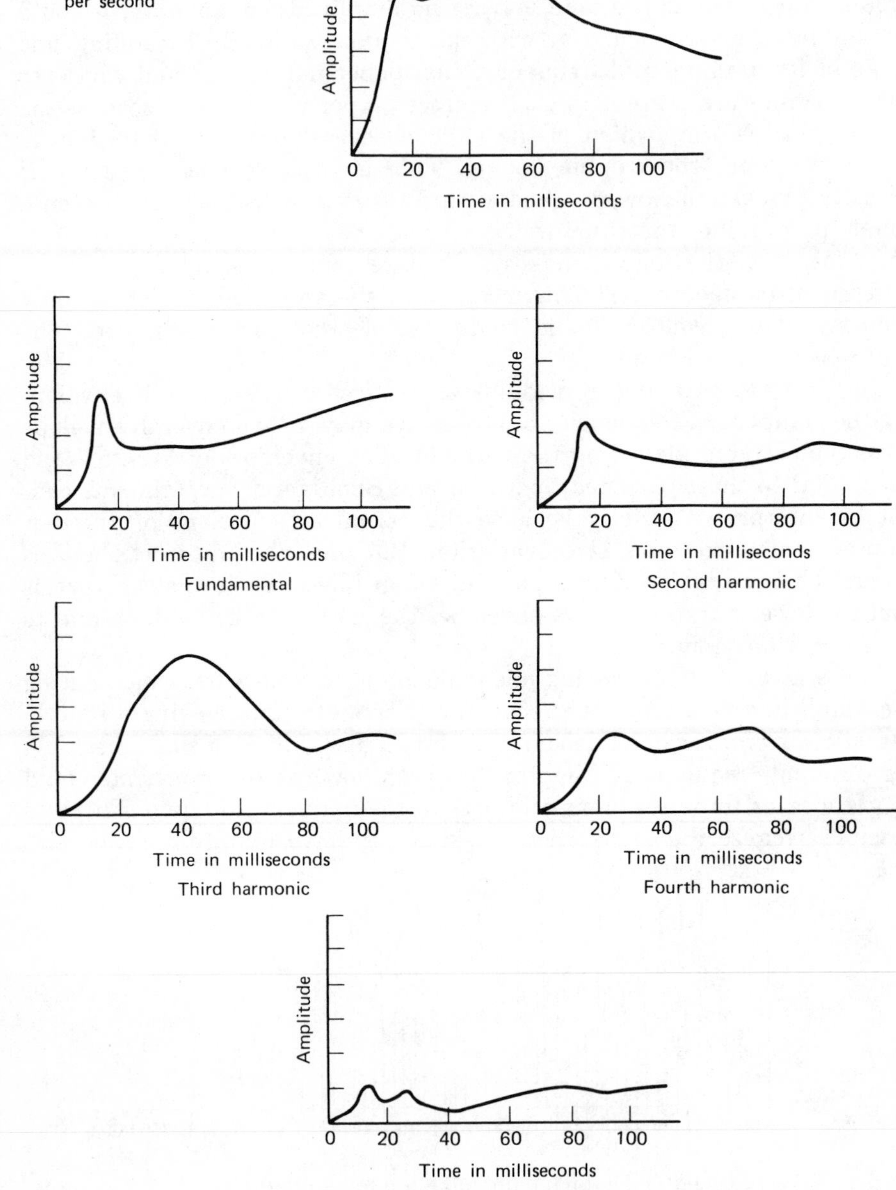

Figure 5.7 Envelopes of trumpet harmonics.

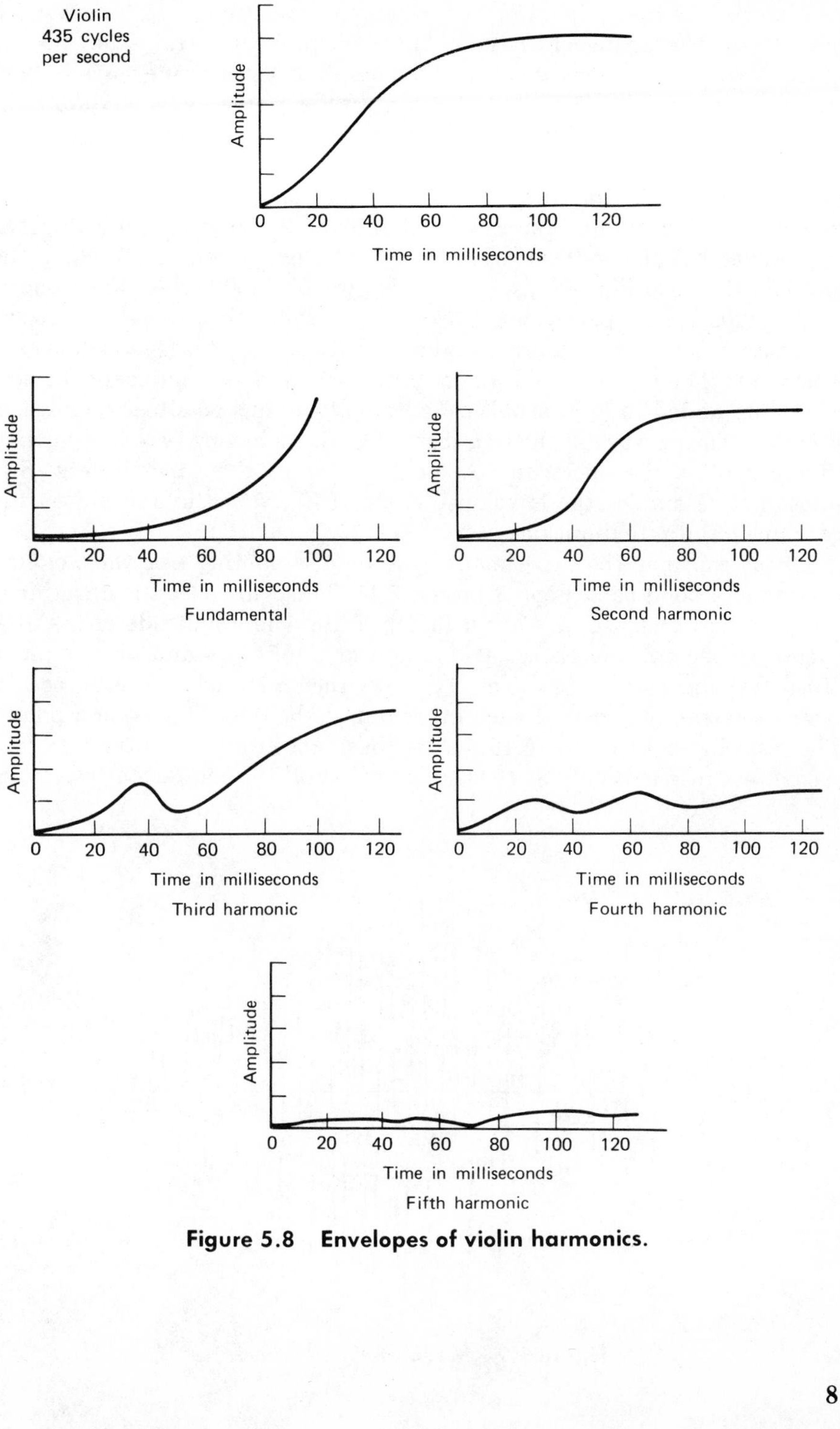

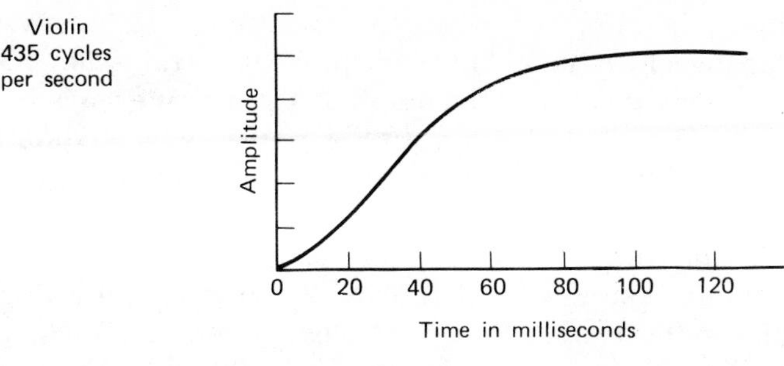

Violin
435 cycles
per second
Amplitude
0 20 40 60 80 100 120
Time in milliseconds
Amplitude
0 20 40 60 80 100 120
Time in milliseconds
Fundamental
Amplitude
0 20 40 60 80 100 120
Time in milliseconds
Second harmonic
Amplitude
0 20 40 60 80 100 120
Time in milliseconds
Third harmonic
Amplitude
0 20 40 60 80 100 120
Time in milliseconds
Fourth harmonic
Amplitude
0 20 40 60 80 100 120
Time in milliseconds
Fifth harmonic

Figure 5.8 Envelopes of violin harmonics.

no change in amplitude. However, when the amplitude of a sine wave is modulated, the change introduces an element of uncertainty in its frequency. We have already displayed the graph of a static sine wave in both the time domain and frequency domain. In Fig. 5.9, we now modulate the sine wave with an envelope. Its graph in the frequency domain, Fig. 5.10, is no longer a singularity, but is a contour of closely spaced frequencies. Why this occurs is somewhat difficult to comprehend at first, but it can be demonstrated by undertaking an experiment. We begin by drawing two sine waves having uniform amplitudes but slightly different frequencies and add them. In Fig. 5.11, we add a sine wave of 900 cycles per second to one of 1100 cycles per second. One may observe that these two curves alternately reinforce each other and go totally out of phase, canceling each other out. Their sum is shown in Fig. 5.12. The two independent sine waves are added to form a pulsating wave. It is thus possible to represent such a pulsating wave in the frequency domain as having two singularities. Figure 5.13 is the spectrum. A single pulse of the wave in Fig. 5.12 somewhat resembles the enveloped wave of Fig. 5.9. But the pulses still continue in infinite duration.

Let us continue the experiment by adding in another sine wave of 1000 cycles per second as in Figs. 5.14 and 5.15. This will cause the duration of the pulses to increase, as shown in Fig. 5.16. The amplitude of the 1000 cycles per second wave is set at double the amplitudes and reverse phase of the 900 and 1100 cycle waves. This way they reinforce at the $\frac{1}{200}$ second point, whereas they cancel each other out at the 0 and $\frac{1}{100}$ second points. The resulting wave of Fig. 5.16 reaches peak amplitudes at intervals of $\frac{1}{100}$ second because it is only at these points that all the component waves are

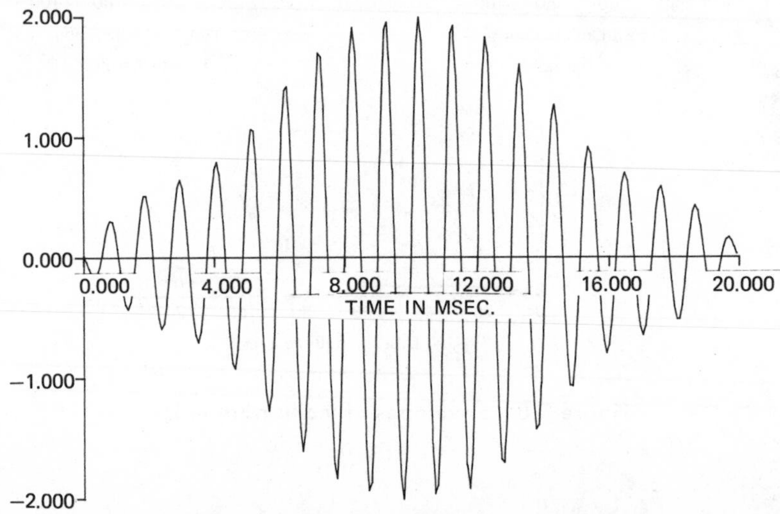

Figure 5.9 Modulated sine wave.

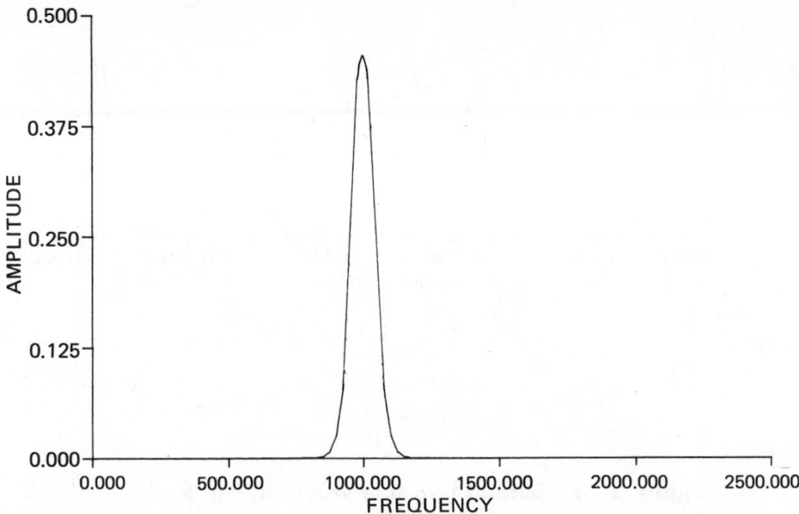

Figure 5.10 Frequency spectrum of modulated sine wave.

in phase reinforcing each other. Now let us add five waves of equal amplitude in Figs. 5.17 and 5.18. Their sum creates a wave whose pulses pulsate. The various pulsations are caused by the effect of the five independent waves either adding to each other or subtracting from each other depending on their relative positions. If the amplitudes of the five waves are strategically chosen, their sum will have a more continuous contour. Figures 5.19 and 5.20 show their graphs in the frequency and time domains.

The important point to notice here is that since the component frequencies are spaced apart at 50 cycles per second intervals, the waveform that their sum produces will only reach a peak amplitude every $\frac{1}{50}$ second. Without drawing more graphs, we may extend the argument to consider another waveform which is the sum of 20 sine waves extending from 900 to 1100 cycles per second in intervals of 10 cycles per second. The resulting wave will reach its maximum 10 times per second. Similarly, a sum of

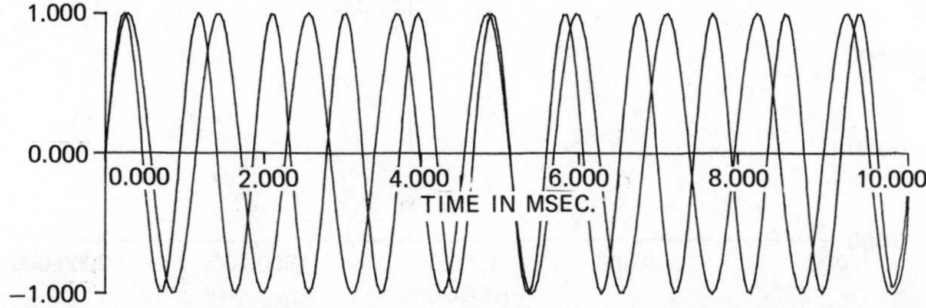

Figure 5.11 Superposition of two sine waves of different frequencies.

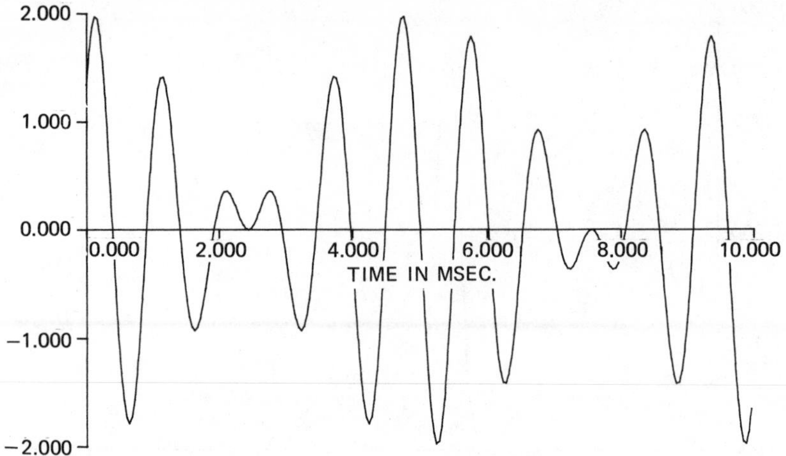

Figure 5.12 Sum of two sine waves in Fig. 5.11.

waves that differ by 1 cycle per second in their frequencies will reach its peak amplitude only once per second. The final extension of this logic assumes that the number of waves being added is no longer finite, being spaced apart at discrete intervals. Instead, we add an infinite number of sine waves having a continuous range of frequencies. The frequencies of these component waves differ infinitesimally, so that their spectrum is a contour rather than an impulse.

This time, the interval between frequency components has decreased until it approaches zero. Consequently, there is only one instant in time when all the waves in the range are in phase so that their sum reaches a maximum. At all other times, the components are out of phase, cancelling each other out. The cancellation causes their sum to diminish at points

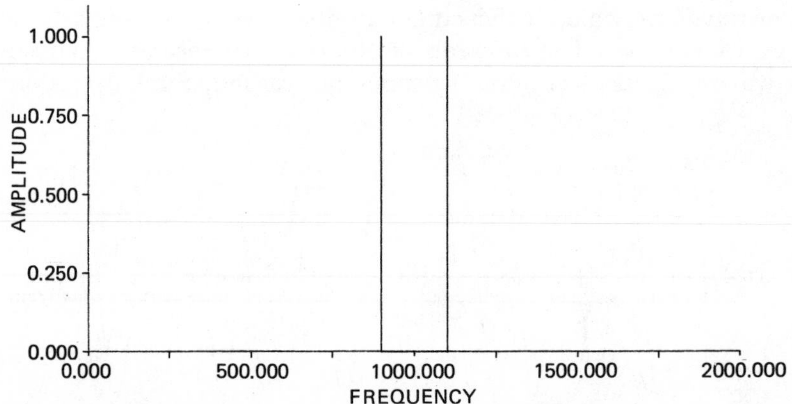

Figure 5.13 Frequency spectrum of two sine waves.

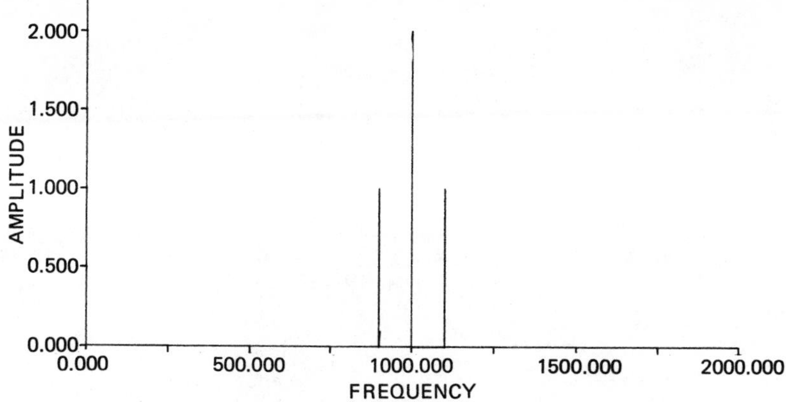

Figure 5.14 Frequency spectrum of three sine waves.

away from this center. Since the central frequency of the spectrum's contour is 1000 cycles per second, the corresponding waveform in the time domain looks like an enveloped sine wave of 1000 cycles per second. Although the wave pulse appears to have a frequency of 1000 cycles per second, its actual frequency is uncertain. This uncertainty is increased if the duration of the pulse is shortened. In Figs. 5.21 to 5.23 we compare the time and frequency domain representations of a long, an intermediate length, and a short wave pulse.

A very long pulse has a narrow frequency range. If it is allowed to be arbitrarily long, the frequency range will narrow to an impulse. Indeed, an impulse represents a static sine wave of infinite duration. Conversely, if the wave pulse is very short, it sounds less like a tone and more like a click, having a broad frequency range. If the pulse is arbitrarily short, its frequency range is indeterminate. Thus we can see that the more abruptly the amplitude of a tone changes, the greater is the uncertainty of the tone's frequency components. (This principle is analogous to the Heisenberg uncertainty principle of modern physics that states that the position and momentum of a particle cannot be simultaneously determined with arbitrary precision.) The loss of definition in frequency resulting from a

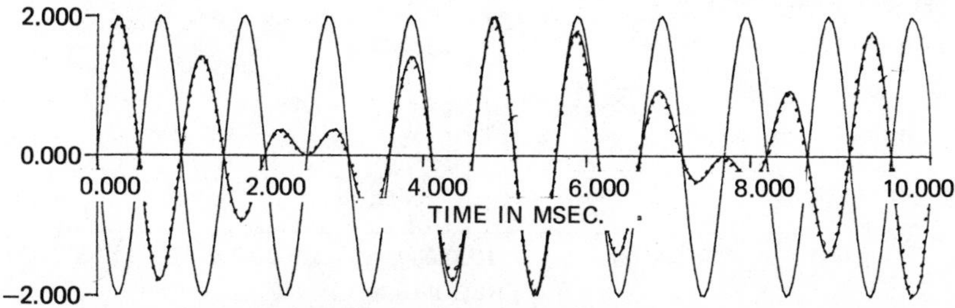

Figure 5.15 Addition of third sine wave to preceding sum.

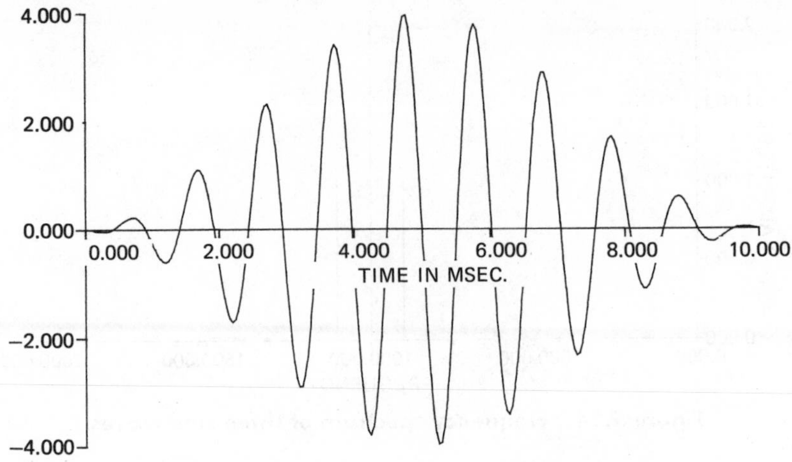

Figure 5.16 Sum of three sine waves.

dramatic and abrupt change in amplitude contributes to the entropy of a signal. The uncertainty of a waveform's frequency corresponds to its noise element. An unmodulated sine wave has no noise content, whereas pure noise has no determinable frequency. This substantiates the idea stated early in the chapter that a signal's modulation is a measure of its entropy.

The discussion above may be extended to include nonsinusoidal waveforms. Chapter 2 analyzed the frequency components of a sawtooth wave. Its graph and spectrum are repeated in Fig. 5.24. In Fig. 5.25, we modulate the sawtooth wave with a broadly contoured envelope. In the frequency domain, the impulses are replaced with contours. The wave pulse of Fig. 5.26 is again shorter, and the peaks in the frequency domain are broader and less defined.

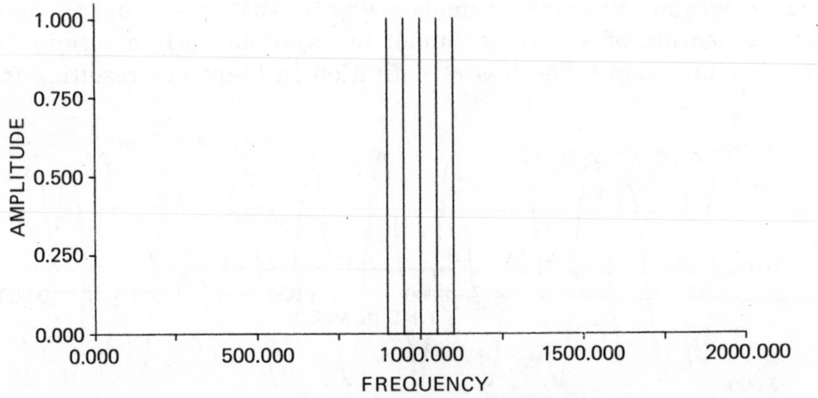

Figure 5.17 Frequency spectrum of five sine waves of equal magnitude.

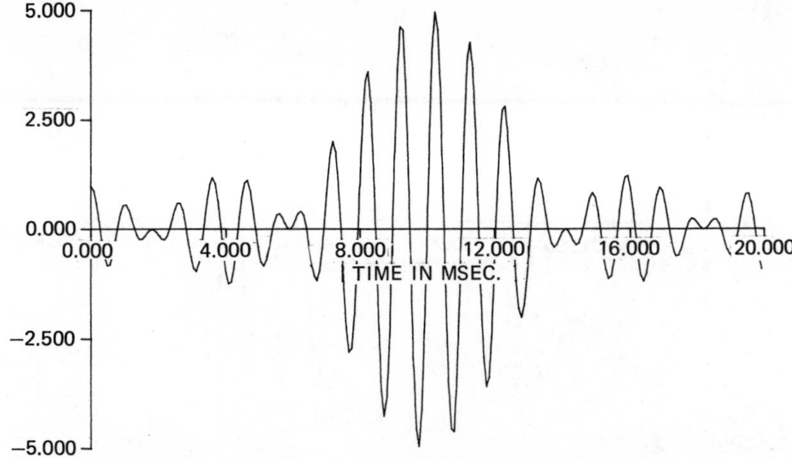

Figure 5.18 Sum of five sine waves of equal magnitude.

The increased uncertainty of the frequency components contributes to the signal's entropy, as shown by the more broadly contoured spectrum. This principle may be extended to state that a signal of pure noise is the sum of an infinite range of continuous frequencies having constant amplitude. Such a signal is termed "white noise" because it contains equal components of all the frequencies of the spectrum in the same sense that white light contains all the colors of the visual spectrum. A white noise signal sounds like a steady hiss if it is extended in time. An abrupt click also has the frequency spectrum of white noise.

Thus far, we have examined a significant principle of amplitude modulation: the dynamic change of a periodic signal multiplies its frequency content. Any signal that is strictly periodic and infinite in duration can be decomposed into a discrete number of sine waves having different

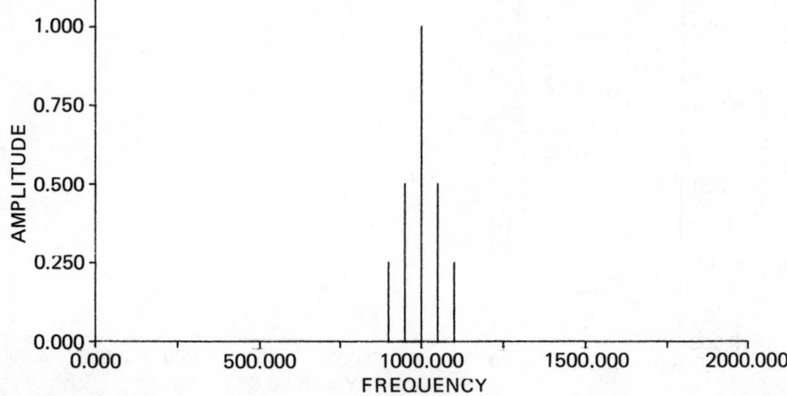

Figure 5.19 Frequency spectrum of five sine waves of unequal magnitude.

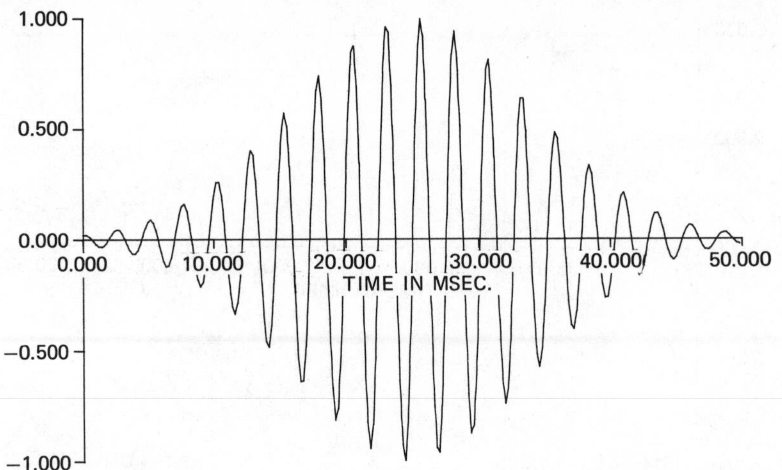

Figure 5.20 Sum of five sine waves of unequal magnitude.

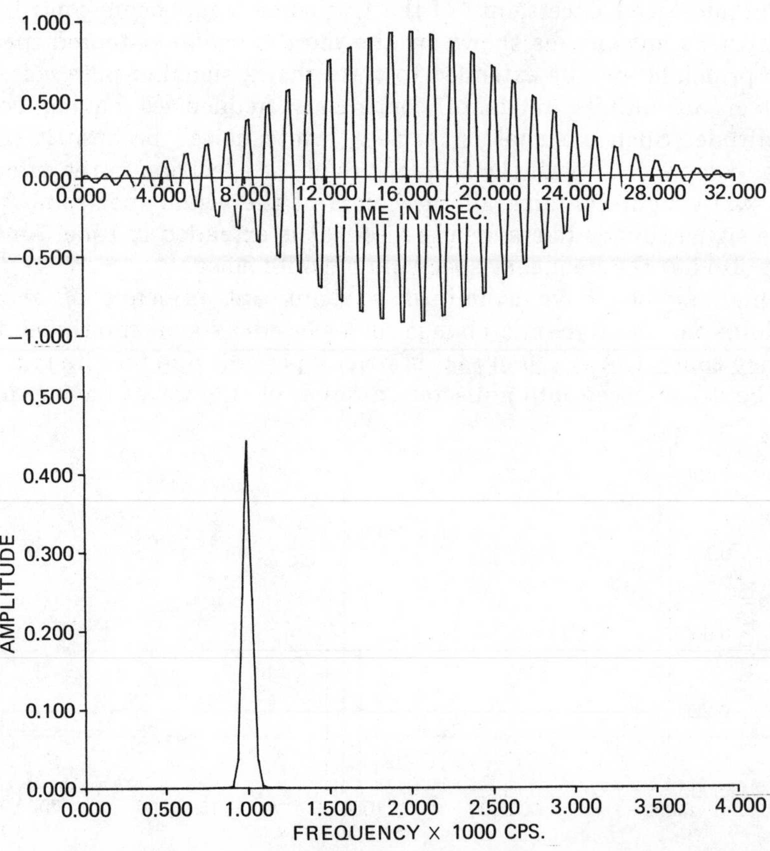

Figure 5.21 Long sine-wave pulse and its spectrum.

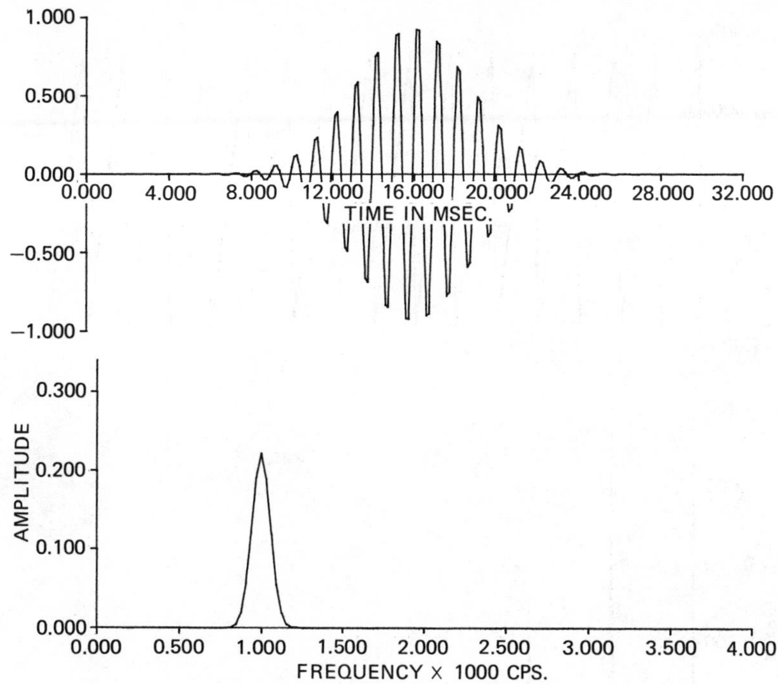

Figure 5.22 Medium-length sine-wave pulse and spectrum.

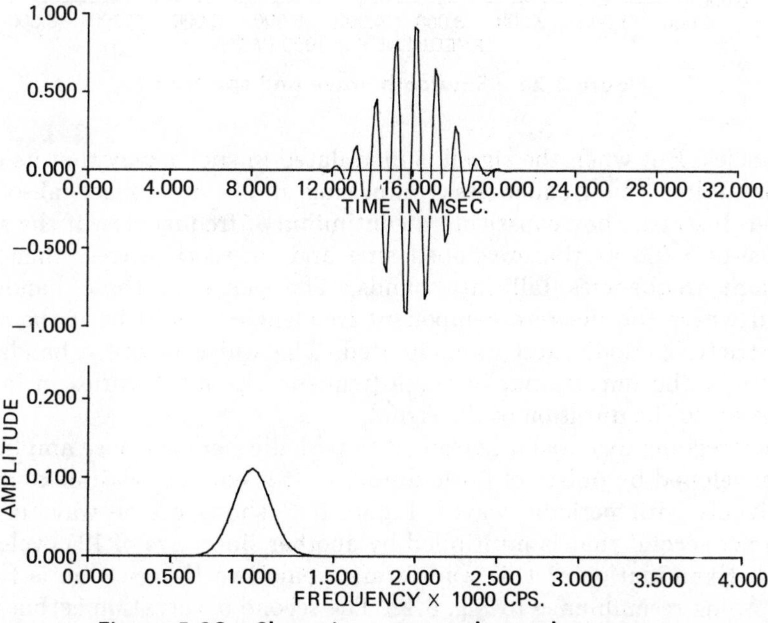

Figure 5.23 Short sine-wave pulse and spectrum.

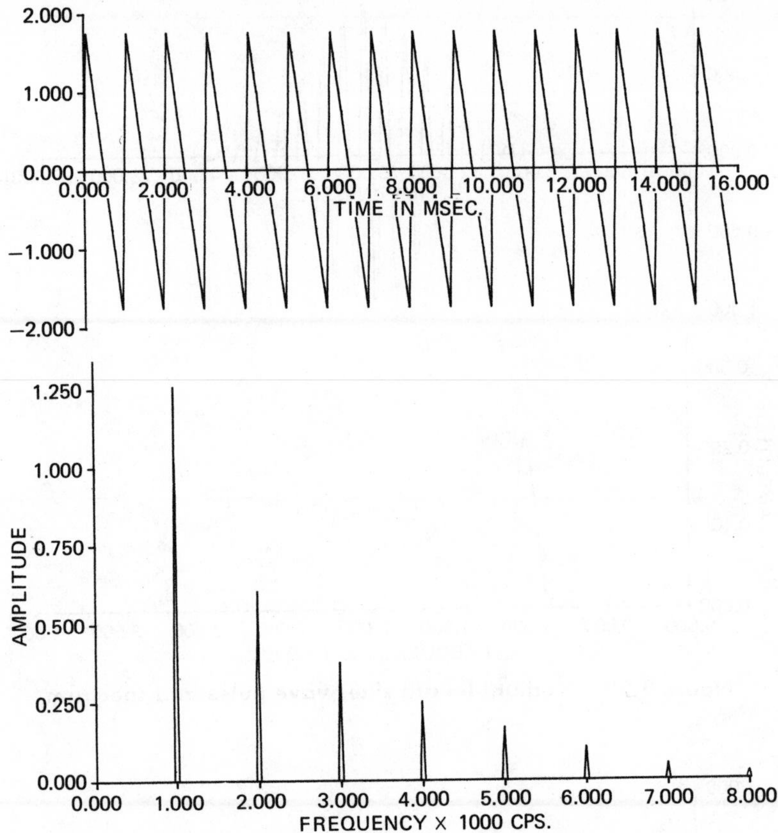

Figure 5.24 Sawtooth wave and spectrum.

frequencies. But when the signal is modulated in such a way that its duration is finite, the frequencies comprising it are no longer absolutely defined. Instead, they constitute a continuum of frequencies. If the signal is quasi-periodic as the enveloped sine and sawtooth waves, then their dominant frequencies fall into bands. The peaks in these bands are located where the discrete component frequencies would be if the signal were strictly periodic and unmodulated. The width of these bands is a measure of the uncertainty of these frequencies, and it varies in inverse proportion to the duration of the signal.

The foregoing discussion pertained to periodic signals whose amplitudes were enveloped by pulses of finite duration. It is equally possible to modulate signals with periodic waves. Figure 5.27 shows a sine wave of 1000 cycles per second that is multiplied by another sine wave of 125 cycles per second. Examination of this waveform reveals two things. One is that it has a strong resemblance to Fig. 5.12. The second observation is that there are now two frequency components introduced in addition to the original

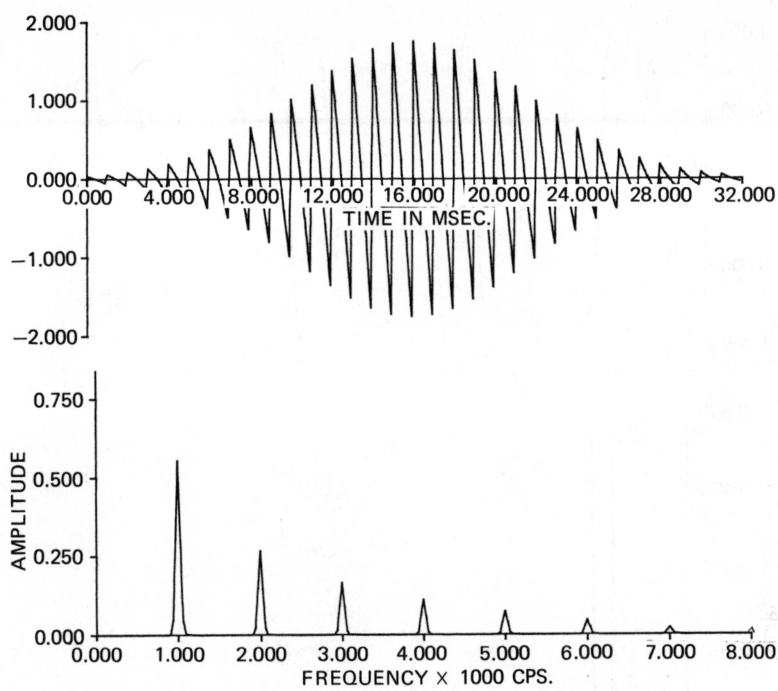

Figure 5.25 Long sawtooth wave pulse and spectrum.

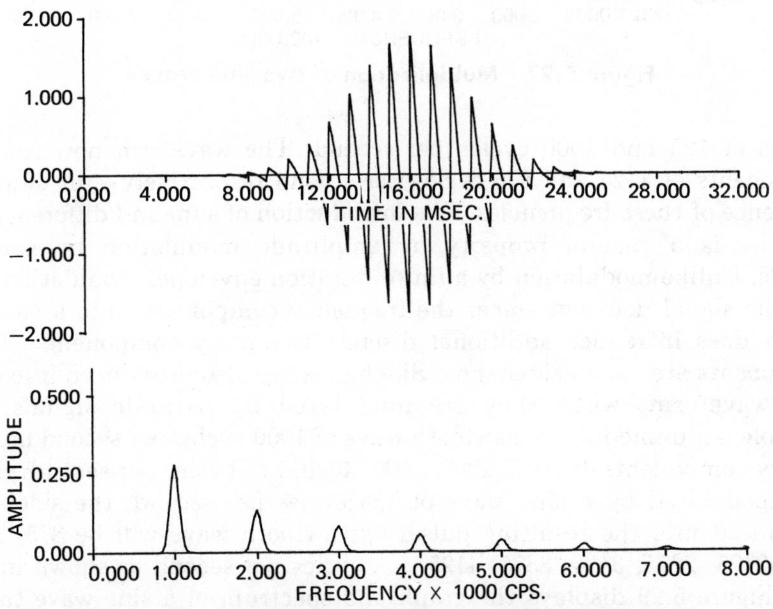

Figure 5.26 Short sawtooth wave pulse and spectrum.

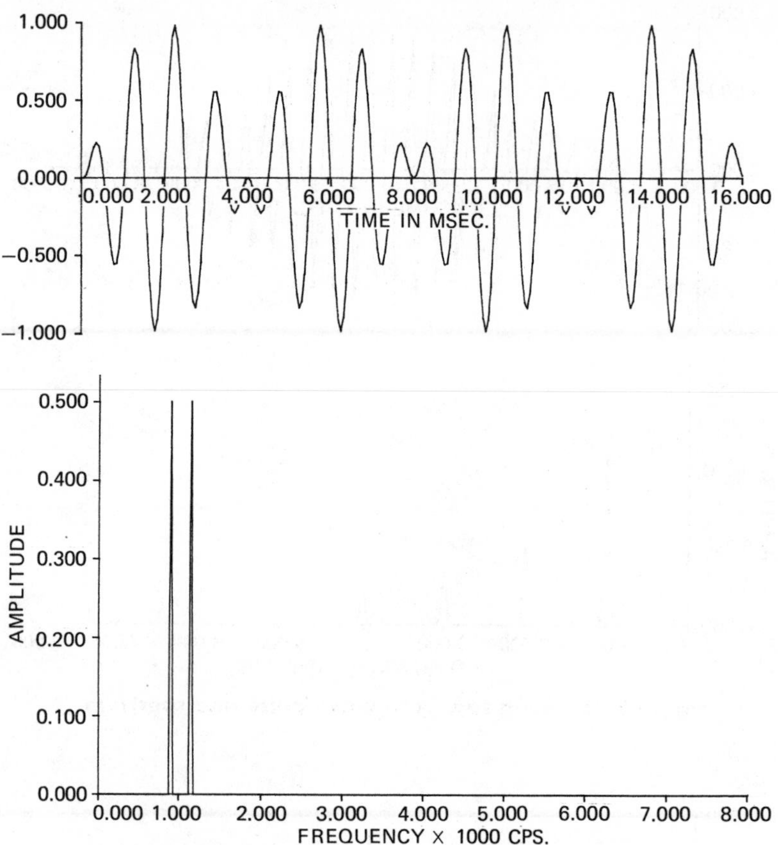

Figure 5.27 Multiplication of two sine waves.

factors of 125 and 1000 cycles per second. The waveform now contains components of 1125 and 875 cycles per second respectively—the sum and difference of these frequencies. The introduction of sum and difference frequencies is a general property by amplitude modulation by periodic signals. Unlike modulation by a finite-duration envelope, modulation by a periodic signal does not smear the frequency components into a contour. But it does introduce additional discrete frequency components. These components are called sidebands. Sidebands are also introduced into complex waveforms when they are modulated by periodic signals. For example, an unmodulated sawtooth wave of 1000 cycles per second has frequency components of 1000, 2000, 3000, 4000, . . . cycles per second. But if it is modulated by a sine wave of 125 cycles per second, the sidebands introduced into the resulting pulsating sawtooth wave will be 875, 1125, 1875, 2125, 2875, 3125, 3875, 4125, . . . cycles per second as shown in Fig. 5.28. Figure 5.29 displays the graph and spectrum of a sine wave that is amplitude-modulated by a sawtooth wave. Then, in Fig. 5.30 we see the waveform and sidebands in the spectrum of a sawtooth wave multiplied by another sawtooth wave.

So far the discussion of sound dynamics and modulation has been focused on changes in a tone's amplitude. It examined how the frequency constituents of a sound are affected by such modulation. Enveloping a signal was shown to render the frequencies partially indeterminate. This indeterminacy must not, however, be mistaken for change in the frequency itself. One must not infer from these illustrations that the frequency is changing in time. For such a signal, the frequency components are static. The contour of the diagram simply implies that the frequency is not perfectly defined at *any* instant of time for a finite wave pulse. Periodic tones that are infinite in duration do not exist. But a tone that lasts for a few milliseconds may be still long enough that its component frequencies are well-established, having negligible uncertainty. It is only when the

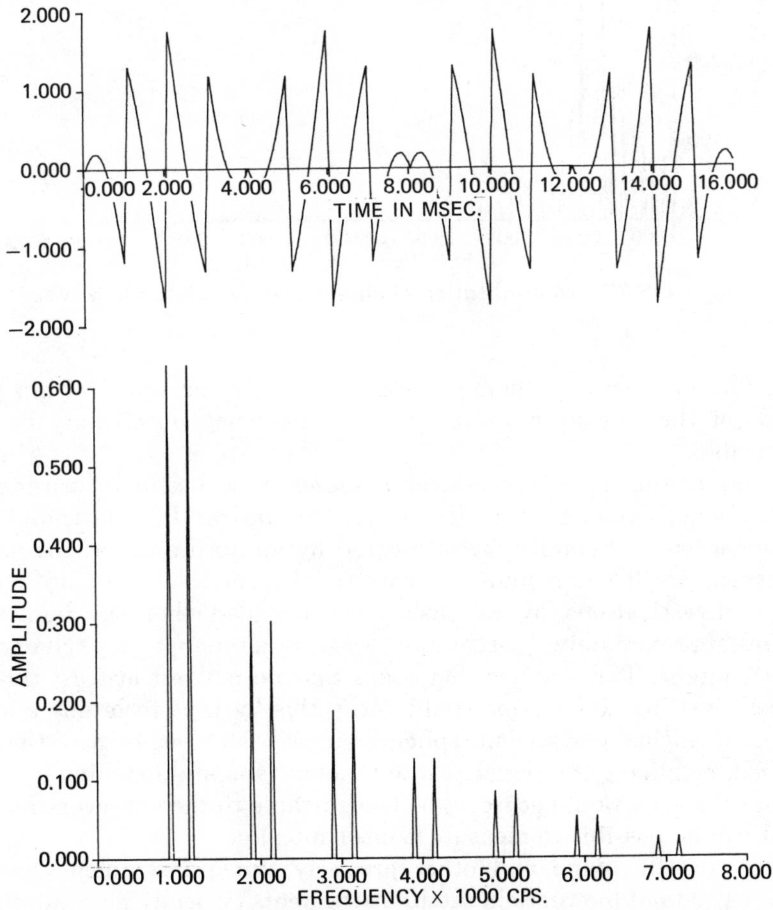

Figure 5.28 Multiplication of sawtooth wave by sine wave.

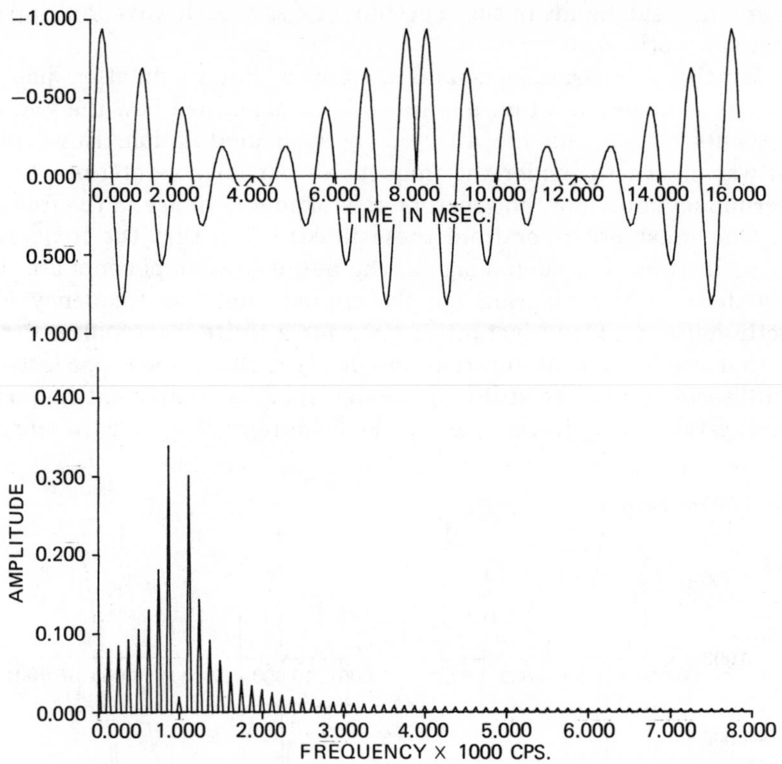

Figure 5.29 Multiplication of sine wave by sawtooth wave.

amplitude of a wave is being changed abruptly, occuring within a few periods of the waveform itself, that the frequency uncertainty becomes appreciable.

As one examines or synthesizes a sound, it is useful to consider the psychoacoustical consequences of its dynamics. In addition to the mathematical uncertainty factor created by an abrupt onset, the hearing mechanism itself compounds the entropy of a modulated sound. Experimental investigations by M. Joos have revealed that the human ear requires approximately 1/20 second to recognize a tone for its pitch and harmonic content. This implies that tones that do not last at least this long are perceived as noises. One could verify this by tape-recording a steady tone at 15 inches per second, splicing out a 3/4-inch segment of the tape, and then resplicing the segment into a blank tape and listening to it. The pitch of the tone would scarcely be recognizable to the ear, even though it would still be possible to measure it mechanically.

Although the piano and other precisely tuned instruments produce tones that do not fluctuate in pitch, instruments typically do exhibit slight pertubations in their intonation. Frequency modulation such as the vibrato of a violin or human voice does not demonstrate any dramatic analytical consequence. Its effect is mostly psychological, rendering the tone more natural and pleasing to the ear. The fluctuation in pitch caused by vibrato adds to the entropy of a sound signal, but in an entirely different manner than the way the frequency is affected by modulating the signal's amplitude. A typical vibrato alters the pitch of a tone by approximately one half of a semitone at a rate of about eight times per second. This rate is too slow and the pitch deviation too slight to significantly alter the tone's actual waveform. Its frequency components simply fluctuate in parallel with the fundamental pitch at this slow rate. Normally, the attack of an instrument does not define the pitch exactly—not only because of the uncertainty principle, but because the instrument itself introduces a portamento into the tone's onset. In synthesizing a musical composition electronically or with a computer, the omission of

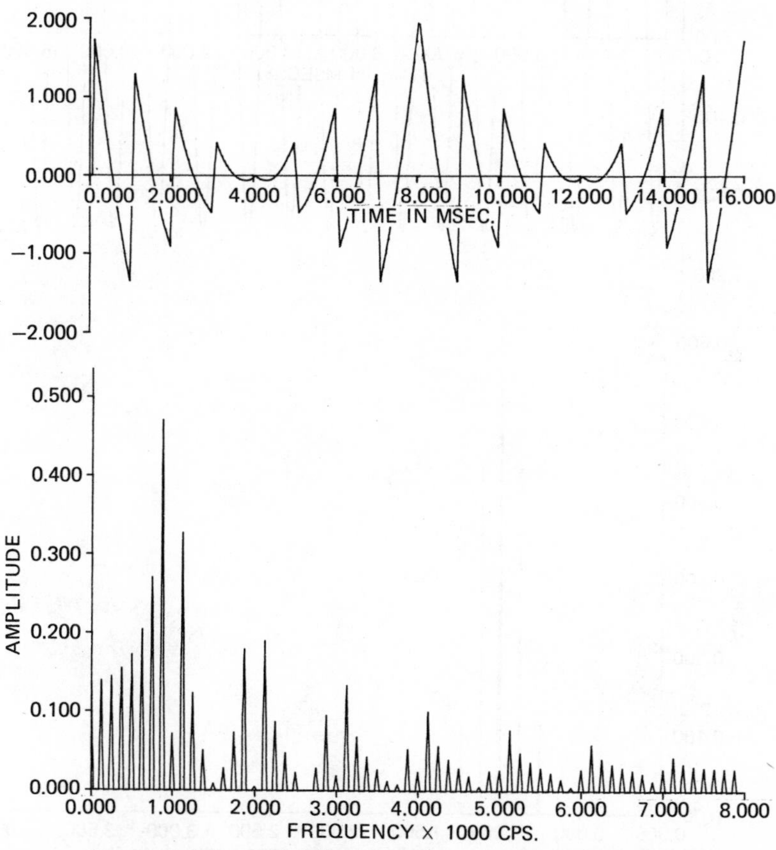

Figure 5.30 Multiplication of two sawtooth waves.

portamento and vibrato in its tonal sounds could easily make them unpleasantly static.

A natural instrument does not produce tones by modulating its sounding frequency. But frequency-modulated electronic signals can be easily generated with interesting results. Whereas an amplitude-modulated signal introduces uniform sidebands which are the sum and difference of the frequencies of the modulating signal and the signal being modulated, the modulation of a signal's frequency introduces several sidebands above

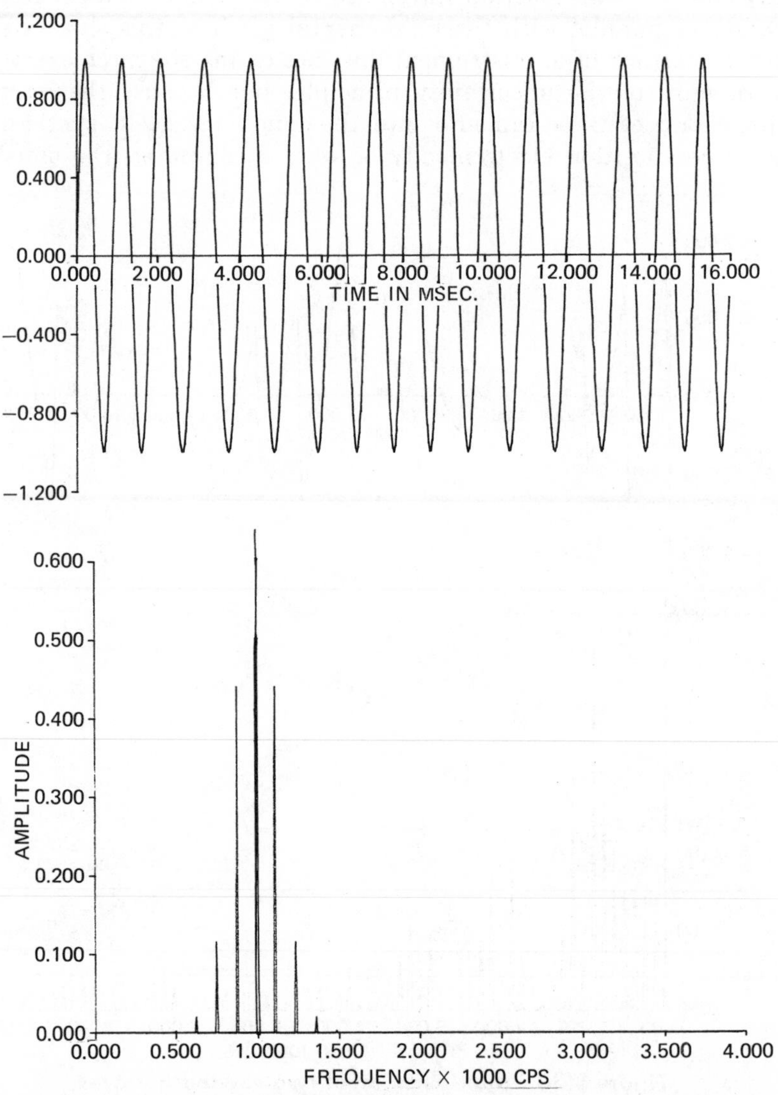

Figure 5.31 Modulation index = 1.

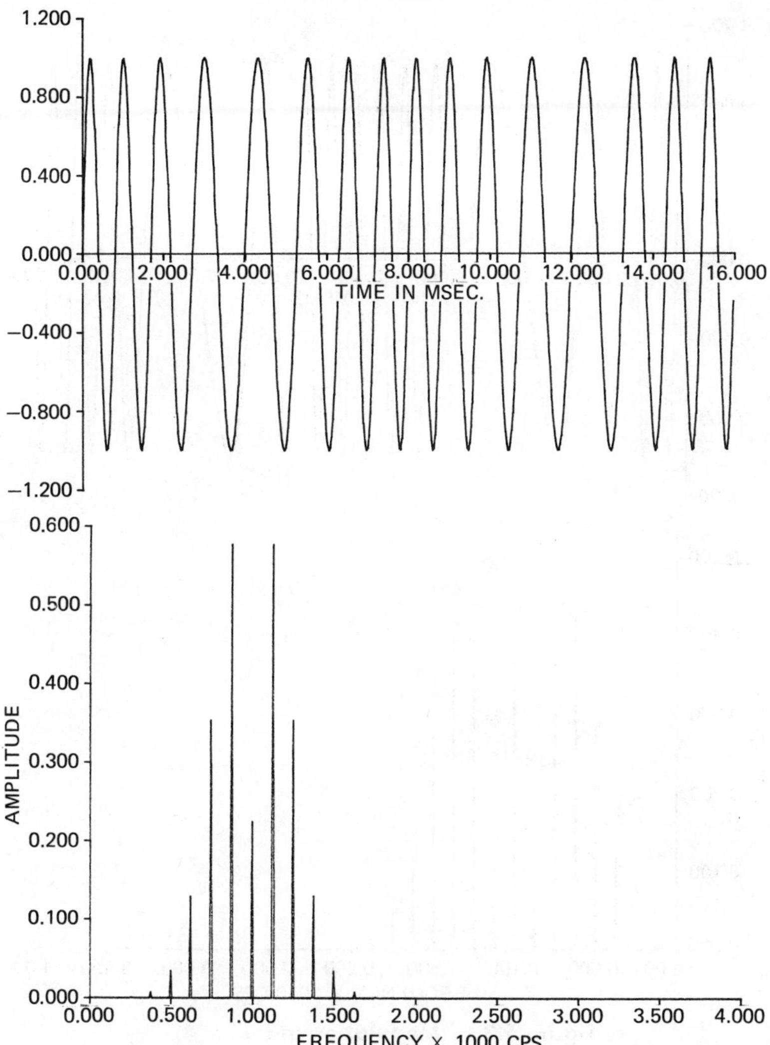

Figure 5.32 Modulation index = 2.

and below the center frequency. The signals diagrammed in Figs. 5.31 to 5.35 are frequency-modulated sine waves whose center, or carrier frequency is 1000 cycles per second. They are modulated by a frequency of 125 cycles per second.

The number and relative amplitudes of the sidebands produced by frequency modulation depend on both the frequency and amplitude of the modulating signal. The significant sidebands occur at multiples of the modulation frequency. The amplitude of the modulating wave determines the amount of deviation in the frequency of the carrier wave. This

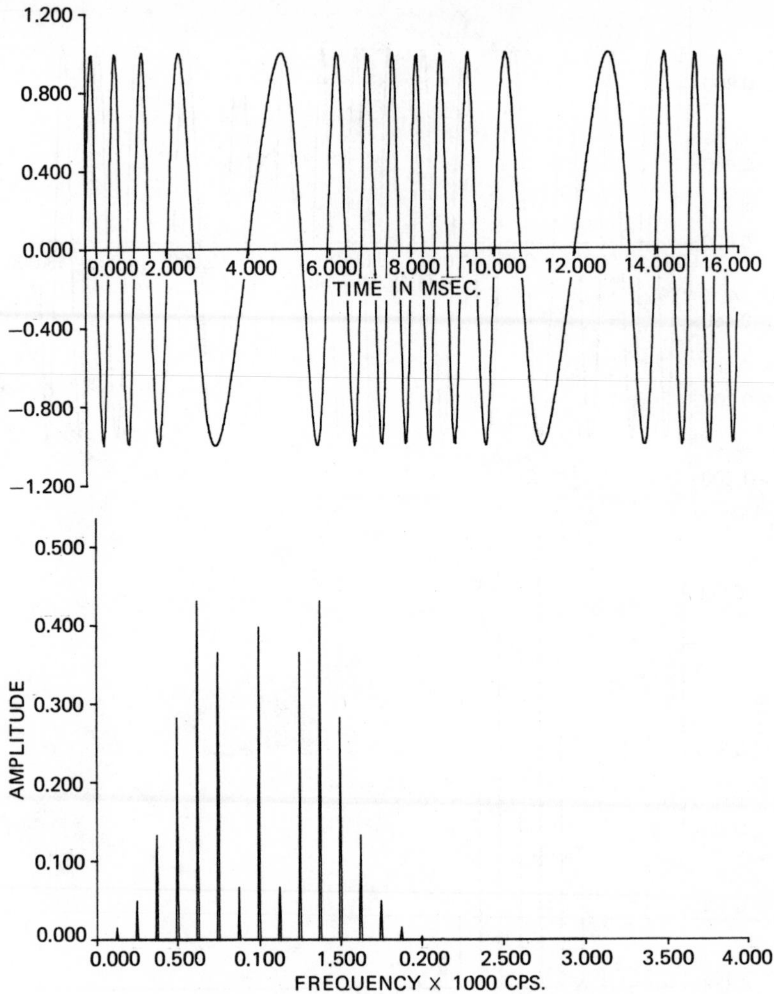

Figure 5.33 Modulation index = 4.

amplitude, which is the ratio of the frequency deviation of the carrier signal to the frequency of the modulating signal, is called the *modulation index*. The mathematical equation used to generate a frequency-modulated signal is

$$\text{signal} = A \sin(2\pi f_c t + I \sin 2\pi f_m t).$$

In this equation, A is the amplitude of the wave, f_c is the carrier frequency, f_m is the modulation frequency, and I is the modulation index. For example, the signal in Fig. 5.3 is fluctuating between 500 and 1500 cycles per second. The carrier frequency is 1000 cycles per second, as mentioned, so the peak deviation is the difference of 1000 cycles per second and either 500 or 1500 cycles per second, which is 500 cycles per second. The modulation frequency is 125 cycles per second, so the modulation index is 500/125 = 4. One can see that as the modulation index is increased, the energy of the signal is spread out into sidebands away from the center frequency. One can also observe that these frequencies are very nonharmonically related, and will consequently produce a noisy, clangorous tone.

Music is often defined as the artistic modulation of sound in time. Whether a musical sound has the 90-minute duration of a Mahler symphony or the ½-second duration of a single tone, its aesthetic qualities are a result of the way its static elements are dynamically modulated. A sound

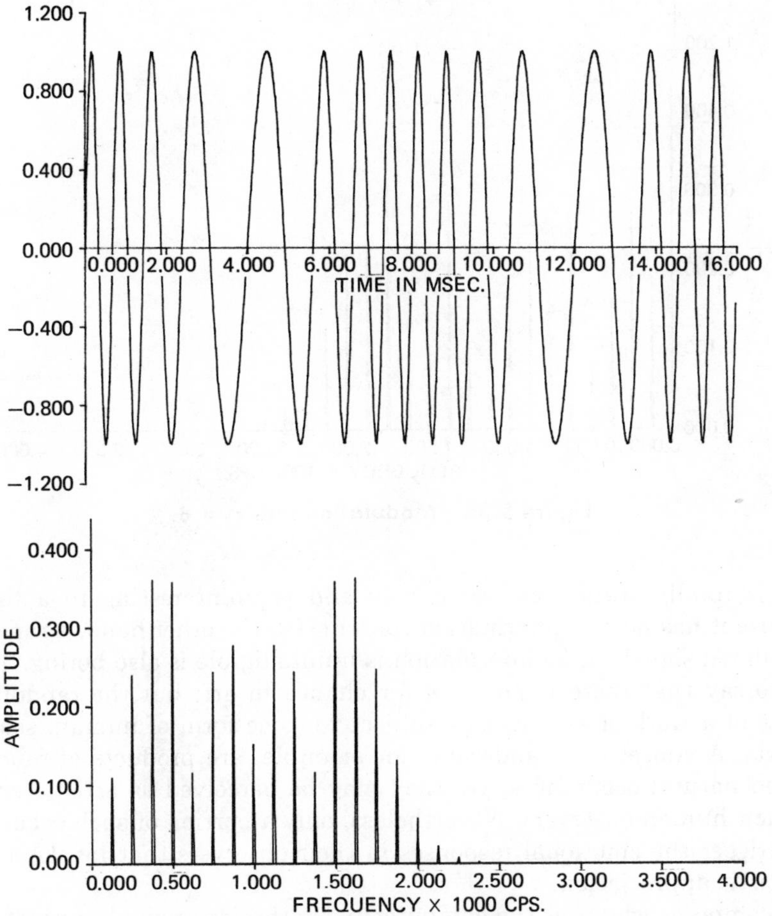

Figure 5.34 Modulation index = 6.

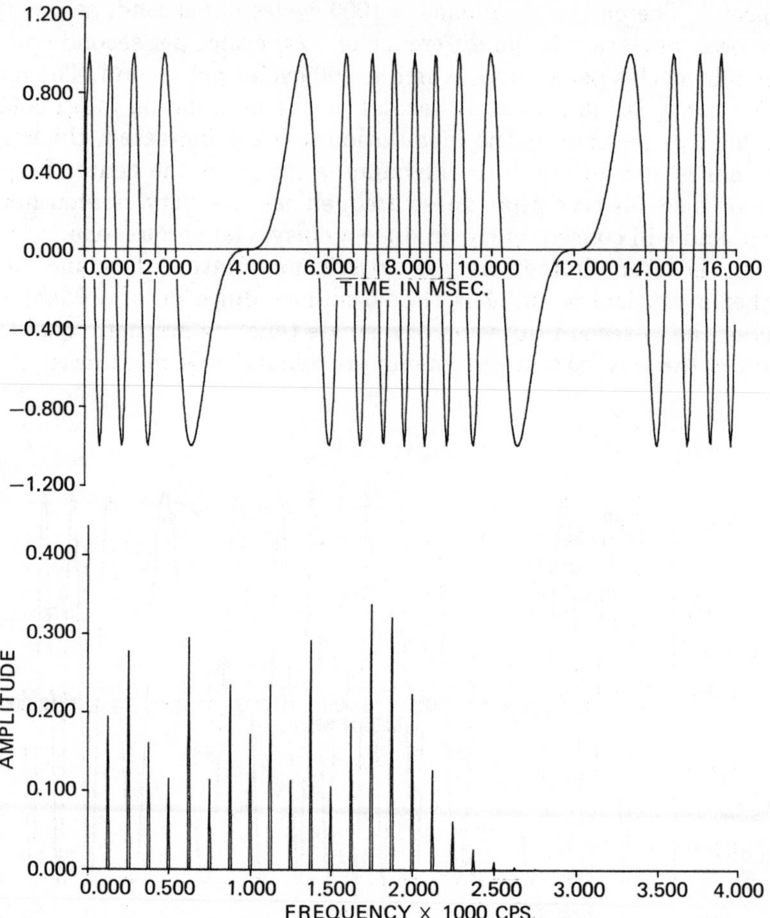

Figure 5.35 Modulation index = 8.

that is totally static has no entropy and is uninteresting to a listener because it has no new information content. On the other hand, a randomly modulated signal whose information is unintelligible is also boring. This is not to say that there is no room for chance in art; but the random elements of a work of art must be subject to some form of human, selective criteria. A sunset or a landscape, for example, are products of randomly caused natural occurances, yet they may be perceived as artistic entities by their human observers. Nevertheless, only a portion of such occurances will trigger the emotional responses in their observers that invoke a sense of artistic appreciation.

A composer who uses the computer to synthesize original musical tones operates in the same creative mode in this area of experimentation as one who is experimenting with new melodies, harmonies, and orchestration techniques. The analysis and creation of interesting musical tones on their fundamental, acoustical level is an extension of the study of music theory and the art of composition.

REFERENCES

Grey, John M., "Timbre Discrimination in Musical Patterns," *Journal of the Acoustical Society of America* **64**(2), 467-472 (Aug. 1978).

Grey, John, "Multidimensional Perceptual Scaling of Musical Timbres," *Journal of the Acoustical Society of America* **61,** 1270–1277 (1977).

Grey, J. & J. A. Moorer, "Perceptual Evaluations of Synthesized Musical Instrument Tones," *Journal of the Acoustical Society of America* **62,** 454–62 (1977).

Helmholtz, Hermann, *On the Sensations of Tone*, Dover, 1954.

Joos, M., *Acoustic Phonetics*, Linguistic Society of America, Baltimore, 1948.

Laske, Otto, "Musical Acoustics (Sonology): A Questionable Science Reconsidered," *NUMUS-W* **6,** 35–40 (1974).

Luce, D. & M. Clark, "Duration of Attack Transients of Nonpercussive Orchestral Instruments," *Journal of the Audio Engineering Society* **13,** 194–199 (1965).

Meyer, E. & G. Buchmann, *Die Klangspektren der Musikinstrumente*, Akademie der Wissenschaften, Berlin, 1931.

Miller, J. R. & E. C. Carterette, "Perceptual Space for Musical Structures," *Journal of the Acoustical Society of America* **58,** 711–720 (1975).

Olson, Harry F., *Music, Physics, and Engineering*, Dover, 1967.

Plomp, R., "Timbre as a Multidimensional Attribute of Complex Tones," in *Frequency Analysis and Periodicity Detection In Hearing*, A. W. Sijthoff (Ed.), Leiden, 1970.

Wedin, L. & G. Goude, "Dimension Analysis of the Perception of Instrumental Timbre," *Scandinavian Journal of Psychology*, **13,** 228–240 (1972).

Winckel, Fritz, *Music, Sound, & Sensation*, Dover, 1967.

Zwicker, E. & B. Scharf, "A Model of Loudness Summation," *Psychology Review*, **72,** 3-26 (1965).

6

WAVEFORM ANALYSIS IN THE FREQUENCY DOMAIN

The average human ear is sensitive to sounds having frequencies up to approximately 15,000 cycles per second. It is thus responsive to changes in air pressure occurring on a time scale of less than $1/10$ millisecond. But if a single pulse of air pressure having $1/10$ millisecond duration were to enter the ear, it would pass unnoticed by the brain even though the eardrum itself would react to it. In fact, a sound pulse of 10 milliseconds would be scarcely noticeable to a human listener. The process of hearing occurs in the human brain rather than the ear itself, and the hearing mechanism of the inner ear merely translates the actual sound into a neurological signal. The conscious brain responds to changes in that signal on a much slower time scale than do the organs in the ear. As mentioned in the preceding chapter, a sound must last approximately 50 milliseconds for the brain to recognize its pitch and timbre. Psychoacoustical experiments have also revealed that sounds must be separated in time by at least this interval of approximately $1/20$ second to be heard as separate events. Yet a sound must have a frequency of at least 30 cycles per second to be audible.

This presents a very interesting paradox! Although the ear is only sensitive to changes in air pressure occurring with a cycle period of less than $1/30$ second, the brain that does the actual hearing, is only responsive to changes over periods of greater than $1/20$ second. Obviously, the brain must interpret sound in an entirely different manner than does the ear. The function of the hearing mechanism is to receive sounds as they occur in the ear canal, then transfer them into another form that is intelligible to the brain. The time scale of the ear, whose limits lie between 1/30 and 1/15000 second, must be mapped into another scale in the brain that is responsive to much slower rates. The hearing mechanism accomplishes this by transforming the mechanical vibrations in the inner ear to nerve impulses that represent pitches in the frequency domain. Consequently, the brain does not interpret sound as instantaneous fluctuations of air pressure, but as a mixture of pure tones on a spectrum of frequencies. Although it perceives the dynamic changes of a tone's onset at each one of those frequencies, it does so at a rate much slower than the time domain representation of a sound. Consequently, a pure tone having constant amplitude and frequency is discerned by the brain as a static entity. If the tone is complex, but strictly periodic, the brain also perceives it statically as a mixture of pure tones having different frequencies. But if the tone is changing in its timbre, the brain then responds to the individual dynamics of its separate frequency components. This is why a strictly periodic sound is heard as a steady tone, a quasi-periodic sound is heard as a modulated tone, and an aperiodic sound is noise.

Since the brain is responsive to sounds in the frequency domain rather than the time domain, it is only pertinent that psychoacoustical analysis of these sounds be conducted in the frequency domain. To create musical sounds mathematically by forming them from pure tones, we must understand the constituent properties of their waveforms. Consequently, we relate them in terms that model the way they are psychologically perceived. Therefore, in developing procedures to synthesize musical tones, we study their properties in the realm of the frequency domain. To perform this analysis mechanically or mathematically, we face the same problem that the hearing mechanism encounters in transforming signals from the time domain to the frequency domain. The electric signal coming from a microphone or going to a loudspeaker is a time-domain signal. The sampled waveforms we generate with a computer are also done in the time domain. We must therefore develop a technique of mapping time-domain signals into frequency-domain representations. We begin by arbitrarily assuming that the waveforms to be analyzed are unmodulated and strictly periodic. Actually, this assumption is unrealistic—like assuming the earth is flat. But in the same way that a small area of the earth's curvature can be considered flat for practical purposes, a slowly varying dynamic sound may be effectively approximated by a static tone in a short time interval. As mentioned previously, tonal sounds are modulated much more slowly than the instantaneous rate of change of their actual waveforms.

One example of a natural tone that is nearly static is a note played on an organ. The combination of frequencies ensuing from an organ pipe are determined by the pipe's length and shape. As we listen to the tone, we wish to investigate its constituent harmonics, and determine each one's relative amplitude. In the last century, Hermann Helmholtz performed harmonic analysis of musical tones without using any electronic apparatus. He performed his experiments by constructing resonators with pipes of various lengths. He used each resonator to detect a particular frequency while isolating other frequencies. This proved him to be a man of colossal patience as well as genius, because this type of harmonic analysis is extremely cumbersome and tedious. Today our analysis can be performed much more easily with a microphone and variable filter. The filter electronically isolates one particular frequency at a time and attenuates the others. Let us suppose that our frequency analyzer has a dial on it that selects the frequency, and a meter that indicates the amplitude of that component frequency. We can then use the analyzer to plot the frequency spectrum of a tone on a graph. We start by setting the dial to 30 cycles per second, and slowly turn it up until the meter jumps. Then we plot the amplitude and frequency at this jump, and continue to plot amplitude and frequencies as the dial is turned. The final plot may resemble Fig. 6.1. We notice in this hypothetical plot that the fundamental pitch is A_{220} and that the odd-numbered harmonics are prominent. The tone would thus sound somewhat like a reed instrument.

The method of analysis just described is far more easily undertaken than one using Helmholtz's resonators, but it still requires special electronic hardware, is fairly inprecise, and requires a few minutes to analyze just one tone. This is acceptable for examining sustained tones, but useless for the analysis of piano, string, or other sharply articulated sounds. To measure the component frequencies of an articulated sound, we must consider its waveform over an interval of only a few milliseconds of its onset. This obviously rules out the use of our electromechanical frequency analyzer.

We now turn to the computer for a way to perform the analysis mathematically. We must obtain a numerical representation of the waveform. Suppose that we have tape-recorded a tone, and have isolated a 20-millisecond portion of it. The analog signal on the tape is not yet in a form suitable for mathematical analysis on the computer. The previous chapters have described how a digital signal is synthesized by the computer and converted to a continuous voltage via D-to-A conversion. Now, we perform the reverse process with an *analog-to-digital converter* (ADC).

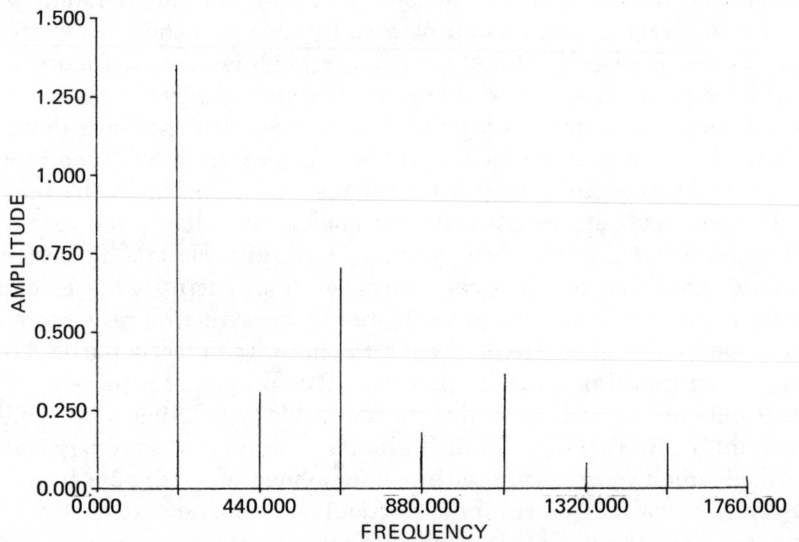

Figure 6.1 Frequency spectrum of a typical tone.

The ADC samples the waveform as it is played back on the tape recorder and stores the samples in the computer's memory. The memory then contains a digitized representation of the signal, which is available for processing and mathematical analysis.

There is a serious hazard associated with digital sampling of analog waveforms. The hazard occurs when the waveform contains frequency components that are higher than one half the sampling rate. To illustrate what this causes to happen, examine Fig. 6.2. In this drawing, the sampled waveform is represented by the heavy line. It is sinusoidal and has a frequency of 12,000 cycles per second. It is being sampled at a rate of 20,000 samples per second, or 1 sample every 0.05 millisecond. The samples taken are thus represented by the heavy dots along the waveform at these intervals. These samples, then, are the only information about the waveform that is stored in the computer. But notice the dashed curve, which also fits through these points along the graph! It represents another sine wave of 8000 cycles per second. This phantom wave was never present in the original signal, but its appearance is implied by the samples. One cannot determine on the basis of the samples alone whether they represent a wave of 8000 or 12,000 cycles per second. This ambiguity is the plague of digital signal processing and is known as "aliasing," or "foldover." The only way to avoid aliasing is to bandlimit the waveform before it is sampled. The waveform must contain no frequencies higher than ½ the sampling frequency, or the higher frequencies will be aliased, or reflected back into the lower range. For example, if a signal is sampled at a rate of 30,000 per second all of its frequency components up to 15,000 cycles per second will be safely represented. But every frequency component above 15,000 cycles per second will be folded back into the range under 15,000 cycles per second. A 20,000 cycles per second wave would be manifest as a 10,000 cycles per second component, a 25,000 cycles per second wave would appear as a 5000 component, and so forth. Consequently, if the waveform under analysis contains any components above 15,000 cycles per second, they must be eliminated with a low-pass filter before the signal can be sampled. Otherwise, the nightmare of aliasing will occur.

Once the signal is sampled and stored, the next task is to identify its frequency components. The mathematical procedure used for this determination is known as *Fourier analysis*. A detailed, rigorous development of Fourier analysis theory is beyond the scope of this writing, but we may present a basic, intuitive description of the technique without elaborate, mathematical complexity. The principle of Fourier analysis states that a time-domain function can be represented as a sum of sine and cosine functions in the frequency domain. This is merely a mathematical generalization of the principle discussed in the previous chapters. A cosine function is identical to a sine function that is time-shifted by an angle of 90° or $\pi/2$ radians. To understand the relationship between sine and cosine functions, imagine that a wheel is turning at a constant rate of 1 revolu-

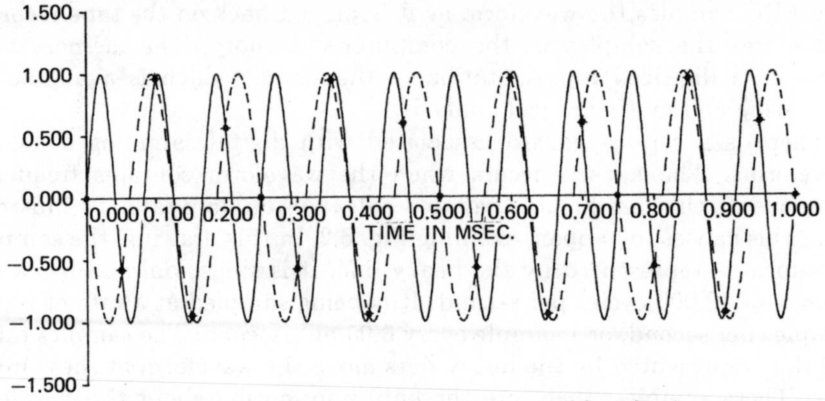

Figure 6.2 Frequency ambiguity caused by aliasing.

tion per second as shown in Fig. 6.3. This wheel has spike attached to its rim at exactly 1 foot from its hub. As this spike revolves, it forms an angle θ with the horizontal axis. Since the rate of rotation is 1 revolution per second and the angle of one complete revolution is 2π radians, the value of θ at any given time is equal to that time multiplied by 2π if the angle θ is equal to 0 at the starting point $t = 0$.

We desire to represent the position of the spike as a function of time. Since the spike is moving in a two-dimensional plane, we represent its position with both a vertical and a horizontal component. At time $t = 0$, the vertical displacement is 0 and the horizontal displacement is the radius of the wheel, which is 1 foot. As the wheel rotates to a position

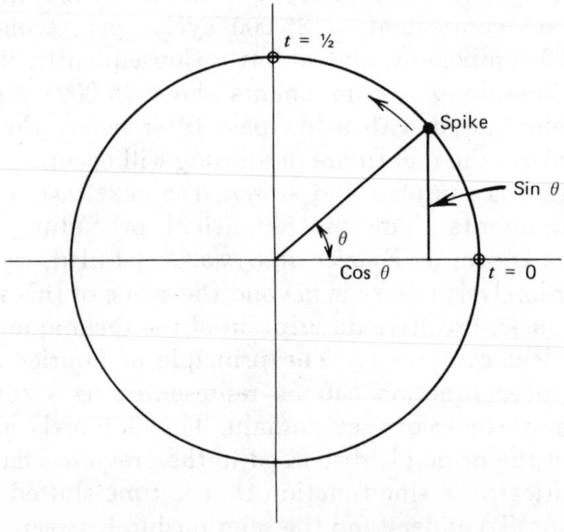

Figure 6.3 Illustration of sine and cosine relationships.

where $\theta = 45°$ or $\pi/4$ radians, the vertical and horizontal components are equal. When θ reaches 90° or $\pi/2$ radians, the vertical component has reached 1 foot and the horizontal component is then zero. This happens at ¼ revolution when t = ¼ second. The sine and cosine functions are defined to be the vertical and horizontal distances, respectively, of the spike from the center of the wheel. In Fig 6.4, we graphically represent the vertical and horizontal position as functions of time.

In Chapter 2 we showed how complex tones can be decomposed into sums of pure tones. A pure tone can be represented by either a sine or a cosine function. So the question immediately arises: why is it necessary in Fourier analysis to decompose complex waveforms into both cosine and sine functions? Although two complex waveforms may have the same frequency components of identical magnitudes, their components may have different phase relationships. Thus to preserve the complete integrity of the waveforms under analysis, the phase of the component waves must be accounted for as well as the amplitudes. This is why the analysis is

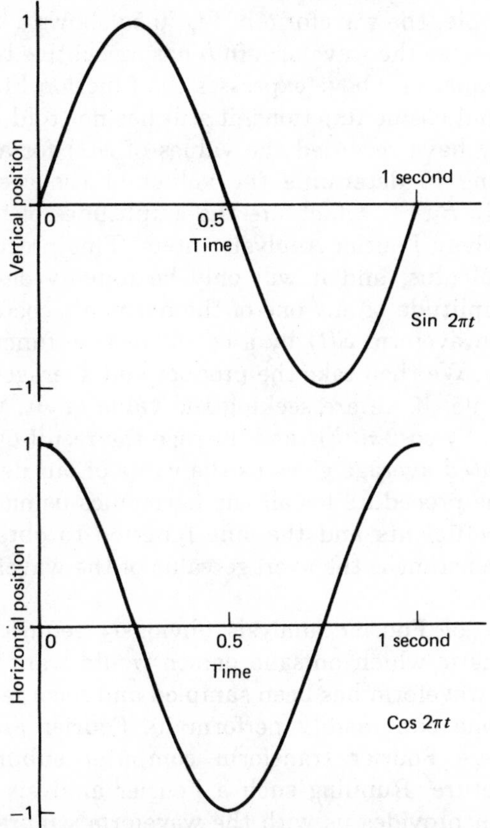

Figure 6.4 Sine and cosine functions.

performed two-dimensionally, using the cosine function as well as the sine function.

Suppose now that we are going to analyze a recorded tone with a Fourier series. We still make the approximating assumption that the tone is strictly periodic and its fundamental frequency is F. Let us say that the waveform of this tone can be represented in the time domain by a function $S(t)$. By Fourier analysis, $S(t)$ can be separated into a sum of cosine and sine functions as expressed by the equation:

$$S(t) = A_1 \cos 2\pi Ft + A_2 \cos 2\pi(2F)t + A_3 \cos 2\pi(3F)t + \cdots + B_1 \sin 2\pi Ft + B_2 \sin 2\pi(2F)t + B_3 \sin 2\pi(3F)t + \cdots + \text{(bias constant)}$$

Here, $A_1, A_2, A_3, \ldots$ and $B_1, B_2, B_3, \ldots$ represent the amplitudes of the fundamental and respective harmonics for both the cosine and sine functions. The bias constant corresponds to a frequency of zero, and is included to represent the component of the waveform whose range is not centered around zero. If the signal is electric, this bias represents direct current. For example, the waveform of Fig. 6.5*a* shows a waveform having a positive bias whereas the waveform in *b* has a negative bias.

Although the equation above expresses the function $S(t)$ in terms of its component sine and cosine functions, it still has not told us all we need to know. We already have recorded the values of $S(t)$ for all time instants. We are now trying to determine the values of the coefficients A_1, A_2, $A_3, \ldots$ and B_1, B_2, $B_3, \ldots$ which are the amplitudes of the separate harmonics. This is where Fourier Analysis enters. This procedure entails the use of integral calculus, and it will only be roughly described here. To determine the amplitude of any one of the harmonic coefficients, we multiply the original waveform $S(t)$ by a cosine or sine function of that harmonic's frequency. We then take the product and average it over one cycle period. For example, if we are seeking the value of A_3, we multiply this original waveform by $\cos 2\pi(3F)t$ and average the result over one complete cycle. The calculated average gives us the value of our desired coefficient. We can repeat the procedure for all the harmonics using the cosine function for the A coefficients and the sine function to obtain the B coefficients. The bias constant is the average value of the waveform itself over a complete cycle.

This procedure of Fourier analysis obviously requires a tremendous amount of arithmetic which no sane person would want to undertake by hand. But once a waveform has been sampled and recorded in the memory of a computer, one can readily perform its Fourier analysis with any number of discrete Fourier transform computer subprograms already available in literature. Running such a Fourier analysis program on our sampled waveform provides us with the waveform's representation in the frequency domain. But one step remains before we can know the absolute

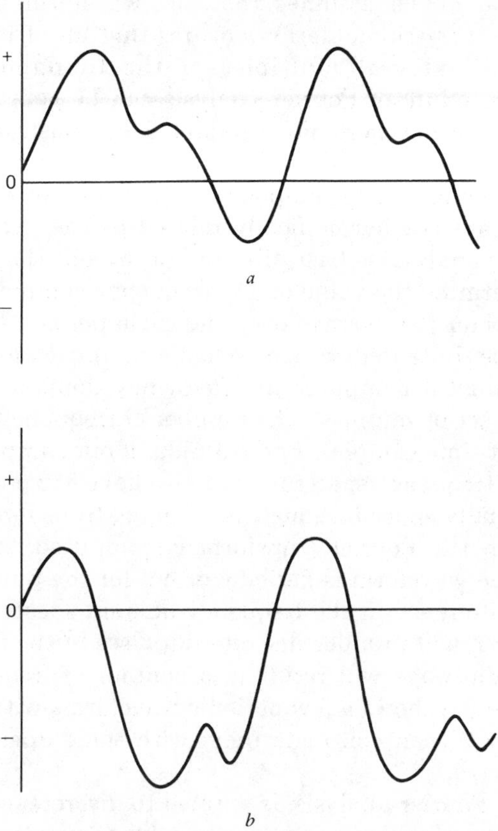

Figure 6.5 *a* Function with positive bias, *b* Function with negative bias.

magnitude of any one harmonic. The Fourier analysis has given us a two-dimensional representation; that is, each frequency constitutes both a cosine and sine function. To find the absolute value of any one harmonic's amplitude, we recall the formula from plane geometry that determines the hypotenuse of a right triangle. We note from Fig. 6.3 that the sine and cosine functions represented there form the sides of a right triangle. The hypotenuse of the triangle is equal to the square root of the sum of the squares of the sides. Therefore, if A_n is the amplitude of the cosine component at frequency nF and B_n is the amplitude of the sine component at nF, the absolute magnitude of the harmonic at frequency nF is given by

$$\text{amplitude } (n\text{th harmonic}) = \sqrt{A_n^2 + B_n^2}$$

We program the computer to calculate the absolute values of the harmonic amplitudes by this relation and plot them on a scale of frequency. Then our harmonic analysis is complete.

The discussion above assumes that the waveform under analysis is strictly periodic. Its periodic nature ensures that all of its component frequencies will be integral multiples of the fundamental frequency. However, the procedure of Fourier analysis can be generalized to include waveforms that are not periodic. Chapter 5 demonstrated that a single wave pulse is represented in the frequency domain as a continuous spectrum of frequencies. The component frequencies of an aperiodic waveform, therefore, are not harmonically related as they are with a periodic wave. Its Fourier analysis is basically similar, except that the sum or integral used to determine the value of any frequency component is taken over all time rather than the average over one cycle period. This requires that the wave pulse be finite in duration. When a sampled waveform is Fourier-analyzed by a digital computer, its frequency domain representation is another discrete set of samples. The number of frequency samples is equal to the number of time samples. For example, if our sampled waveform has 512 samples, its frequency spectrum will also have 512 points, representing 512 discrete, equally spaced frequencies ranging from zero to the sampling frequency. When the Fourier transform is computed, it will not matter whether this time waveform is periodic or not for the purposes of the computation. The difference in the frequency-domain spectrum will be that a periodic waveform will produce discrete impulses in the frequency domain while an aperiodic wave will result in a contour of frequencies along the spectrum. Figure 6.6 shows a few periodic waveforms with their amplitude spectra. Figure 6.7 then contrasts them with some aperiodic signals and their energy spectra.

The theory of Fourier analysis as applied to discrete, sampled functions differs from its application to continuous functions in certain technical aspects. They will not be developed here, but we may mention that sampling and discrete analysis leads to some loss of precision and distortion. But the error inherent in the mathematics of discrete Fourier analysis is scarcely a fraction of the imprecision that would result from using analog equipment such as the hardware frequency analyzer described earlier. Let us return to our 512 sample waveform. It is worth remarking that the number 512 is chosen because it is a power of 2. Most popular discrete Fourier transform computer programs are designed for arrays whose lengths are powers of two, because the computation is easier to carry out. If the sampling frequency is 30,000 per second 512 samples will represent approximately 17 milliseconds of sound. Whether or not the original sound is periodic, the computer performs the discrete Fourier analysis of the 512 samples in the same way. It divides the frequency spectrum of 0 to 30,000 cycles per second into 512 equal intervals. Then it performs the analysis and determines coefficients for each of the 512 different frequencies. Consequently, the output spectrum is another array of 512 points that represent frequencies rather than time instants. If the waveform is approximately periodic, it harmonics will be clearly visible in its frequency

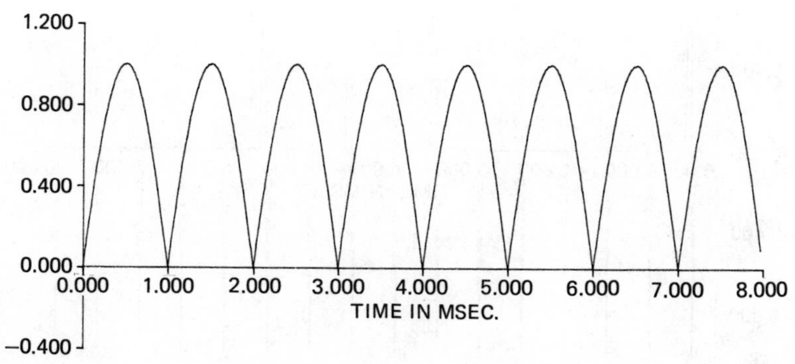

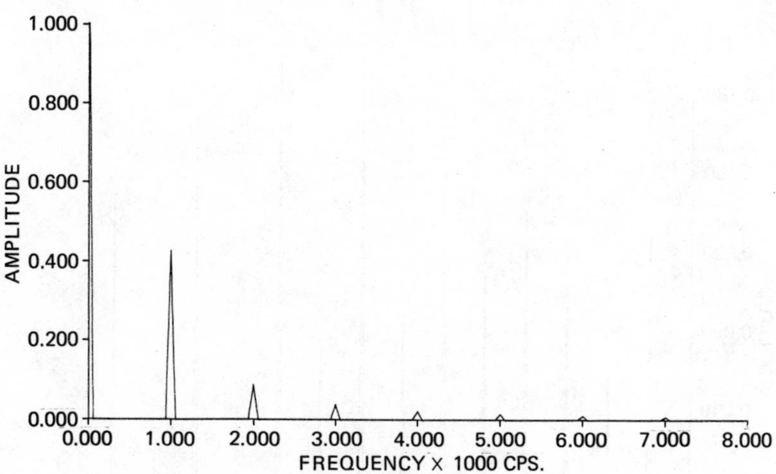

Figure 6.6 Sample periodic signals and their spectra.

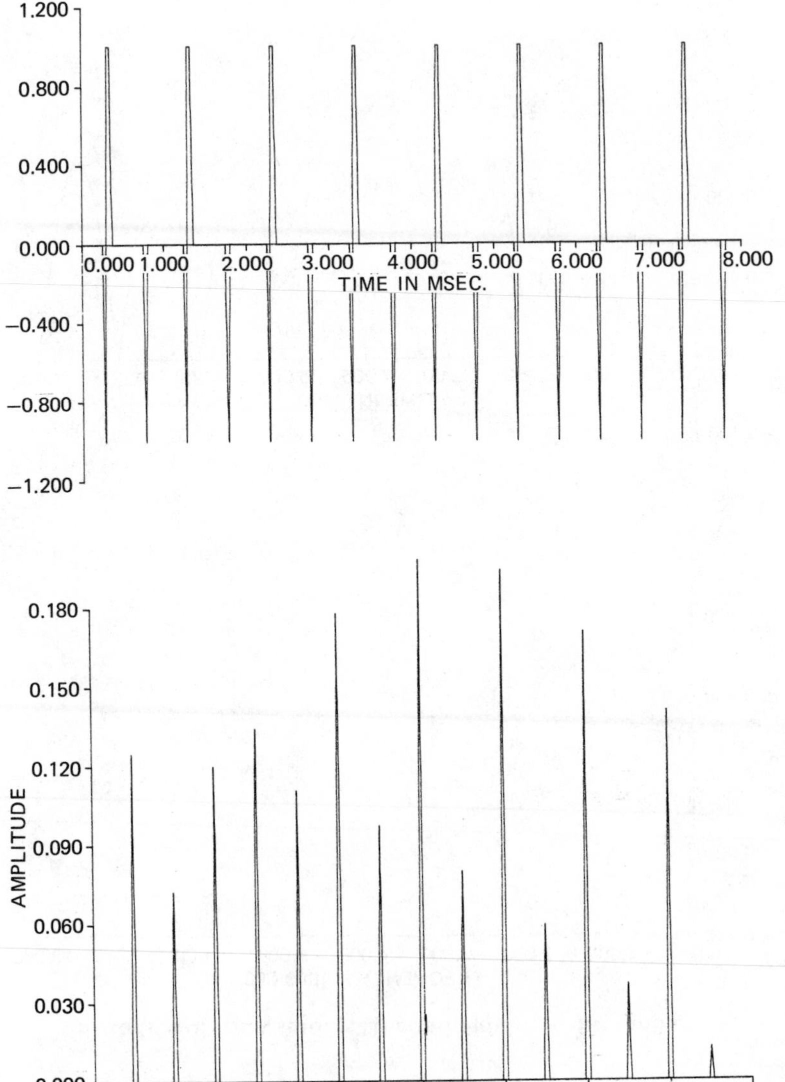

Figure 6.6 (*Continued*).

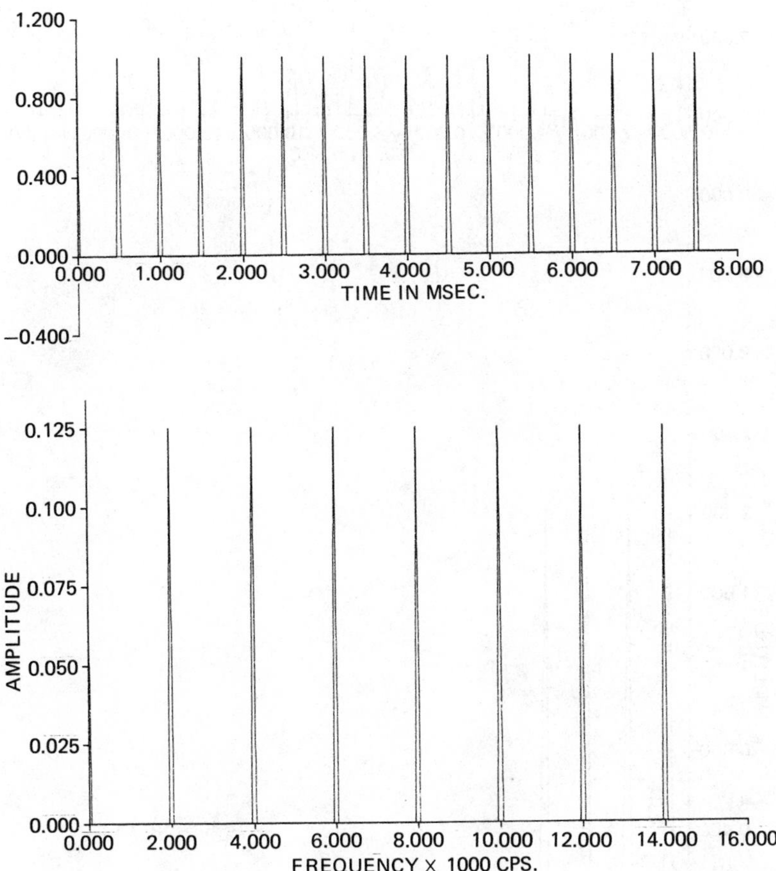

Figure 6.6 (***Continued***).

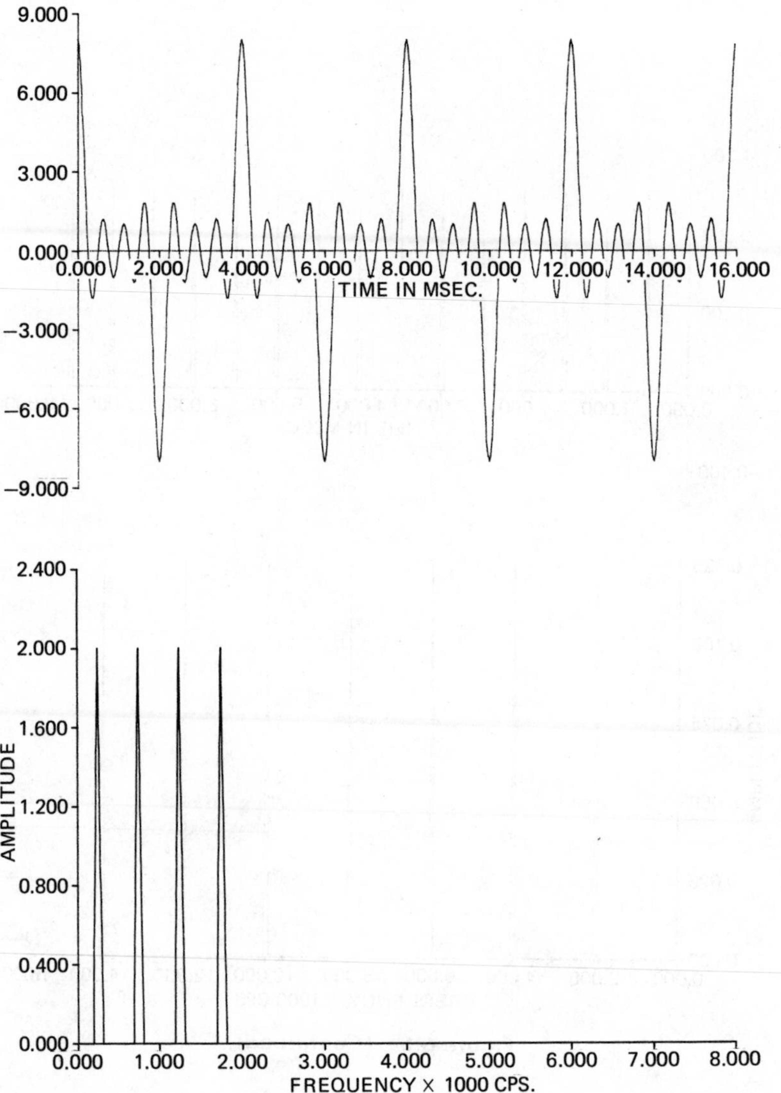

Figure 6.6 (***Continued***).

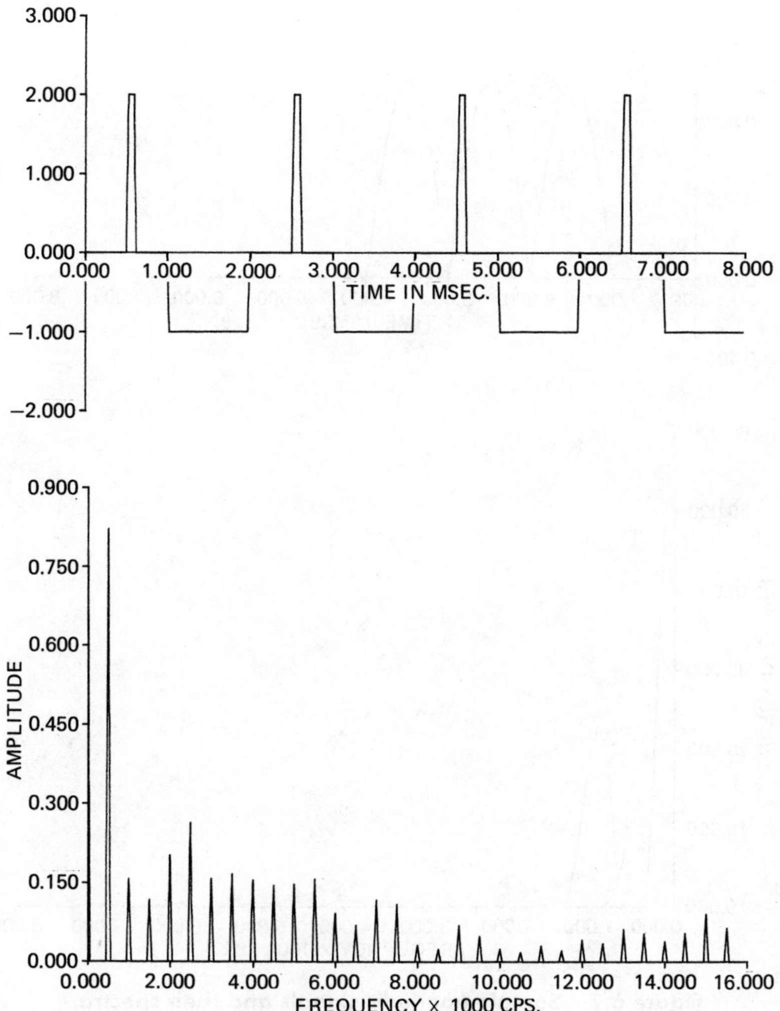

Figure 6.6 (***Continued***).

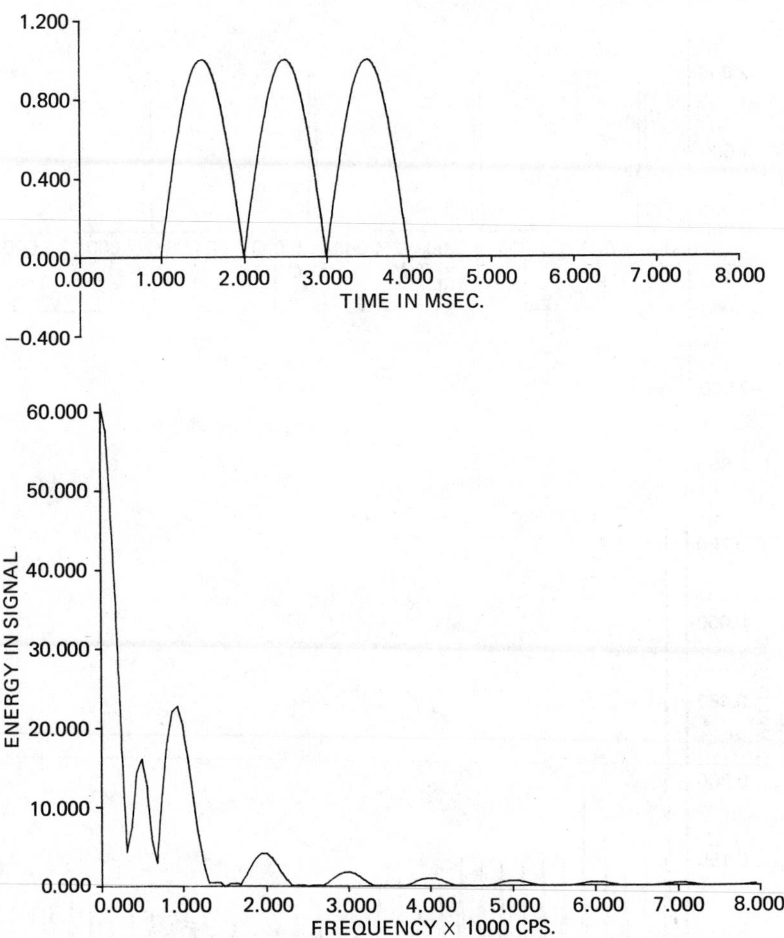

Figure 6.7 Sample aperiodic signals and their spectra.

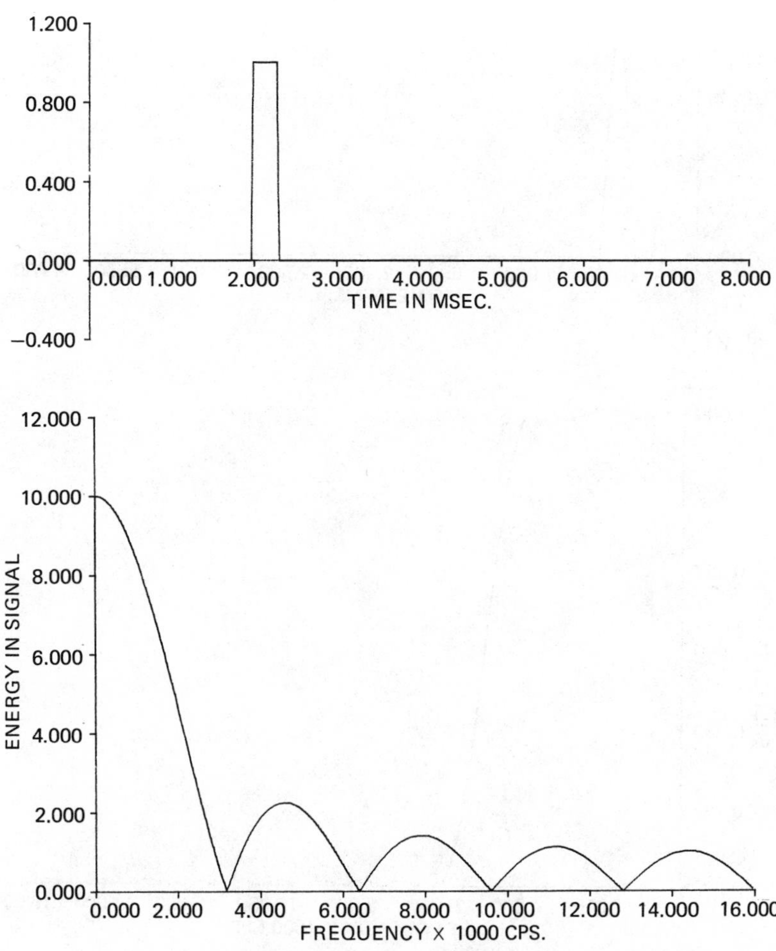

Figure 6.7 (***Continued***).

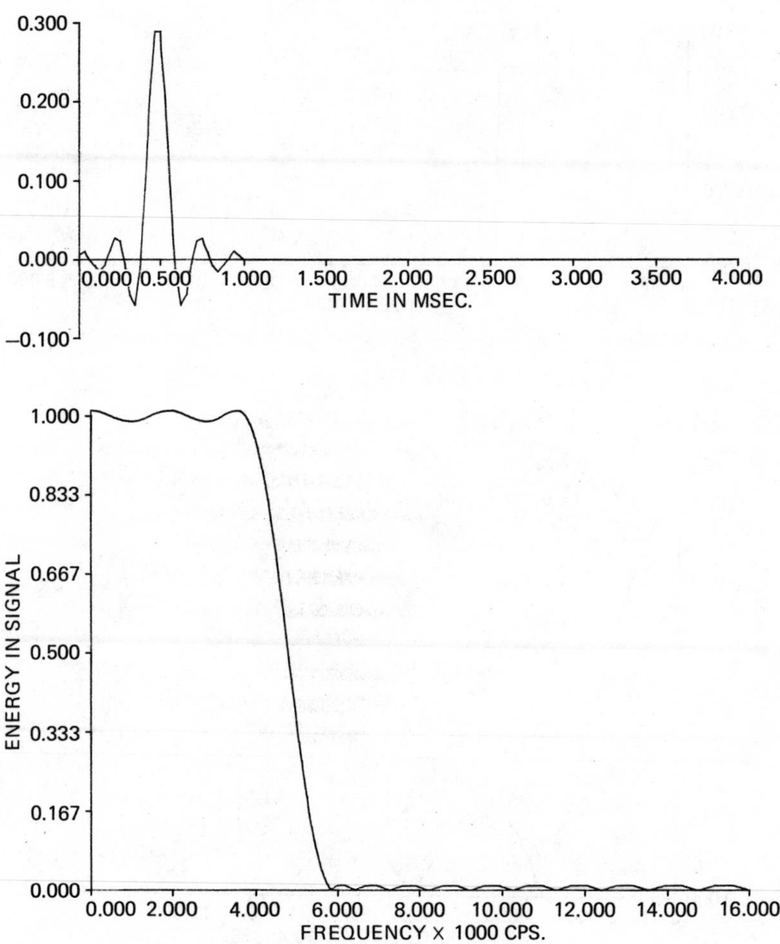

Figure 6.7 (*Continued*).

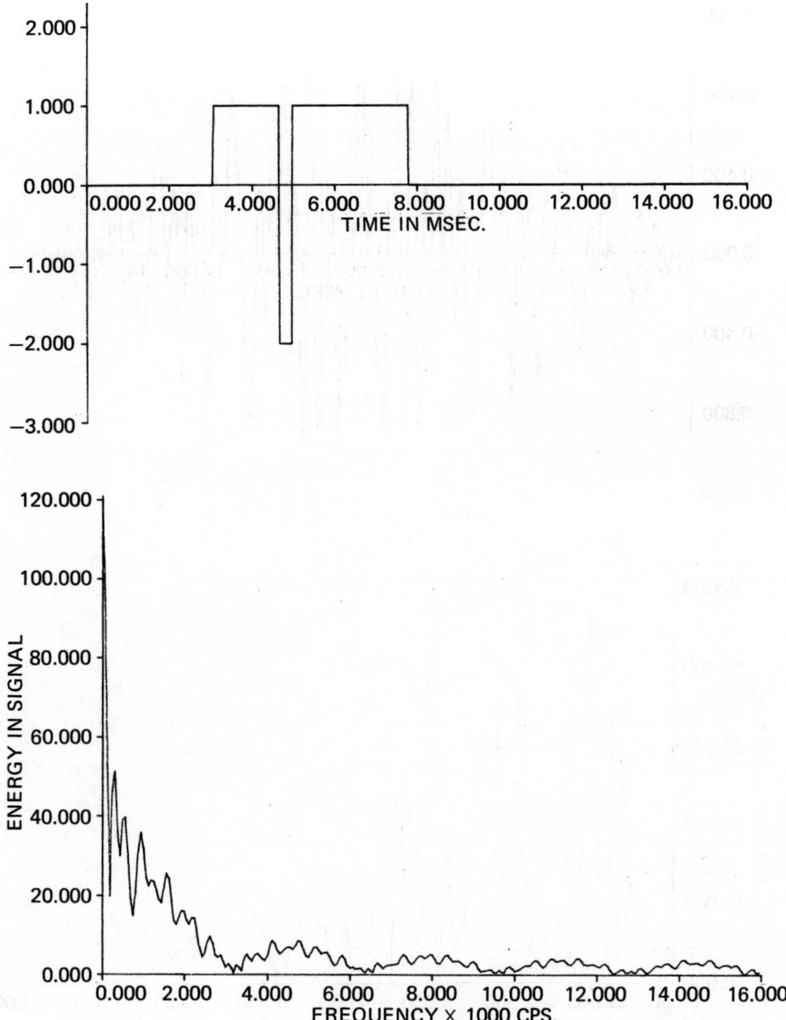

Figure 6.7 (***Continued***).

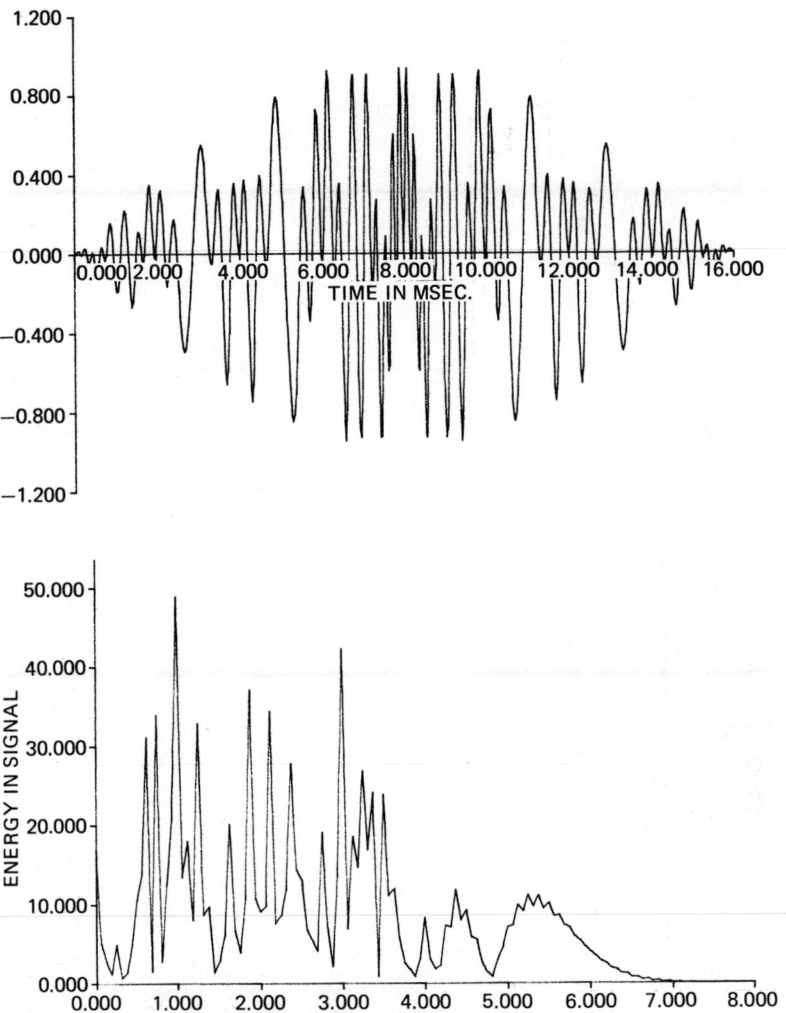

Figure 6.7 (***Continued***).

spectrum as can be seen from Fig. 6.6. This is because the Fourier transform coefficients at the frequencies that are not at or near these harmonics are nearly zero in magnitude.

The capability of performing discrete Fourier analysis by digital computer offers a distinct and very important advantage over mechanical methods. Mechanical harmonic analysis requires at best several seconds to perform, and also demands that the tone be nearly static in timbre. It would clearly be futile to attempt such an analysis of a tone made by a plucked string or percussion instrument. Plotting the spectrum of a tone is analogous to taking a photograph. If the camera's shutter speed is fast enough, one can take a picture of a rapidly moving object. Like the camera shutter, a 512 sample Fourier transform isolates a 17-millisecond segment of sound and provides a frequency-domain "photograph" of it. The 17-millisecond interval is short enough that one may obtain a good picture of a dynamically changing tone at any point of its onset.

Let us suppose that we intend to harmonically analyze a piano tone for 1 full second of its onset. We will not only study what harmonics are present in the tone, but how each individual harmonic changes with time. We first tape-record the note. Then we sample one second of the recording with an ADC at a sampling rate of 30,000 per second. The 30,000 samples in the computer's memory represent the tone in the time domain, but they reveal nothing about its harmonics. To perform a 30,000 sample Fourier analysis of the tone would be impracticable on the computer, and it would be useless even if it were feasible. It would be like taking a 1-second time exposure of a football play! What we can do, in effect, is take a short "motion picture" of the tone—taking one frame, or separate discrete Fourier transform, of the tone every 17 milliseconds. If each of these separate transforms are plotted on graphs, we are not only able to analyze the tone's harmonics as they occur statically in a small time interval, but we may trace the dynamics of any particular harmonic as it changes over 17-millisecond intervals. We can then use this information to plot the individual envelopes of the various harmonics. If we had relied on a picture of the waveform in the time domain only, we could view the contour of its overall envelope, but we would discern nothing of its harmonic character. The diagram in Fig. 6.8, obtained by James Moorer, illustrates a few examples of harmonic analysis that were performed on the tones of various instruments.

The value of studying the harmonic spectra of various musical tones is that we may discover the measurable properties of the tone that determine its color. Helmholtz, using his resonators, tuning forks, and other interesting mechanical devices, was able to make extensive examinations of the tones of many different instruments. He was restricted in his study to the analysis of unmodulated tones having static timbre for reasons we have discussed. But his work pioneered the development of psychoacoustical research as it continues today with the extensive use of the computer.

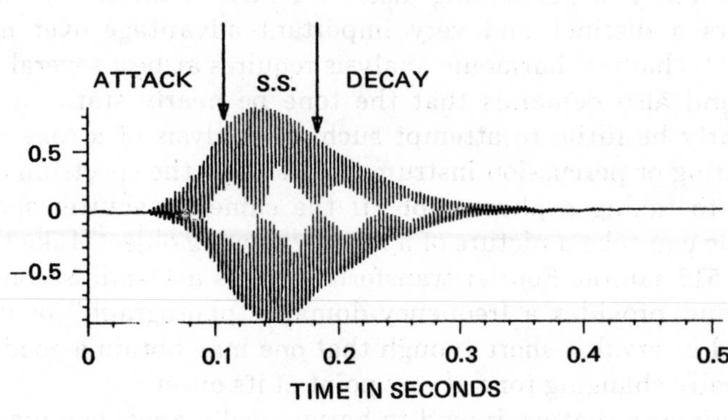

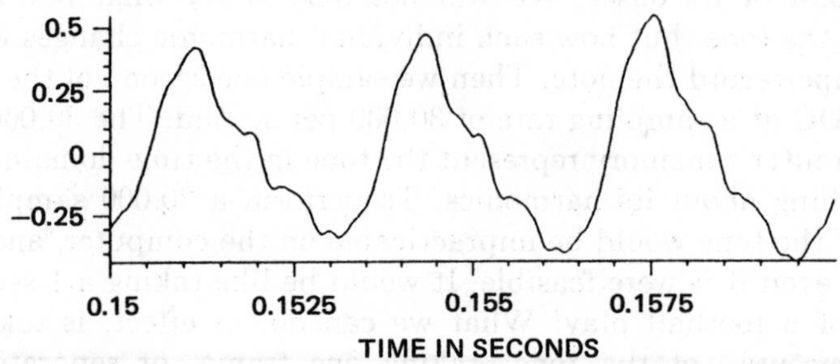

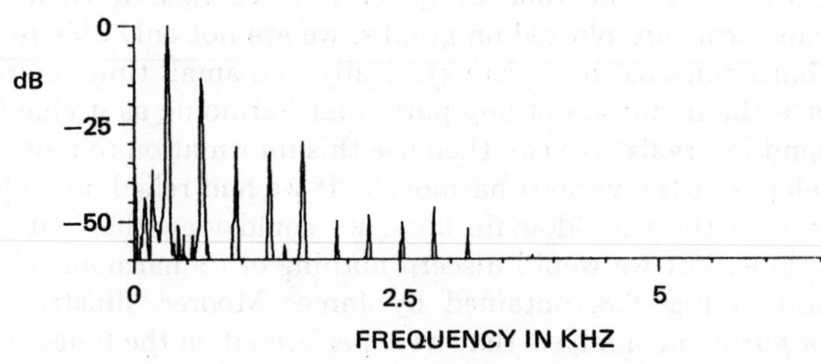

A

Figure 6.8 ***a*** **isolated cello tone,** ***b*** **isolated clarinet tone,** ***c*** **isolated trumpet tone, and** ***d*** **isolated bass drum note. Photographs obtained courtesy of the** ***Computer Music Journal.***

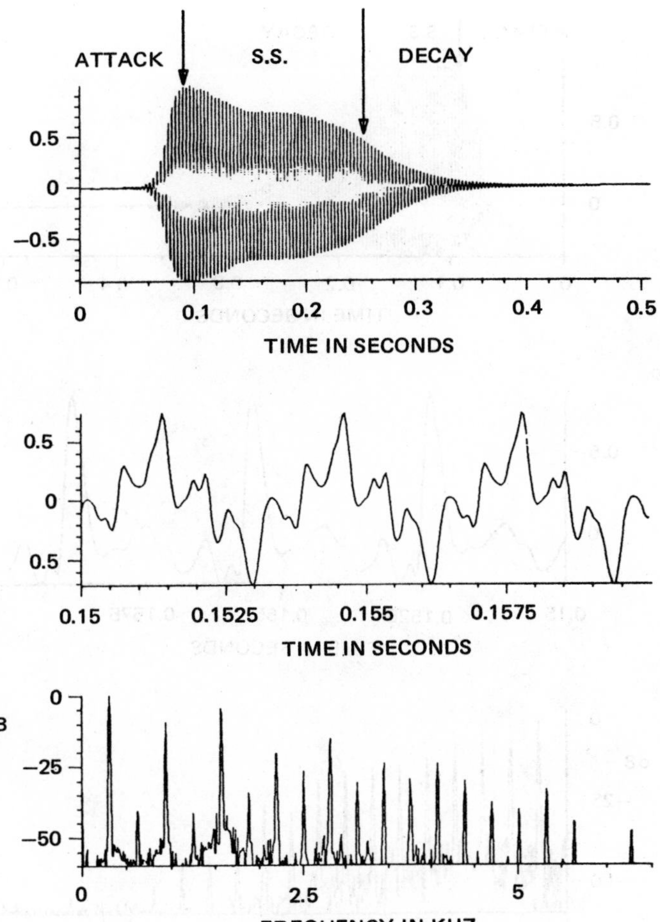

Figure 6.8 (***Continued***).

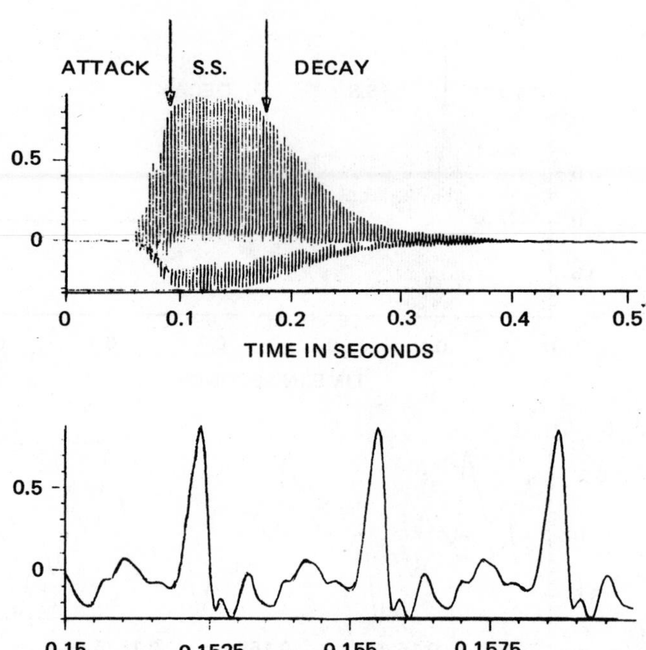

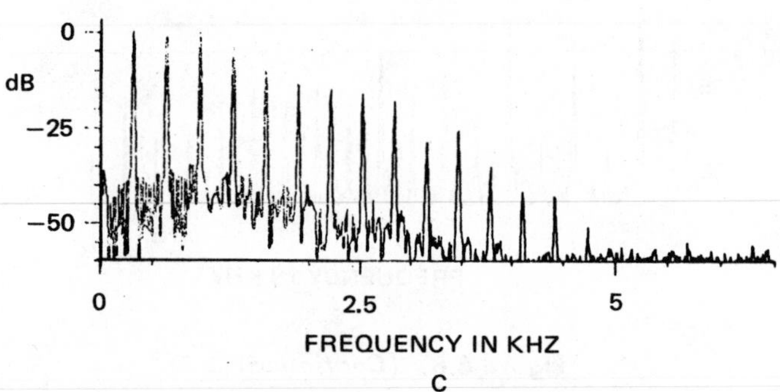

C

Figure 6.8 (*Continued*).

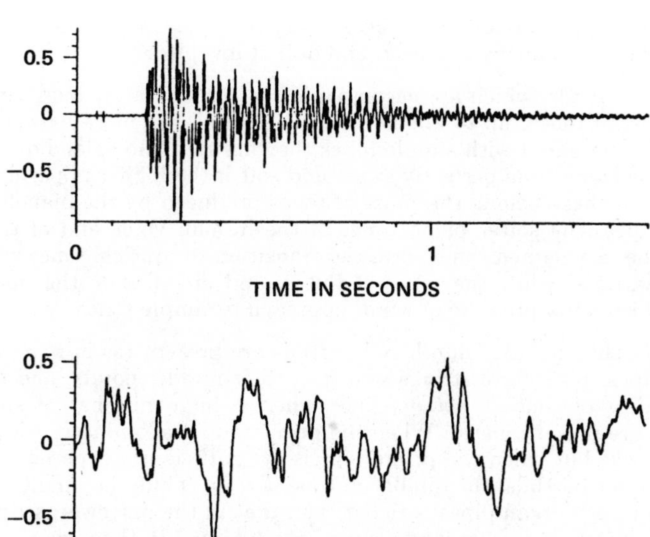

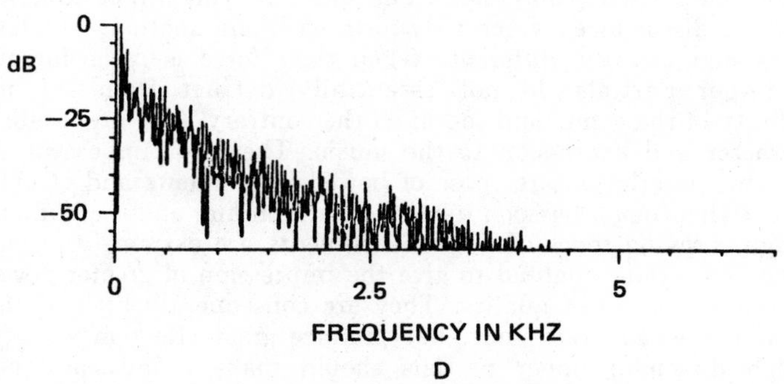

Figure 6.8 (***Continued***).

Helmholtz discovered that the psychological perception of tone color depends largely on the relative amplitude relationships of the tone's harmonics. He generalized the results of his investigation into some fundamental rules:

> 1. *Simple tones*, like those of tuning-forks applied to resonance chambers and wide stopped organ pipes, have a very soft, pleasant sound, free from all roughness, but wanting in power, and dull at low pitches.
>
> 2. *Musical tones*, which are accompanied by a moderately loud series of the lower partial tones, up to about the sixth partial, are more harmonious and musical. Compared with simple tones they are rich and splendid, while they are at the same time perfectly sweet and soft if the higher upper partials are absent. To these belong the musical tones produced by the pianoforte, open organ pipes, the softer piano tones of the human voice and of the French horn. The last-named tones form the transition to musical tones with higher upper partials; while the tones of flutes, and of pipes on the flue-stops of organs with a low pressure of wind, approach to simple tones.
>
> 3. If only the unevenly numbered partials are present (as in narrow stopped organ pipes, pianoforte strings struck in their middle points, and clarinets), the quality of tone is *hollow*, and, when a large number of such upper partials are present, nasal. When the prime tone predominates the quality of tone is *rich*; but when the prime tone is not sufficiently superior in strength to the upper partials, the quality of tone is *poor*. Thus the quality of tone in the wider open organ pipes is richer than that in the narrower; strings struck with pianoforte hammers give tones of a richer quality than when struck by a stick or plucked by the finger; the tones of reed pipes with suitable resonance chambers have a richer quality than those without resonance chambers.
>
> 4. When partial tones higher than the sixth or seventh are very distinct, the quality of tone is *cutting* and *rough*. The reason for this will be seen hereafter to lie in the dissonances which they form with one another. The degree of harshness may be very different. When their force is inconsiderable the higher upper partials do not essentially detract from the musical applicability of the compound tones; on the contrary, they are useful in giving character and expression to the music. The most important musical tones of this description are those of bowed instruments and of most reed pipes, oboe (hautbois), bassoon (fagotto), harmonium, and the human voice. The rough, braying tones of brass instruments are extremely penetrating, and hence are better adabted to give the impression of greater power than similar tones of a softer quality. They are consequently little suitable for artistic music when used alone, but produce great effect in an orchestra. Why high dissonant upper partials should make a musical tone more penetrating will appear hereafter. Hermann Helmholtz, *On the Sensation of Tone*, pp. 118–119.

Helmholtz also experimented with tonal perception by producing different tones that had identical harmonic amplitude relationships, but whose harmonics varied in their phase orientation. He discovered that despite the phase differences, the tones were audibly indistinguishable from each other. From this, he concluded that although the human ear is extremely pitch sensitive, it has no phase perception. Since then, in more sophisticated experiments, researchers have determined that the ear is actually phase sensitive to a slight degree. Yet the sensitivity is small enough that Helmholtz was essentially correct in stating that the ear perceives tonal character in terms of harmonic amplitudes rather than phase. For this reason, although it is necessary in Fourier analysis to account for the phase of the waveform being analyzed, once the analysis is complete, its two-dimensional sine and cosine spectrum may be simplified to a single, one-dimensional spectrum of absolute magnitude whereas the phase is ignored.

To further understand how the harmonic content of various instrumental tones determines their timbral color, we may investigate their spectra in relation to the physical construction of the instrument. The analysis of reed instruments, strings, the flute, and the human voice leads to particularly interesting revelations. All of these instruments form their sound by exciting a resonating cavity with a vibrating medium. The resonating cavity of a brass or woodwind instrument is the tube or pipe that is stopped with holes or valves that vary its effective length. The length of the cavity determines the note's pitch. As a result, the partials of the tone it produces are closely harmonically related. One finds in a flute tone that the fundamental frequency is very dominant whereas the upper harmonics are only slightly present. Consequently, the flute's tone is very pure, sounding similar to a sine tone. However, although a sine tone generated by an electronic oscillator and loudspeaker has no fluctuation or variation, the tone of a flute is appealing to the ear because of its articulation and slight pertubations of pitch and intensity. A flute tone also contains a small amount of random noise introduced by the air blown across the mouthpiece.

The tone of an oboe or clarinet is much richer in upper harmonic content. Superficially, this instrument sounds much like square or triangle waves. Recalling the discussion in Chapter 2, those waveforms contain the fundamental and odd-numbered harmonics in decreasing amplitudes. The action of the reed itself is able to excite the higher modes of the air column which are not emphasized in a flute. It is not necessary here to undertake an extensive discussion of the physics of reasonating air columns, but we may state that a pipe closed at one end resonates in frequencies such that the length of the column is an odd-numbered multiple of ¼ the wavelength of the harmonic. Figure 6.9 illustrates this by depicting a pipe resonating in its first three modes. This explains why the odd-numbered harmonics prevail.

The acoustics of a violin are much more complex. The violin's resonating cavity is fixed whereas the length of the string determines the fundamental pitch. As a result, the body of the instrument acts as a filter which emphasizes certain partials while attenuating others. The action of the string, being alternately drawn back and snapped forward as it is bowed,

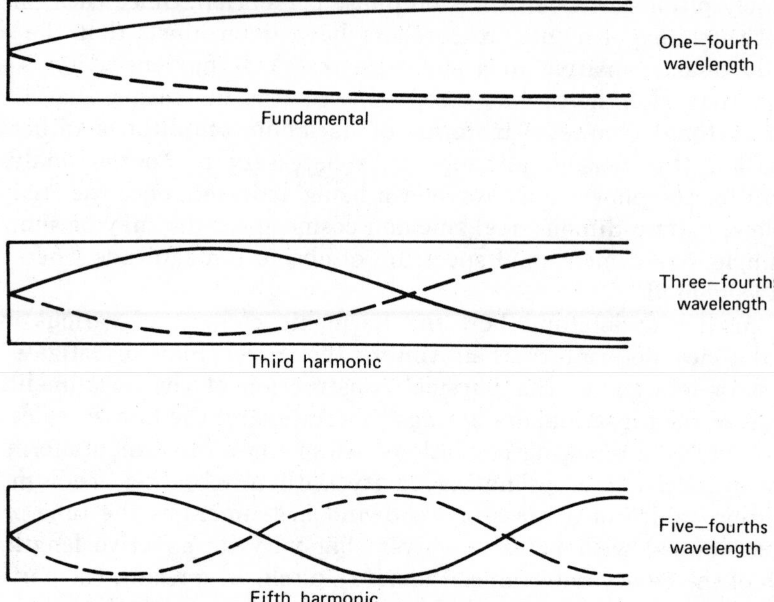

Figure 6.9 Closed-end pipe resonating in three modes.

approximates the action of a sawtooth wave. Recall that a sawtooth wave contains even as well as odd-numbered harmonics. Listening to a sawtooth wave from an electronic synthesizer reveals its rough similarity to a violin's tone. The fixed character of the violin's resonating body dictates the partials that are emphasized. They will not vary from note to note, nor will they necessarily be related harmonically to the pitch being played or to each other. The fricative noises created by bowing of the string will excite frequencies in the instrument cavity that are independent of the note's pitch. The violin's spectrum is thus considerably more complex than that of the wind's.

Turning to the human voice, we find that its tone is subject to yet another degree of variability. The pitch of the voice is determined by the vocal chords, but the partials of its tone result primarily from the shape and position of the throat, nasal cavity, diaphram, and chest. All of these factors vary independently one from another. The filtering capacity of resonating chamber performs the same function as the body of a mechanical instrument, except that most instruments lack this variability. The vocal chords themselves produce a broad spectrum of frequencies not harmonic to the actual fundamental pitch. Most of them are then filtered away by the vocal tract while a few are emphasized. The partials that are emphasized are called *formants*, and determine the character of vowel sounds they produce. Much of the research currently being done in speech synthesis by computer involves the simulation of vocal sounds by variable filters. The filters are excited by impulse-train functions that approximate the action of vocal chords. Then the filter characteristics are modeled to imitate the frequency response of the vocal tract as it produces a particular vowel sound. Although the formant theory of vocal sounds is applied primarily to speech analysis and production, it is also used extensively in the study of the timbre of musical instruments. By understanding the determining factors of an instrument's timbre in mathematical detail and specificity, one can model its acoustical characteristics on a computer. However, it is not the ultimate aim of computer music to perfectly imitate musical instruments. Indeed, it is much easier to hear the sound of a violin by calling upon a violinist. The challenge of computer music is in the creation of original tones not producible by conventional instruments. Meeting this challenge requires the knowledge to be gained by the study of existing instruments.

The method of Fourier analysis discussed thus far is intended primarily for the analysis of a tone's frequency spectrum. To gain information concerning the dynamic properties of a particular timbre, one must regard its spectrum as a changing function of time. If one attempts to perform a time-varying analysis by the "motion-picture" method just described, it requires the separate computation of a new Fourier transform once every few milliseconds. This is very problematic, and requires great expense in computer time. Moreover, if one wishes to inspect the results in terms of how each of the tone's partials are separately enveloped, the sequence of spectra are inconvenient to interpret into this form.

James W. Beauchamp at the University of Illinois and James A. Moorer at Stanford University have utilized a method of timbral analysis that

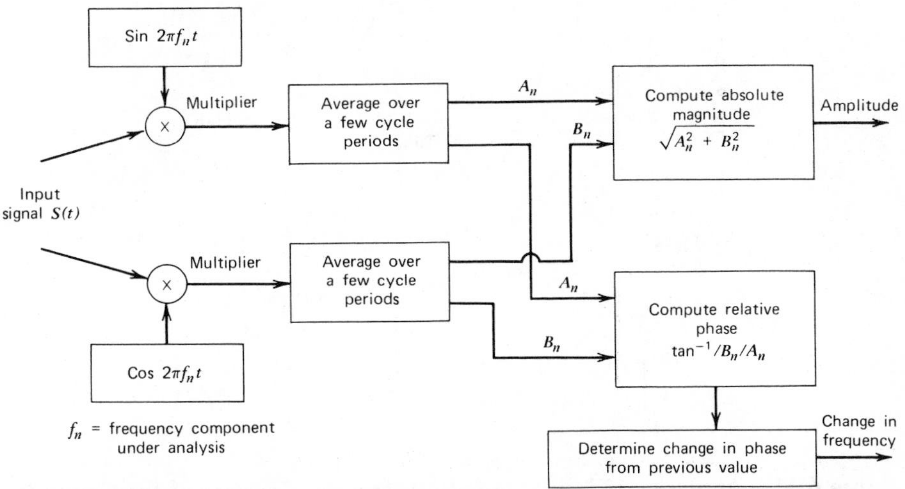

Figure 6.10 Method of timbral analysis using hetrodyning.

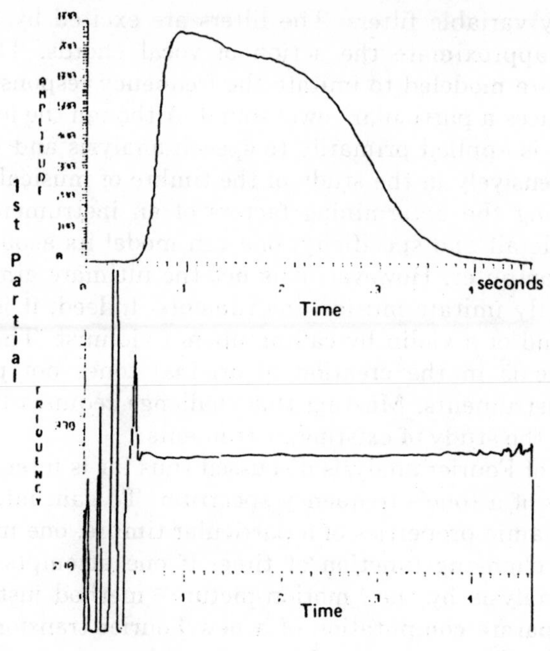

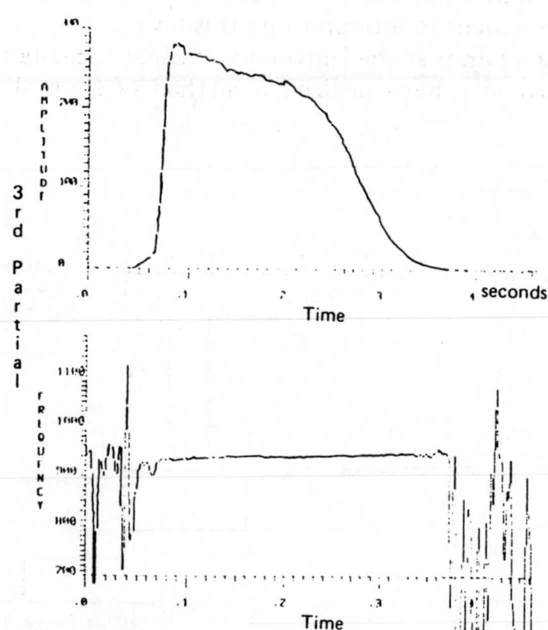

Figure 6.11 Analysis of Clarinet tone by J. Moorer. Courtesy of the *Computer Music Journal*.

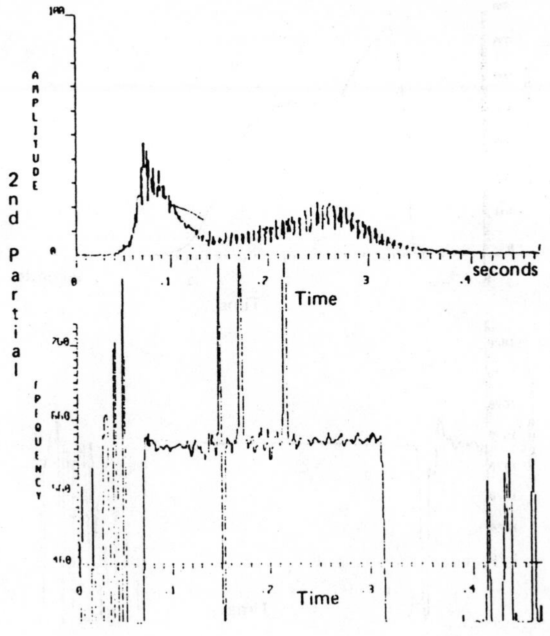

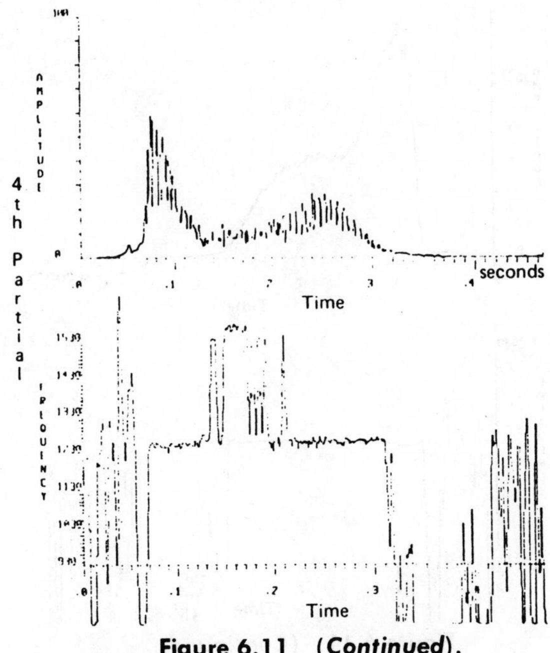

Figure 6.11 (***Continued***).

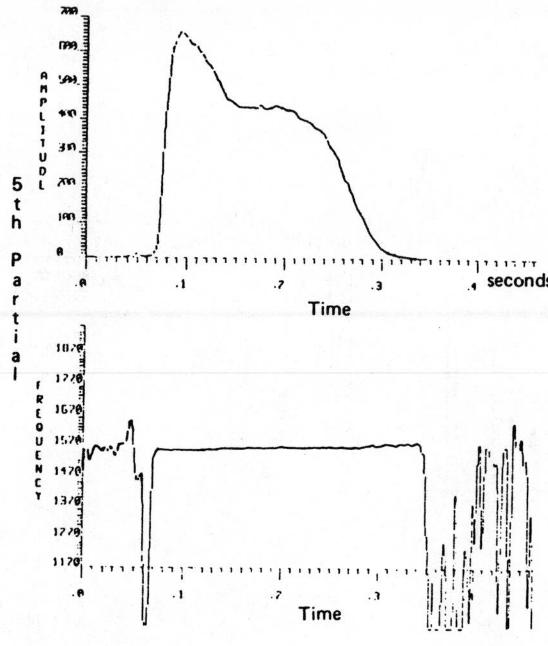

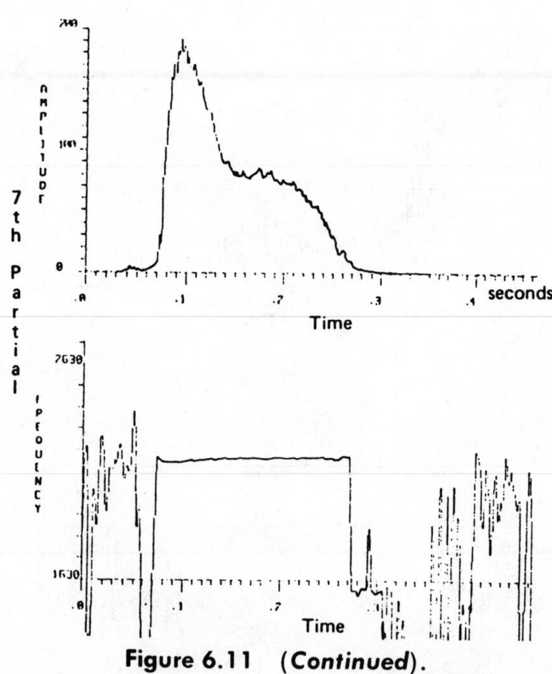

Figure 6.11 (*Continued*).

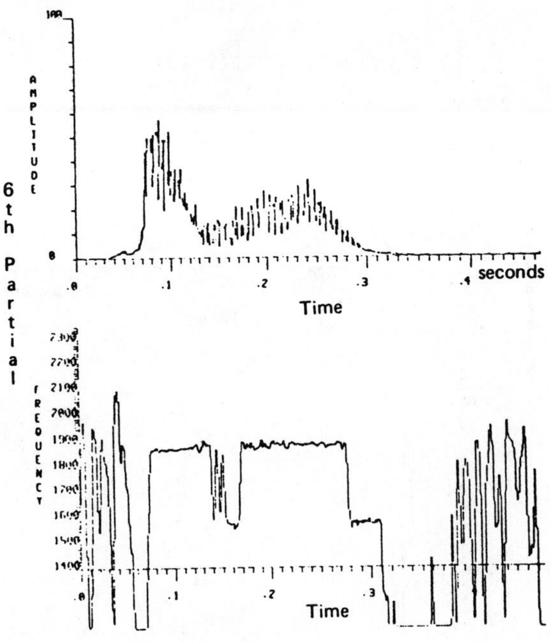

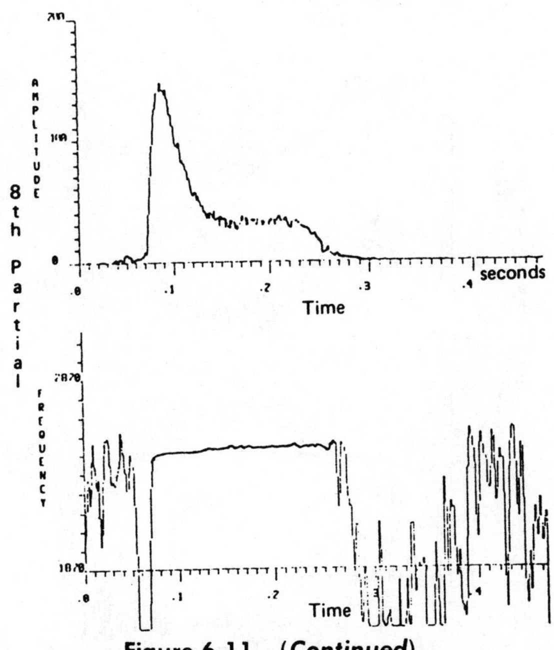

Figure 6.11 (*Continued*).

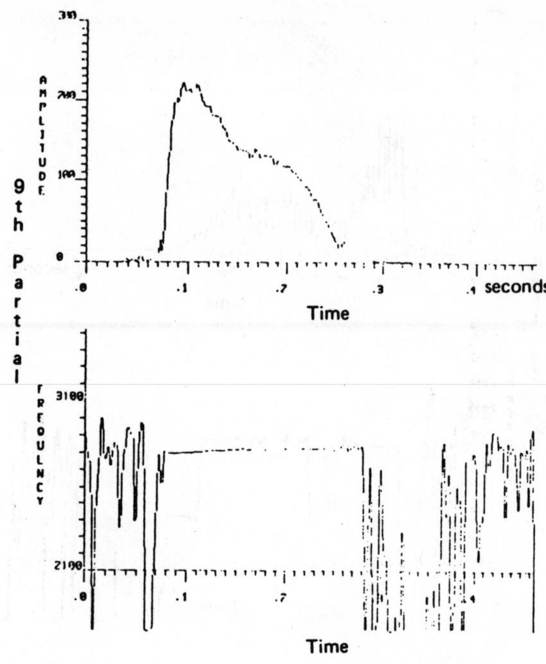

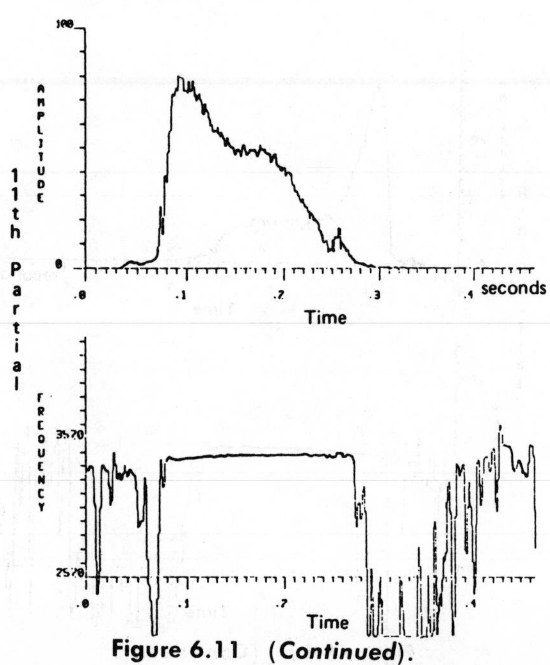

Figure 6.11 (*Continued*).

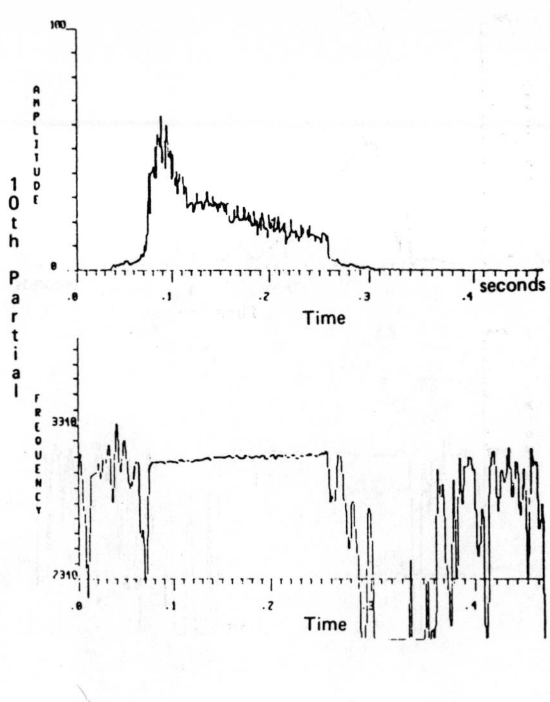

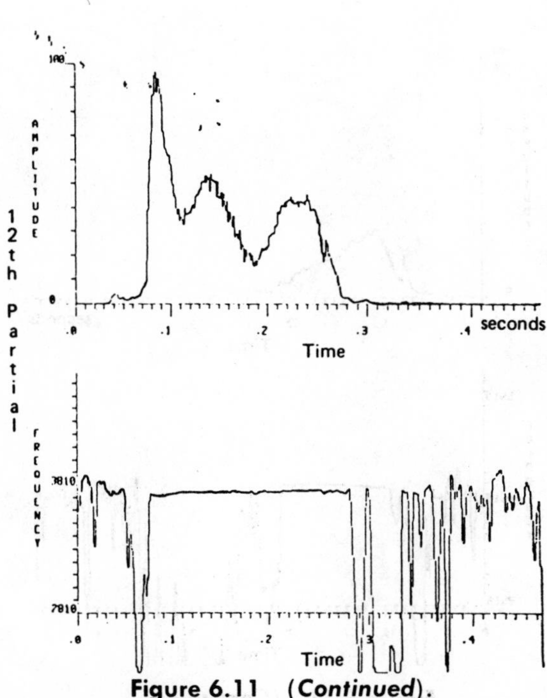

Figure 6.11 (*Continued*).

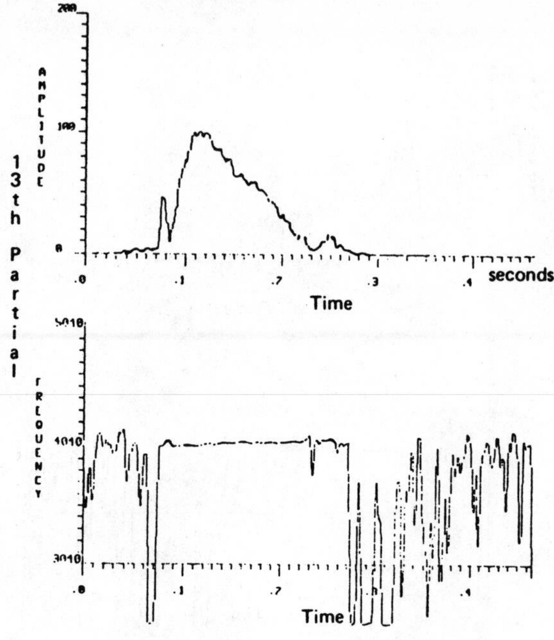

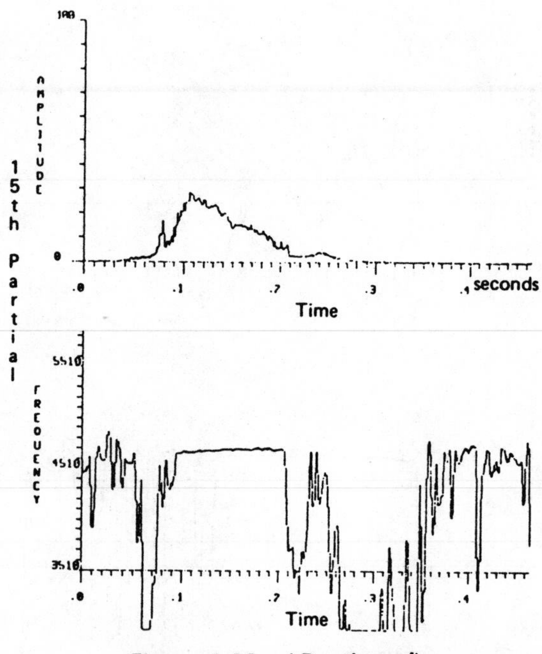

Figure 6.11 (*Continued*).

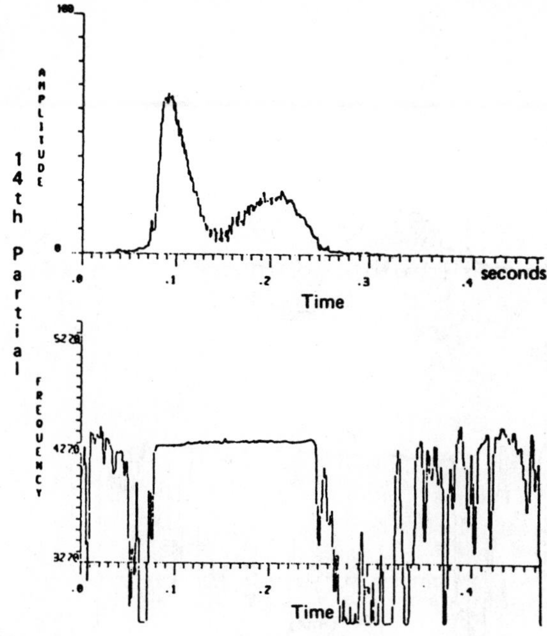

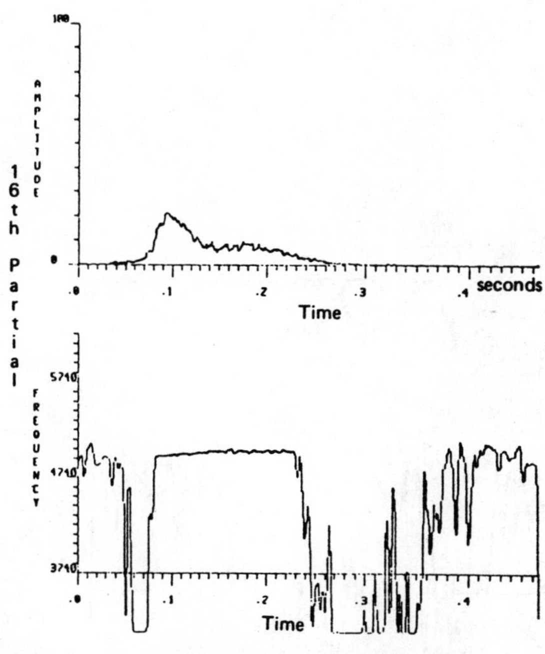

Figure 6.11 (*Continued*).

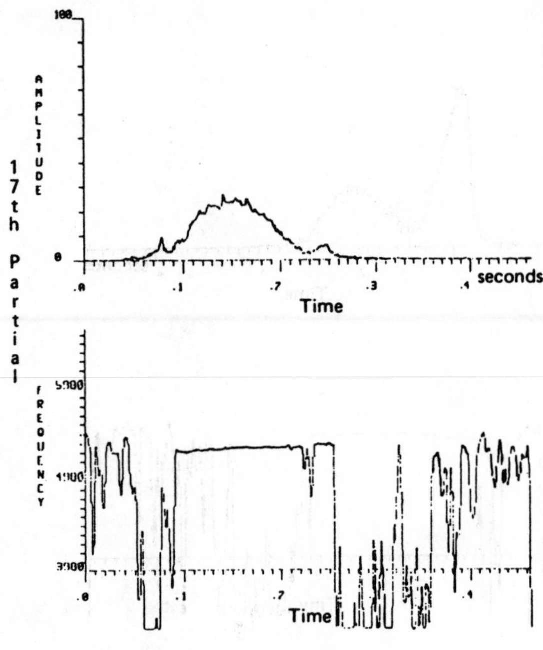

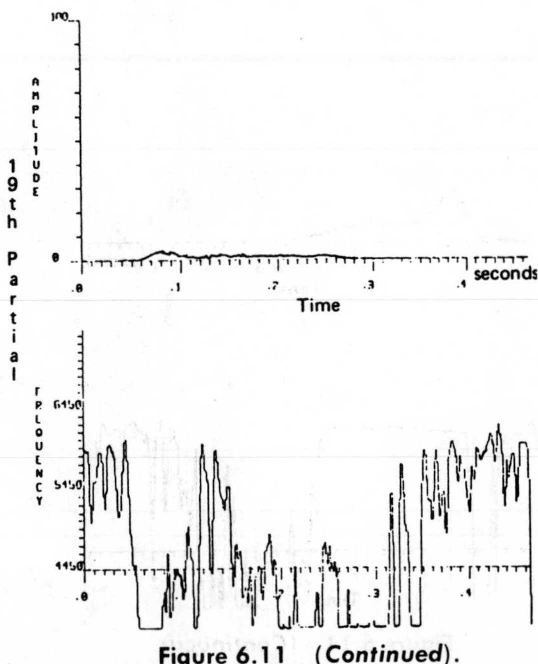

Figure 6.11 (*Continued*).

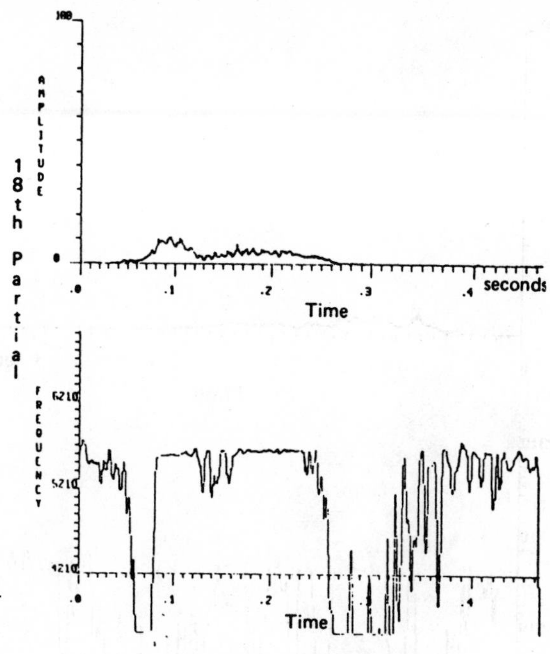

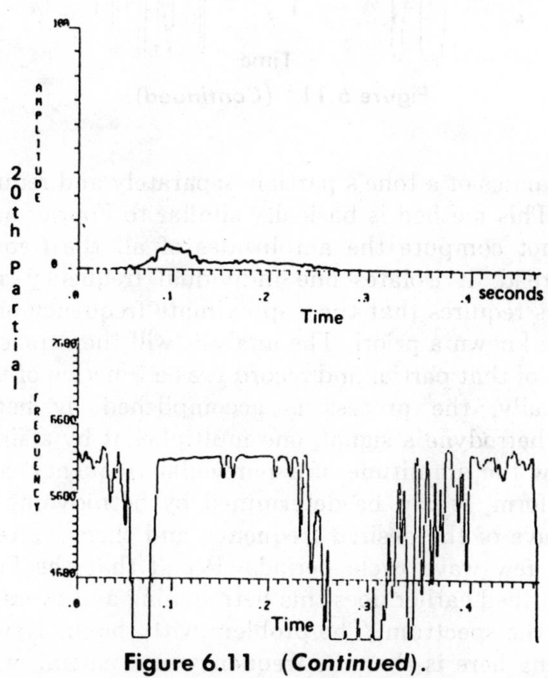

Figure 6.11 (*Continued*).

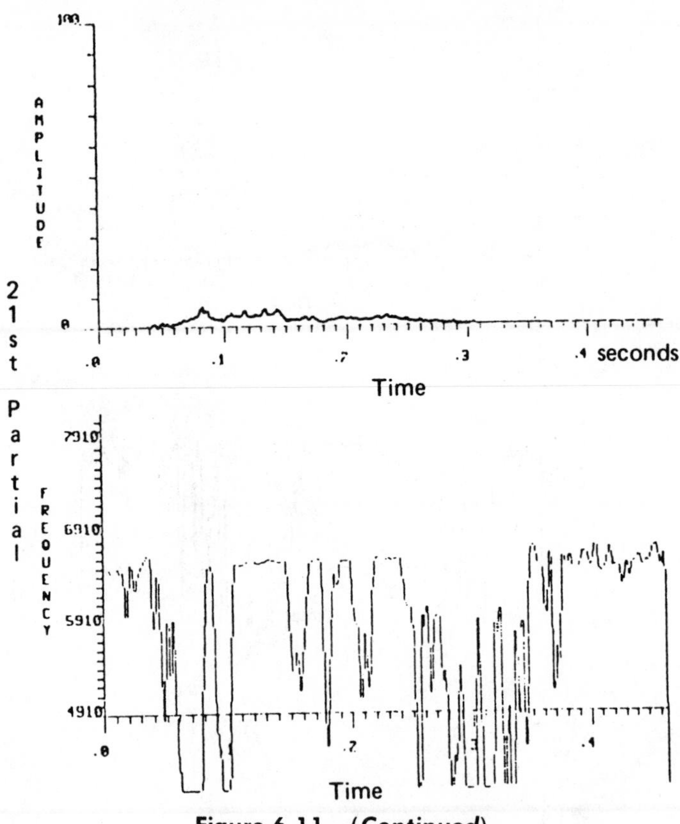

Figure 6.11 (***Continued***).

traces the dynamics of a tone's partials separately and requires much less computation. This method is basically similar to Fourier analysis, except that it does not compute the amplitudes of all the frequencies of the spectrum. Instead, it isolates one individual frequency and follows its dynamics. This requires that the approximate frequency of the partial to be analyzed be known a priori. The analysis will then trace the frequency and amplitude of that partial and record it as a function of time.

Mathematically, the process is accomplished by hetrodyning and averaging. To hetrodyne a signal, one multiplies it by a sine wave. If one desires to know the amplitude of a particular frequency component in a complex waveform, it can be determined by hetrodyning the waveform with a sine wave of the desired frequency and then averaging the result over one or a few wave cycle periods. Recall that the Fourier analysis procedure described earlier does this hetrodyning and averaging for all the frequencies of the spectrum. The problem with the analysis procedure we are investigating here is that the frequency of a partial, while remaining *approximately* constant in time, does fluctuate to some degree. Thus to keep track of this frequency as it changes in time, it is necessary to periodically update the frequency of the sine wave used to hetrodyne the signal. But how does one determine how far and in what direction to modify this frequency? It is known that as the frequency of any signal changes, its phase also correspondingly changes. The phase of a signal may be tracked by expressing it two-dimensionally as a sum of sine and cosine functions as is done in Fourier analysis. Knowing the amplitudes of the sine and cosine components separately relative to each other permits one to determine the phase of the signal at any instant. This phase is the inverse tangent of the quotient of these two amplitudes. As the phase changes in time, the difference is computed over a short time interval of approximately 10 milliseconds. This difference determines the degree and direction that the frequency of the hetrodyning sine and cosine waves must be modified and updated. The procedure may be expressed as in Fig. 6.10.

The analysis method described above is limited in that the frequency f_n of the partial under analysis must be fairly stable. If it changes too abruptly, the process will lose track of it. The partial must also be well-defined with no other prominant frequency components too close to it. If two partials of a tone are close enough together, the hetrodyning and averaging procedures will not sufficiently distinguish them from each other. Consequently, this method would be ineffective for percussive, clangorous, or noisy sounds, or for tones with excessive vibrato. Nevertheless, the procedure has been used successfully with interesting results. The graphs of Figs. 6.11 and 6.12 were obtained by James Moorer, and illustrate the first 20 harmonics of clarinet and oboe tones. Notice the prominence of the odd harmonics characteristic of these instruments!

One can make an interesting comparison between the harmonic analysis of a clarinet tone illustrated in the figure and the harmonic analysis of a Haydn sonata. The term "harmonic analysis" is anachronistically used to designate two entirely different procedures—one in acoustics and one in music theory. However, the utility of the two procedures is essentially similar. One analyzes the harmonic, contrapuntal, and rhythmic style of a Haydn sonata to learn how an important artist composed. After analyzing many works of Haydn, a skilled music student can compose works in the style of Haydn. One can even program a computer to imitate the style of various composers. This topic will be explored later. But imitation is not the object of analysis. It is merely a stepping-stone used to gain the understanding and compositional skill necessary to create original, artistic works. Our purpose in developing the mathematical techniques of dynamic, spectral analysis of musical tones presented in this chapter is to apply the knowlege gained thereby to the synthesis of original tones that are not in the repetoire of ordinary instruments. One may analyze the tone of an instrument and use the results of the analysis to perform a nearly perfect imitation of the tone with the computer. But to

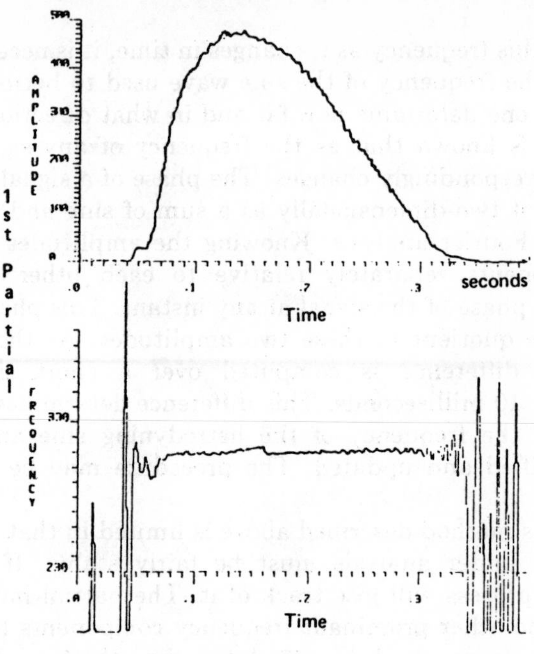

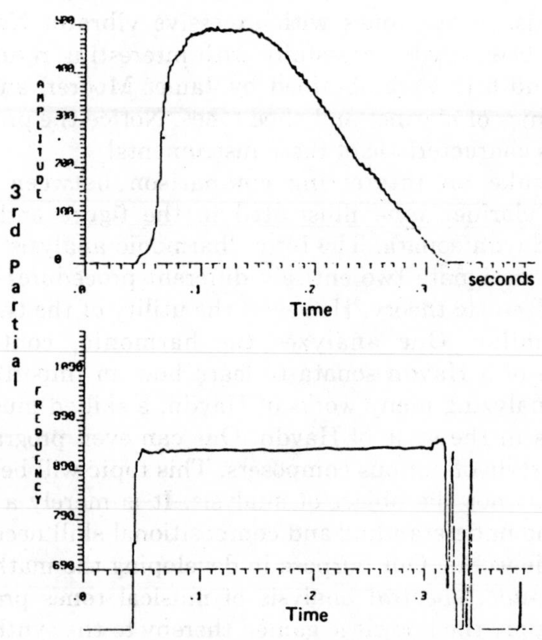

Figure 6.12 Analysis of Oboe tone by J. Moorer. Courtesy of the *Computer Music Journal*.

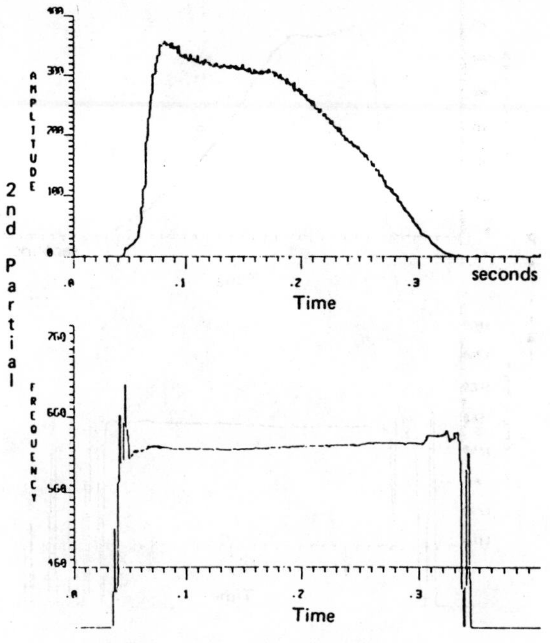

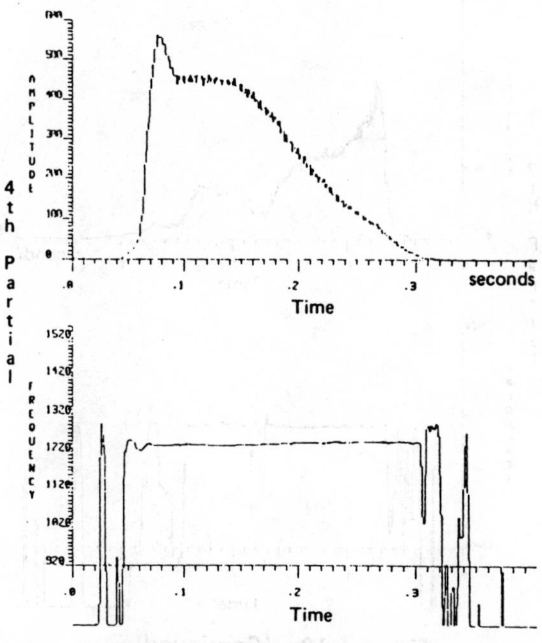

Figure 6.12 (*Continued*).

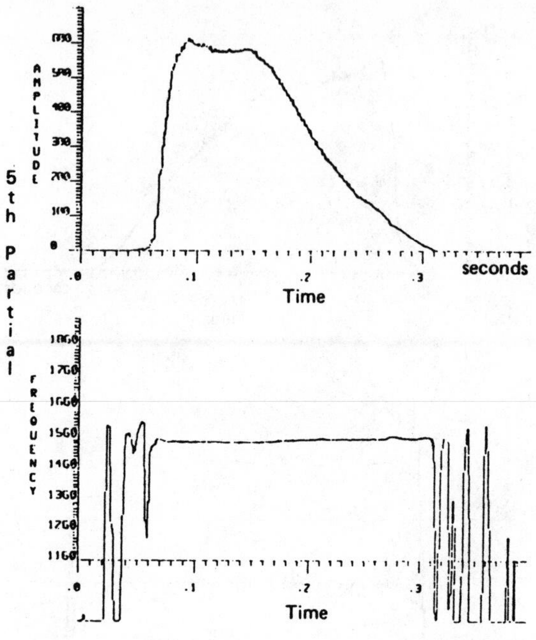

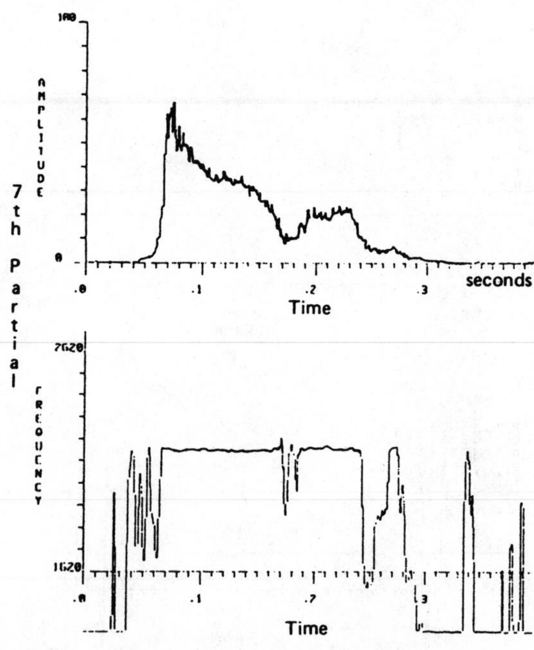

Figure 6.12 (*Continued*).

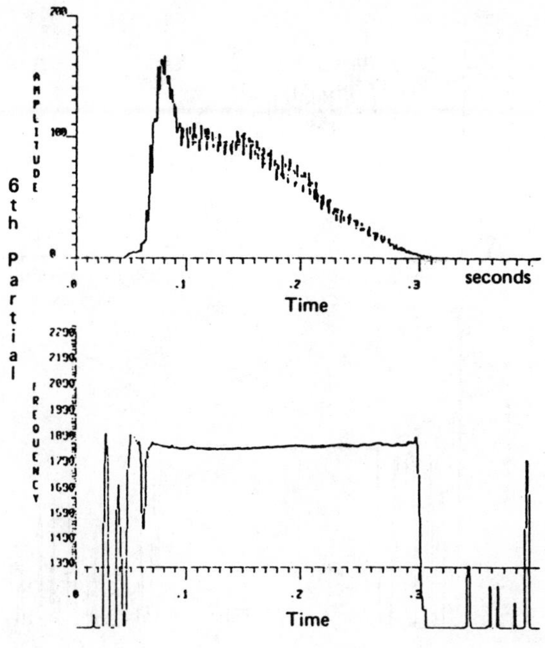

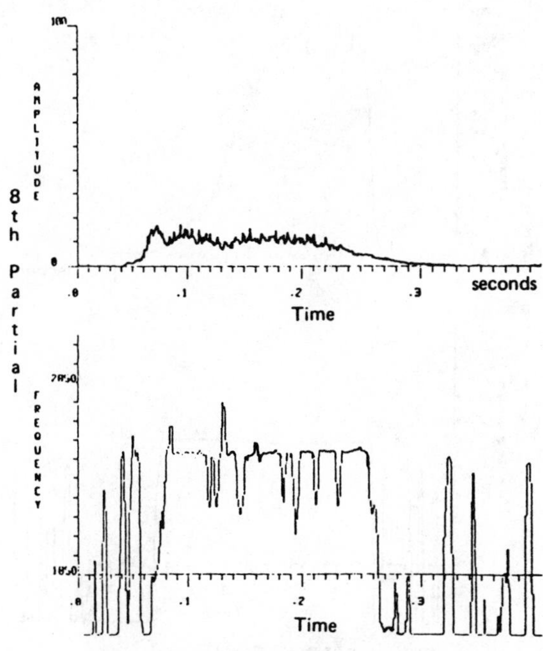

Figure 6.12 (*Continued*).

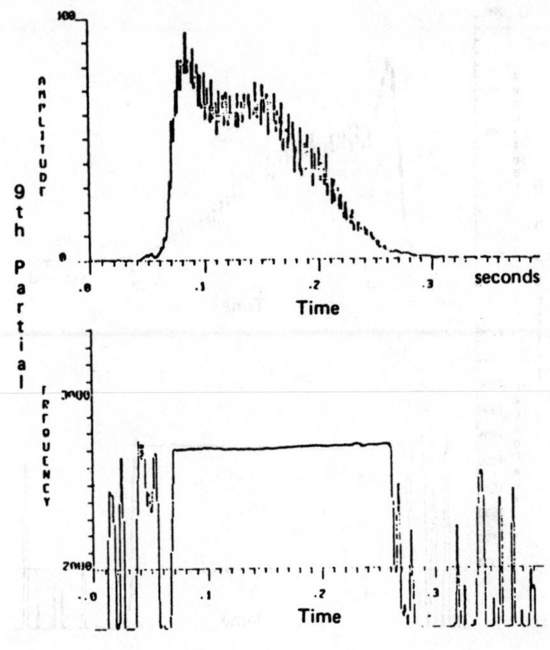

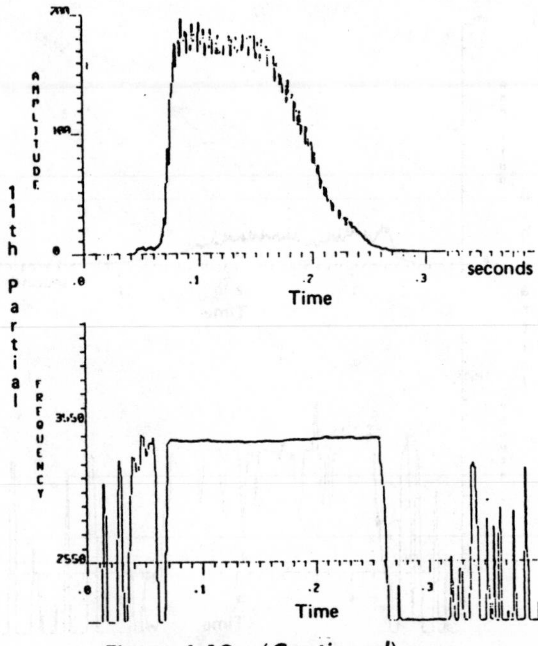

Figure 6.12 (*Continued*).

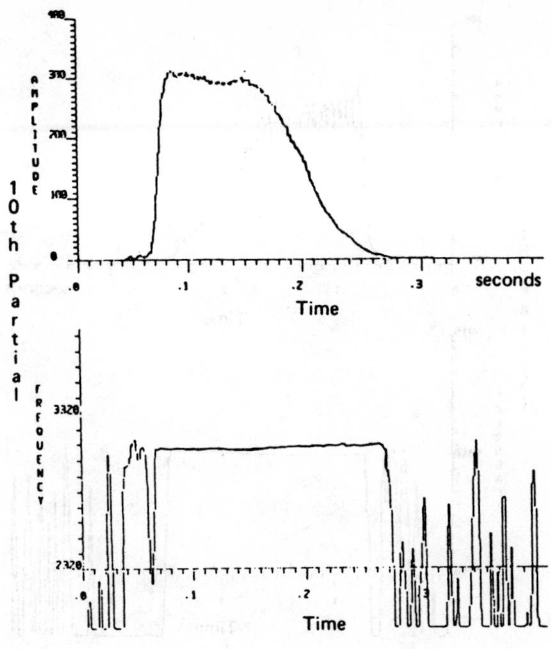

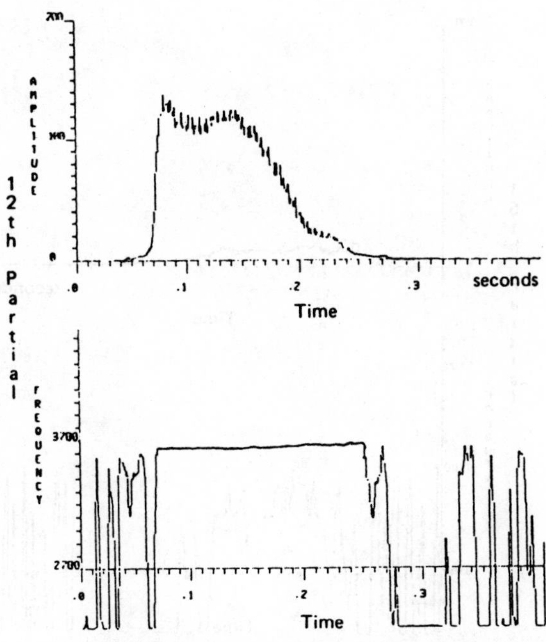

Figure 6.12 (*Continued*).

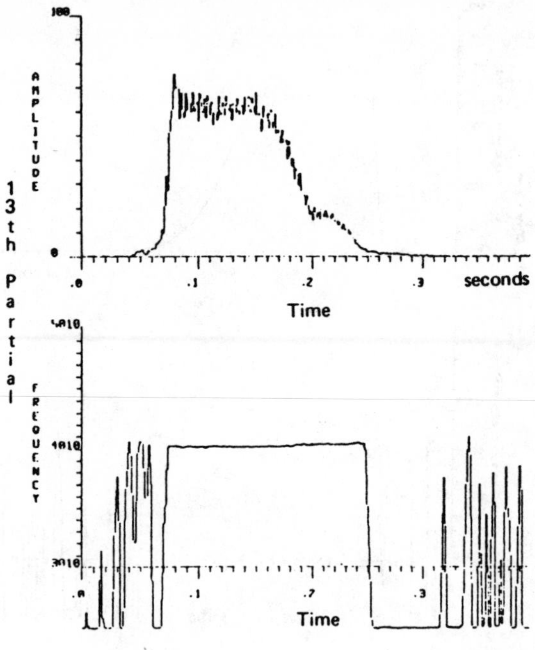

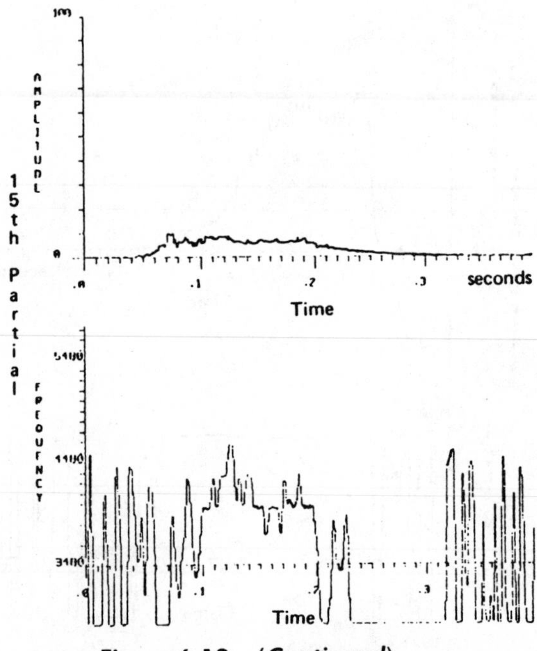

Figure 6.12 (***Continued***).

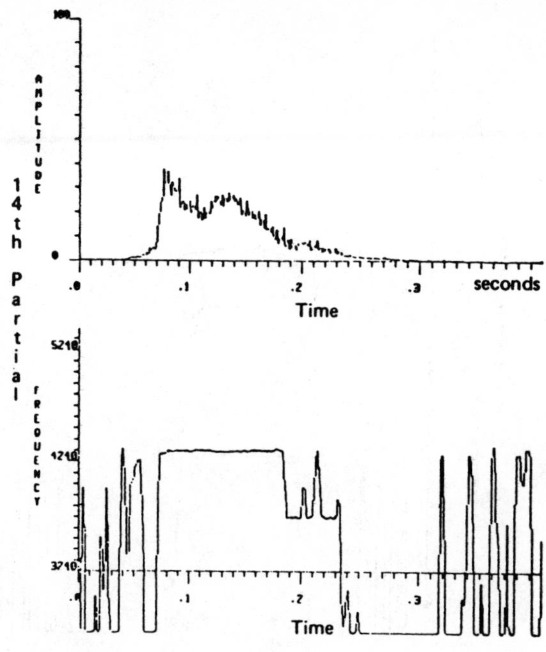

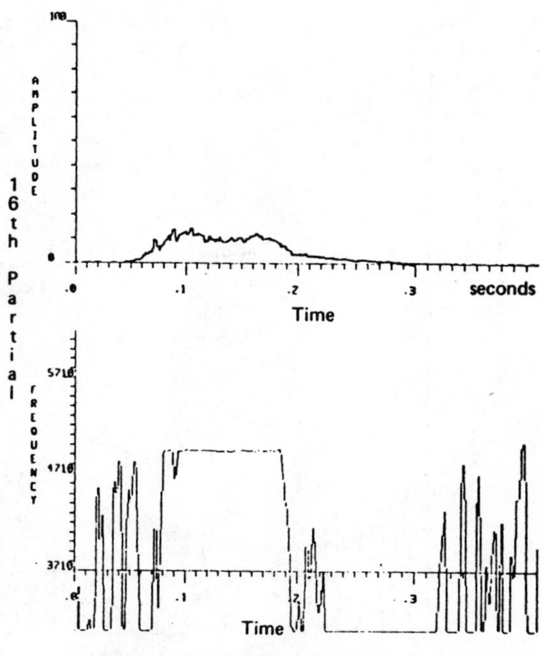

Figure 6.12 (***Continued***).

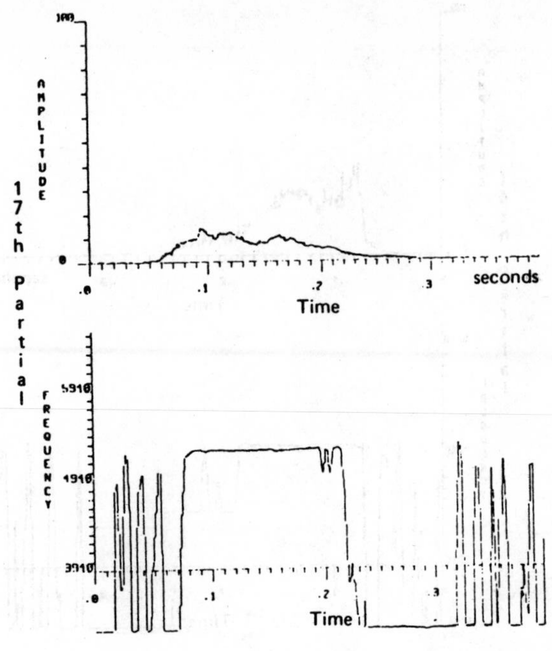

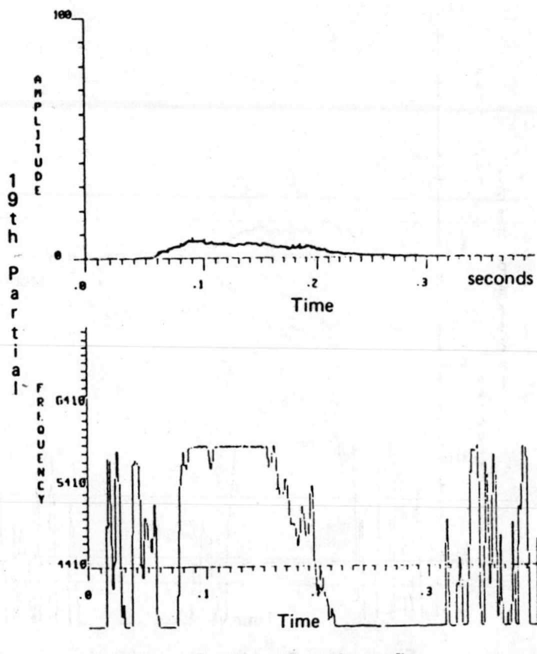

Figure 6.12 (*Continued*).

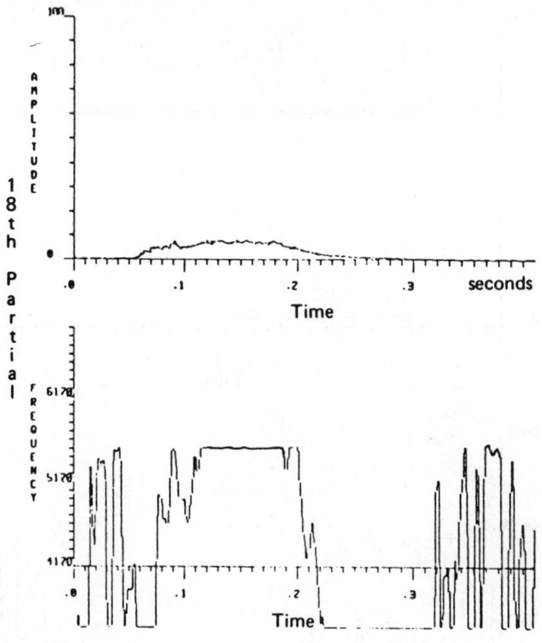

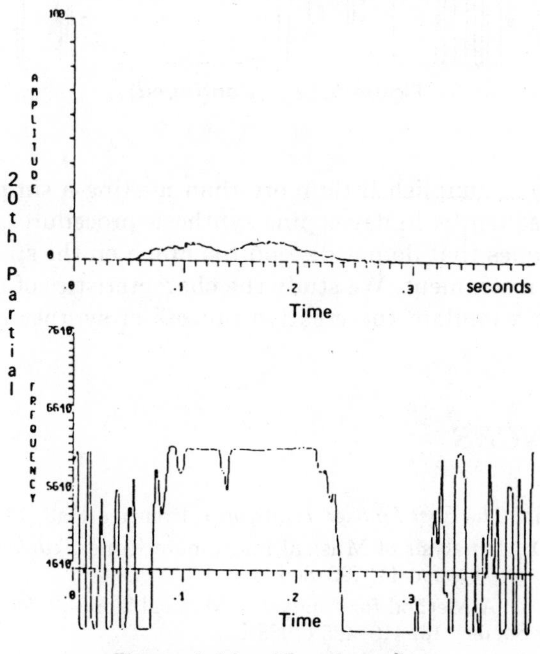

Figure 6.12 (*Continued*).

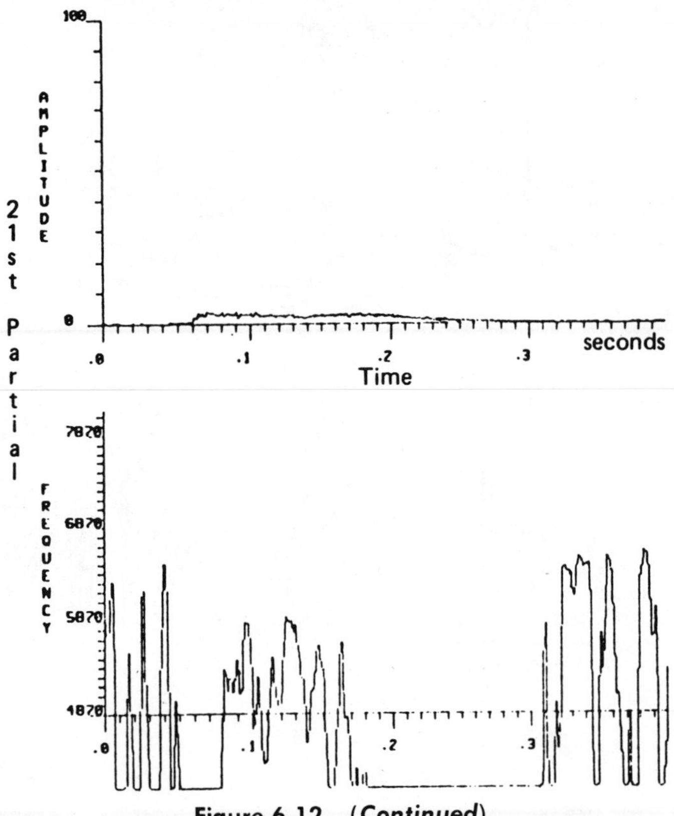

Figure 6.12 (*Continued*).

stop there is to accomplish little more than making a simple recording of the tone. Consequently, in developing synthesis procedures, we will seek to develop techniques that do not depend too much on the specific properties of a particular instrument. We study the characteristics of a known instrumental tone to stimulate the creative process of synthesizing an original timbre.

REFERENCES

Brigham, E. Oran, *The Fast Fourier Transform*, Prentice-Hall, 1974.

Freedman, M. D., "Analysis of Musical Instrument Tones," *Journal of the Acoustical Society of America* **41,** 793–806 (1967).

Freedman, M. D., "A Method for Analysing Musical Tones," *Journal of the Audio Engineering Society* **16,** 419–425 (1968).

Grey, John, *An Exploration of Musical Timbre*, PhD thesis, Stanford University, 1975.

Helmholtz, Hermann, *On the Sensations of Tone*, Dover, 1954.

Hoeschele, D., *Analog-to-Digital Digital-to-Analog Conversion Techniques*, Wiley, 1968.

Liu, C. L., & Jane W. S. Liu, *Linear Systems Analysis*, McGraw-Hill, 1975.

Luce, David, *Physical Correlates of Nonpercussive Musical Instrument Tones*, PhD thesis, Massachussetts Institute of Technology, 1963.

Moorer, James A., "On the Segmentation and Analysis of Sound by Digital Computer," PhD thesis, Stanford University, 1975.

Moorer, J. A., J. Grey, & J. Snell, "Lexicon of Analyzed Tones," *Computer Music Journal* **1**(2), 39–45 (1977).

Moorer, J. A., J. Grey, and J. Snell, "Lexicon of Analyzed Tones," *Computer Music Journal* **1**(3), 12–29 (1977).

Moorer, J. A., J. Grey, and J. Snell, "Lexicon of Analyzed Tones," Computer Music Journal **2**(2), 23–31 (1978).

Oppenheim, Alan V., & Ronald W. Schafer, *Digital Signal Processing*, Prentice-Hall, 1974.

Piszczalski, Martin, "Spectral Surface from Performed Music," Computer Music Journal III (1) pp. 18–24, 1979.

Rabiner, Lawrence R. & Bernard Gold, *Theory and Applications of Digital Signal Processing*, Prentice-Hall, 1975.

Risset, J. C. & M. Mathews, "Analysis of Musical Instrument Tones," *Physics Today* **22** 23–30 (1969).

7

SYNTHESIS OF COMPLEX TONES

Computer music is an art that has not yet been defined. Though the computer's application to musical analysis and composition is very broad and includes a wide range of issues, this book has so far emphasized just one of its major aspects. Potentially, the computer may be an infinitely versatile musical instrument. But this capability is only being realized with the advent of integrated circuits and the accompanying explosive development of digital technology. Consequently, although the physical machinery is now becoming available to the composer interested in computer music, the techniques for its use have scarcely been explored. It is as though the piano had just been invented, and because of its newness was wanting in compositions and techniques of performance.

As a result, the composer who engages a computer in generating musical sounds is a pioneer. He or she has very little of the previous experience of others for use as a background. This book has therefore established a foundation for computer sound synthesis by examining related subjects in acoustics, waveform analysis, computing, and music theory. One must well understand these concepts before he or she can extend and apply them to techniques of sound production. Consequently, the previous chapters have discussed analytical theory as an introduction to waveform synthesis.

In attempting to discuss techniques and procedures of waveform synthesis, we may approach the topic from two directions. One is to explore methods already undertaken and experimented with by today's composers of computer music—few in number though they exist. This approach suffers a serious drawback, however. Even the best techniques in computer music composition and waveform generation are as yet in their experimental stage of development. The art has not had more than a mere few years to allow the best discoveries and works to establish themselves while the failures die out. Whereas in conventional music composition one may study the works of the masters, the masterpieces of computer music have yet to be created! It would indeed be possible to investigate extensively and describe the programs in computer music at Columbia University, the

University of Illinois, Bell Laboratories, and other establishments. Several machines and specialized computer programming languages such as Music 360 and Music IV-B have been invented and successfully implemented in some places. However, the greater part of these current developments are highly esoteric to the institutions which sponser them. A comprehensive description of a computer music system at one school is of little use to the students at another location where that system is not available. Although the engineers who design and implement computer music systems will inevitably use the technical information that is gained from studying existing facilities, students and composers will find that information to be outside their demands.

For this reason, we assume here that the engineers interested in designing new facilities for computer music will obtain the necessary technical information from the literature. The individuals who subsequently utilize these systems will not be required to understand their internal workings in technical detail. They will instead require a theoretical understanding of how waveforms are produced from mathematical computation. Consequently, the following exposition examines the theory of waveform synthesis without detailing its application in different institutions.

The previous chapters have emphasized that complex waveforms may be treated as the composition of various pure, sinusoidal waveforms. In terms of actual sound, this means that complex timbres may be decomposed into sums of pure tones of different frequencies. We now seek to apply this background to the generation of arbitrary waveforms having particular timbral or dynamic characteristics. Complex waveforms may be generated in several ways. Two of the most fundamental techniques are known as *additive* and *subtractive synthesis*. Additive synthesis generates complex waveforms by adding simple waves together in varying proportions. Subtractive synthesis starts with a signal containing nearly all frequency components in a random mixture, and filters out the unwanted components leaving the desired mixture.

The concept of additive synthesis has already been introduced in previous chapters. The example of a waveform-generating computer subprogram presented in Chapter 4 employs a simple form of additive synthesis. We now develop this concept further. Before doing so, however, a few remarks should be made about computation economy and efficiency. As emphasized before, there is often an enormous tradeoff between conceptual simplicity and computational economy in computer programming. Thus this chapter is mainly concerned with establishing concepts rather than implementing techniques, and these methods will not be representative of great computer economy. Their application will always require some adaptation to fit the constraints and limitations of particular, available computer facilities.

Chapter 4 formulated a subprogram that could generate a sound by adding the first 10 harmonics of a tone in varying amplitudes. This produced a complex tone whose timbre was far more interesting than one of a simple, pure tone of its fundamental frequency. The resulting waveform, nevertheless, was still strictly periodic, and lacked the dynamic characteristics of natural sounds described in Chapters 5 and 6. Our present goal is to expand upon this additive synthesis technique, making it capable of simulating natural sounds and creating interesting, new, and artistic timbres.

To begin with, we recall from our discussion of dynamics that the amplitude of a tone fluctuates in time through its onset. The dynamic "shape" of this amplitude variation is the envelope of the tone. Although the overall amplitude of a tone may be described by a single envelope function, such a single function does not provide a complete picture of the sound. Indeed, we discovered in our time-varying harmonic analysis of instrumental tones that their individual harmonics each had separate envelopes. Our synthesis procedure must therefore comprise a method of generating and enveloping each harmonic component separately *before* summing them into a single tone.

Our synthesis procedure must also account for another unpleasant fact of acoustics. Although *ideal* resonators produce harmonics in exact multiples of the fundamental frequency, resonators in real life—be they strings, pipes, rods, bars, or membranes—have physical nonlinearities that cause the tones they produce to have slightly nonharmonic characteristics. The piano is a prime example of this. It must be intentionally mistuned slightly to sound in tune! An instrument may also produce partials that are not harmonically related to the sounding fundamental pitch. To be completely versatile, our tone generator must be capable of producing nonharmonic overtones as well as harmonics.

Procedures for generating tones by additive synthesis are mathematically straightforward. The timbre of virtually any quasi-periodic, complex tone can be approximately modeled by the following function:

$$W(t) = A_1(t) \sin (2\pi f_1 t) + A_2(t) \sin (2\pi f_2 t) + A_3(t) \sin (2\pi f_3 t) + \cdots + A_n(t) \sin (2\pi f_n t)$$

In this equation $W(t)$ represents the waveform being computed and f_1, f_2, f_3, . . . represent the component frequencies. As mentioned above, these frequencies are not necessarily exact multiples of the fundamental f_1, nor do they need to be static in time. One may assume that f_1, f_2, f_3, . . . are not constants, but are slowly varying functions of time. For example, varying f_1 periodically approximately eight times per second with a relative fluctuation of a few percent, and correspondingly varying f_2, f_3, f_4. . . . will introduce vibrato to the tone. The frequencies may commence at one initial value and climb to a final value during the onset or attack portion of the tone to introduce portamento. If the frequency variables are allowed very slight, random pertubations, this will render the tone a more natural quality.

The functions $A_1(t)$, $A_2(t)$, $A_3(t)$, . . . represent the envelopes of each of the partials. They may be input to the computer in any one of several ways. One fairly simple way is to let each envelope function $A_n(t)$ consists of several line segments whose breakpoints are entered sequentially in a data list or file. For example, suppose the envelope for a particular harmonic is represented as in Fig. 7.1. One enters the number pairs (0.04, 1) (0.06, 0.6) (0.16, 0.3) (0.28, 0.4) (0.36, 0.2) and (0.5,0) on a line designated to specify the envelope function of that particular harmonic. Then the program calls a linear interpolation subroutine to compute the values of the function between the breakpoints. Another more elegant method requiring more hardware and a more sophisticated computing facility is a graphics display terminal. The terminal is configured so that the composer enters the envelop function by drawing its outline on the face of the screen with a light pen. On such a system, a composer enters the envelope function by drawing its outline on the face of the screen with a light pen. On such a system, a composer forms a note by specifying the fundamental pitch f_1, the upper partials f_2, f_3, f_4, . . . , and drawing outlines for each of the envelope functions A_1, A_2, A_3, ... The computer then sums them into a final waveform $W(t)$, represents this waveform in memory as a sequence of discrete samples, and stores the samples for digital-to-analog conversion. Finally, it outputs the signal to a tape recorder and loudspeaker.

The additive synthesis procedure described here is probably the most versatile method of creating nearly periodic musical tones. It would be difficult, however, to use this method to generate clangorous, noisy, or percussive sounds. One advantage to additive synthesis is that it may be conjoined with the results of harmonic analysis. For example, if a composer wishes to create tones that sound somewhere between a trumpet

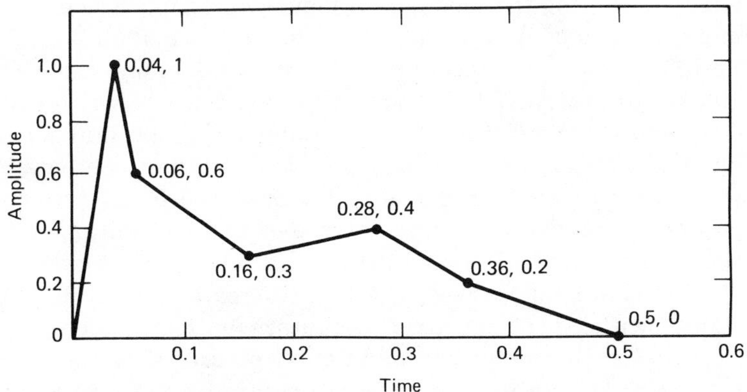

Figure 7.1 Specification of envelope by breakpoints.

and an english horn, he or she can synthesize them directly on the basis of their time-varying harmonic analysis. The composition is straightforward, since the tone's waveform is specified in terms modeling the results of the analysis. Until recently, additive synthesis suffered a major drawback in the amount of computation time required to generate so many sine functions necessary for its implementation. However, one can now instill digital oscillators on a computer system at a reasonable cost. Such digital oscillators are commercially available that can generate and envelope up to 256 sine waves simultaneously, and do it fast enough to operate in real time.

An alternative method of tone generation related to additive synthesis has been investigated at Stanford University by John Chowning. Although it lacks the versatility of the method described above, the technique is computationally much more efficient and can be used in more restrictive applications. Its experimentors call it *discrete summation formulae* and employ it in the frequency-modulation equation:

$$W(t) = A(t) \sin \{2\pi f_c t + I(t) \sin (2\pi f_m t)\}$$

The implications of this equation are not as obvious as the formula used for direct additive synthesis. But the equation does show that the frequency of one sinusoid (represented by the carrier frequency f_c) is being modulated by another sinusoid (represented by a modulation frequency f_m). The amount of modulation is controlled by a modulation index represented by $I(t)$. This modulation index may be a slowly varying function of time having its own envelope. $A(t)$ is the overall time-varying amplitude, or envelope of the tone.

This chapter will not attempt to analyze the equation above in any more mathematical detail, since some of its important consequences were already enumerated in Chapter 5. The most important feature of this equation is that varying the modulation index will change the distribution of the tone's harmonics, producing a form of timbre modulation. Chowning's experiments with this technique have produced some lifelike imitations of brass-like tones. If the modulation frequency is set to twice the carrier frequency, the resulting tone contains only odd-numbered harmonics, making it sound somewhat clarinet-like. Other combinations of frequency ratios between f_m and f_c may be employed to produce still different timbres. The overall timbre of the sound is controlled by the modulation index function $I(t)$, and the amplitude is enveloped by $A(t)$.

Thus to the composer in need of a tool to create interesting, natural-quality sounds without the extended computational requirements of direct additive synthesis, the frequency modulation procedure offers a versatile alternative. Unlike additive synthesis, summation formulae is not analysis-based. Consequently, in using it for composing new timbres, one must rely on experimentation and trial-and-error to obtain interesting results. One also sacrifices the separate control of each individual harmonic. Frequency modulation synthesis also allows one to define fractional ratios of f_m and f_c. This results in nonharmonic sounds, which may resemble bells, gongs, or drums, depending upon how they are formulated and enveloped.

The frequency-modulation equation is actually only one of any number of possible formulae that can be used to generate complex waveforms resulting in interesting sounds. Triangle, pulse, exponential, or other periodic functions may be substituted for the sine function. Actual physical vibrating bodies are usually nonlinear, and their action is thus only approximated by the trigonometric functions. In fact, it is the nonlinear behavior of physical instruments that is typically responsible for the complexities of the sounds they produce. To further understand the nature of this behavior and the meaning of the mathematical term "nonlinear," let us return to the example of a vibrating string. If the action of this string were mathematically "linear," it would displace the surrounding air in *exact proportion* to the tension exerted on it. But in actuality, the proportion of a string's displacement to its change in tension is not exactly uniform, although it remains approximately the same. The deviation in this proportion from absolute uniformity is the meaning of the string's "nonlinearity."

Consequently, a string vibrating in its fundamental mode is producing a tone that is "pure" only to a close approximation. The sine function used to describe or simulate the string's action is also just a close approximation of the real behavior. With this in mind, we may design an electronic instrument whose behavior will be nonlinear and use it to produce signals that are nonsinusoidal. Imagine that this instrument is like an amplifier from a stereo or P.A. system. A high-quality audio amplifier should be linear, that is, it should deliver current at its output, which is directly proportional to the voltage at its input. If it does this, the waveshape of the output signal will be an exact replication of the input waveshape. But if the gain of the amplifier is nonlinear, the output signal will be distorted. Its waveshape will be different, and it will contain frequency components in its spectrum not present in the input signal.

One can readily see that nonlinear behavior is extremely undesirable for faithful audio reproduction. However, for the purpose of synthesizing tones having complex spectra, nonlinear waveshaping is a viable and productive technique. Like additive and frequency modulation synthesis, it has been widely exploited in many computer music systems. Although the mathematics underlying the techniques of its implementation are complex, the fundamental conception of nonlinear waveshaping is fairly simple. Let us suppose that our "instrument" is a digital oscillator. The oscillator will typically (although not necessarily) be outputting a sine wave as an input to our nonlinear waveshaper. The device then distorts the wave according to the nature and specifications of its nonlinearity, giving it its desired spectral complexity. If the nonlinear waveshaper is to be an analog device, it would have to be implemented by designing a circuit network that meets its desired standards. The network would then be physically constructed with the appropriate electronic components. The digital world, on the other hand, would simply require the specification of a mathematical function that defines the nonlinearity. It is possible, as shown by Schaefer, to arrive at such a function given the specification of the desired frequency spectrum. The sine wave from a digital oscillator would be multiplied by the function or processed by a short subprogram to obtain the reshaped signal.

The techniques described so far have been exploited successfully to simulate musical tones, and are particularly amenable to computer music synthesis. The method of subtractive synthesis, however, has not enjoyed extensive application in this area. It has instead been developed primarily for use in synthesizing human speech. Nevertheless, by virtue of the parallels between synthetic speech production and waveform synthesis in musical tone generation, subtractive synthesis can be applied to computer music with nominal modification. Indeed, subtractive synthesis offers great possibilities for creative use in musical composition. Unfortunately, the mathematics that it entails are far more complex than the elementary trigonometry associated with the additive method. In fact, the complete mathematical foundation of speech-production algorithms is beyond the scope of most graduate-level college textbooks. Nevertheless, many researchers in acoustic waveform processing and speech synthesis have developed software and hardware for subtractive synthesis that can be expeditiously installed on most any general-purpose computer. Once such an installation has been made, composers may use it to great advantage without being expert in its underlying mathematics. For example, designing a digital filter requires fluency in advanced calculus and complex linear algebra. But once a digital filter has been installed in a computer system, it can be accessed and used by a person without extensive technical training.

In discussing subtractive synthesis, this chapter attempts to present its concepts intuitively without pursuing them in mathematical detail. Before attacking the subject directly, however, it is first necessary to address the topic of filtering and signal processing as a foundation. Following this, it introduces time-varying filters and their use in speech synthesis. The study of these filters is important to the composer as their use may be extended to musical tone generation.

Subtractive synthesis is conceptually the opposite of additive synthesis. In subtractive synthesis, one starts with a noise signal—for example, one that is rich in its mixture of component frequencies. It then extracts a desired harmonic spectrum by eliminating unwanted frequencies. The device used to expunge the unwanted frequencies while preserving the desired components is a filter. A filter may be visualized as a black box

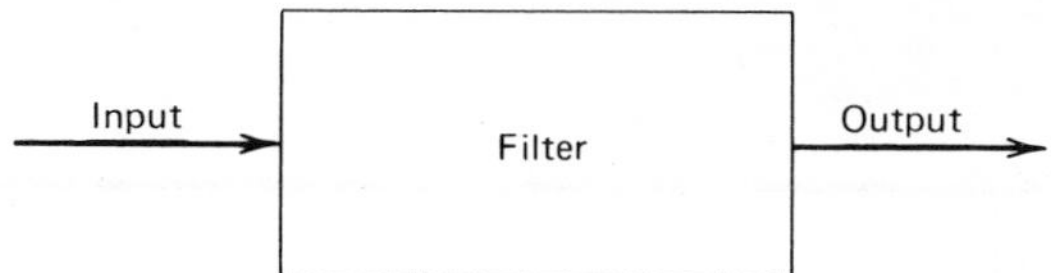

Figure 7.2 Representation of filter.

having an input signal and an output signal, is suggested in Fig. 7.2. Let us assume (Fig. 7.3) that the input to the filter is random noise having a perfectly flat frequency spectrum. Suppose then, that the filter is a cardboard tube whose resonant frequency is f_r. As one places the tube to the ear and listens to the noise, its spectrum is no longer flat, but is "colored" by the acoustical characteristics of the tube. Suppose that the frequency response of the tube can be diagrammed as in Fig. 7.4 One may notice immediately from this diagram that whereas all the frequencies of the spectrum are allowed to pass through the filter to some degree, the frequencies not near the resonant frequency f_r are appreciably suppressed. This partially explains the ringing type of acoustic distortion produced by such a tube.

One good example of an electroacoustic filter is a low-quality radio receiver or phonograph. Although such an instrument does not have the resonant peak of a tube or pipe, its bandwidth, or frequency range, is considerably smaller than that of the human ear. The frequency response of a typical inexpensive loudspeaker is shown in Fig. 7.5. Such a frequency response is satisfactory for most general purposes. But as any high-fidelity critic well knows, the quality of sound reproduced by such a system is vastly inferior to a live performance. This is because the signal's low and high frequency sound energy are lost in transmission and the listener can only hear the midrange frequencies.

In the early days of recording, phonograph records were cut directly with a stylus connected to an acoustic horn. The horn was able to capture enough of the energy of a singer's voice to vibrate the stylus. But in the process, it introduced a terrible amount of distortion to the sound it was capturing. Recordings of Enrico Caruso were made in this manner. As one

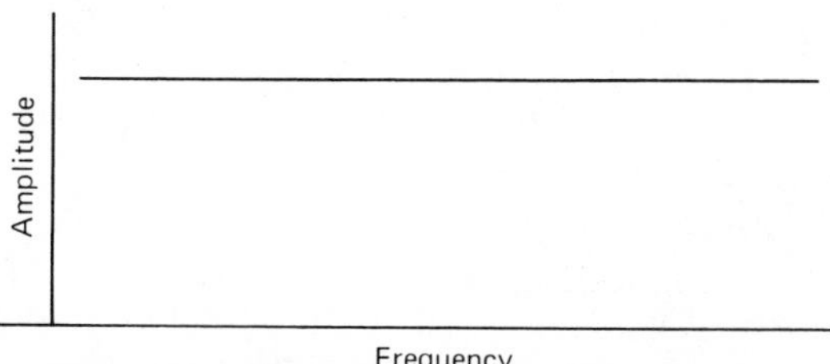

Figure 7.3 Spectrum of random noise.

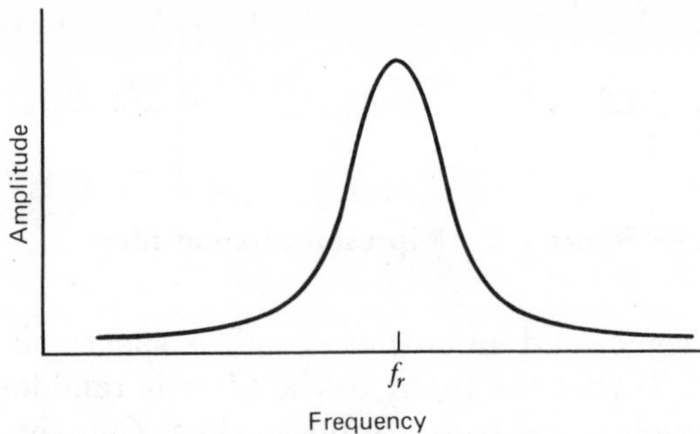

Figure 7.4 Frequency response of tube.

listens to reproductions of these recordings, he or she immediately notices the tinny quality that degrades Caruso's natural voice. This distortion was caused by the filtering action of the horn he was singing into as well as the nonlinearities of the recording device. In capturing the sound of Caruso's voice, the horn transmitted some frequencies with special emphasis, while it attenuated others.

Some of the recordings of Caruso were used at the University of Utah by Dr. Thomas G. Stockham in an interesting experiment with digital filtering. Dr. Stockham analyzed these recordings in conjunction with modern recordings of operatic tenors to determine the acoustic characteristics of Caruso's horn. He then attempted to approximate the frequency response of this horn. From this information he was able to digitally "construct" a filter whose frequency response was the inverse of Caruso's horn. The recording of Caruso was then sampled by an ADC and the samples were processed by this filter in a computer. The resulting output, although not a high-fidelity reproduction, was a considerable improvement over the original recording and rendered a much more natural quality to Caruso's voice.

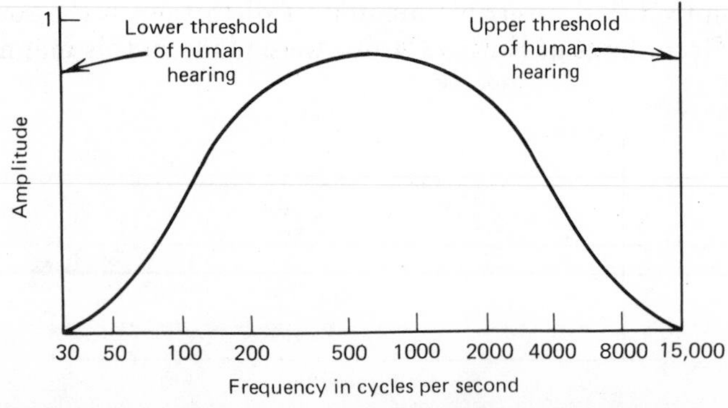

Figure 7.5 Frequency response of mediocre loudspeaker.

The preceding discussion has spoken of acoustic filters in terms of their nuisance value. But this is not to imply that a filter's only place in the world is to produce annoying distortion to good sound. The subject is intended to introduce the speech production model and a description of the vocal tract as a time-varying acoustic filter. As speech is produced in the vocal tract, the sound is generated in one of two ways. In vowels, semivowels, and voiced consonants, the vocal cavity is excited by quasi-periodic pulses of air passing through the glottis. The air stream is pulsated by the action of the vocal chords. In fricative, plosive, or other unvoiced consonants, the cavity is excited by some form of turbulant noise created in the mouth. In either case, the sound created is "processed" by the vocal cavity, which is an acoustic filter. The vocal tract is a resonating cavity—a horn that emphasizes some frequencies of the spectrum while it suppresses others. The frequencies emphasized are called formants.

As a person speaks, the physical shape of the vocal tract is continuously changing. Thus the formants and overall frequency response of the vocal filter also continuously change. An analysis of the waveform produced by the vocal chords themselves in the time domain reveals that it closely resembles a series of impulses. On an oscillograph, the waveform would appear like Fig. 7.6 The frequency spectrum of such an impulse series is nearly flat. Consequently, the spectrum of a spoken vowel is approximately the same as the frequency response of the vocal tract. In the case of unvoiced sounds, the air turbulance produced in the oral cavity is similar to random noise. Its frequency spectrum is also nearly flat, but without the fundamental pitch period associated with voiced sounds.

From this discussion, one can readily see that human speech is a

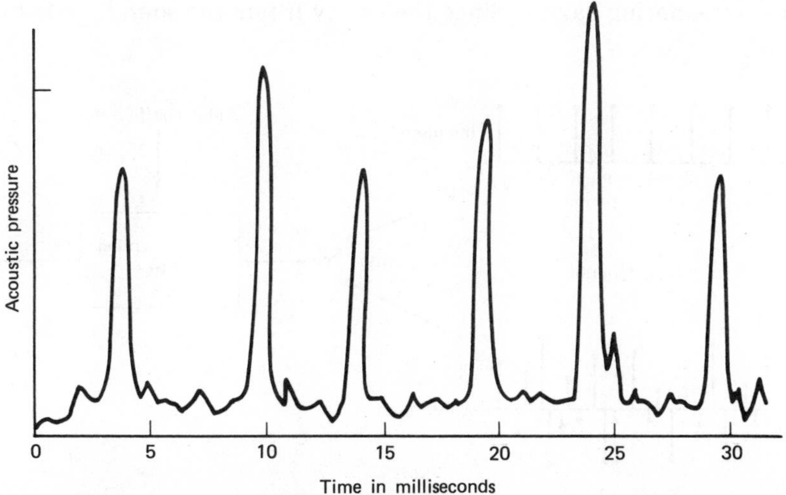

Figure 7.6 Wave form of sound produced by vocal chords.

excellent example of subtractive synthesis by an acoustic mechanism. It first generates a sound containing a rich content of frequencies, then passes that sound through a filter to shape its spectrum, rendering it a particular color. We now describe a mathematical model of subtractive synthesis which imitates the speech model. The mathematical subtractive synthesizer can be realized in a computer processor and its results can be converted to actual sound by D-to-A conversion as was done with additive synthesis. The synthesizer used in digital speech production is a time-varying digital filter. The filter accepts as input the coefficients that specify its frequency response and a driving function, as shown in the diagram of Fig. 7.7. The filter coefficients are represented by the subscripted variables A_1, A_2, A_3, . . . A_n for an n-point filter. Each of these coefficients may be considered a slowly varying function of time (slowly compared to the pitch period of the output samples). The frequency response of the filter is thereby made to vary as the coefficients A_1–A_n are periodically updated approximately once every 5 milliseconds.

Thus, in any 5-millisecond interval, the filter is responding to the driving function at its input. The driving function is either a series of impulses or nonperiodic white noise, depending upon whether the speech segment being imitated is voiced or unvoiced. A selector switch is provided to determine which source is to be used as input to the filter. We may also mention at this point that there is no teleological necessity that the driving function be an impulse sequence or white noise. Nor does its frequency spectrum need to be flat. It can, in fact, be any function at all! This implies that if a subtractive synthesizer is not going to be used for artificial speech, it may use any number of input driving functions, with a multitude of musical possibilities. For example, as mentioned in Chapter 6, the tone of a violin is produced by the action of a bowed string which excites a resonating cavity. Since the cavity filters the sound made by the

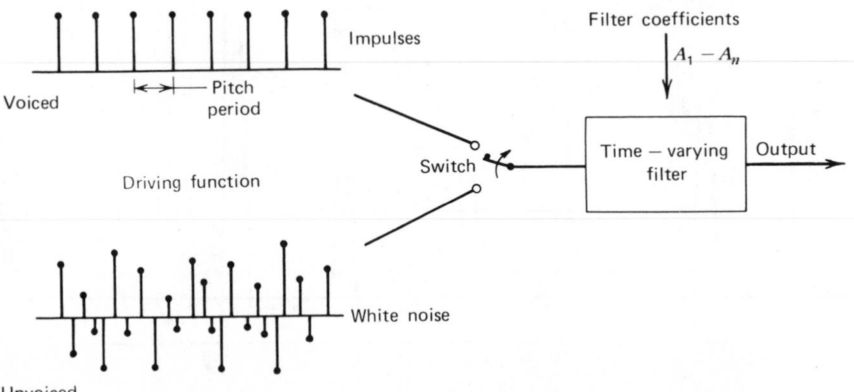

Figure 7.7 Synthetic vocal sound production using subtractive synthesis.

string, the violin is a good example of a subtractive synthesizer. If, therefore, we want to digitally imitate a violin tone, we may use a driving function that models the action of the violin string. A sawtooth wave is such a function. The filter we use, then should have the same frequency response as a violin body, and it need not vary with time.

The preceding paragraphs have described how subtractive synthesis is employed to generate speech. But nothing has been said about how the coefficients A_1–A_n of the time-varying filter are determined and implemented. This is where the mathematical complications enter the picture. The mathematics need not be outlined here, but it will suffice to say that much computer software is available in the signal processing literature for speech synthesis by time-varying digital filters. These programs are able to accept an array of numbers as parameters to a digital filter and use that filter to process an input signal. Many systems can do this in real time.

The question still remains, however, as to how one determines what values to provide the filter coefficients for its implementation. To accomplish this, it is necessary to sample a segment of real-life speech with an ADC, and mathematically analyze the samples. The analysis takes advantage of the fact that the speech waveform is approximately periodic. This implies that although two adjacent pitch periods of voiced speech are not identical, they are closely similar. It is therefore possible to make a comparison between pitch periods in a short interval of time and compute an error function which represents their difference. This mathematical procedure is known as *Linear Prediction* because it employs linear algebra to predict future samples of a quasi-periodic function based on samples of its past history. It selects a set of predictor coefficients A_1–A_n, then uses that set to generate a function similar to the sampled speech segment. It is impossible to find coefficients that produce a function *exactly* like the speech samples. But with enough number crunching, the computer finds optimum values for the predictor coefficients. The values are chosen so that the difference between the function that they generate and the current samples of the actual speech waveform are forced to a minimum. It is this minimization of the difference, or error function, that determines the values assigned to these predictor coefficients A_1–A_n. The linear prediction procedure is diagrammed in Fig. 7.8.

At this point one may wonder what is the utility of going to so much mathematical trouble to analyze a segment of speech simply to resynthesize it later! The purpose of developing linear prediction algorithms and digital speech synthesis techniques is to find ways to transmit speech along communications channels having very limited bandwidth. It requires a much smaller quantity of information to send a set of predictor coefficients along a channel than it does to trasmit a live, analog signal. Thus, digital speech synthesis per se is now investigated primarily by the military for communication links that have special, unusual restrictions in their information capacity. Digital speech analysis,

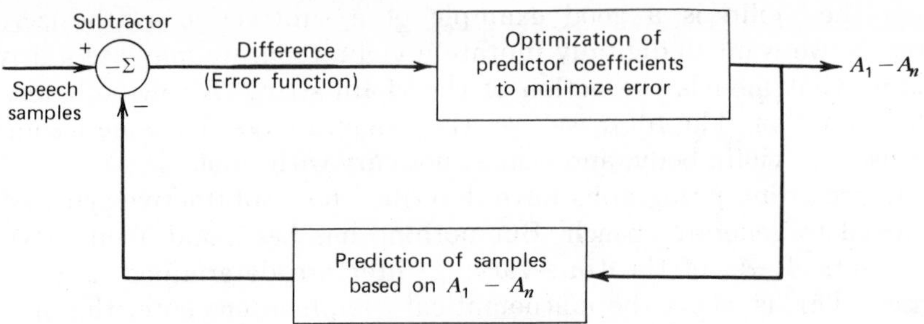

Figure 7.8 Procedure of linear prediction.

however, has enormous theoretical interest in voice and word recognition. One of its most dramatic applications is the recent development of machines that can talk.

The combination of a speech analyzer, communication channel, and synthesizer is known as a *vocoder*—an acronym for a voice coder. A vocoder is logically comparable to a telephone or P.A. system in which the analyzer is included with the microphone and the synthesizer is included with the earphone or loudspeaker. If the communication channel is a simple electric wire, the vocoder simply adds unnecessary complexity to the system. But when the communication channel is a radio wave with strictly limited bandwidth, the conservation of transmitted information provided by a vocoder justifies its utilization and expense.

Having thus far introduced and briefly described the use of subtractive synthesis as it has been developed for speech production, we may now investigate its possibilities for synthesis of musical tones. Although vocoders were invented for speech transmission, they can be used for other purposes as well. A clever composer interested in waveform processing should find many creative uses for a vocoder in computer music. Of course a musician does not need a vocoder to conserve information for narrow bandwidth channels. Nor would he or she need it to faithfully reproduce musical tones that already exist—simple recording equipment can do that! But once a sound at the input of a vocoder is analyzed and its predictor coefficients are computed, the information going into the communication channel (or storage) may be "doctored" in any number of ways. Depending on how this information is modified or rearranged, the output at the synthesizer may be distorted in interesting and colorful ways without being utterly destroyed. A composer will have to perform much experimentation and trial-and-error to discover different ways that information along a vocoder channel can be processed to create sounds of musical interest.

This kind of experimentation obviously has enormous potential, but the concept is yet so new that the use of a vocoder as a musical instrument remains an idea waiting to become a reality. Vocoders have only existed for a few years. It is therefore up to the next generation of musicians to determine what their contribution will be in the future of music composition. One musician-engineer who has nevertheless begun development of an interesting technique in vocoder music is Tracy Petersen at the University of Utah. Petersen uses two vocoders simultaneously operating in parallel as they each analyze two separate sounds. He then crosses the pitch information from one vocoder with the other before the two sounds are resynthesized. The procedure is called *cross-synthesis* and is diagrammed in Fig. 7.9. As one can see from this diagram, each vocoder transmits two modes of information along its channel. One code is the parameters used to construct the synthesis filter. In the linear-prediction model described in the preceding paragraphs, the filter parameters are the predictor coefficients A_1–A_n. Other kinds of vocoders use filter parameters that are different mathematically, but are used to produce the same result. The other mode of information output by the vocoder analyzer and sent along the channel to the synthesizer is the pitch-period of the input source. This pitch period is the length of time between impulses in the driving function. In speech synthesis, it corresponds to the pitch of the voice. At the synthesizer end of the vocoder, the filter information is used to construct the digital filter that processes an impulse sequence generated at intervals determined by the pitch information.

In the vocoders of Fig. 7.9, the pitch information of each channel is crossed with that of the other unit. Imagine then, that the input signal to vocoder #1 is receiving filter information corresponding to a speaking voice. Vocoder #2 is then associated with a violin. The first vocoder will be constructing the formants of vowels as the voice speaks. But its pitch information will be coming from the violin. One can imagine what the output of the synthesizer is going to sound like—a violin trying to talk! Correspondingly, the output of vocoder-synthesizer #2 will be the pitch modulation of a voice, but filtered to the frequency spectrum of a violin.

Subtractive synthesis is a concept that emphasizes the frequency

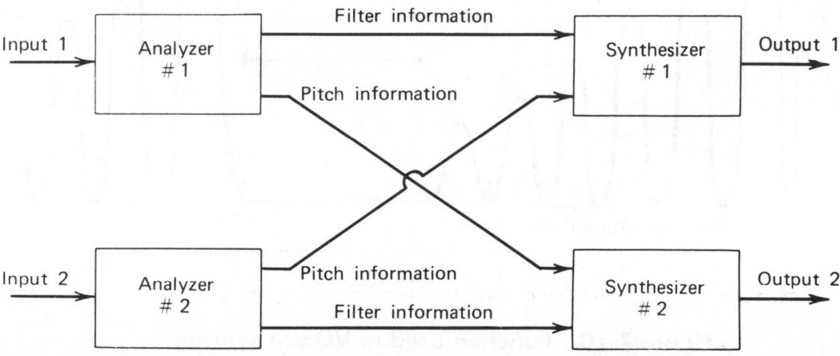

Figure 7.9 Cross synthesis with two vocoders.

domain. Its chief use is in the simulation of human speech, and as has been discussed here, it also has widespread potential for musical tone production. Another method of speech and music synthesis somewhat related to the concepts introduced in this chapter has been developed at the University of Utrecht, The Netherlands by Werner Kaegi and Stan Tempelaars. It is called VOSIM, a contraction for voice simulation.

The VOSIM technique was developed for the synthetic production of both speech sounds and musical instrument tones. It differs from additive synthesis in that it does not produce sounds by summing sinusoids, and it differs from subtractive synthesis in that it does not require filters. It produces a signal that has a rich harmonic spectrum, but controls the spectrum by directly shaping the signal itself. Thus it is a technique that emphasizes the time domain rather than the frequency domain.

Fundamentally, the VOSIM strategy is to take a quasi-periodic sound such as a vowel sound, and observe its waveform in the time domain. It then isolates one period and generates an artificial waveform to imitate its timbral characteristics. Several functions were investigated in search of one that could be used somewhat universally to imitate a wide variety of speech and musical sounds. The function found to have the most success in its imitative capability and versatility is a sequence of decaying sine-squared pulses followed by a short delay. Such a function is illustrated in Fig. 7.10.

As one examines this function, he or she can readily see that one of its outstanding features is its fundamental pitch period, which in the diagram is 10 milliseconds. Consequently, this would represent a tone whose funda-

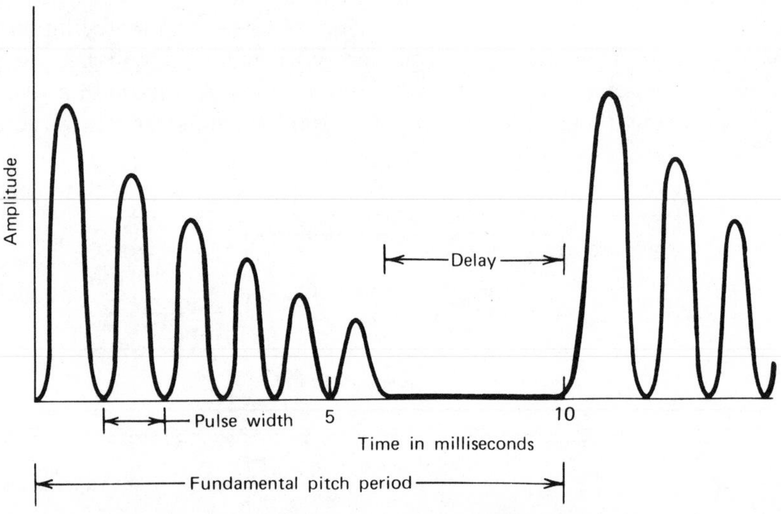

Figure 7.10 Function used in VOSIM synthesis.

mental frequency is 100 cycles per second. One also notices that the period of the sine-squared pulse is approximately 1 millisecond. The tone's most prominent harmonic will thus be 1000 cycles per second. Due to the decay of the pulses and the delay associated with each period, the function introduces additional harmonics to the tone's spectrum. As mentioned earlier, the spectrum is not controlled through the frequency domain. It is determined by the selection of the VOSIM function's variable parameters. The static parameters are the width of the sine-squared pulse, the delay time, the rate of decrease in the sine-squared pulses, the amplitude of the first pulse, and the number of pulses per period. These parameters affect just one fundamental period. But one may assume that each period will not be identical. Therefore, additional dynamic parameters are comprised in the VOSIM function that govern the change from period to period of the static parameters.

Unlike additive and subtractive synthesis, the choice of the controlling parameters is not based on analysis in the frequency domain. Instead, a pulse width and amplitude are chosen that approximate the pulse width and amplitude of the first pulse of one cycle of the original waveform. Of course, if the VOSIM model is being used to generate an original musical tone rather than to imitate speech, the parameters are simply selected arbitrarily. Once the VOSIM function has been specified and the synthesis undertaken, the tone can be represented by a table of numbers corresponding to the static and dynamic variables. The compositional procedure, then, is the choice of the parameters that results in artistically interesting sounds.

The concepts of waveform synthesis introduced in this chapter are intended to illustrate how a computer can be used as a new, versatile musical instrument. The composer who uses the computer to produce musical sounds is working in a medium that has not existed in conventional music before now. The scores written for the piano and other instruments, for example, contain information specifying the notes of the scale to be played along with their rhythm and dynamics. The composer is operating in the fields of harmony, counterpoint, rhythm, and form—the subjects that composition students study exhaustively. However, the tonal qualities of the sounds made by these instruments are determined by the mechanism of the instruments themselves without regard to the composer. Consequently, it has not been incumbant upon musicians to study physics, mathematics, and acoustics to describe how musical tones are produced and perceived by the human ear.

With computer music this is no longer the situation. Here, the composer is in direct control of the timbral quality of all the sounds in the composition. Consequently, he or she must understand the fundamental constitution of these sounds and the principles governing the methods of their production. This is why extensive study of acoustics and waveform analysis must now take a prominent place in music theory as the electronic medium is brought into the art.

As composers begin to experiment with computer music synthesis, they will be doing it on computer systems that are much more complex, expensive, and sophisticated then any conventional musical instrument. The design, implementation, and even maintenance of such equipment requires specialized technicians and engineers. But is is the responsibility of these engineers to install these systems so that their general use does not require more than a minimum of technical training. A composer is not expected to be an expert in systems software or solid-state electronics. For this reason, this text has not attempted to outline the features of existing computer music systems, or describe their components. Such components and systems, while important for study by their designing engineers, vary greatly from one installation to the next, and are subject to rapid obsolescence. But the mathematical and psychoacoustical concepts underlying their use are universal and are not subject to change. These, in fact, are the ideas pertinent to music theory, and are the composer' new domain.

REFERENCES

Atal, B. S., & S. L. Hanauer, " Speech Analysis and Synthesis by Linear Prediction of the Speech Wave," *Journal of the Acoustic Society of America* **50,** 637–655 (Feb. 1971).

Boll, Steven F., *A Priori Digital Speech Analysis*, University of Utah, 1973.

Boll, Steven F., E. Ferretti, & T. Petersen, "Improving Speech Quality using Binaural Reverberation," *IEEE International Conference on Acoustics, Speech, and Signal Processing*, 705–798. April 12–14, 1976.

Callahan, Michael W., *Acoustic Signal Processing Based on the Short Time Spectrum*, University of Utah, 1973.

Chowning, John, "The Synthesis of Complex Audio Spectra by Means of Frequency Modulation," *Journal of the Audio Engineering Society* **21**(7), 526–534 (1973).

Chowning, J., John Grey, Loren Smith, & James Moorer, *Computer Simulation of Music Instrument Tones in Reverberant Environments*, Stanford University, 1974.

Fant, Gunnar, *Speech Sounds and Features*, MIT Press, 1973.

Ferretti, Ercolino, "Sound Synthesis by Rule," *Proceedings of the 2nd Annual Music Computation Conference*, University of Illinois, Urbana—Champaign, part 1, p. 1 (Nov. 1975).

Kaegi, W., & S. Tempelaars, "VOSIM—A New Sound Synthesis System," *Journal of the Audio Engineering Society* **26**(6), 418–425 (1978).

LeBrun, Marc, "A Derivation of the Spectrum of FM with a Complex Modulating Wave," *Computer Music Journal* **1**(4), 51–52 (1977).

LeBrun, Marc, "Digital Waveshaping Synthesis," *Journal of the Audio Engineering Society* **27**(4), 250–266 (1979).

Makhoul, John, "Linear Prediction: A Tutorial Review," *Proceedings of the IEEE* **63**(4), 561–580 (1975).

Makhoul, J., & J. J. Wolf, "Linear Prediction and the Spectral Analysis of Speech," Bolt, Beranek and Newman, Inc., Cambridge, Mass., Report number 2304 (Aug. 1972).

Markel, J. D., & A. H. Gray, Jr., *Linear Prediction of Speech*, Springer-Verlag, 1976.

Markel, J. D., & A. H. Gray, Jr., "A Linear Prediction Vocoder Simulation Based Upon the Autocorrelation Method," *IEEE Transactions on Acoustics, Speech, and Signal Processing* **ASSP-22**(2), 124–134 (April 1974).

Mathews, M., and J. Kohoul, "Electronic Simulation of a Violin," *Journal of the Acoustical Society of America* **53,** 1620–1626 (1973).

Moorer, James A., *The Synthesis of Complex Audio Spectra by Means of Discrete Summation Formulae*, Stanford University, 1975.

Moorer, James A., "The Use of the Phase Vocoder in Computer Music Applications," Preprint no. 1146 (E-1) presented at the 55th convention of the Audio Engineering Society, Los Angeles, (1976).

Moorer, James A., "Signal Processing Aspects of Computer Music—A Survey," *Proceeding of the IEEE* **65**(8), 1108–1137 (1977).

Moorer, James A., "The Use of Linear Prediction of Speech in Computer Music Applications," *Journal of the Audio Engineering Society* **27**(3), 134–140 (1979).

Oppenheim, Alan V., "Speech Analysis-Synthesis Systems Based on Homomorphic Filtering," *Journal of the Acoustical Society of America* **45**(2), 458–465 (1969).

Oppenheim, A., & R. W. Schafer, *Digital Signal Processing*, Prentice-Hall, 1974.

Petersen, Tracy L., "Vocal Tract Modulation of Instrumental Sounds by Digital Filtering," Presented at the Music Computation Conference 2, University of Illinois, Nov. 7–9, 1975.

Petersen, Tracy L., "Analysis-Synthesis as a Tool for Creating New Families of Sounds," *Preprint no. 1104* (*D-3*), presented at the 54th convention of the Audio Engineering Society, Los Angeles, (May 1976).

Petersen, Tracy L., *Cross Synthesis—A New Avenue for Experimental Music*, University of Utah, 1976.

Portnoff, Michael R. "Implementation of the Digital Phase Vocoder Using the Fast Fourier Transform," *IEEE Transactions on Acoustics, Speech, and Signal Processing* **ASSP-24**(3), 243–248 (1976).

Rabiner, L., and B. Gold, *Theory and Applications of Digital Signal Processing*, Prentice-Hall, 1975.

Risset, J., and M. Mathews, "Analysis of Musical Instrument Tones," *Physics Today* **22**(2), 23–30 (1969).

Saunders, Steven E., "Real-time FM Digital Music Synthesis," *Proceedings of the Music Computation Conference 2*, Urbana Illinois, (November 1974).

Schaefer, R. A., "Electronic Musical Tone Production by Nonlinear Waveshaping," *Journal of the Audio Engineering Society* **8**(4), 413–416 (1970).

Schottstaedt, B., "The Simulation of Natural Instrument Tones using Frequency Modulation with a Complex Modulating Wave," *Computer Music Journal* **1**(4), 46–50 (1977).

Snell, John, "Design of a Digital Oscillator which will Generate up to 256 Low-Distortion Sine Waves in Real-Time," *Computer Music Journal* **1**(2), 4–25 (1977).

Tempelaars, S., "The VOSIM Signal Spectrum," *Interface* **6,** 81–96 (1977).

Truax, Barry, "Organizational Techniques for C:M ratios in *Frequency Modulation*," Computer Music Journal **1**(4), 39–45 (1977).

von Foerster, Heinz, and J. Beauchamp, Eds. *Music by Computers*, Wiley, 1969.

8

MODIFICATION AND PROCESSING OF RECORDED SOUNDS

Up until now, this text has devoted its discussion to waveform analysis and synthesis. We now expand our study and investigate how musical materials may be processed once they have already been recorded. These source materials may be sounds that were synthesized directly from "scratch" by methods like those described in the preceding chapter. Alternatively, these sources may be recorded "concrete" sounds from vocal, instrumental, or other natural origin. They may be sounds whose waveforms are already represented digitally in a computer's memory, or they may be tape-recorded sounds ready for analog-to-digital conversion.

Much experimental work has been done in electronic music in processing tape-recorded sound materials. Pioneered by Vladimir Ussachevsky of Columbia University, modern composers use sophisticated electronic equipment to generate interesting and provocative musical compositions. The field of electronic music created with this equipment was virtually unknown in the early 1950s, but it has in the last two decades expanded into modern music's leading frontier. The introduction of the digital computer to this scene promises to even further expand and advance its proliferation.

Fundamentally, the operations performed by a computer in digital waveform processing are similar to those undertaken in an electronic music studio with analog equipment. But the way a computer accomplishes the synthesis, modification, processing, and recording of sounds is radically different. Electronic music produced with analog equipment is still new, yet it is not nearly as new as digitally processed and generated music. Digital sound processing offers distinct advantages not realized by analog processing. The foremost advantage is its versatility. A computer may be programmed in an infinite variety of ways while analog equipment is relatively constricted in the number of operations it can perform. Computer equipment is almost completely automatic, whereas analog hardware ordinarily requires manual operation. Although both computer and electronic music is primarily an experiment of trial-and-error, the composer has much more definite control of computer algorithms than the hit-or-miss settings of level controls on an analog synthesizer. One could scarcely duplicate a sound produced by a synthesizer with arbitrary control settings because it would be nearly impossible to reset all the knobs *exactly* to their original positions. But a computer program or subprogram can be identically duplicated and run any number of times with the same results. This makes computer programming much more controllable than synthesizer patches and settings.

A computer has much greater processing capacity than does analog electronic equipment. A digital synthesizer can produce many times more waveforms at once than can even the largest, most expensive analog synthesizer. A digital filter implemented on a computer has greater precision, variability, and versatility than any analog electronic filter. Moreover, its cost is nominal, since it is actually an element of software—a written program rather than an expensive physical device. A further advantage to computer systems for sound processing is that digital technology is advancing at a much faster rate. Whereas the expense of most electronic studio equipment steadily increases along with almost everything else on the market, the integrated circuits of digital processors and memory continue to skyrocket in their capabilities while they plummet in cost. At this date, digital and analog equipment are more or less comparable in their expense. But the trend is clearly in favor of digital electronics reaching dominance in applications heretofore held by analog circuitry.

The techniques of sound mixing and modification with tape recorders, filters, frequency shifters, reverberators, and other processing equipment are well known to the composer of electronic music. The objective of this chapter is to describe these techniques and explain how they are employed on a computer system. Although the aims and concepts of digital and analog processing are theoretically similar, their implementation is much different. Since the analog techniques are now well established, they will be cited here as an introduction to digital procedures.

As an electronic music composer assembles a composition, he or she records a collection of source materials onto magnetic tape. These elements of the composition are then arranged into their desired form. The technique of sound-arranging is tape splicing. The composer manually slides the tape back-and-forth across a unit's playback head until he has located a certain position for the splice. A finished tape will often have splices occurring only inches apart. The timing for any segment on the tape may be determined by measuring its length with a ruler.

On a computer system, the sounds are represented digitally as a sequence of samples stored on a file in secondary memory. The memory on the disk of a computer is generally divided into tracks, pages, and sectors. A composer, then, needs to know the memory mapping system to access the sound sources. He or she may know, for example, that the beginning of a particular section starts on sector #3 of page #2 in disk memory. He or she must also know how much memory space is required for a particular duration of time. He can then instruct the computer to relay the contents of that memory section into the DAC. This is done at the user's terminal. By issuing the appropriate commands to the system through this terminal, the composer may address the files and manipulate their contents in any manner. Thus a lengthy portion of sound samples may be figuratively "cut" and "spliced" to any particular sequence. Although the protocol for memory-manipulation instructions varies from one computer to the next, this type of memory management programming is generally not very complicated or difficult to learn.

The second widespread practice of tape manipulation is the mixing and overlaying of more than one sound source onto a single recording. One way to accomplish this is to use two or three tape recorders. The operator plays back separate programs while combining their outputs through a mixing panel and recording the mixture on another machine. This mixing requires careful syncronization of several tape units and demands high precision of the equipment. As an alternative to operating several machines at once, one may use a multichannel tape recorder. A well-equipped studio should have one with 8 or 16 tracks. Using such a machine, a composer may play back and monitor some of the channels while recording on another track. This allows him or her to record as many "takes" of any isolated part of the composition. It also provides great flexibility in deciding how the different parts of the composition are arranged and controlled. He or she may isolate a small section of the work for modification or improvement without disturbing the other parts that have already been recorded. Since the channels in the record mode are selected individually, and the tape may be stopped and started at any point, segments can be recorded or deleted at any arbitrary location along the tape.

The availability of high-quality, sophisticated recording equipment has given the modern composer capabilities not even dreamed of by artists of past generations. Yet notwithstanding these enormous capabilities, magnetic tape recording suffers some serious drawbacks. One of them is noise that comes mainly from the granularity of the magnetic oxide on the tape surface. Fortunately, good studio tape recorders are capable of making recordings whose background tape noise level is scarcely noticeable. But as sound sources are mixed and rerecorded from one machine to another, the background noise accumulates. Each successive generation of recording and mixing doubles the noise level, raising it 3 decibels. Each additional track that is added to a program on multi-channel equipment also adds 3 decibels of noise. Consequently, tape noise is a major problem on even the best professional studio equipment.

The second major restriction of tape-recording equipment is its enormous cost. Ironically, the bulk of the expense required for the manufacture of a high-quality tape deck does not lie in the electronics. The amplifier represents only a small portion of the machine. The expense falls mainly in the mechanical elements. The motors, capstain, brakes, idlers, and other parts of the transport mechanism need to be extremely durable and mechanically precise. They must move the tape at a constant speed, since the ear is extremely sensitive to the slightest fluctuation. The tape heads themselves are also expensive, subject to wear and accumulation of dirt, and require precise mechanical alignment and constant maintenance.

As this book is written, the tape-recording equipment described above remains the state of the art in spite of its inherent shortcomings. There is not yet a superior alternative on the market. But digital electronics is on its way! Digital recording equipment is not yet commercially available on a large scale, but at its current rate of development, it will be very soon. A digital recorder virtually eliminates the problem of background noise. Actually, sampling does introduce a certain level of random noise called quantization noise to the recording. But if the register length used to represent the sample is 16 bits, the level of this quantization noise is a mere fraction of a tape recorder's noise. The signal-to-noise ratio of a 16-bit digital recording can be higher than 90 decibels, reducing the noise level to where it cannot be heard at all. A good tape recorder can reproduce sounds with very little distortion, but a digital recorder reduces this distortion even further. Moreover, the effect of noise and distortion on digital recordings is not cumulative. Their levels do not increase as more sources are added and successive regenerations made. Any reproduction of a digital recording is identical to the original.

The elements required in the construction of digital recording equipment are electronic logic circuitry such as gates and flip-flops, and memory. As mentioned earlier, the logic elements are nonmechanical and are inexpensively manufactured on LSI chips. Once constructed and tested, they require no alignment or maintenance. The single obstacle to the proliferation of digital recording equipment now is the memory required to store all the samples. For high-fidelity reproduction, 40,000 16-bit words of memory are required for one second of sound. Fortunately, memory does not have to be the type of random-access memory used in a computer's primary memory. Indeed it cannot since a mere 32,000 words of semiconductor or core random-access memory is extremely expensive. The commercialization of digital recorders requires the development of memory systems that store large volumes of information, are mechanically simple, physically compact, and low cost. Such systems are still in their stage of development, but one may safely predict that they will soon be commercially available and prelude the eventual obsolescence of mechanical tape recorders and phonographs.

The process of mixing digitally recorded sounds is conceptually simple. But it is performed much differently than mixing is done in a tape studio. One must constantly think of the recording as being a long sequence of samples represented by numbers. Each number is typically a 16-bit word in memory. Although the samples of a recording may be stored on tape, this is still radically different from the way sound is recorded on an analog device. It is not economical to store several minutes of sound samples on a computer's disk memory at one time, because space is limited. However, for purposes of manipulating sound programs, several seconds of sound may be loaded onto files in disk memory from an external memory device such as digital magnetic tape. Once the sounds are on file, they may be edited, processed, or mixed with other sources via commands from the operator's console.

To illustrate how this is done, let us suppose that we have two 5-minute tape recordings of sounds we want to use as sources for a 2-minute composition. Indeed, if we merely wanted to mix them, it would be much simpler to use the standard recording-studio method without involving the computer. The example here is presented to illustrate how digital processing is advantageous when more than simple mixing is required. The first step in our procedure is to convert the recordings from analog to digital representation. If the sounds were originally derived from digital synthesis on a computer as described in the previous chapters, then the analog-to-digital conversion would not be necessary. The tape-recorded sounds are taken from the playback unit and go to an ADC. The samples from the converter are then placed in the computer's memory, and can be stored digitally, probably on another tape. But unlike analog recordings, digital records may be transferred from one storage unit to another *any number of times* with no accumulation of noise or distortion. A composer mixing tapes in a recording studio knows that a third generation rerecording of his or her sources will have noticeable background noise, yet has no similar worry at a computer console. He or she may watch the sounds go from one disk track to another, and back and forth between disk, external memory, and primary memory as many times as he likes, and the final copy will still be an undistorted, noise-free duplication of the original. The principle is the same as one that can be demonstrated in photography. If one photographs a photograph of a photograph, the original quality is lost. But if the original photograph is of a table of numbers, the numbers in the table can be copied and remain intact no matter how many times the table is rephotographed.

Suppose in our example, then, that our 5-minute sources are each represented in the form of long number tables stored on tape. We are then ready to begin at our computer terminal. We assume that the terminal is located in a studio where the composer can monitor his results out of a loudspeaker as he is working. To listen to our sources, we type a command into the console to output the samples to a DAC and from there to the sound system. The computer does this instantly, and the action is equivalent to pressing the "play" button of a tape recorder. Using a stop watch, we decide that we want the first 18 seconds of source #1 to introduce the composition. Then we listen to our #2 source and decide that we want a 40-second segment of it to begin at the one minute mark. We want the second source to come in mixed with the first source after ten seconds. We also want it to start softly and crescendo for 5 seconds before it reaches full volume.

We create two files: one for the first 18 seconds of source #1, and another one starting with 10 seconds of silence followed by the section of source #2 from its 60-second point to its 100-second point. The first portion of this segment is multiplied by an exponential sequence that increases from 0 to 1 in 5 seconds. Then the two files are added sample for sample, and the sum is stored in a third file. The first two files are now free for us to discard their contents and subsequently reuse them for further mixing and processing. We continue this kind of file manipulation until we end up with a final digital record of our 2-minute composition. We can then output it through the DAC for monitoring and tape-recording.

The description of this process may make it appear more complicated than it really is. Actually, the file-manipulation commands on modern computers are easy to learn, and with a little experience, sound sources may be processed and mixed at a computer terminal with greater ease, control, precision, and speed than can be done in a tape studio.

A typical mixing studio can channel about 12 different sources separately. Each of these have a separate volume control. It is easy to set such a simple control, or even to set all 12 of them—as long as they can be set one at a time. But if one is mixing several sources onto a single recording and wants to change the volume of the individual sources independently but simultaneously while the tape is going, he or she is out of luck! It takes two hands to control two dials, but there are often much more than two things to be done at one time while a recording is being processed. The computer allows the composer to plan everything that is to be done in advance, then format the instructions with as much detail as he or she likes before the processing is actually done. When these instructions are executed, they are performed automatically. So if one is mixing six separate sources in a digital recording, the amplitude, or "volume" of each one of them can be varied at will. If then, after listening to the results, the composer wants to change the control of just one of the sources, this can be done by modifying the instructions for that channel while the control of the other sources will remain. This eliminates the need to repeat many "takes" of a mix just to get the physical coordination required to properly handle all the controls while a tape is running.

One controls the amplitude of a digital recording simply by multiplying the samples by whatever factor is necessary to obtain the desired volume. In performing such volume control, one must remember that the relationship between loudness and amplitude is exponential rather than linear. So when programming a crescendo or dimenuendo, the sequence of amplitude factors used to scale the source sequence should increase or decrease according to the exponential function rather than in uniform steps. This phenomenon was discussed in Chapter 5.

The process of multiplying a sound sequence by a controlling function sequence is simple amplitude modulation, or envelope control. On an analog synthesizer, this is performed with envelope generators and voltage-controlled amplifiers. These modules are more automatic than simple volume controls. The envelope generator is activated by an electric trigger pulse that may come from a keyboard or another module on the synthesizer. The envelope control is easy to set if the desired envelope is simple, but complex envelopes require several envelope generators, and are difficult to configure. The procedure required for digital envelope generation may be more or less time consuming than the analog process. It depends on the particular computer system one is using. But in either case, an envelope or amplitude contour can be specified with much greater variability, precision, and consistancy using computer control.

The concept of amplitude control is fundamental to signal processing. It stipulates that the numbers of one sequence are each multiplied sample for sample by the corresponding numbers of another sequence. In the processing described above, the first sequence represents a sound source whereas the second sequence is a modulating function or envelope. If each multiplication had to be carried out manually, the task would take days to accomplish. But the computer will have file-manipulation software that can do it expediently and conveniently. In performing simple envelope control, the modulating sequence is normally a slowly varying positive function of time. But multiplication of two sequences may also be done wherein both signals are sound sources. If one waveform consisting of a particular set of component frequencies is multiplied by another waveform consisting of a second set, the signal that is the product of the two will consist of a third set of components. The third set will contain the sums and differences of the frequencies of the first two sets. For example, a sine wave of 800 cycles per second multiplied by a sine wave of 300 cycles per second, will yield a result that is a mixture of a 1100-cycles per second component with a 500-cycles per second component. Consequently, if a complex, periodic wave is multiplied by a sinusoid of any given frequency, the effect of the multiplication is to shift all the component frequencies of the complex wave both up and down by an amount equal to the frequency of the modulating wave. These shifted frequencies are called sidebands. Thus, as two waveforms are multiplied, every frequency in the first waveform produces two sidebands for every frequency in the other waveform. For example, a signal having 10 harmonics multiplied by another signal with five harmonics will form a product having 50 partials. Those 50 components will not be harmonically related unless the original frequencies are specially chosen. One can readily anticipate that this waveform multiplication can lead to very complex, clangorous sounds. On an analog synthesizer, this kind of four-quadrant multiplication of two signals is performed with a ring modulator. A ring modulator multiplies continuous voltages electronically, rather than multiplying discrete samples numerically as is done with a digital computer.

Another analog signal-processing device is closely related to the ring modulator, called a *frequency shifter*. It merits discussion here because it is of great utility to composers of electronic music. A frequency shifter functions identically to a ring modulator except that a ring modulator produces both an upper and lower sideband for each component of its program signal and a frequency shifter produces just one sideband while it suppresses the other. The modulating frequency is set or varied either by an externally applied control voltage or by a dial on its front panel. Since only one sideband is generated for each frequency component of the input waveform, the output signal will have the same set of frequencies as the input, but they will have been all shifted by a uniform amount; either up or down. For example, a tone sounding an A pitch at 220 cycles per second and having harmonics at 440, 660, 880, 1100, . . . cycles per second, may be input to a frequency shifter. If the dial controlling the modulating frequency is set to 50 cycles per second, the output will be a tone with a pitch of 270 cycles per second having nonharmonic partials at 490, 710, 930, and 1600 cycles per second.

One may note that the effect of frequency shifting is radically different than simple transposition. Transposing a signal can be done on a tape recorder by changing its speed, or on a digital instrument by changing the sampling frequency of the DAC. If the harmonic tone A-220 were transposed by a frequency of 50 cycles per second, the result would still be harmonic, having a fundamental frequency of 270 cycles per second. Its overtones would then fall at 540, 810, 1080, and 1350 cycles per second—multiples of the fundamental. The duration of the tone would be shortened. But the tone entering a frequency shifter is processed in real time. Thus, it comes out as it goes in, and its duration is not changed. Unlike a transposed tone, its frequencies have a nonharmonic relationship which is entirely different than the original signal. The sound of the output, although similar to the original, will typically have a peculiar ringing distortion to it. This distortion can be artistically exploited to give ordinary sounds interesting, colorful qualities; consequently, frequency-shifting techniques are used abundantly by composers in the electronic medium.

Filtering is another topic of major interest in recorded sound processing. The preceding chapter described how time-varying digital filters are used in vocoders to synthesize speech. However, they are not limited to this application. Although filters are employed in electronics, communication, and signal processing primarily for noise reduction, they are used extensively in electronic music to color and modify the timbre of recorded or synthesized sounds. A typical filter widely found in electronic music studios is s third-octave equalizer. An equalizer is actually a combination of several simple filters, so before attempting to explain how one works, it is helpful to first come to understand some basic filters.

The most fundamental kind of filter is a *low-pass filter*. It is called low-pass because it permits low frequencies to pass through it while it blocks higher frequencies. Figure 8.1 shows the frequency response of what would be an ideal low-pass filter. However, as an astute reader may suspect, a novelty such as an *ideal* filter does not exist. The physical reasons and philosophical implications of this fact of life are beyond the range of this discussion, but it will suffice to say that the closer one seeks a filter with ideal characteristics, the more difficult and expensive will be its design and construction. Figure 8.1 shows that this nonexistent filter has perfect unity gain for all frequencies from 0 up to a specified cutoff frequency f_c. Then all frequencies above this cutoff value are perfectly attenuated—that is, they don't pass through it at all. The lower region of unity gain is called the passband, and the upper region of perfect attenuation is called the stopband. In real life, the frequency response of a practical filter will have a contoured or rippled frequency response as diagrammed in Fig. 8.2. As mentioned above, the quality of a filter is related to how closely its actual frequency response resembles an "ideal" response.

A second typical filter that is the reverse of a low-pass filter is a *high-pass filter*. It is so named because it passes the high frequencies and attenuates the lows. Figure 8.3 depicts the frequency responses of an ideal, and two practical high-pass filters. A *bandpass filter* may be considered as a combination of a low-pass filter and high-pass filter connected in series. It has both a lower cutoff frequency f_{c1} and an upper cutoff frequency f_{c2}. It passes all frequencies in the region between f_{c1} and f_{c2} while it attenuates the frequencies outside as shown in Fig. 8.4. The inverse of a bandpass filter is a *bandreject filter*. Its ideal frequency response is diagrammed in Fig. 8.5.

The third-octave equalizer mentioned earlier is actually a cascade of bandpass filters. Each filter has a bandwidth (the width of the passband)

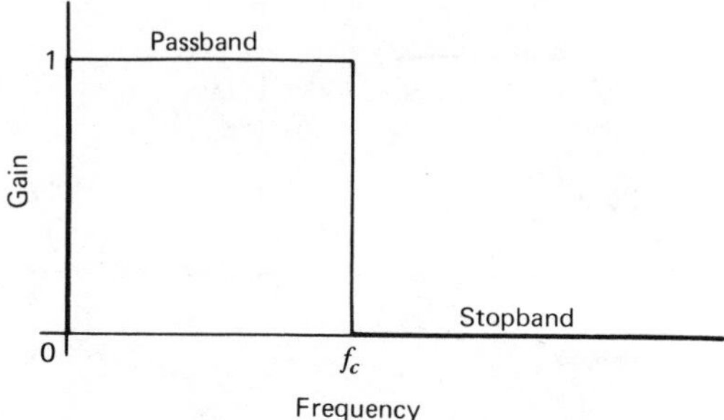

Figure 8.1 An ideal lowpass filter.

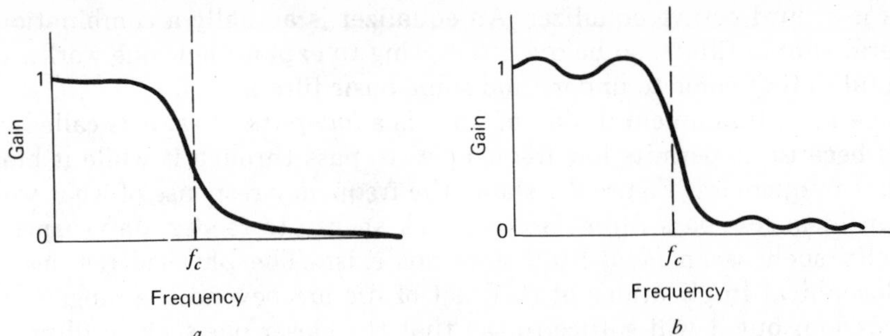

Figure 8.2 Practical lowpass filters.

of approximately one third of an octave, and there are three separate filters for every octave in the audible frequency range. The gain of each individual third-octave filter is variable and is controlled by a small slide switch. The slide switches are arranged along the front panel of the equalizer unit so that they conveniently depict the overall frequency response of the entire equalizer by their physical positions. As one uses an

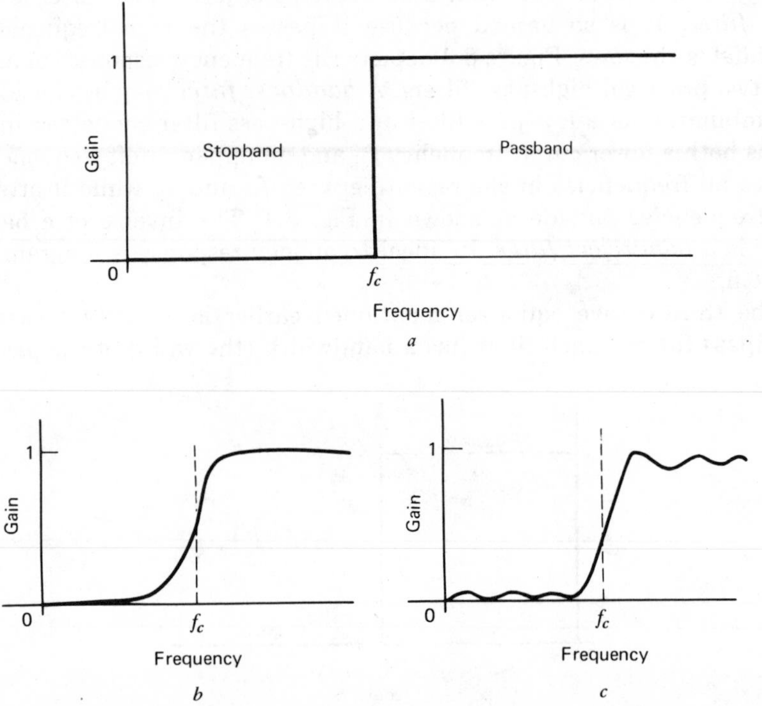

Figure 8.3 Highpass filters: *a* ideal, *b* and *c*, practical.

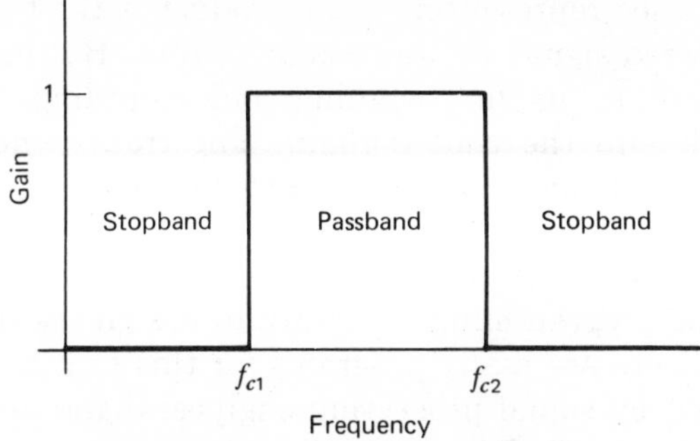

Figure 8.4 Ideal bandpass filter.

equalizer in a recording studio, he can position the slide switches of the individual filters in any arbitrary configuration, obtaining virtually any frequency response with one-third octave resolution.

On the computer, digital filters perform the same operation as analog filters, but their implementation and use are much different. A digital filter is not actually a physical device. It is actuated by a computer program that accepts a number sequence as an input representing the samples of the signal to be filtered. There are several different ways that this sample sequence can be mathematically manipulated and processed. One common method uses the discrete Fourier transform (DFT) introduced in Chapter 6. The computer performs this DFT on the original sequence. The signal is then represented in the frequency domain as another array stored in memory. This frequency-domain sequence, that is the transform of the original signal, is then multiplied by another sequence representing the frequency response of the digital filter. One then has a third sequence representing the product of the first two. Since the original signal and the digital filter are both represented in the frequency

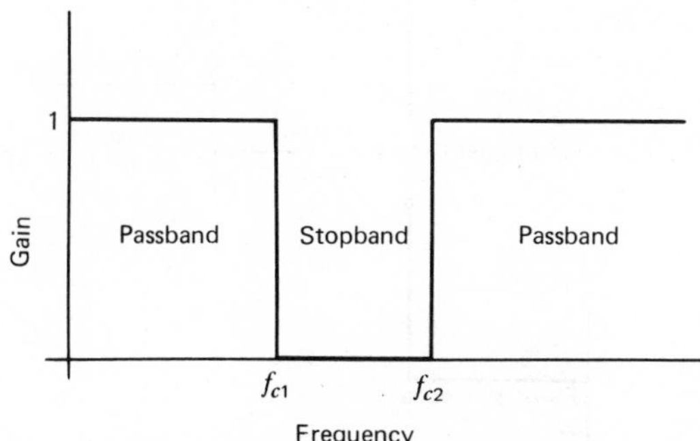

Figure 8.5 Ideal bandreject filter.

domain, the sequence representing their product is the frequency domain version of the filtered signal we want as an output. But before this output sequence is of use to us for listening and recording, it must be re-transformed back into the time-domain. The transformed time-domain signal is then the final one available for d-to-a conversion, monitoring, and recording. Figure 8.6 diagrams the process.

The person who uses this process to filter digital signals does not need to worry about the programming necessary to design the filters or perform the transforms. There are many programs for this that have already been written and tested by signal-processing engineers, and are widely available. They can be installed on virtually any general-purpose computer system. To obtain a digital filter having a certain, desired frequency response, a user simply calls a filter design program on file in the computer's software library. As input to the program, he or she specifies the parameters describing the type of filter he or she wants. These parameters will usually include the number of passbands and stopbands in the filter, as well as their bandwidths, upper and lower cutoff frequencies, relative attenuations in each band, and required tolerances. The computer program then uses this data to calculate the sequence representing the desired filter. It is this computed sequence which is subsequently used to process the input sequence. If this process is carried out in the frequency domain as indicated in Fig. 8.6, the computer does it by complex multiplication and the product is inverse-transformed back into the time domain as shown. The computer programs that perform the DFT and

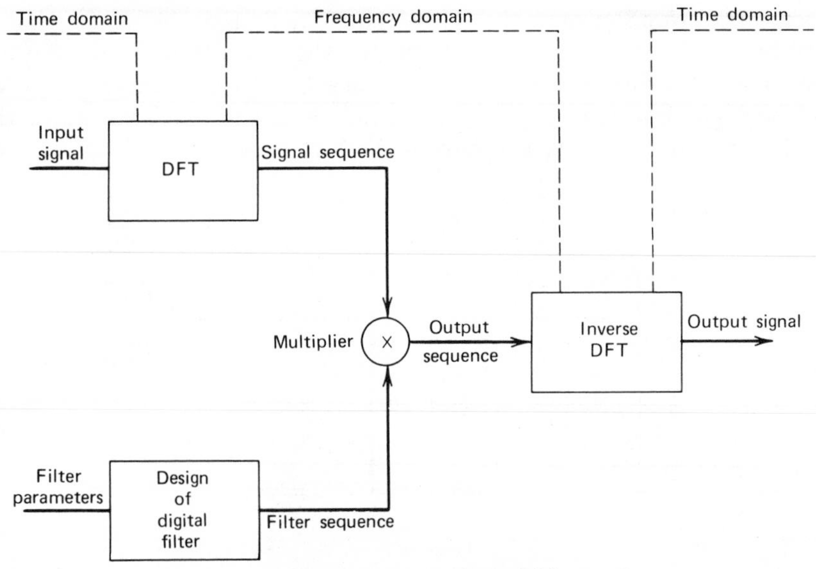

Figure 8.6 A digital filter.

inverse DFT should be available on file in the system library. The user calls and runs these programs by simple commands at his terminal.

The filtering process described above is somewhat similar to the filter of a vocoder described in Chapter 7. The important difference is that the vocoder's filter has a time-varying frequency response. The parameters determining its response are the information carried by the vocoder channel. But these parameters are set by the vocoder's analyzer rather than by arbitrary selection. A standard digital filter, like the third-octave equilizer, is essentially a static device. The user selects the characteristics and frequency response he or she wants, then designs the filter accordingly. This can be done with a hand calculator if the user has the mathematical knowhow. Nevertheless, with obvious preference, he or she can leave the task of filter design to the computer, who can do it much faster. This will require no more effort of the user than to supply the filter's simple description. One should not infer from this discussion that these filters are necessarily static devices. Analog synthesizers, for example, usually contain low and high-pass filters whose cutoff frequencies are voltage controlled. In the digital world, it would not be too difficult to design a filter whose frequency response varies according to a preprogrammed input or even a set of variable parameters supplied to it in real time by a user through an input device.

The digital filter, like the multiplier and mixer, has been described here in context with its analog counterparts. The analog devices of electronic synthesizers such as voltage-controlled oscillators, filters, and amplifiers, envelope generators, ring modulators, and the like are well familiar to the composer of electronic music. Their roles and capabilities are well-established. This chapter has intended to present the principles of their use in terms of the functions they accomplish. These principles apply universally to signal processing devices—analog or digital. They may be 10 years obsolete, state of the art, or 20 years into the future. The difficulty in discussing devices whose technology evolves so rapidly is that explanation of how one device functions may not apply to another device, even though both of them perform the same operation. This is especially true of analog versus digital equipment. Consequently, a composer who is already familiar with analog hardware, or one who is unfamiliar with the electronic music studio, must learn a new battery of techniques when composing with the computer as an instrument. But the new techniques that must be learned are the mechanical procedures that vary from one machine to another. The principles underlying them exist apart from the technicalities of their operation just as the principles of harmony and counterpoint exist apart from the pedagogy of the instruments of the orchestra. The line to be drawn between the technician and the artist then, is the same line that separates the machine itself from the master of its use.

REFERENCES

Blesser, Barry A., "Digitization of Audio: A Comprehensive Examination of Theory, Implementation, and Current Practice," *Journal of the Audio Engineering Society* **26**(10), 739–771 (1978).

Olson, Harry F. *Music, Physics, and Engineering*, Dover, 1967.

Pain, H. J., *The Physics of Vibration and Waves*, Wiley, 1968.

Roederer, Juan G., *Introduction to the Physics and Psychophysics of Music*, Springer-Verlag, 1975.

Stephens, R. W. B., & A. E. Bate, *Acoustics and Vibrational Physics*, Arnold, 1960.

Stockham, Thomas, "A/D and D/A Converters: Their Effect of Digital Audio Fidelity," in *Digital Signal Processing*, Rabiner & Rader (Eds.), IEEE Press, 1972.

9

SIMULATION AND REPRODUCTION OF NATURAL SOUNDS

Much has been said thus far about the computer's role in synthesizing new and complex sounds. The discussion has maintained that any sound may be modeled mathematically as a function of time. The actual waveform represented by this function is physically created by a vibrating source and then transmitted by the surrounding air to the ear of a listener. The variation of instantaneous pressure at any point in the air is the function of interest in the analysis or reproduction of sound. One uses a microphone to convert the variations of air pressure into identical vairations of electric current or voltage. The role of a loudspeaker is the reverse of the microphone, transforming fluctuations of electric current back into sound.

When the patterns of fluctuating air pressure that constitute a sound are represented electrically, they are in a form readily usable for analysis, recording, or reproduction. In this condition, they can be viewed graphically on an oscilloscope. They may be used to drive a magnetic tape head for storing their representation on a moving tape surface. They may also be electronically amplified and transmitted to a remote location. Or they may be sampled at short intervals of time to be represented digitally in a computer memory.

This text has naturally focused on the latter process. The aim of computer music is the production of sound by the origination of a mathematical representation describing that sound. This book has presented some ways by which computer equipment can synthesize waveforms from mathematical functions. It has explored various techniques of defining functions that may be used to generate musical tones or simulate the sounds of musical instruments. It has also discussed some of the psychoacoustical characteristics of sound and the constitution of tones versus noise.

It is puzzling that most schools of music theory, analysis, and composition are dedicated to the study of form, harmony, and counterpoint, yet many of them almost totally neglect the study of sound itself. In some music curricula, the subject of acoustics is not only not required, but is not even offered! An interested music student must find an acoustics course in the schools of physics or engineering. Be that as it may, when a composer penetrates the field of mathematics to create original sounds by the formulation of their representative functions, he or she must have preparation that goes beyond standard music theory. There must be a clear understanding of the physical properties underlying the sounds that are being created.

In exploring the possibilities of computer music composition, one may accumulate a mass of technical know-how and skill in computer programming. One may be familiar with all of the state-of-the-art devices and processes under development that are available to the computer musician. Yet technical skill in the operation of a device is not now, nor has it ever been, the foundation of an art. In the field of electronic music, there are hundreds of technicians who are tremendously skilled in designing, maintaining, and operating electronic equipment for each composer who can use it to create a work of art. The skill requires knowledge deeper than that of simple electronics. It is important to understand what makes one sound an interesting musical source and another sound a mundane noise.

The study of acoustics is even more essential in computer music where the control of timbre is absolutely determined by the composer. This is an altogether different type of control than is exercised by an orchestrator. An expert in instrumentation knows the character of sound that each instrument of the orchestra makes. He or she also knows how to combine those sounds to create the right mood and tone color for the piece that is being orchestrated. The art of instrumentation demands years of study and experience as well as natural talent. But an orchestrator does not need to know what a cello tone looks like displayed on an oscilloscope or what the graph of its power spectrum looks like in the frequency domain. The acoustical characteristics of instrumental tones are determined by the mechanical characteristics of the instruments. Therefore, the instrumentalist may direct concern to the familiarity of the various sounds as they are naturally created by these instruments without having to ascertain their mathematical description.

This is not true for computer music! When analyzing an instrumental tone, one starts with the physical sound itself, and then uses electromechanical devices to go from the real entity to the mathematical model. The essence of scientific inquiry is the search for and discovery of rules that consistently describe and predict the phenomena of nature. The rules are generally expressed in mathematical formulas. Creation of sound or even visual art using the computer as an instrument involves the reverse process. The artist invents the mathematical model; then the instrument becomes its realization.

Acoustics is the study of how sounds are produced, transmitted, and perceived. Although the computer is a mechanical object, its mechanical properties have no correlation with the way it is used to synthesize sound. Its only "natural" sound is the noise made by its cooling fans and disk drive. Therefore, what the computer is actually doing is mathematically simulating the way sounds are mechanically produced. The sounds that the computer simulates may or may not actually have their counterparts in nature. The computer may simulate an actual trumpet tone, a tone that is a cross between a trumpet and a bassoon, or a sound of a totally imaginary instrument. For the computer to do any one of these things, its programmer must provide it with the exact, logically formatted, procedural description of how that sound is to be created. For the computer to simulate an oboe, its programmer must understand and be able to describe how an oboe player makes an oboe tone.

Sounds are produced by vibrating objects. As the objects vibrate, they disturb the air molecules in their surrounding environment. Due to the elastic property of air, these disturbances are transmitted in every direction at an approximate speed of 1100 feet per second. The disturbance is perceived when the sound waves cause someone's eardrum to vibrate in nearly the same patterns created by the original vibrating source. To understand how and why the source may vibrate in such an infinite variety of modes, it is necessary to explore the mathematics of harmonic motion. This topic was examined in Chapter 2 and is pursued again for further understanding. The fundamental properties of a given sound are its pitch, its intensity, and its timbre. The pitch and intensity are simple, measurable quantities that can each be represented by a single variable. But the timbre of a sound is a complex, multidimensional property. To describe the timbre of a sound. one must decompose that sound into a changing spectrum of all its frequency components. Each of the components must be dynamically and separately considered.

As any one of these components is individually measured and analyzed, it may be described by an equation of simple, harmonic motion. To understand the model of simple harmonic motion, we may describe a mechanical system that oscillates in a simple mode. Chapter 2 described an imaginary system that generates a sine tone. But an ideal electric motor driving an ideal piston is hardly a natural phenomenon! A much more realistic example of a body vibrating in simple harmonic motion is a mass suspended from a spring and disturbed from its equilibrium position as pictured in Fig. 9.1.

When the mass is at equilibrium, the spring exerts an upward force on it that exactly balances its downward force imposed by gravity. When the mass is displaced, the forces are no longer in balance; consequently, the mass moves towards its equilibrium position. But due to its inertia, it passes that position and proceeds beyond it where the force is reversed and arrests its motion. The reverse force pulls it back to where the process

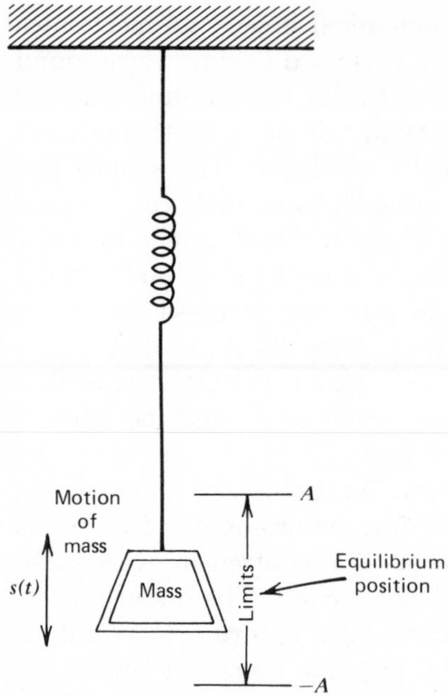

Figure 9.1 A simple mechanical oscillator.

repeats itself. When we study the motion of the mass on the spring, we discover that it can be described by the sine function,

$$S(t) = A \sin 2\pi ft$$

Although this equation is not an exact model of the system, (the equations never are) it is close enough for practical purposes. The function $S(t)$ represents the position of the mass at some instant of time t. A represents the maximum displacement of the mass and is the amplitude of the function. Its frequency is represented by f, and is determined by the weight of the mass and the tension of the spring. This equation actually ignores the fact that friction causes the oscillations to diminish and die out, but it is presented in this form to illustrate the mechanism of simple vibration rather than to be a comprehensive description.

A mass on a spring is a good example of simple harmonic motion because it is so easily visualized. It is not an example of a sound-producing source because its rate of oscillation is obviously much too slow. A vibrating string, on the other hand, is an easily visualized, clear example of a sound source. But its motion is generally not simple harmonic. The forces that cause its periodic vibration are similar in principle to a mass on a spring, but the mass of the spring is distributed over its entire length. This distribution allows it to vibrate in several modes at once as was shown in Chapter 2, producing a complex tone of several harmonics. The motion of any one of the individual modes, nevertheless, may be considered simple harmonic and describable by the sine function.

The science of acoustics would be mundane if it were restricted to the mere study of sound-producing sources. The real complications arise when one begins to analyze what happens to sound when it reflects different surfaces. It is the reflective property of sound that causes open pipes to be good resonators. It is interesting to examine the way sound is reflected inside a pipe or tube and see why the reflection causes resonance. When the pressure front of a sound wave enters an open tube, the pressure of the wave is exerted along the inside wall of the tube as it travels down its length. This wave is thus contained along the inside of the tube and is not allowed to dissipate as it would if the tube were not there to restrict it. This reflection reinforces the wave motion. By contrast, a sound wave in open air is not reinforced, but is dissipated into the surrounding space.

The impedance of a sound-conducting channel such as a pipe is a measurable quantity and is a significant factor in determining the channel's acoustic properties. One can readily see that open air has much greater impedance than a pipe, and that narrow pipes have less impedance than wide ones, since their small diameter allows them to conduct sound more easily. Let us suppose that a sound wave front is traveling down an open pipe of low impedance and suddenly reaches the end where it is faced with the wide open air at once. The open air has much greater impedance as the wave is allowed to dissipate in every direction as it leaves the pipe. The abrupt change in impedance causes a portion of the sound to be reflected back into the pipe in the opposite direction as shown in Fig. 9.2. Once the reflected wave travels to the opposite end of the pipe, it is reflected again, whether that end is open or closed. Once a sound enters a pipe, it will consequently be reflected back and forth along the inside several times before it dies out.

Since sound travels at a constant speed, a periodic sound wave of any fixed frequency has a particular wavelength. For example, a sound wave

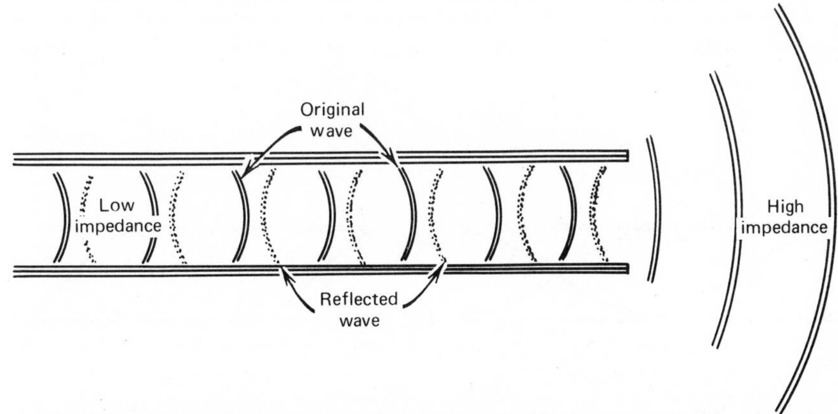

Figure 9.2 Reflection of a sound wave in an open-ended pipe.

having a frequency of 1100 cycles per second has a wavelength of 1 foot. This is because sound travels at 1100 feet per second. Given this fact, we may now see what happens when a sound enters a pipe open at both ends. Suppose that the sound's wavelength is 1 foot and the pipe is 6 inches long. Figure 9.3 diagrams how the sound reflects inside the pipe. The ends of the pipe reflect the waves back to the inside so that the reflected waves mutually reinforce each other. For these reflected waves to all be in phase with and reinforcing each other, the length of the pipe must be a multiple of one-half the wavelength. Otherwise the reflected waves will not be in phase, and will dampen each other. The result of this situation is that the open pipe selects only a set of frequencies that are harmonics of a fundamental whose one-half wavelength is the length of the pipe. Consequently, our 6-inch pipe will respond and resonate at sounds whose frequencies are 1100, 2200, 3300, 4400, . . . cycles per second.

A pipe closed at one end reflects the wave at its mode at the closed end. Consequently, it resonates at odd-numbered multiples of the frequency whose one-fourth wavelength is the length of the pipe. This was illustrated in Chapter 2, and is repeated in Fig. 9.4. If this pipe is 3 inches long, the resonant frequencies will be 1100, 3300, 5500, . . . cycles per second.

The preceding discussion presents the basic concept of an acoustic resonator. However, it did not consider an important complication. When a sound wave is reflected at the open end of a pipe, the point of reflection does not occur exactly at the pipe's end. It is actually reflected at a loca-

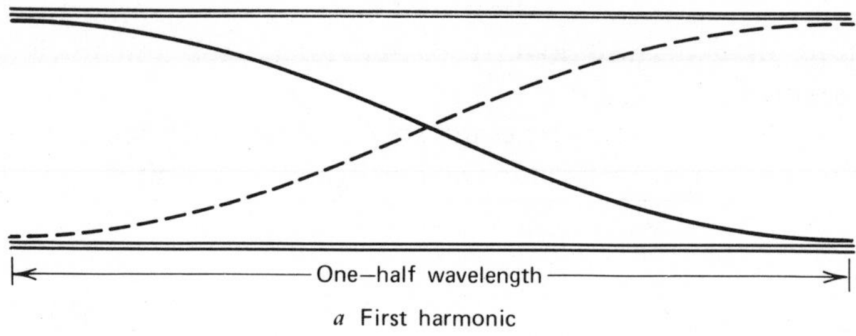

a First harmonic

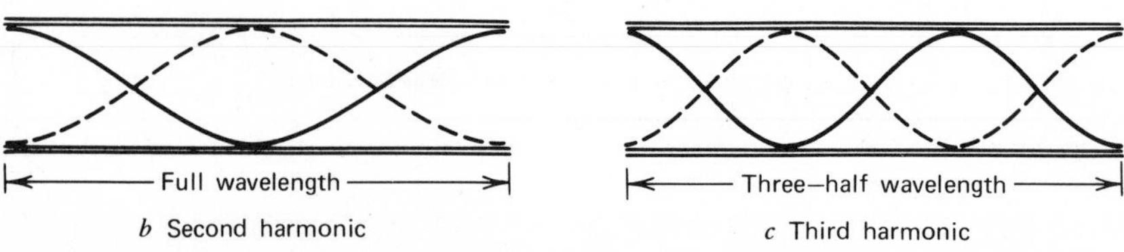

b Second harmonic

c Third harmonic

Figure 9.3 Resonation in open-ended pipe *a* first harmonic, *b* second harmonic, and *c* third harmonic.

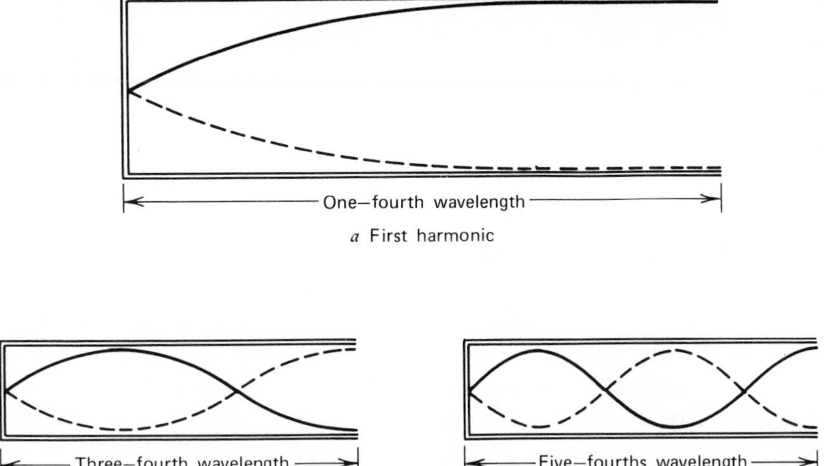

Figure 9.4 Resonation in close-ended pipe *a* first harmonic, *b* third harmonic, and *c* fifth harmonic.

tion slightly beyond the opening. This effective reflection point is determined by both the wavelength of the sound and the diameter of the pipe. As a result, all of the harmonics are not reflected at the same point, and the pipe resonates the harmonic poorly. For musical instruments, this is very undesirable. To compensate for this, brass and reed instruments attach a bell on their open ends. The bell has the effect of smoothing the abruptness of the impedance gap between the instrument and the open air. The effective reflection point is spread out through a short region and allows the upper harmonics of the tone produced by the instrument to stand out more than they would if the bell were not there. The tone is thus rendered a richer quality.

To enable these instruments to sound the notes of the scale, their effective lengths must be variable. With the exception of the trombone, this variability is usually effectuated by placing holes or valves along the length of the column. The degree whereby such an opening changes the pipe's resonant frequency is determined by the area of the hole, its position, and diameter and length of the pipe. Consequently, by placing several holes along the length of the instrument's body and allowing them to be individually opened or closed, the instrument may sound a variety of pitches. In summary, the pitch of a wind instrument is determined by the relative intensities of the tone's harmonics. This is affected by the nature of the exciting source (the lips or reed), and the shape of the instrument—particularly its bell.

We have seen how a column of fixed length resonates a particular set of harmonic frequencies. This is true as long as it has a uniform diameter.

Let us now suppose that a narrow tube is joined to a wide tube as shown in Fig. 9.5. Here we see that reflections occur not only at the open end, but at the region where the two sections of the tube join and there is a change of impedance. If these two sections are not the same length, they will not have the same resonant frequency. So instead of resonating only one fundamental pitch, the combination will sound two frequencies that are not necessarily harmonically related. The acoustics of the resonating system can be further complicated by introducing a configuration of several pipe sections of varying lengths and diameters. Figure 9.6 is an example. The lengths, positions, and diameters of the sections not only determine which frequency partials will be projected, but what their relative intensities will be. A resonating system of this kind thus has two degrees of variability—each partial's frequency and amplitude are determined by the overall shape of the resonating body.

We may now attack the problem of how to model the physics of acoustical resonators mathematically. It is possible, although quite complicated, to formulate equations that describe the frequency response of a joined-pipe system such as the one pictured in Fig. 9.6. One specifies the dimensions of each section, and from this information predicts what frequencies it will propagate. It is even possible to use this kind of a resonator to simulate the acoustic behavior of a person's vocal tract. Of course, it is highly unfeasible to try to measure the physical dimensions of one's throat and sinus cavity while he is speaking or singing! There would certainly be no practicality in the physical construction of such a model when its shape changes continuously, anyway. But when we are dealing with computers, the resonators we "build" are mathematical rather than physical entities. Some very interesting research has been done in this area by Atal, Hanauer, Wakita, and Gray and is described in Markel and Gray [1976]. Their studies show how a hypothetical configuration of several sections of pipe each having uniform diameter and equal lengths may be formatted to simulate a vocal tract. One assumes that the length of the hypothetical joined-pipe system is approximately the same as the distance between one's lips and glottis. The diameters of the sections approximate the diameter of the vocal tract at corresponding intervals along its length. The equations that one derives from the dimensions of the hypothetical pipe system predict a frequency spectrum that would be expected from the vocal tract it is simulating.

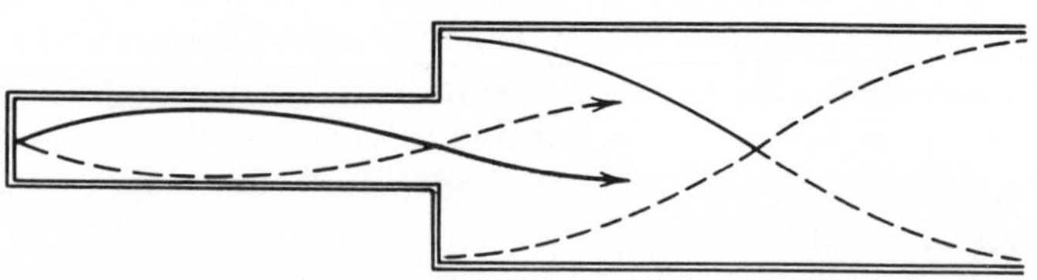

Figure 9.5 Resonation in two joined pipes.

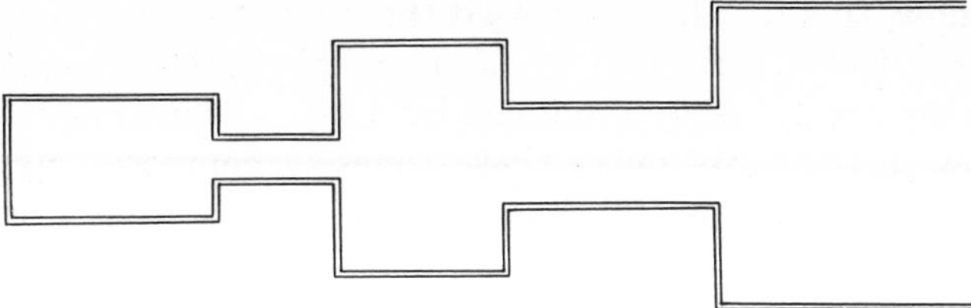

Figure 9.6 A complex resonating system.

At this point one may justifiably object to this line of reasoning. We have only said that the vocal tract may be simulated, but we do not have any practical way of reaching inside a person's mouth to make the measurements necessary for the simulation! Without the physical measurements of the shape of the vocal tract that would be continuously changing, the affair seems rather pointless. But the problem is still worth pursuing. So far, we have only talked about the mathematical prediction of the system's frequency response from its physical shape. Now we reverse the procedure and measure the frequency spectrum of a human voice. Then we derive the mathematical model from the spectrum. In spite of the enormous difficulties involved with this process, the researchers have undertaken it with success. Their procedure works similarly to the linear prediction system in vocoders introduced in Chapter 7. A short interval of recorded speech is sampled and analyzed by a computer program. From this analysis the program determines the spectrum of the sound and outputs a set of "reflection coefficients." The significance of these reflection coefficients is that they correlate with the actual physical dimensions of the vocal tract projecting the sound. As mentioned earlier, the change in impedance that occurs between two adjacent sections of pipe causes sound to be reflected at their junction. The reflection coefficients derived from the acoustical spectrum of a short speech interval define the hypothetical pipe system in terms of the actual vocal tract it is modeling. Experimentation has shown that the pipe-section dimensions derived from the reflection coefficients actually correspond to vocal tract shapes observed in X-ray photographs.

The discussion of reflection coefficients and hypothetical resonators may be summarized by stating that one may take a recording of speech, analyze it, and from the analysis formulate an approximate description of the shape of the vocal tract that produced the sound. The presentation is not suggesting itself as a practical method of making computers talk or sing. It is offered instead as an example to demonstrate one way to undertake a mathematical simulation of a natural physical system. When a composer synthesizes tones with a computer, he or she is mathematically "creating" instruments. The nonphysical instruments created by the composer and realized by the computer may simulate the acoustical behavior of a physical device, be it real or imaginary.

Up until now, this text has discussed the properties of sound in terms of their mathematical description. It has also briefly described some of the ways that tones are naturally produced by musical instruments. By understanding how instruments make these tones, a composer may have the facility to invent ways of simulating them or creating original tones mathematically. The previous chapters have described how the computer is used to formulate a discrete function representing a sound waveform based on its mathematical description. DAC is then used to transform the table of numbers in the computer's memory into a voltage. It is now important to consider the way that an electric signal is converted to sound, and conversely, how sound is transformed into an electric signal.

An electromechanical device used to transform mechanical energy to electric energy or vice versa is called a transducer. The transducers involved with the conversion between electric and sound energy are microphones and loudspeakers. However, a simple microphone or speaker by itself is incomplete in a sound production system. This is because the energy of a signal generated by a microphone is very insufficient to drive a loudspeaker or other transducer without amplification. Similarly, the electric outputs from a tape head, phonograph pickup, DAC, or radio tuner is not strong enough for a loudspeaker, either. Therefore, an amplifier must be included as an essential component. This chapter does not attempt to describe the operation of microphones, amplifiers, and loudspeakers in the technical detail of an engineering text, but describes their basic characteristics so that the reader may have an overall conception of how these devices work.

There are several different ways that mechanical vibration can stimulate electric current. Consequently, a wide variety of differrent designs are used in the construction of microphones. One kind commonly utilized in telephone communication systems is a carbon microphone. It is used because it is very sensitive and produces a high output requiring much less amplification than other less efficient kinds of microphones. Its grave disadvantage is its low quality. It is highly nonlinear and suffers a great deal of distortion. It also has poor frequency response. A carbon microphone consists of a diaphragm coupled to a chamber full of carbon granules is illustrated in Fig. 9.7. The carbon granules are used as a conducting path for an electric current. As sound is captured by the diaphragm, the mechanism is set to vibrate. The motion is transmitted to the chamber containing the granulated carbon. As the granules are compressed, their electrical conductivity increases because of the packing. As the pressure on them is made to fluctuate by the sound coming into the diaphragm, the electric current passing through the chamber is also made to fluctuate. The variations in electric current constitute the output of the microphone.

A crystal microphone is another microphone commonly used in inexpensive devices. It employs a piezoelectric crystal such as rochelle

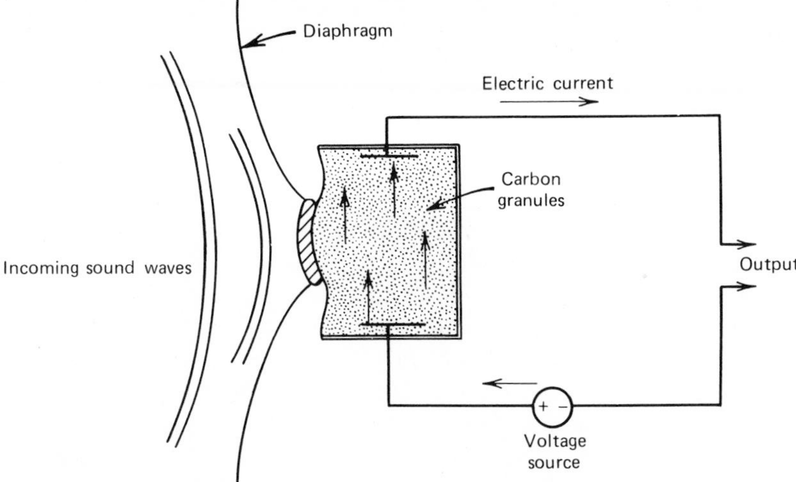

Figure 9.7 A carbon microphone.

salt, and operates on the principle that the crystal emits an electric current when it is deformed. Unlike the carbon microphone, it generates its own voltage, not requiring the application of a battery or current source from the outside. The crystal may be coupled to a diaphragm similar to the carbom microphone so that the sound may be captured to vibrate the crystal. As the crystal is forced to vibrate, the voltage sensed at its boundaries fluctuates in a corresponding pattern to the incoming sound waves.

One interesting microphone design employs a variable-plate capacitor. A capacitor is a small device used to store electric charge. It consists of two parallel plates separated by an insulator. The insulator separating them may be air or empty space. The capacitance of the plates is a measure of the amount of charge that they store at a given voltage. It is determined by the area of the plates, the properties of the material (if any) separating them, and the distance between them. Consequently, if one constructs a capacitor in such a way that the distance between the plates may be subject to variation, he or she may use it as a transducer. A condensor microphone is such a device. A battery contained inside the microphone casing is used to apply a charge to the capacitor plates. Since the battery is only needed to supply a voltage, but not to pass any current through the capacitor, it may be used for a long time without dying out. As the charge is stored on the capacitor, sound waves entering the microphone vibrate one of the plates and cause the voltage to vary with the vibration. Condensor microphones are often used where high quality and low distortion is required.

The dynamic microphone is the most common design in high quality applications. It generates electric current from the motion of a conductor through a magnetic field. It is a well-known fact of electrodynamics that electric current passing through a wire induces a magnetic field around the wire. Conversely, if a loop of wire is made to move across a magnetic field, the motion will generate current in the loop. A dynamic microphone is constructed from a permanent magnet and a coil of wire called a voice coil coupled to a diaphragm. As in the case of the other microphones we have mentioned, the diaphragm captures the sound energy and causes the voice coil to vibrate in the field surrounding the magnet. The output from the coil of wire is sent through a cable to an amplifier.

These four types of microphones just introduced by no means constitute all the different ways that modern microphones are manufactured. They do, however, represent the most common design methods. We may now turn our attention to the design of loudspeakers. Although there are a near infinite variety of loudspeaker constructions, most are fundamentally a variation of one basic design principle. This design is the same as the one used in the dynamic microphone. However, rather than using the motion of the diaphragm to generate electric current in the voice coil, the coil is supplied a fluctuating current to induce motion in the diaphragm. A dynamic microphone and a loudspeaker could be theoretically interchangeable. Other criteria prevent this from being true in practice. For a dynamic microphone to be acoustically sensitive, the components must be extremely flexible and lightweight. The voice coil of a loudspeaker, on the other hand, must be able to handle several watts. The diaphragm must be large enough to radiate sound at a satisfactory volume level. The permanent magnet must also be larger and stronger to accommodate the more massive voice coil and diaphragm. Figure 9.8 shows a cross-sectional side view of a typical loudspeaker.

A phonograph pickup is a transducer that operates almost the same way as a microphone. As with microphones, most cheaper phonograph cartridges use a crystal to generate an electric signal while high-fidelity pickups employ a dynamic element. Whereas a microphone element is coupled to a diaphragm to capture sound out of the air, the phonograph element is made to vibrate by the motion of a stylus. The other principal difference between a microphone and phonograph cartridge is that the stereo phonograph is actually two elements built into one unit. As the stylus sits in the groove of a rotating phonograph disk, it is made to vibrate in two perpendicular directions simultaneously, as shown in Fig. 9.9.

The grooves of a stereo phonograph record are cut so that the faces of their two sides are perpendicular. As the record turns, the surface of each side varies independently of the other side. As one can see from Fig. 9.9, the fluctuations of the left side of the groove cause the stylus to vibrate diagonally in the direction of the arrow at the upper right. This vibration stimulates element #1, but does not affect element #2. Similarly, the vibrations caused by the right side of the groove move the stylus in the

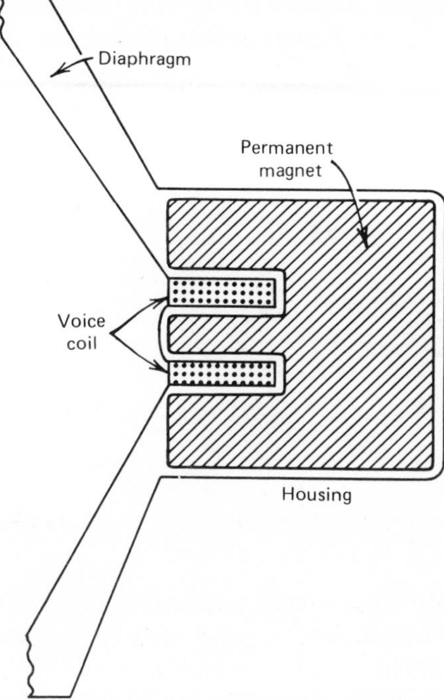

Figure 9.8 A typical loudspeaker.

other diagonal direction and stimulate element #2 while element #1 is unaffected. The two sides of the groove carry two different channels of sound that are captured separately by the two-dimensional motion of the stylus. The two signals are transduced independently by two separate elements built into the pickup.

In spite of the enormous popularity of the phonograph, it is subject to severe mechanical drawbacks. The worst of these is the wear and deterioration suffered by disks as they are handled and played. An electromagnetic tape has much longer life than a phonograph record, and it may record a signal with much less noise and distortion. It also has the capability of repeated recording as well as playback. Its disadvantage is that tape recordings cannot be mass produced as easily and cheaply as phonograph records. The signal on an electromagnetic tape is recorded onto an emulsion of fine magnetic particles on the tape's surface. The tape head is a small electromagnet over which the tape surface move. When the tape recorder is in the recording mode, an electric signal is supplied to the coil of the head from an amplifier as illustrated in Fig. 9.10. The current induces a fluctuating magnetic field in the head that radiates to the tape as it slides across a narrow gap in the electromagnet. The magnetic particles along the tape are thus polarized in a direction and intensity that varies along the length of the tape as shown in Fig. 9.11. This diagram

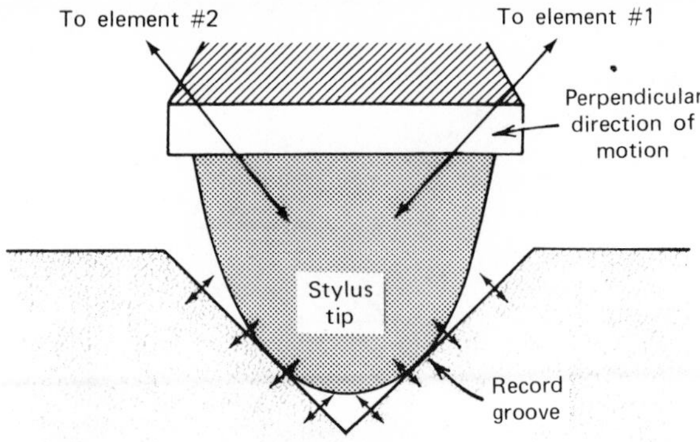

Figure 9.9 A stereo record stylus in groove.

shows approximately one cycle of a recorded sine wave. If the frequency of the sound were 750 cycle per second and the tape speed 7½ inches per second, the length of the tape for one cycle would be $\frac{1}{100}$ inch.

The tape head used for recording can also be used for playback. Once the tape is recorded and the magnetic domains of its surface particles are established, as shown in Fig. 9.11, when it moves across the tape head gap it sets up a fluctuating magnetic field in the head. The varying field in turn induces current in the coil that may be sent as a signal to an amplifier. Whereas one head may be used for both recording and playback—and is, in fact, on most tape recorders, a separate head is included for playback on high-quality equipment.

The quality of sound available on a tape recording is directly proportional to the area of the surface on the tape where it is recorded. Obviously a greater surface area can sustain a stronger signal. Consequently, the proportion of signal to noise is greater, permitting a wider dynamic range in the recording. This is why recording studios use a wider section of the tape and run it at a higher speed than commercial recorders. It is also why the

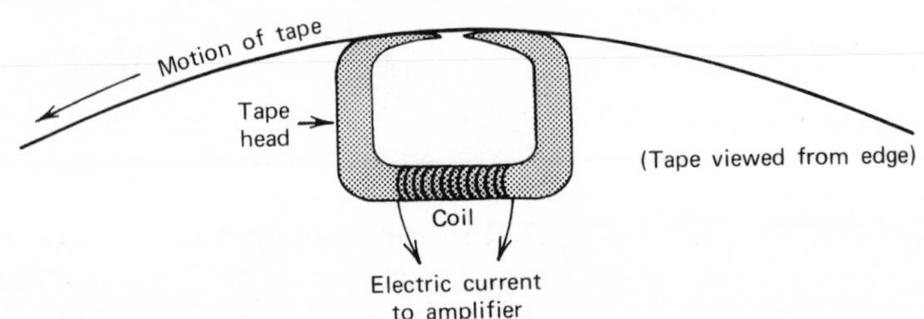

Figure 9.10. A magnetic tape head.

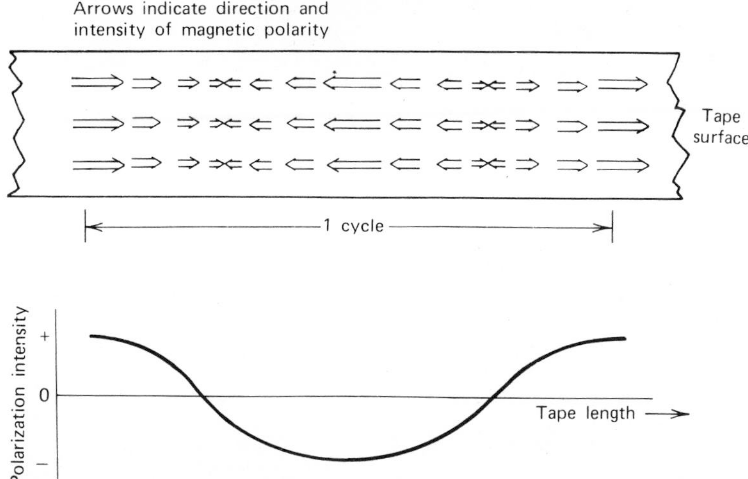

Figure 9.11 Magnetic polarity imposed on recording tape surface.

popular cassette tapes, although convenient and economical, suffer low output and high noise levels because of their narrow width and slow speed.

A discussion of transducers is not complete without further mention of electronic amplifiers. As stated earlier, a loudspeaker requires much more power to drive it than is available from a microphone. The signal from a microphone must also be amplified before it can be strong enough for magnetic tape recording or digital sampling. We thus conclude our presentation of electronic sound equipment with a description of how amplifiers work. Originally, amplifiers were made out of vacuum tubes, but the invention of the transistor has made vacuum tubes virtually obsolete. A transistor may be best thought of as a passageway for electric current. In the middle of this passageway is a gate that controls the amount of current allowed to pass through it. There are many ways a transistor can be designed and configured in an amplifying circuit, but the most common and easily understood method is shown in Fig. 9.12. The transistor is constructed out of three separate layers of silicon or germanium crystal. The layers are each chemically doped with certain impurities that give it the transistor's required properties. It is not necessary here to expound on the theory of solid-state electronics, but it will suffice to say that the transistor in this example is a sandwich of these three doped crystal called the *emitter*, *base*, and *collector*. The current from the voltage source enters the transistor at the emitter. It then flows through the base into the collector and then returns to the voltage source through a resistor. The resistor is included in the circuit so that the signal output may be tapped between it and the transistor without being short-circuited to the voltage source. To vary the output voltage at this point, the transistor must be able to control the amount of current that flows through the circuit. It

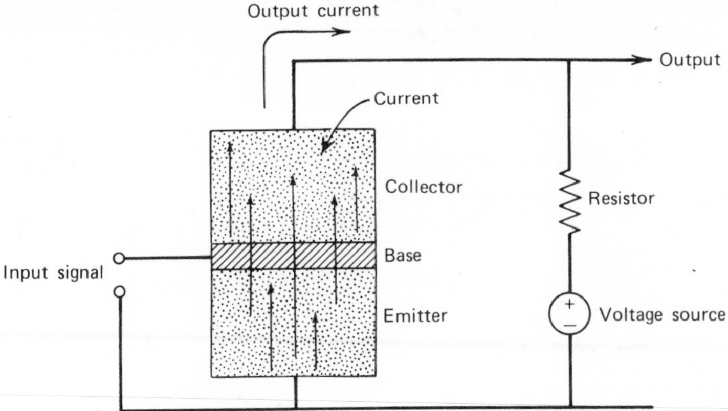

Figure 9.12 A transistor in operation.

thus acts as a variable resistor. The key to the transistor's variable resistance is the interaction of free electrons in the region of the base section where it joins with the emitter and collector. It is the base that acts as a "valve," controlling how much current can flow from the emitter to the collector. The amount of current allowed by the base to pass through is determined by an electric signal entering it. The input signal causes a small, fluctuating current to flow between the base and emitter. This input current is much weaker than the emitter-collector current of the output circuit. But the slight fluctuations of the input base current cause large corresponding variations in the current coming out of the collector. This is how the amplification is achieved.

When several transistors are configured in series or cascade along with other appropriate electronic components to couple and balance them, one has a complete amplifier. The power of the signal input to the amplifier may be only a few microwatts, but the output signal may be many watts. An amplifier of good quality should produce an output having the same waveshape as the input. It should not distort the signal appreciably, and should pass all audible frequencies equally. It also should not introduce unwanted noise to the signal. When excess amounts of current flow through a transistor, the crystals can overheat and burn out. A good amplifier must be designed to disperse the heat in high-power operation to avoid this danger. These are some of the criteria that are most pertinent in amplifier design and of greatest interest to the consumer.

In our discussion of electroacoustics, we have considered some of the ways that natural sounds may be captured, analyzed, and simulated by electronic devices. The presentation has included an introductory explanation of how sounds may be transformed to electric current, amplified, recorded, and reproduced. It has also explored some methods whereby a computer can mathematically imitate the acoustical characteristics of musical instruments and the human voice. An interesting topic remains for analysis, however, It is well known that sound behaves much differently in closed rooms where it can reflect off walls and other surfaces than it does in an open area. Musical performers and organizations have always recognized the importance of the acoustics in the halls where they perform. In fact, it is convincingly argued that throughout musical history, the styles of a particular period and location have been greatly influenced by the characteristics of the halls where music was performed. For example, the light music of Haydn and Mozart was acoustically well-adapted to the smaller orchestras and auditoriums of their times. Conversely, the bombastic music of the late romantic era is much better suited to large, live concert halls.

Consequently, the architectural design of performance halls is a highly sophisticated science. Engineers go to great pains to equip music halls with microphones, amplifiers, and loudspeakers properly placed and balanced for optimum acoustical performance. As anyone who has experienced an outdoor music concern is aware, the sound is dead without a reverberant environment. Conversely, the echo in a large cathedral, although especially suitable to renaissance choral music, would blur a Prokofiev piano concerto beyond recognition.

When one listens to a musical performance, the natural reverberation of the hall is taken for granted, unless the acoustics are unusual or poor or the performance is outdoors. Even recordings of performances retain the reverberation from the environment where the recording was made. It is the specific responsibility of the engineers monitoring such recordings to optimize their reverberation by proper microphone placement and location of sound-absorbing or sound-reflecting bodies in the room. What happens, then, when one is creating music with electronic sound generators? The only way that a performance of electronic or computer music may enjoy the advantage of natural reverberation is if the loudspeakers are located in a live room or concert hall. Yet this is an unrealistic expectation. People do not normally listen to their stereos in large, reverberant rooms. As a result, unless the composer of electronic or computer music introduces artificial reverberation into the recording of it, it will not be present. In this medium, the composition, recording, and performance are all the same event—the reverberation must be programmed into the composition itself. Of course, many compositions call for dry, unreverberated sounds, but normally, some reverberation proves desirable. The advantage of programmable, artificial reverberation is that it is entirely controllable by the composer. He or she may omit it or use it to any degree at any point in the composition.

To understand the behavior of sound in reverberant environments, we may begin by examining the reflection of a sound in a room with smooth walls. Suppose, for example, that a sound source is placed in a rectangular room having the dimensions indicated in Fig. 9.13. Here we see that the

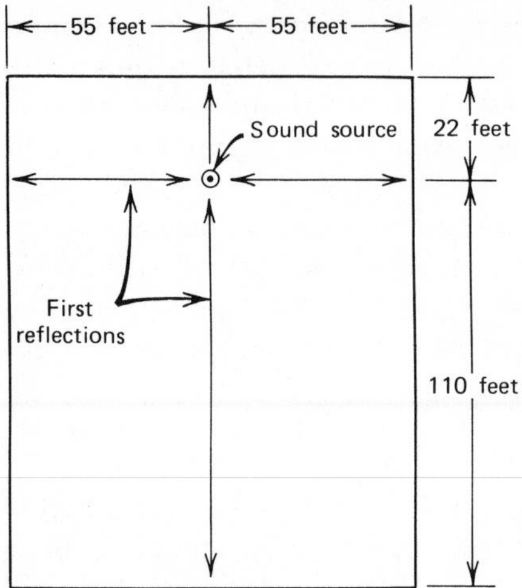

Figure 9.13 Sound reflection in a closed, rectangular room.

sound source is located in such a position that its distance from one wall is 11 feet, its distance from two other walls is each 55 feet, and the distance to the remaining wall is 110 feet. Now suppose that the sound source emits a loud impulse—an abrupt pop or click. Let us also assume that the walls are smooth and are perfectly reflective. The first reflections occur frontally on each of the four wall faces. We predict how the sound impulse returns to its point of origin after reflecting off the walls. Recalling that the speed of sound in air is 1100 feet per second, and noting that the closest wall is 22 feet from the source, the wave front travels 44 feet before it returns. The time that it takes to return is therefore 44 feet/(1100 feet per second) = 0.04 second or 40 milliseconds. Similarly, the time to return from the side-walls is 100 milliseconds, and it takes 200 milliseconds to return from the rear wall. The intensity of the reflected wave decreases with the distance it travels according to an inverse square proportion. The sound and its first reflections are diagrammed in Fig. 9.14. After the sound pulse is reflected

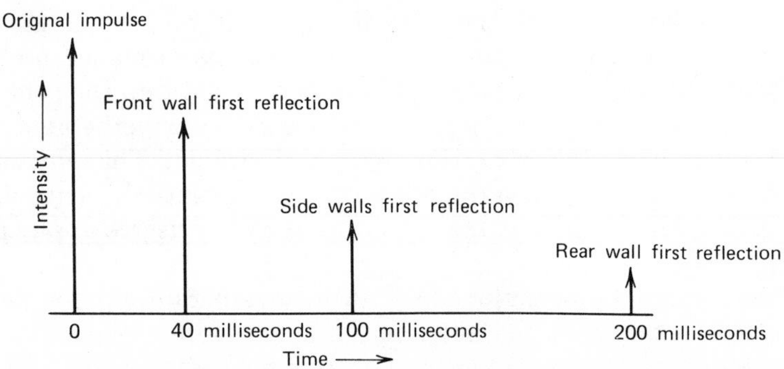

Figure 9.14 First reflections of sound impulse in room shown in Fig. 9.13.

once off each of the walls, it continues to reflect back and forth both frontally and diagonally through the room until it finally dies out. Consequently, a generalized picture of the reverberation of a sound impulse in a room of arbitrary dimensions would look similar to Fig. 9.15.

This picture is complicated when the sound is not an abrupt click represented by a single impulse but is instead a continuous wave form. To construct a diagram of the form of Fig. 9.15 for a continuous sound, one would begin with a picture of the original wave function, then superimpose on it a copy shifted to the right and reduced in magnitude for each reflection that occurs. The summation of the original and all the reduced and shifted copies constitutes the total sound.

If the sound source were an electric organ playing a note that has no rise time or decay time, its envelope would be a rectangular pulse as in Fig. 9.16. However, its envelope in a reverberant environment will be given an onset and decay time. This is because as the reflections begin to occur and build up, they add to and reinforce the original sound which is continuing. When the original sound is turned off, it will take a few milliseconds for the reflections of its residue to die out. The envelope of such a sound coming from the source in the room of Fig. 9.12 would look like the diagram in Fig. 9.17. One notes that the sound does not build up continuously, but does so in steps. Each step corresponds to one reflection or echo. It is important to realize that echo and reverberation are not the same thing. Reverberation is the total effect of the combined echoes, which quickly blend together into a continuous sound.

As one investigates the reverberant characteristics of a particular hall, there are two primary considerations. One is the intensity of the reflected sound. This is determined by the reflectivity of the walls and surrounding surfaces. A highly reflective room will result in strong reverberation that takes a long time to die out. Conversely, a "dead" room, having curtains and uneven surfaces that readily absorb sound, will behave as though the

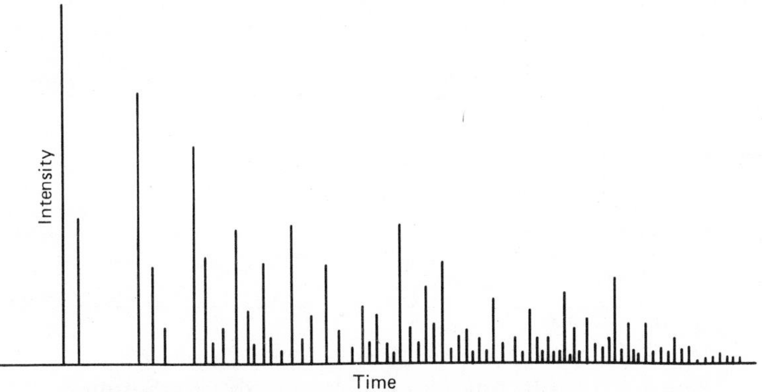

Figure 9.15 Typical indoor sound reverberation.

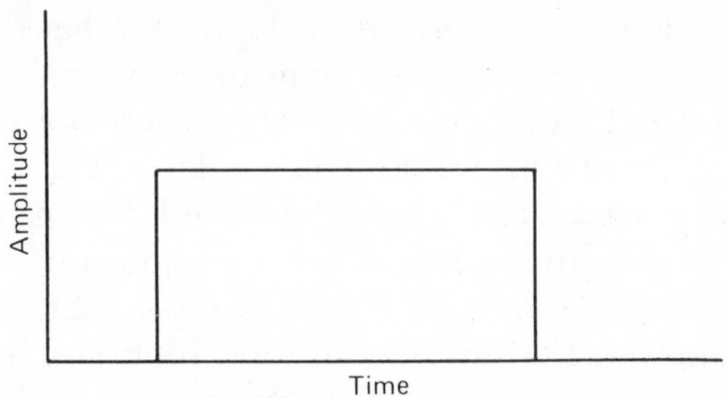

Figure 9.16 Rectangular sound envelope without reverberation.

sound were made in open air. The other factor of interest is the elapsed time between successive echos. This time length is determined by the room's size. Recalling the example cited earlier, the response time for the first echo was 40 milliseconds for a wall 22 feet from the sound source. There is a special significance associated with reverberation times greater than 50 milliseconds. This is because 50 milliseconds is the minimum length of time required by a normal ear to separate sound events in time. If two sound events occur less than 50 milliseconds apart they are perceived as happening simultaneously. But if they are more than 50 milliseconds apart, they are heard separately. Consequently, if the response time of a reverberant environment is not less than 50 milliseconds, the echos will be individually audible. This is normally quite undesirable.

Let us now explore some of the ways to artificially simulate reverberant environments. One conceptually simple method is available with a tape recorder that has separate heads for recording and and playback. With such a tape unit, one may record a signal and simultaneously monitor what is being recorded with the playback head. Since the two heads are placed a few inches apart, there will be a fraction of a second time delay between the recording and the monitoring. By expeditiously feeding the signal monitored by the playback head back into the record head, it will

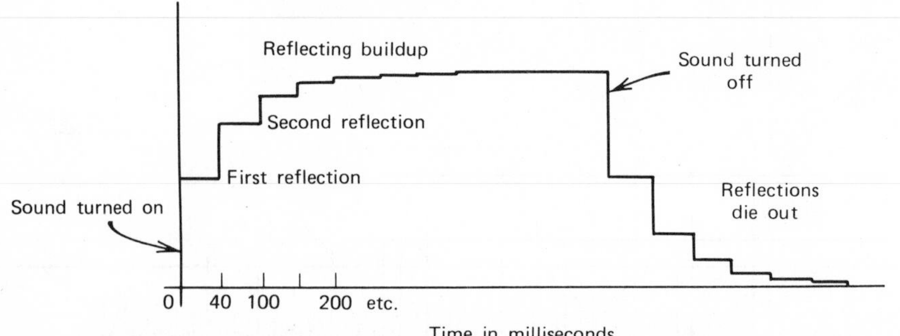

Figure 9.17 Rectangular envelope with reverberation.

be rerecorded on top of itself but with a slight delay. This causes a distinct echo in the recording. The amount of echo can be adjusted by varying the level of the monitored signal being fed back to the record head. The echo time will be determined by the distance between the two tape heads and the tape speed. For example, if the tape speed is 15 inches per second, and the heads are 1½ inches apart, the echo time will be ⅒ second. Unfortunately, this is twice the length of time to be under the "critical" interval of 50 milliseconds. Another disadvantage to this method is that the successive rerecording associated with the feedback loop builds up unwanted noise.

Most recording studios use methods of artificial reverberation that are much superior to tape-recorder feedback. A typical reverberator that is expensive, but yields very satisfactory results is comprized of two transducers and a large, metal plate. The first transducer produces sound at one location on the plate. The sound may then travel down the plate's surface to where it is picked up by the other transducer. The sound reflects back and forth off the edges of the plate, causing the desired reverberation.

We may now turn our attention to the simulation of reverberation with a digital computer. Suppose, for our example, that the sampling rate is 30,000 per second, or 30 samples per millisecond. We design our reverberator so that the time between successive echos is 30 milliseconds. The "reflected" signal is 25% of the original in amplitude. The delay time, then, corresponds to $30 \times 30 = 900$ samples. For a delay unit, we use a buffer memory of 900 words. Our strategy is diagrammed in Fig. 9.18. In this simple reverberation system, the samples of the input signal are input to an adder, where they are combined with the output from the delay unit. Initially the delay unit is empty—for example, its contents are all set to zero. Thus, as the first 900 samples pass through the system, they are left unchanged. But as the 901st sample comes in, it will be added to 25% of sample #1 that is now coming out of the delay unit. The 902nd output sample is likewise a sum of the original 902nd sample plus 25% of the 2nd sample. The process continues through to sample #1801. At this point, the

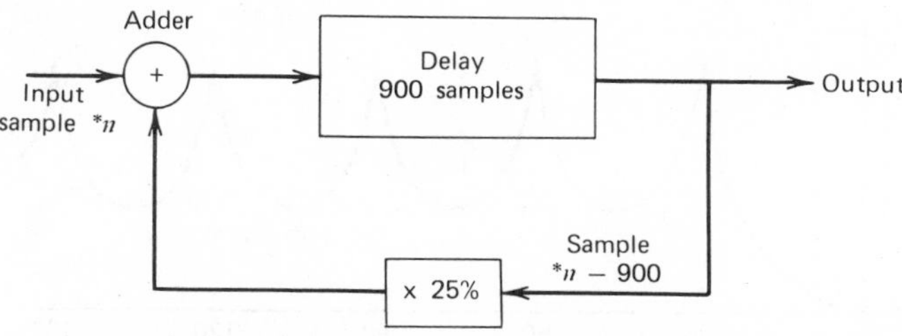

Figure 9.18 Comb filter reverberator.

delay unit is outputting the modified 901st sample. The output sample is #1801 plus 25% of sample #901, plus 5% of the first sample. Generally speaking, the output of the nth sample will be expressed by the formula:

$$\text{output } \#n = S_n + \tfrac{1}{4} S_{n-900} + \tfrac{1}{16} S_{n-1800} + \tfrac{1}{64} S_{n-2700} + \cdots$$

In this equation, S_n represents the original nth sample. If the subscript $n - 900$, $n - 1800$, $n - 2700$, . . . is less than zero, that signifies the number of samples thus far input to the unit is not yet equal to the number required for computation of that reverberation cycle, and the term is taken to be zero.

One can readily see that this digital reverberator is mathematically simulating an "ideal" physical reverberation chamber. However, the term "ideal" is used here in a mathematical sense rather than an aesthetic one. In fact, its very "ideal" behavior will render it some undesriable characteristics as we may presently examine. The numbers of 25% gain and 900 samples delay time were arbitrarily chosen and could easily be replaced by other parameters. But regardless of which values are chosen for the feedback gain and delay interval, this kind of a reverberator has a grave drawback. In fact, an ideal physical reverberator would also have the same problem. The fact that the delay time between each echo is identically the same each time causes the reverberator to resonate. If the signal input to the unit is periodic, having any frequency components that are multiples of the reverberator's fundamental resonant frequency, those components will be greatly amplified at the exclusion of other frequencies. The resonant frequencies are determined by the delay time. For example, if the delay time is $\frac{1}{30}$ second the resonant frequencies will be 30, 60, 90, 120, . . . cycles per second. The reason for this resonance is that as signals of these frequencies are fed back through the delay unit and stacked on top of each other, they reinforce each other and accumulate. Signals of other frequencies, however, will not reinforce and accumulate, but will diffuse. The frequency response of such a reverberator is shown in Fig. 9.19. Such a system is often called a "comb filter" for obvious reasons.

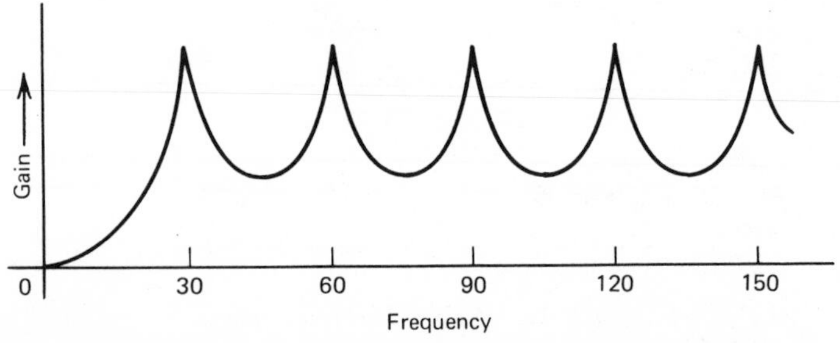

Figure 9.19 Frequency response of comb filter.

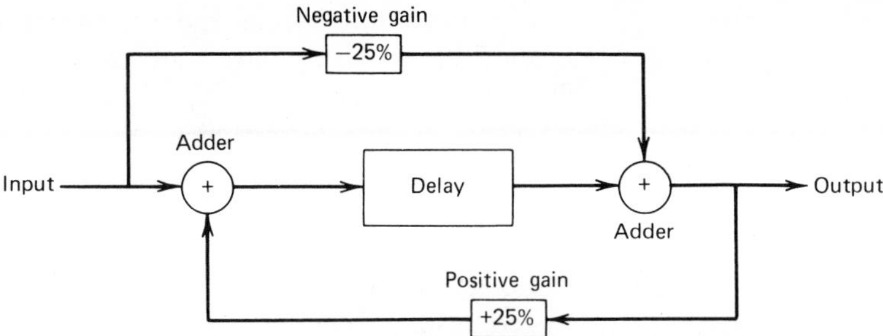

Figure 9.20 Reverberator modified for flat frequency response.

The type of room that this reverberator is actually simulating would be perfectly cubical and have no sound-reflecting objects within it. Such a room would resonate in much the same way as a long, closed pipe. A realistic reverberant room will not resonate perfectly at a single set of harmonics. Nevertheless, its frequency response will not be perfectly flat, either. One may argue that a reverberant environment that emphasizes different frequencies unequally is acoustically undesirable. On the other hand, a reverberation simulator may be considered more "natural" if it models the resonant characteristic of an actual room. Be that as it may, it is possible to construct a digital system that will function similarly to the one described above, but whose frequency response will be perfectly flat. Figure 9.20 shows how the reverberator of Fig. 9.18 may be modified so that it will not resonate, but will transmit all frequencies equally.

As in the preceding example, the value of the feedback gain was arbitrarily chosen to be 25%, but could be any positive number less than 1. In this modified system, a reduced version of the signal is subtracted from the delayed portion. This negative part cancels the positive feedback, but is separated from it by the delay. Because of the delay, only the periodic portion of the signal is affected by the cancellation, and the reverberation still takes effect.

It should be emphasized that when a computer is used to simulate a reverberation chamber, it is only approximating its behavior. This is true of any artificial simulation of a natural event. It is generally impractical if not impossible to account for all the variables of a system when one formulates its mathematical description. One therefore chooses the parameters of most interest and constructs his or her model around them. Although the model's behavior is functionally similar to the actual event, it is not an exact duplication of it. In many applications of computer simulation, only a few out of many characteristics need to be modeled and studied. For example, if one were trying to simulate a violin performance, the simulator would not necessarily incorporate the extraneous sounds of the musician turning the page, shifting in the chair, or coughing. The difference between the simulation of a sound and the reproduction of the sound is that the simulation selects only a certain set of the original sound's characteristics, models them mathematically, and then creates a new sound based on the model. The model is free to be altered or modified in any way. Conversely, a phonograph or tape recording is merely a transmission of the original sound delayed in time.

Computer simulation of sound sources is very new and experimental. Computers have, nevertheless, been used for nearly three decades in science, industry, and technology to simulate molecular behavior, planetary motion, bacteria reproduction, stock prices, aircraft dynamics, electric circuits, and thousands of other things. Consequently, their introduction to the musical scene is but a new application of an already well-developed science.

REFERENCES

The Phonograph and Sound Recording after One Hundred Years," *Journal of the Audio Engineering Society—Centennial Issue* **25**(10–11) (1977).

Blesser, B. A., K. Baeder, & R. Zaorski, " A Real-Time Digital Computer for Simulating Audio Systems," *Journal of the Audio Engineering Society* **23**(10), 698–707 (1975).

Chowning, John M., "The Simulation of Moving Sound Sources," *Computer Music Journal* **1**(3), 48–52 (1977).

Markel, J. D. & A. H. Gray, Jr., *Linear Prediction of Speech*, Springer-Verlag, 1976.

Maxfield, J. P. & H. C. Harrison, "Method of High Quality Recording and Reproducing of Music and Speech Based on Telephone Research," *Journal of the Audio Engineering Society* **26,** 327–342 (1978).

Olson, Harry F., *Music, Physics, and Engineering*, Dover, 1967.

Olson, Harry F., *Modern Sound Reproduction*, Robert E. Kreiger Publishing Co., 1979.

Pain, H. J., *The Physics of Vibration and Waves*, Wiley, 1968.

Roederer, Juan G., *Introduction to the Physics and Psychophysics of Music*, Springer-Verlag, 1975.

Sato, N. "PCM recorder—A New Type of Audio Magnetic Tape Recorder," *Journal of the Audio Engineering Society* **21**, 542–548 (1973).

Stephens, R. W. B., & A. E. Bate, *Acoustics and Vibrational Physics*, Arnold, 1960.

10

SCALES AND TONALITY

The introduction of computer music as a new art form has opened avenues of creative possibilities that composers have never before seen. As this book has emphasized, a computer may be employed as a tremendously versatile musical instrument. Computers have been compared and contrasted with conventional instruments, thereby revealing some of their special aspects and distinctions. The juxtaposition of the computer with a piano or organ is especially appropriate in this chapter to introduce the topic of musical scales and tonality.

A keyboard divides an octave into 12 intervals. Each note is set to a specific pitch at the time the instrument is tuned. Consequently, keyboard music is generally restricted to the 12-note scale that the keyboard defines. The computer, by contrast, has no such restriction. A computer may, of course, be optionally interfaced with a keyboard so it can be played like an organ. Yet as one programs a computer to synthesize musical tones, their pitches may be set to any arbitrary value with tremendous precision. A computer music composition consequently does not need to adhere to the confines of any prescribed tonal system. The intervals, scales, and harmonic relationships on a composition for a computer may be defined in any imaginable way at the time of composition.

A composer may write a tonal piece that strictly conforms to the rules of counterpoint and may specify pitches to the exact intervals of the conventional 12-note tempered scale. He or she may, on the other hand, compose in the mode of the avant-garde and generate tones with pitches selected at random or even aperiodic sounds having no tonality. Ironically, the "chance" music that has enjoyed such a rise in the last decades is becoming a form and tradition in its own right, even though it was introduced as a break from form and tradition. The composer of contemporary music is faced with an interesting paradox: the more he or she conforms to the norms and rules established by tradition, the more restricted the originality of the work will be. This is not to say that great music cannot be traditionalistic! The well-loved masterpieces of Brahms and Rachmaninov, for example, were the culmination of an established musical form rather than the innovation of a new one. Nevertheless, an art must continuously redefine itself to progress. Consequently, rules and traditions will continue to break down, as they have done throughout musical history. But this breakdown, although necessary, poses a real threat to an art's survival. The concept of entropy in information theory referred to in Chapter 5, applies to the arts as well as statistics and communication. This is to say that if a musical composition becomes entirely an unstructured sequence of random, sonoral events, it is by definition an agglomeration of noise with no basis of communication.

An artist is thus obliged to replenish art with some form of logic and organization if it is to endure. When he or she obviates one artistic pattern, it must be supplanted with another. This way the art may evolve without disintegrating. As a computer music composer faces the possibility of arbitrarily defining the harmony, scales, and tonality of the composition, he or she is also faced with the responsibility of inventing some form of logic for their definition. To intelligently and artistically formulate the rules that will be used for the selection of pitches and intervals, he or she should well understand the natural harmonic foundation of the traditional 12-tone system, even if not planning to strictly conform to it. The reason for this becomes clear as we study 12-tone harmony.

The purpose of this chapter is to examine the mathematical roots of the 12-note scale. We find this scale to be the outgrowth of a natural harmonic system that was built on pitch intervals derived from simple numerical ratios. The tonal system formed from these pure ratios though, cannot be configured into practical musical instruments in different keys. The equally tempered scale was invented as a compromise between the purity of the natural scale and the physical limitations of these instruments. The reason for this disparity is that the intervals of a justly intoned scale are not exactly equal. As a result, a scale tuned to the key of C would be out of tune in any other key. However, if the octave is divided into 12 equal steps, the result is a close approximation of a just scale, and may accommodate any key.

The essential difference between consonant and dissonant intervals lies in the ratios of their pitches. The term "dissonance" describes a subjective quality that depends on the context of the musical passage where it is found, as well as the preference of a listener. However, as a general rule, dissonant intervals arise from complex harmonic ratios whereas the simplest ratios define the most consonant intervals. A prime, being the perfect consonance, has a ratio of 1:1. The ratio of the octave is 2:1. The ratio of 3:1 forms a perfect twelfth, and 4:1 is two octaves. A 5:1 ratio forms an interval of two octaves plus a major third. One can readily see that the intervals of perfect fifth and major third within an octave are formed from the pitch ratios of 3:2 and 5:4. The inversions of these intervals—namely the perfect fourth and minor sixth, are formed from the

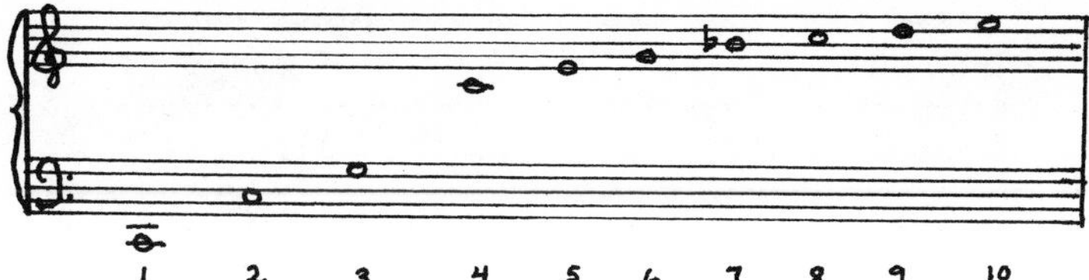

Figure 10.1 Note representation of tone's harmonics.

inverse of these ratios. A perfect fourth has a ratio of 4:3 whereas a minor sixth is 8:5.

The reason for the "pleasantness" of consonant intervals is that one note is a harmonic of the other. As discussed in Chapter 5, tones of different pitches produce sum and difference tones of different pitches when sounded together. These difference tones, or beats, add to the complexity of the sound, and to its dissonance if they are not harmonically related to the original tones. The relationship between intervals and their harmonic ratios can be best seen by plotting them on a musical staff as in Fig. 10.1. As the intervals with the simplest harmonic ratios are collected and arranged in ascending order within an octave, the just scale is formulated. It is listed in Fig. 10.2.

In connection with this, we may also look at Fig. 10.3 as it displays the frequency ratios of adjacent tones in a major scale. One may quickly notice from examination of these charts that if the C scale is tuned according to these ratios, the intervals of that scale will be harmonically in tune. But when the composer wants to use the same instrument to play in another key, the scale will have to be retuned for that key. Of course, this cannot be done for each key modulation in a musical performance! Consequently, about three centuries ago musicians decided to compromise the just scale for equal temperament. The tempered scale divides the octave into 12 intervals whose pitch ratios are exactly equal. Since the octave interval ratio is 2:1, one-twelfth that interval is the twelfth root of 2, or 2 to the $\frac{1}{12}$ power. Symbolically, this is represented as $\sqrt[12]{2}$ or $2^{1/12}$. The chart in Fig. 10.4 displays the frequency ratios of the equally tempered scale and compares them to their justly intoned counterparts. One can see from this table that the intervals of fourth and fifth in the tempered scale are almost exactly equal to their corresponding intervals in the just scale. This is because $2^{7/12}$ is almost exactly equal to $\frac{3}{2}$. As a result, the difference in intonation between a perfectly tuned fifth and a tempered fifth is so slight that it is barely perceptible. But the intervals of major and minor third, as well as their inversions minor and major sixth, are mistuned enough in the tempered scale from the harmonic ratios of the just intonation that the difference is conspicuous. If one listens alternately to these just and tempered intervals, he or she immediately perceives that the just intervals

Interval	Pitch Ratio
Unison	1:1
Semitone	16:15 = 1.066667
Minor step	10:9 = 1.111111
Major step	9:8 = 1.125000
Minor third	6:5 = 1.200000
Major third	5:4 = 1.250000
Perfect fourth	4:3 = 1.333333
Augmented fourth	45:32 = 1.406250
Diminished fifth	64:45 = 1.422222
Perfect fifth	3:2 = 1.500000
Minor sixth	8:5 = 1.600000
Major sixth	5:3 = 1.666667
Harmonic seventh	7:4 = 1.750000
Grave seventh	16:9 = 1.777778
Minor seventh	9:5 = 1.800000
Major seventh	15:8 = 1.875000
Octave	2:1

Figure 10.2 Pitch ratios in just scale.

sound noticeably more pure. The mistuning of the tempered scale is mostly manifested on an organ where the keys are fixed in pitch and the tone is sustained. It is less conspicuous on a piano, whose tones decay rapidly after the string is struck. Of course, vocal and string tones are not fixed in pitch, and they fluctuate enough that if their sounding pitch were precisely measured on any note, it would be difficult to determine if any interval were exactly just or tempered. Many musicians with sensitive ears have nevertheless contended that singers trained on the piano sing mistuned "tempered" thirds and sixths.

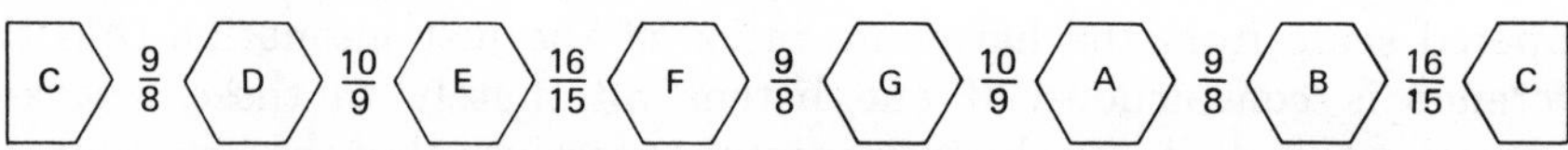

Figure 10.3 Pitch ratios in step intervals of just scale.

Interval	Pitch Ratio	Deviation from Just Scale
Prime	1	0
Semitone	$2^{1/12}$ = 1.059463	−0.007204
Whole step	$2^{2/12}$ = 1.122462	From minor +0.011351
		From major −0.002538
Minor third	$2^{3/12}$ = 1.189207	−0.010793
Major third	$2^{4/12}$ = 1.259921	+0.009921
Perfect fourth	$2^{5/12}$ = 1.334840	+0.001507
Tritone	$2^{6/12}$ = 1.4.4214	From augmented fourth +0.007964
		From diminished fifth −0.008008
Perfect fifth	$2^{7/12}$ = 1.498307	−0.001693
Minor sixth	$2^{8/12}$ = 1.597401	−0.012599
Major sixth	$2^{9/12}$ = 1.681793	+0.015216
Minor seventh	$2^{10/12}$ = 1.781797	From harmonic +0.031797
		From grave +0.004019
		From minor −0.018203
Major seventh	$2^{11/12}$ = 1.887749	+0.012749
Octave	2	0

Figure 10.4 Pitch ratios in tempered scale.

It is fairly safe to assert that if it were practical to build an organ with 12 different keyboards—one of them justly tuned to each note of the scale—the resulting intonation would be a considerable improvement over one single, tempered scale. Unfortunately, the impracticalities of such an instrument prohibit its construction for other than experimental purposes. With this in mind, we now return our attention to the computer. One may freely compose music for the computer as an instrument with reference to the 12-tone system, yet he or she does not need to perform on it with a keyboard. The pitches that a computer is programmed to synthesize are ultimately indicated to the machine by the numerical value of their frequencies in cycles per second. As a result, equal temperament is not necessary. Actually, if one wants to interface a computer to a keyboard for use in real time like an electronic synthesizer, convenience may dictate that a tempered scale be used. For this discussion, we are assuming that all the notes of a particular composition are to be programmed in advance so that each pitch may be individually indicated by its numerical value.

We may illustrate this principle with an example. To show how the notes of a composition can be programmed according to just intonation, we will suppose that our computer is to "perform" a rendition of Bach's Chorale #2, "Ich Dank dir, Lieber Herre." For this demonstration, we will not attempt to formulate an entire computer program to generate the tones, but will merely decide what exact pitches should be used for each note. If we were doing this according to the tempered scale, the task would be trivially simple. It would merely require looking up each pitch in a table. But in the just scale, the intervals will change with each modulation, and must consequently be calculated separately. In spite of the extra calculation, the process can be done for several bars in a few minutes with a hand calculator.

The opening measures of the chorale are represented in Fig. 10.5. The chorale is in the key of A major and the opening chord is an A major triad. The soprano note is appropriately tuned to A-440. The bass tone, an octave lower, is then 220 cycles per second. The alto note E is a perfect fifth above A-220, and is $220 \times 3/2 = 330$ cycles per second. The tenor note C# is a major third, having the interval ratio of $5/4$. Its pitch is thus $220 \times 5/4 = 275$ cycles per second. In the bass voice, we calculate the pitch of the passing tone G# as a major seventh with ratio $15/8$ above the unsounded root A-110. It is thus 96.25 cycles per second.

In the second measure, the root of the first triad F# - A - C# is the sixth of the A scale. So its pitch is $5/3 \times 110 = 183.33$ cycles per second. The alto F#, being one octave higher, is 366.7 cycles per second. The tenor C# and soprano A are still 275 and 440 cycles per second. The second chord is back to the tonic in the first inversion with the same pitches as the first chord except for the bass tone which is an octave beneath the tenor at $1/2 \times 275 = 137.5$ cycles per second. The tenor passing tone B is a major second above A-220, being that pitch times $9.8 = 247.5$ cycles per second. In the third

Figure 10.5 Chorale #2—J. S. Bach.

beat, the D in the bass is the root of a subdominant triad. Its pitch relative to A is 110 × $\frac{4}{3}$ = 146.67 cycles per second. The tenor and soprano A's remain at 220 and 440 cycles per second, and although the F# is now a third in D major, its pitch has not yet changed. The passing tone G# could be arbitrarily calculated as an augmented fourth or diminished fifth of D or even as a sixth of the B in the next chord. But being a nonharmonic tone, it does not matter very much, so we choose the augmented fourth of D which is $\frac{45}{32}$ × 146.67 = 206.25 cycles per second.

Beginning in the fourth beat of this measure, the chorale modulates to E minor. Although the fourth beat is in B major first inversion, it is nonetheless the dominant of E to which it is leading in the following bar. The pitch of E is 165 cycles per second (A-110 × $\frac{3}{2}$), and the soprano above it is 165 × 3 = 495 cycles per second. We calculate the D# and F#, with reference to the unsounded root B-123.75 two octaves below. The D# is 123.75 × $\frac{5}{4}$ = 154.69 cycles per second, and the F#'s are 185.63 and 371.25 cycles per second respectively. This may seem disconcerting considering that the alto F# was 366.67 cycles per second in the previous beat. But with the change of tonality, the fractional rise in pitch does not sound unnatural. Neither tone clashes with its neighbor, because they are not sounded simultaneously. To calculate the E minor triads in the next measure, we use the same method as before but with E-165 as a base rather than A-110. The B and G# are thus 247.5 and 2 × 165 × $\frac{6}{5}$ = 396 cycles per second. The B major triad in the second beat has the same pitches as the fourth beat of the previous measure with the voices and octaves interchanged. The pitches of the third beat with the fermata are likewise the same as the first beat with the G# and Bass E an octave lower. The G# in the fourth beat functions both as the major third of the E triad and the leading tone to A in the next chord. Either way it is considered, its pitch is calculated as 165 × $\frac{5}{2}$ or 110 × $\frac{15}{4}$ = 412.5 cycles per second.

With the beginning of the next measure, we are back to A-220, and continue the procedure. Since all the chords in this measure as well as the following one are the same as the chords already calculated, it is unnecessary to recalculate them. We summarize our results by displaying the score of these bars again with the pitches entered by each note in Fig. 10.6.

One may well question the value of spending time computing pitches for seventeenth-century music to be performed on a computer in just intonation. Indeed, this text does not intend to advocate the computer as a substitute for choirs, harpsichords, pianos, or orchestras. The example was presented to demonstrate the mathematical foundation of traditional harmony. When one performs classical music on conventional instruments, these relationships are transparent because the instrument is already tuned before the performance. Moreover, it is tuned by ear rather than by calculator, so the performer does not need to be concerned with the pitches' numerical values. The only concern is that they *sound* in tune.

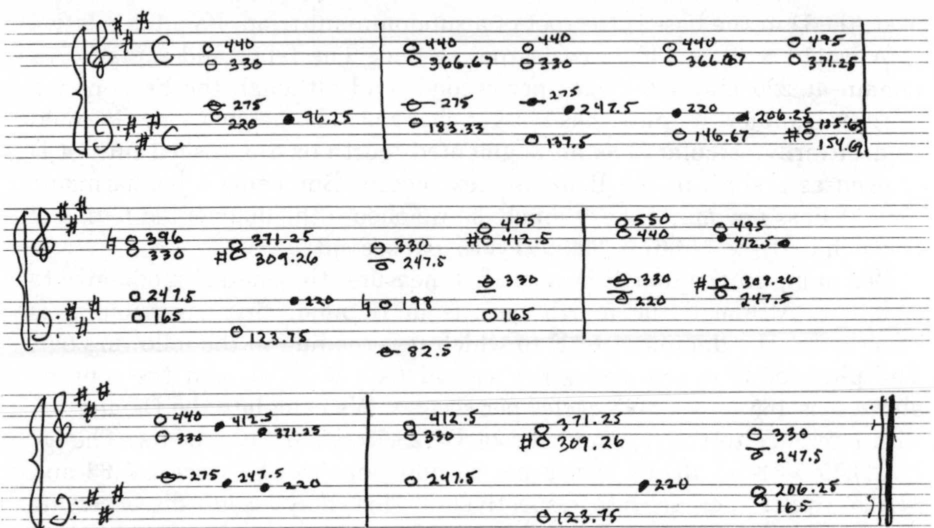

Figure 10.6 Calculated pitches of chorale notes.

The computer, however, must be given a number for every pitch, and the numbers do not need to correspond to any known scale. For the same reason that composers study the counterpoint of Palestrina and the harmony of Mozart and Beethoven, even though they do not themselves compose in those styles, a computer programmer-composer should understand the principles of harmony from a mathematical viewpoint.

As an exercise, a student could choose passages from classical and romantic compositions and perform a harmonic analysis of them as would be done in a music theory course. In addition to indicating the chord's tonality, inversion, and degree of the scale, he or she can calculate each note's pitch in just intonation as we did with the Bach chorale. The procedure would be straightforward for eighteenth-century music, but considerably more complex for nineteenth-century composition. For twentieth-century music, it would be impossible in many cases. The reason for this is that music has undergone a trend toward atonality through the years. The early composers strictly adhered to rules imposed by the harmonic relationships of the major and minor scales, even though the equally tempered tuning of these scales deviated slightly from that harmony. But as time progressed into the late romantic and impressionistic periods of music, composers began to experiment more and more with chromatic, whole-tone, and pentatonic scales. They introduced these as well as other entities that emanate from the equal intervals of the tempered 12-tone system rather than from simple harmonic ratios. The excerpt from Debussy's "Pour le Piano" in Fig. 10.7 illustrates an interesting interposition of tonality and atonality as a series of inverted seventh chords descend in parallel motion. The notes are diatonic in E, but as the chords progress, the tonal center is quite unapparent. Another example by Ravel in Fig. 10.8 employs triadic harmony in parallel motion. Unlike the Debussy passage, the progressions do not stay in any key and their parallel motion is strict. The tonality thus shifts with each chord and seems to float. The harmony of any individual chord may be figured for only that chord but not with relationship to its neighbors.

In the early part of the twentieth century, the movement toward atonality took a major stride with the introduction of serial music. Arnold Shöenberg was particularly interested in this mode and from it invented the 12-tone row. The objective of this form of music is to abolish tonality by employing the 12 tones of the chromatic scale with perfect equality. The notes of the composition are arranged so that none of them appear any more or any fewer times than the other notes, and the appearance of any tonal center is obscured. The 12-tone row is generated by arranging the 12 notes of the scale in an arbitrary sequence and numbering them from 1 to 12. Then, as the composition progresses, the notes must appear in the order they were numbered. For the sake of variety, they may appear in reverse order, they may be inverted, and the rows may overlap. But in

Figure 10.7 Sarabande from Claude Debussy, *Pour le Piano*.

Figure 10.8 *Sonatine for piano,* Maurice Ravel.

the sequence of any one row, every tone must be used exactly once, although one tone may be held over several beats. Figure 10.9 is an example of a 12-tone row and a few bars which it can generate. The reader may perform it at his or her own risk, but for whatever it may be lacking in aesthetic merit, it serves to illustrate the mechanics of the technique.

The evolution of music composition as it has transpired from the time of Bach to the present day has followed an intriguing path. As we have shown, the 12-note scale was a natural, mathematical consequence of simple, harmonic relationships. But as time has progressed, the correlation between the use of the scale and the tonal harmony from which it was born has gradually disintegrated. Finally, the 12-tone row abolishes the relationship altogether. Indeed, one may inquire why the octave need be divided into 12 equal intervals and not some other number. In the mode of atonality, a chromatic scale of 10, 11, 13, or 20 notes per octave may have just as logical a base as the familiar 12-note scale. These other scales would not approximate the harmonically based just scale, but if the 12-

Figure 10.9 Example of twelve-tone row.

note tempered scale is not used harmonically, it makes no practical difference! As a satire of serial music, this author wrote and recorded a composition based on a 13-tone row. The recording was made with a synthesizer and a keyboard tuned so that each octave was divided into 13 equal steps. Although the result of the experiment sounded somewhat comical and aesthetically gross, it dramatized the possibility of alternatives to the 12-tone system.

The idea and employment of scales having an arbitrary number of nonharmonic intervals is the logical extension of atonal serial music. Yet as music composition is extricated from the necessity of a fixed scale, as it is with computer music, one may just as well extend the logic in the reverse direction and return to mathematical harmony without the interjection of any musical scale. One could write a composition with one or a series of tonal centers specified in terms of their pitches given in cycles per second. Then all the notes would be built on these centers by a harmonic pitch ratio rather than their position on a scale. We may well imagine a four-part chorale whose score might appear something like Fig. 10.10. The

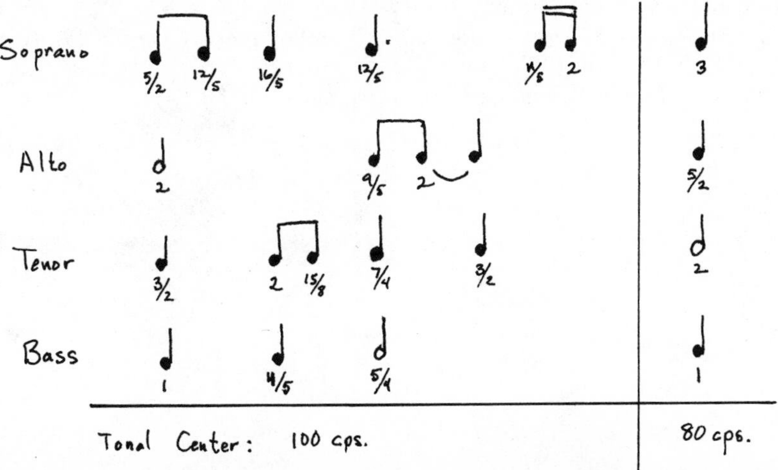

Figure 10.10 Alternate representation of four-part chorale.

indication of note pitches in this manner would be easier to program on the computer, but much more difficult to "hear in one's head" without a lot of practice.

One must not infer from this discussion that an artist experimenting with computers and music would have an obligation to follow techniques illustrated in this or any other text, or to adhere to the rules of harmonic or serial music. The "rules" of any art are not laws; nor are they moral imperatives. They are merely the common denominators of artistic techniques that have already been proven in the past. Usually, they serve more as pedagogical devices than systems of procedure. They may freely be broken as long as they are broken intelligently and circumspectly. The analysis of scales and intonation in this chapter follows the development of a 12-tone system from strict harmony to serial atonality. Each system has its own set of canons. Although a composer need not conform to the rules, he or she is still wise to understand them. The adherance to a uniform scale has been imposed primarily by the mechanical limitations of conventional musical instruments. Since these limitations do not exist in computer music, the topic of new, alternative tonal systems is particularly interesting to this medium.

REFERENCES

Barbour, James M., *Tuning & Temperament, A Historical Survey*, Michigan State College Press, 1951.

Fokker, Adriaan D., *Just Intonation and the Combination of Harmonic Diatonic Melodic Groups*, M. Nijhoff, 1949.

Graham, George, *Tonality and Musical Structure*, Praeger, 1970.

Link, John W., *The Mathematics of Music*, Gateway Press, 1977.

Piston, Walter, *Harmony*, 3rd ed., Norton, 1962.

Regener, Eric, *Pitch Notation and Equal Temperament: A Formal Study*, Occasional Papers No. 6, 1973, University of California Press.

Winckel, Fritz, *Music, Sound, and Sensation*, Dover, 1967.

11

COMPOSITION WITH THE COMPUTER

Mozart once composed music with a pair of dice. Presumably he used the dice to select notes at random from the scale and then constructed a melody and its supporting harmony from that selection. He might also have used a random number pattern in composing the rhythm. Of course, this was done as a novelty and never became a common practice in music composition in that time. In the past 30 years, however, a growing number of composers have taken up an interest in what they call "stochastic music"; that is, music composed from random numbers. This interest in random music has grown largely as a philosophical outgrowth of the avant-garde movement, and its practice is facilitated by the introduction of the digital computer to the arts. Although computer music composition began essentially as a vehicle for assembling note patterns from random processes, in the last few years composition with the computer has broadened to include a wide base of techniques that attempt to embody modern analytical and compositional procedures. It is very tempting to overdramatize the power of the computer in composing music, however. The computer is an awesome machine, and its capabilities can easily be exaggerated if one does not understand how it operates. It is particularly easy and dramatic to envision the computer as an electronic supermind capable of creating art. Yet to claim that a computer has actually composed music is little different than asserting that Mozart's dice composed music. One is at pain to attribute dice with creative intelligence!

A computer system is, of course, many orders of magnitude more complex and powerful than a pair of dice. But as a computer system is employed in music composition; it is actually doing no more than producing number patterns and then translating those patterns into sequences of sonic events according to a fixed set of rules defined by the computer programmer. When Mozart played with his dice, he did not have a computer to help him transmute the random numbers to a written score. Yet one may reasonably suppose that he invented a systemized procedure and used it as a framework to obtain the notes of his composition from the numbers on the dice. Whatever procedure he did use might well have been coded in the language of a computer program had computers existed in his time.

In contrast with the previous chapters, this one does not discuss the computer as a musical instrument or a tool of sound synthesis. The bulk of this text has described how a computer can be programmed to generate musical sounds and simulate natural instruments. Computer music is not limited to this application. Many works of music have been composed with a computer and then performed instrumentally by professional musicians. This book does not attempt to debate whether this kind of music is composed by the computer or by the programmers. Instead, it seeks to explain the computer's role in music composition and illustrate some simple ways whereby algorithms are used to generate musical patterns from number sequences and data structures.

Computer music composition has been pioneered largely by Lejaren Hiller and Leonard Isaacson at the University of Illinois. Their work, described in a 1959 book called *Experimental Music*, resulted in two significant compositions called *Illiac Suite for String Quartet*, and *Computer Cantata*. The techniques of composition involved in these early works focus on the generation of note sequences from random number patterns similar to Mozart's dice game. The method of music composition from random or quasi-random processes has also been widely developed and exploited by Iannis Xenakis of Paris, France. Xenakis uses the term "stochastic music" and describes his techniques and philosophy in a monograph that is translated into English called *Formalized Music*. Although Xenakis uses random numbers to generate musical sound structures, he generally employs various mathematical probability distributions and other "rules" to fit the final sonic structure into certain stylistic constraints. In the past two decades many other composers have begun and continued with experiments in music composed with random numbers and have utilized the computer as a central tool in their work.

This chapter does not attempt to survey the works of these composers, but since the development of computer composition began principally with random note patterns, we begin the discussion with a general description of some fundamental ways that random number sequences are used to generate musical structures. One very simple procedure to generate a note sequence is to number all the notes of the scale, then randomly select the numbers. Obviously, a melody generated like this is not very interesting to most people. As emphasized in Chapter 5, a work of art requires some repetition and redundancy as well as variety in its form. Only a very trivial computer program is needed to generate a sequence of purely random or pseudorandom numbers. The actual programming effort goes into shaping the random number sequence into a particular probability distribution, and restricting the possible choices to certain sets, to meet special criteria. To illustrate this idea, let us propose a simple strategy to compose a melody whose notes are not taken entirely at random, nor chosen deterministically. To begin with, we restrict the notes to lie within the range from middle C to the C two octaves higher. The first note is the C in the middle of the range. Thereafter, each note in the sequence is chosen from a number taken at random between −12 and +12. This number determines the interval of the new note from the previous note. For example, +1 corresponds to a half step up, −3 is a minor third down, and +7 is a perfect fifth up. If a note falls outside the two octave range, it is automatically transposed up or down one octave to place it within the range. Thus the number sequence 2, 4, −3, −8, −6, 1, −9, 3 produces the melody shown in Fig. 11.1. Now we stipulate that certain intervals are selected with preference to other intervals. We construct a table listing each interval with a value representing the probability or desired frequency of its choice. In Fig. 11.2 we give preference to short and consonant intervals over longer and dissonant intervals. This probability distribution function is more easily visualized by a graph as in Fig. 11.3. As with all probability distributions, the sum of all the values must equal 100%.

How, then, does one get a number sequence whose members occur with the probabilities, hence relative frequencies specified by the table? One simple way is to use a device (or instruction of a computer program) that chooses numbers between 1 and 100 purely at random. The probability of any one selection must be no greater or less than any other selection. The next step is to devise a function that maps the domain of numbers between 1 and 100 into the desired distribution. This is quite easily accomplished with the chart of Fig. 11.4.

One can readily see that this is merely a slight modification of the table in Fig. 11.2. The only difference is that the random variable is now chosen from the domain 1 to 100 with the indicated mapping into the range of −12 to +12. To show how our intervals are chosen with the desired weighting factor, consider the interval of + perfect fifth. It is called by any of the numbers 82, 83, 84, 85, 86, 87, or 88. This represents seven choices out of the possible 100, so this interval is therefore selected with a probability of 7%.

This probability distribution tailors a random sequence of notes so that some intervals are chosen with varying degrees of preference over other intervals. But this is a long way from shaping the melody into something that could be characterized as a style. As we work to further constrain the possible choice of notes to fit into a stylistic pattern, we still want to retain a range within which the random choices may vary. The probability dis-

Figure 11.1 Melody produced by random number sequence.

Interval Number	Relationship	Probability of Selection
−12	− Octave	3%
−11	− Major seventh	1%
−10	− Minor seventh	2%
−9	− Major sixth	3%
−8	− Minor sixth	3%
−7	− Perfect fifth	7%
−6	− Tritone	1%
−5	− Perfect fourth	6%
−4	− Major third	4%
−3	− Minor third	5%
−2	− Whole step	6%
−1	− Half step	7%
0	Unison	4%
+1	+ Half step	7%
+2	+ Whole step	6%
+3	+ Minor third	5%
+4	+ Major third	4%
+5	+ Perfect fourth	6%
+6	+ Tritone	1%
+7	+ Perfect fifth	7%
+8	+ Minor sixth	3%
+9	+ Major sixth	3%
+10	+ Minor seventh	2%
+11	+ Major seventh	1%
+12	+ Octave	3%

Figure 11.2 Example of probability distribution function.

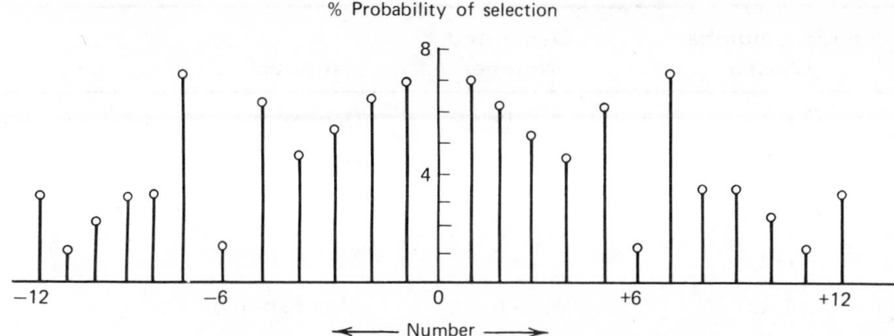

Figure 11.3 Graph of probability distribution.

tribution allows for this range, but the melody that it generates needs more structure before it is stylistically interesting. The distribution function just described is termed "first order" because each note choice is affected only by one other parameter—in this case the note preceding it. We now explore a way to construct a second-order system. As such, the choice of intervals is made from a probability distribution that is based on two other variables in the system. They may be the two notes preceding the note under selection. There are multifarious ways that second-order systems can be devised—indeed the imagination is the only limit to their variety. But for this discussion, we present one simple example for the purpose of illustration.

Whereas the first-order system uses the same probability function for every choice of intervals in the note sequence, we now create 10 such distributions having the same form or a form similar to Fig. 11.4. As the intervals are chosen, they are used to determine which of the 10 distributions selects the next interval. To implement this, we devise another table that maps the interval choices into the 10 functions. One may note in Fig. 11.5 that the perfect intervals all point to distribution #3, and the intervals of major and minor third and sixth map into the same distribution as their inversions. Of course, such a feature is an option and not a rule. The mapping of such a system is in any case up to the preference of the composer. The composer's next choice is the constituencies of the 10 probability functions. He or she may devise each one to be particularly appropriate to the interval selecting it. For example, in traditional music a tritone is usually followed by a stepwise interval. Thus in the example of Fig. 11.5 distribution #1 might be heavily weighted to half- and whole-step intervals. Similarly, stepwise contrary motion may be given probabilistic favor over other intervals following melodic leaps.

This chapter need not pursue in great detail the possible "rules" that can be programmed into compositional algorithms. The point to be made is that stochastic music is not normally produced purely from chance.

Random Number Chosen	Generated Number	Interval
1–3	−12	− Octave
4	−11	− Major seventh
5–6	−10	− Minor seventh
7–9	−9	− Major sixth
10–12	−8	− Minor sixth
13–19	−7	− Perfect fifth
20	−6	− Tritone
21–26	−5	− Perfect fourth
27–30	−4	− Major third
31–35	−3	− Minor third
36–41	−2	− Whole step
42–48	−1	− Half step
49–52	0	Unison
53–59	+1	+ Half step
60–65	+2	+ Whole step
66–70	+3	+ Minor third
71–74	+4	+ Major third
75–80	+5	+ Perfect fourth
81	+6	+ Tritone
82–88	+7	+ Perfect fifth
89–91	+8	+ Minor sixth
92–94	+9	+ Major sixth
95–96	+10	+ Minor seventh
97	+11	+ Major seventh
98–100	+12	+ Octave

Figure 11.4 Implementation of probability distribution.

Preceding Interval	Probability Distribution for Choice of Next Interval
Octave	#9
Major seventh	#5
Minor seventh	#2
Major sixth	#10
Minor sixth	#8
Perfect fifth	#3
Tritone	#1
Perfect fourth	#3
Major third	#8
Minor third	#10
Whole step	#4
Half step	#6
Unison	#7

Figure 11.5 Example of a second-order system.

Rather, it is a product of random events operating under a set of restrictions. The nature of the restrictions define the stylistic characteristics of the composition. In stochastic music the composer specifies rules directly rather than chooses notes as would be done in conventional music. This raises some interesting psychological questions which are beyond the reach of this author to solidly answer. For example, to what degree does chance play a role in the creative mental process, and how "stochastic" is the conventional music of classical and contemporary composers? When a composer chooses the intervals, modulations, rhythms, dynamics, and form of a work, the choices are neither deterministic nor random, but are the result of free decisions operating within a set of rules. One may argue that a second- or third-order probability system analogous to what is illustrated in this chapter can model an artistic process. Undoubtedly, much more experiment, evaluation, and time is required before these ideas can be respectably tested.

Thus far this chapter has described a system for use in stochastic music composition that involves a second-order routine for choosing melodic intervals based on probability distributions. As such, it is still simple enough to be used without the help of a computer. But to make it more interesting, we expand it, incorporating some more compositional rules. One example of a rule that can be added to the system is the exclusion of no more than three consecutive melodic leaps. Another possibility is the substitution of short "miniroutines" for the simple intervals heretofore entered in the probability tables. Such "miniroutines" generate short melodic phrases or stepwise sequences based on their own respective smaller probability functions and sets of rules. If the composer is working on a harmonic piece, he or she may devise a strategy for choosing the sequence of harmonic changes before determining the melody. The rules and distribution functions for generating the melody with reference to the underlying harmony are then chosen.

In this framework, the procedure for stochastic music composition becomes analogous to a game of chess. At any point in a chess game, the player has a variety of possible moves that he or she can make under the circumstances of the game. But the set of the possible moves is a variable that changes with each move and depends on the history of previous moves. Since the rules of chess can be explicitly defined, the game is amenable to computer programming, and many chess programs have been written that can beat all but the best players. Nevertheless, when one plays chess with a computer, one must bear in mind that the opponent is not actually the machine, but the program. The chess program is a logical sequence of instructions that are written on a piece of paper. It is expressed in a flow diagram or even in English statements. Naturally any set of instructions that is run on a computer can also be easily carried out by a human being. Although the task is so menial that it can be accomplished by a machine, the total process requires millions of arithmetic calculations. Thus a computer can accomplish it by virtue of speed rather than intelligence.

As a composer undertakes computer music composition, his or her task is to formulate an assembly of rules that can be explicated and logically diagrammed. The free choices permitted within that framework of the rules are then left to chance. When the composer finishes designing a compositional algorithm, it may be too complex and involve far too many (though purely menial) operations to be done by a human being in a reasonable amount of time. But once they are outlined, it is not particularly difficult to translate them from a logical diagram into BASIC, FORTRAN, PASCAL, or a music programming language. While the discussion has so far concentrated on generating melodic sequences using probability distributions for the transitions from one note to the next, this is only one of an unlimited number of systems that the composer can devise. One related method selects notes at random, but constrains the selection to a set of rules defined by the composer. As an example of such a procedure, let us suppose that we have compiled a list of several strict specifications such as the following:

1. Melodic leaps must not be larger than a major tenth.
2. A melodic leap may not be followed by another melodic leap larger than a major sixth.
3. No more than three consecutive melodic leaps are allowed.
4. No ascending or descending passage may contain more than one melodic leap.
5. No ascending or descending passage may last longer than six notes.

These rules are arbitrary, and we suppose that the list is much longer in an actual compositional program. In fact, an interesting system undoubtedly contains many rules that are in themselves complex, involving several contingencies and exceptions.

The job of a compositional computer program in this context is to automatically test the melodic sequence to determine if it conforms to all or a certain proportion of the rules in the list. It makes the determination each time a new note is selected by the random number generator and rejects the choice if the criteria are not met. This method does not use a distribution function for transition probabilities as did the procedure defined earlier. But given an understanding of both these approaches and some practice in their implementation, a composer may combine them both into one system.

Once we have devised a strategy for composing the melody, we must undertake the composition of the harmony, rhythm, and dynamics. Indeed, we may well opt for establishing the rhythm or harmony before the melody. For example, we can initiate one procedure to generate a series of harmonic progressions that would form an outline or skeleton of the composition. Like the melody, these progressions and modulations are selected by random number sequences according to a probability function, a list of rules, or a combination of the two. Then, after the harmonic progressions are outlined, the melodic entities are created according to their own rules and transition probabilities that are specially adapted to the particular scale and key in which they lie. If the composition is modeling a style of traditional music, this would be the most logical method. On the other hand, it would be inappropriate for contemporary atonal music.

The rhythm can be composed by random numbers in a manner completely analogous to the way the melody and harmony are formed. Like the melodic intervals, the note durations are chosen by chance, but constrained to fit a certain set of standards. When a composer integrates the compositional procedures for the melody, harmony, and rhythm, he or she may allow each entity to be created autonomously. This way, the melody and rhythm are not affected by each other, but are combined by "brute force." But composers seldom want these entities to be entirely separated and independent of each other. For this reason an imaginative composer normally designs the procedures for melodic and rhythmic generation to be interactive. For example, one of the compositional rules may be something like "All sequences of sixteenth notes must proceed stepwise and be followed by an interval in contrary motion." Another typical rule is that all notes falling on certain beats in the measure must fit into the harmony in a particular way. The rules may also require that nonharmonic tones be restricted to parts of the measure not emphasized by the rhythm. Of course, such rules have to be formatted in a way that can be programmed on the computer.

It is possible to pursue this topic in greater detail and to outline many other procedures for combining random number selections, probability functions, and procedural rules for the stochastic composition of music, including its melody, harmony, rhythm, and dynamics. Yet it is not the intention of this book to dictate any method of composition to its readers. The composers active in computer composition today each have their own unique methods that do not constitute any unified system. Their value is in inspiring other composers to develop more new and original techniques. Thus to critically review or compare these composers and their methods against each other here would do them and the reader a disservice as well as escape the purpose of this chapter. Their evaluation should be left to tomorrow's musicologists. In its present stage, computer composition has not defined itself into a body of canons. One might sardonically quip that the rules of stochastic music composition are "stochastic" in and of themselves. Each composer must consequently rely on the fertility of his or her imagination rather than look to any established norms or traditions when such do not yet exist. The previous discussion has sought instead to present an overall perception of what stochastic music is, and to offer a few possible means of its exploration with the aid of the computer.

This chapter has presented computer composition in a somewhat limited framework. It has addressed stochastic composition as a starting base for a tutorial discussion. The composition of simple melodies from random number patterns is actually more useful as a pedagogical device than a serious compositional method, however. In recent years computer composers have developed schemes whose sophistication far exceeds the basic concepts introduced here. Students interested in investigating the latest techniques can profit by frequently checking the literature in the current music and computer science periodicals.

The basic methods of composition introduced in this discussion work distinctly in two stages. The first stage is the development of the rules and compositional procedures that define the stylistic properties of the composition. This stage thus represents the human element. The second stage, the machine element, is the number generation and the imposition of the constraints dictated by the first stage. While it is important conceptually to view these two stages separately, it is not necessary to strictly detach them in practice. In fact, few composers would want to release their work without its careful and extensive review and revision. This implies that once the machine has performed its task and "cranked out the notes," the result may or may not be what the composer wants to hear. Thus, in practicality, an artist who is composing music with a computer does so interactively—in effect, alternating the human and the machine stages of composition as his or her tastes ultimately decide the final outcome. Even in conventional music that involves neither computers nor random numbers, the compositional process entails review, regeneration, and some trial and error. This is so with any creative undertaking.

A musical composition, to be a work of art, comprises an aggregate of phrases and patterns that are interwoven into an overall structure. The form that this structure assumes varies among artists and is different for each style, period, and culture. Yet the logical manner whereby microscopic elements are constructed into a whole work determines the artistic consistancy of the piece. As one composes conventional music, the criteria that determine the logical arrangement of the compositional elements into forms and patterns are an outcome of the composer's intellectual activity. Although this mental function manifests itself in the form of the musical composition that it produces, it is not an explicit algorithm that needs to be formalized. However, when a compositional procedure enlists the computer, its formalization becomes essential. It can be argued that such formalization impairs or even destroys a work's artistic integrity. This book neither refutes nor defends the argument, but leaves aesthetic and subjective judgments of this kind to the reader. The point to be made here is that a formalized, effective procedure for music composition should have a structure of its own that is hierarchal—an overall procedure that contains several subprocedures.

A hierarchal approach to formalized music composition is particularly amenable to computer programming because of its special affinity for modularity in its construction. In fact, modularity is the staple of computer programming. Virtually all sophisticated computer software is hierarchal—programs that call subprograms which in turn call other subprograms. Consequently, in developing algorithms that shape number patterns into the structure of a musical composition, the adoption of a hierarchal procedure is greatly advantageous over a straight, nonmodular approach. In fact, as while analyzing the harmonic, melodic, or contrapuntal structure of virtually any work of classical music, one discovers that it is hierarchal in some way, even if its form is not strictly defined.

An excellent example of this idea is the partially completed representation of a classical sonata shown in Fig. 11.6. Here an entire musical composition as a hierarchy of subunits, each containing its own subunits is viewed. Moreover, the subunits of one branch are generally found in identical or varied form in other branches. For example, the themes from the exposition are also heard in the development, recapulation, and coda, but in different orders, keys, and tonalities. Similarly, the motives from one theme also appear throughout the movement, but transposed,

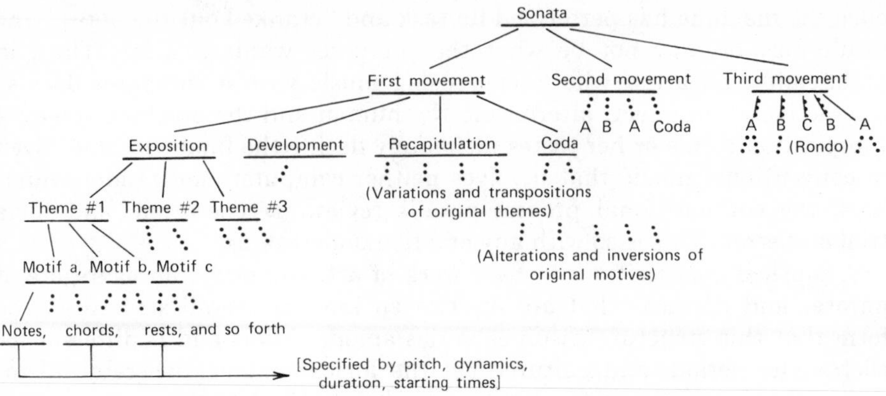

Figure 11.6 Hierarchial diagram of classical sonata.

inverted, stated in retrograde, diminished or agumented, or otherwise altered.

Although the formal structure of a musical composition varies widely from one composer or style to another, the hierarchal nature of the form remains nearly universal. Thus one can generalize the diagram of Fig. 11.6 to appear as the one in Fig. 11.7 with the nested substructures being given the terminology "musical event."

The musical structure illustrated in Fig. 11.7 is tremendously significant in terms of computer composition because as such it can be represented in a data base. Let us suppose that a composer wishes to develop a composition with a data structure. Each musical event must be associated with a description of its parameters or properties. For example, at the note level, the description of a particular sound comprises the specification of its pitch, loudness, duration, timbre, and envelope. The musical event at this level of the hierarchy then consists of an array or data structure where these parameters are assigned numerical values. The musical events at one level of the hierarchy are defined by the combination of musical events that they contain. Suppose that in the composition of Fig. 11.7 each musical event is assigned a record in computer memory. The record may consist of identifiers and pointers to other records of other musical events within its own substructure. It may also contain descriptors of the event itself.

This representation of musical events is particularly adaptable to programming languages like PASCAL that emphasize hierarchy, block form, and data structures. Several computer music programming systems such as Barry Truax' P.O.D. and the work of Buxton, Reeves, Baecker, and Mezei at the University of Toronto also greatly facilitate the use of hierarchy and data structures in music composition.

One interesting aspect of musical structure and composition is being explored by Otto Laske at the Massachusetts Institute of Technology. It involves the description of musical structures as a grammar. The events or sonic entities define the semantics of the grammar, and their interrelationships denote the syntax. While this may sound superficially simple, one may quickly realize that with a "language" or set of expressions so abstract as musical ideas, the formalization of a precise grammar to define it is no trivial matter. In connection with this, Laske has also studied the behavior of student composers working interactively at computer terminals to model the compositional process after human thought and memory patterns.

Although the foregoing discussion illustrates a model for the representation of a musical event as a data structure, it does not define any explicit procedure for generating the parameters or descriptors of that event. This is up to the composer. This book cannot dictate how these structures should be manipulated, yet it can make a few general observations concerning how they may be treated.

One simple, rather obvious method for inventing a hierarchal system for music composition is to write a group of routines to generate short melodic fragments. They function in a manner similar to the one introduced earlier in the chapter, or any other way one may want to design. These short routines are then combined into an overall framework that integrates them into entire phrases. Other routines may establish the rhythmic patterns, set the harmony, and overlay the segments contrapuntally. Each time a step in the compositional procedure is undertaken, the resulting note patterns are checked by other subroutines and modified as necessary to fit a set of criteria that stylistically define the work.

The compositional methods illustrated so far are capable of generating an unlimited variety of note patterns from a single algorithm. The choice

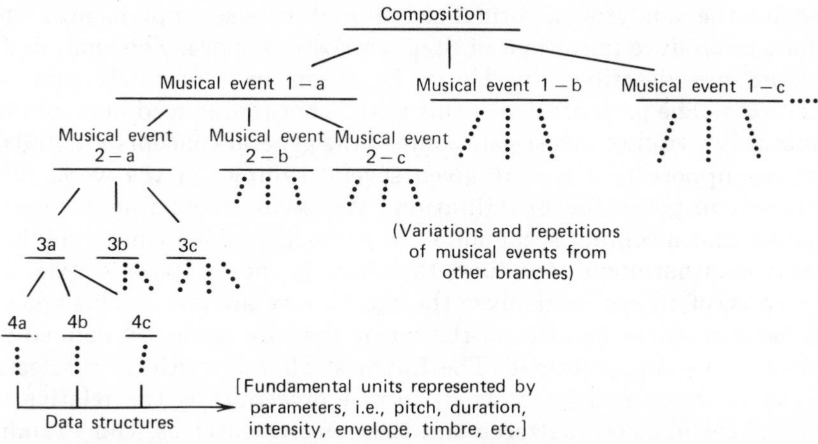

Figure 11.7 Generalized diagram of musical composition.

of the notes (and other compositional entities) are made from random number selection or predefined arrays, but constrained by rules and probability distributions to fit prescribed patterns. In this approach, the rules and patterns represent a fixed element whereas the number selection represents a variable element. It is possible, nevertheless, to reverse this logic so that a single number sequence or matrix may be used to generate a variety of melodic, harmonic, and rhythmic patterns. In this case, the structuring routine becomes the variable element while an initial number array or set of arrays is chosen once and then remains fixed and while a variety of routines map the fixed sequence into different, interrelated patterns. In some respects, the latter approach to composition is much more conformal to traditional music practice. It is the logic of variations upon a single theme, the rules of canon and fugue, and even the 12-tone row. In formalizing the procedures that a computer follows in translating a number array into a complexity of variations of musical patterns, one may feasibly incorporate random variables in the definitions of the routines themselves. Indeed, this would practically complete a reversal of variable and fixed elements and the two compositional stages previously defined.

Now that we have perused a few of the possible ways that a composer can invent new algorithms for generating musical structures, we may inquire if these methods are directed to imitate already existent musical styles. The term "style," as it is loosely used in this chapter, refers to the formal structure that constrains random choices to fit certain criteria. The question now is whether the formatted "style" referred to here can be correlated with an actual, artistic style of an individual composer. More specifically, we inquire if it is feasible to write an effective procedure to be programmed on a computer to produce music that sounds closely similar to the works of a particular composer. One interesting experiment in this regard undertook a detailed analysis of several Stephen Foster melodies. Based on the analysis, a formalized procedure was implemented on a machine to produce imitations of Stephen Foster's songs. The analysis and procedure are described by Harry F. Olsen in *Music, Physics, and Engineering*. The presentation of this work is not reproduced here, but it is instructively useful to investigate some of the general concepts it entails.

Let us suppose that we are given several samples of the works of an arbitrary composer for examination. We wish to outline a specific procedure that a computer can follow to produce note sequences, rhythmic patterns, and harmonic structures that imitate the composer's style. The first step is, of course, to analyze the samples we are given. This analysis must focus on those features of the music that are explicitly defined and listed in a statistical format. The foremost characteristic of a selection that can be examined by a strict, formal procedure is the relative frequency of certain note patterns and the notes themselves. Our examination may begin with a list of the 12 notes of the chromatic scale in which every note is followed by a number or percentage indicating how many times it occurs in the melody. To make the test more meaningful, it may be advisable to list the notes as intervals relative to a harmonic base if the selection is modulating among different keys. When completed, this list takes the form of a probability distribution similar to the one described earlier in the chapter. Once such a table is compiled for note or interval frequencies, we proceed to construct more tables that list other features of the composition as random variables. For example, we inspect the piece for frequently occurring melodic patterns and list them with their respective probabilities of occurrence. We follow the melodic analysis by a harmonic and rhythmic examination. We inspect the rhythm for the relative frequencies of whole, half, quarter, eighth, and sixteenth notes, and so forth, as well as for ties, triplets, dotted notes, syncopations, and any special peculiarities distinctive of the work.

When the examination is completed, it may comprise many complex charts and listings. In fact, for comprehension, the body of music to be examined and the number of its stylistic features to be considered may be far too extensive to permit its accomplishment by a person in a reasonable amount of time. But while it is not a trivial task, it is feasible to program on a computer. In fact, for several years, many institutions have used computer programs for the statistical analysis of musical styles. Data for these programs are the scores of compositions coded in a format appropriate for computer input. The analysis programs then inspect the scores for specified features and patterns and list the frequencies of their occurrence.

Once we have this list and as much information as we need to statistically describe the style of our composer, we translate the statistical description into a compositional algorithm such as a flowchart. The computer may begin to "roll the dice" and map the random number sequence into note sequences and patterns according to the probability tables that resulted from the prior analysis. As it generates the notes of the composition, the program inspects and reviews them automatically to determine if they conform to the required criteria. This involves many "pass-fail" tests for each new note. Those note selections that fail the examinations are rejected. They then are replaced by new random choices until by successive hit-or-miss trials, an acceptable note sequence or pattern emerges. Then after it successfully produces a group of patterns in this manner, another routine is programmed to overlay and configure them into larger units according to explicit and stylistic criteria. The process continues in hierarchal order until the fundamental units are structured and brought together into a complete composition.

The most immediate danger in this approach to music composition, whether it is imitating the style of an existing composer or initiating an original style, is that the stylistic parameters may be overspecified or underspecified. If they are underspecified, that is, if not enough criteria are defined, the resulting composition has too weak a stylistic identity. It merely sounds like random notes with no expressive significance. On the other hand, if the parameters are overspecified, and too excessive, the music they define is not composable—the notes chosen at random and tested to meet the criteria all fail and are rejected.

The second danger is more aesthetic than logistic. Even if a compositional algorithm is stylistically "tight" enough to engender its output with readily identifiable stylistic features, the resulting music sounds mechanical and boring. Indeed, one can offer no assurance that it is even possible to compose music according to an explicit, inflexible, formalized procedure that in the long run is artistically satisfying to most people. This is not to discount the value of experimental stochastic music! Like any other new art form, it deserves much more exploration, testing, and consideration. My own greatest fear is that as this chapter describes compositional procedures and styles in such mechanistic terms, the reader may infer that a computer program can be made to substitute for the original creativity of a composer's mind. This is not the case. Even if one supposes that a computer program could be invented that would perfectly imitate the style of Brahms, it would in no way be the originator of Brahms' style. One could rightfully say in such an instance that Brahms initiated whatever music the program generates as much as he did his own concertos and symphonies, since it was he who in fact originated the style to begin with. Furthermore, such a hypothetical "Brahms imitation" computer program would be incapable of self-enrichment and progressive modification. The living Brahms continuously developed and added layers of innovation to his own style. A formalized compositional procedure is not regenerative in this way. Consequently, any music that is composed mechanistically can at best be considered an extension of the mechanism's development. The invention of the mechanism is the creative act requiring the human intellect.

It is hoped that the reader is impressed with the scope and variety of techniques that can be explored in the area of stochastic music composition. The details of exactly how formalized routines are translated into actual computer programs are somewhat mundane and technical, and are not essential to their description. The reader is advised to consult the appendices and other programming manuals to become acquainted with programming procedure. It is foolish to dogmatically contend that any particular system, procedure, or philosophy, constitutes the "essence" of stochastic music. The methods pioneered so far by modern composers can only represent a fraction of the possibilities open to future composers. The primary usefulness of their ideas is their propensity to stimulate more divergent ideas. It is hoped that this book has successfully uncovered some of the potentialities of what computer music can be rather than pretentiously attempting to dictate what it is.

REFERENCES

Alonso, S., J. Appleton, & C. Jones, "A Special Purpose Digital System for Musical Instruction, Composition, and Performance," *CHUM* **10**(4), 209–215 (1976).

Ashton, Alan C. "A Computer Stores, Composes, and Plays Music," *Computers and Automation* **20** 43 (1971).

Baker, R. A., "MUSICOMP, *MU*sic-*SI*mulator-for-*COM*positional-*P*rocedures for the IBM 7090 Electronic Digital Computer," Technical Report No. 9, University of Illinois Experimental Music Studio, Urbana, 1963.

Buxton, William, "A Composer's Introduction to Computer Music," *Interface* **6,** 57–72 (1977).

Buxton, W., W. Reeves, R. Baecker, & L. Mezei, "The Use of Hierarchy and Instance in a Data Structure for Computer Music," *Computer Music Journal* **2**(4), 10–20 (1978).

Clough, John, "Computer Music and Group Theory," *American Society of University Composers: Proceedings* **4,** 10–19 (1971).

Clough, John, "TEMPO: A Composer's Programming Language," *Perspectives of New Music* **9,** 113–125 (1970).

Hiller, L. A. Jr., & L. M. Isaacson, *Experimental Music*, McGraw-Hill, 1959.

Hiller, L. A., & L. M. Isaacson, *Illiac Suite for String Quartet*, Vol 30(3), *new music Ed.* Theodore Presser Co., 1957.

Hiller, L. A., & R. A. Baker, *Computer Cantata*, Theodore Presser Co., 1968.

Hiller, L. A., & R. A. Baker, "*Computer Cantata*: An Investigation of Compositional Procedures," *Perspectives of New Music* **3,** 62 (1964).

Howe, Hubert, "Composing by Computer," *CHUM* **9**(6), 281–290 (1975).

Howe, Hubert, "A General View of Compositional Procedure in Computer Sound Synthesis," *American Society of University Composers: Proceedings* **7,** 25–30 (1974).

Koenig, Gottfried, "The Use of Computer Programmes in Creating Music," *Music and Technology*, Stockholm Meeting, organized by UNESCO, Stockholm, Sweden, 1970.

Koenig, Gottfried, "Notes on the Computer in Music," *World of Music* **9,** 3–13 (1967).

Laske, Otto, "Musical Semantics—A Procedural Point of View," International Conference on the Semantics of Music, Belgrade, 1973.

Laske, Otto, "Toward a Musical Intelligence System," *NUMUS-W* no. 4 11–16 (1973).

Laske, Otto, *Music, Memory, and Thought: Explorations in Cognitive Musicology*, University Microfilms, 1977.

Laske, Otto, "Considering Human Memory in Designing User Interfaces for Computer Music," *Computer Music Journal* **2**(4), 39–45 (1978).

Laske, Otto, "Understanding the Behavior of Users of Interactive Computer Music Systems," *Interface* **7,** 159–168 (1978).

Lerdahl and Jackendoff, "Toward a Formal Theory of Tonal Music," *Journal of Music Theory* **21**(1), 111–172 (1977).

Lincoln, Harry B. Ed., *The Computer and Music*, Cornell University Press, 1970.

Lincoln, Harry B., "Uses of the Computer in Music Composition and Research,"

In M. Rubinoff, (Ed.) *Advances in Computers*, pp. 73–114, Academic Press, 1972.

Lindblom, B., and J. Sundberg, "Music Composed by a Computer Program," *Speech Transmission Laboratory, Stockholm*, **4,** 20–28 (1972).

MacInnes, Donald, "Sound Synthesis by Computer: MUSIGOL, A Program Written Entirely in Extended ALGOL," *Perspectives of New Music* **7,** 66–79 (1968).

Mathews, M. V. et al., "Computers and Future Music," *Science* **183,** 263–268 (1974).

Moorer, James A., "Music and Computer Composition," *Communications of the Association for Computing Machinery* **15,** 104–113 (1972).

Olson, Harry F., *Music, Physics, and Engineering*, Dover, 1967.

Olson, H. F., & H. Belar, "Aid to Music Composition Employing a Random Probability System," *Journal of the Acoustical Society of America* **33,** 1163 (1961).

Roads, Curtis, "Grammars as Representations for Music," *Computer Music Journal* **3**(1), 48–55 (1979).

Seay, Albert, "The Composer of Music and the Computer," *Computers and Automation* **13,** 16 (1964).

Smith, L., "Score: A Musician's Approach to Computer Music," *NUMUS-W* no. 4 21–28 (1973).

Smoliar, Stephen W., "Music Theory: A Programming Linguistic Approach." *Proceedings of the ACM Annual Conference*, 1001–1014, (1972).

Smoliar, Stephen W., "Basic Research in Computer Music Studies," *Interface* **2,** 121–125 (1973).

Smoliar, Stephen W., "A Data Structure for an Interactive Music System," *Interface* **2,** 127–140 (1973).

Smoliar, Stephen W., "Music Programs: An Approach to Music Theory Through Computational Linguistics," *Journal of Music Theory* **20,** 105–131 (Spring 1976).

Strang, Gerald, "The Computer in Musical Composition," *Computers and Automation* **15,** 16 (1966).

Tanner, Peter P., *MUSICOMP: An Experimental Aid for the Composition and Production of Music*, National Research Council, Document ERB-862, Ottawa, 1971.

Tanner, Peter P., *Some Programs for the Computer Generation of Polyphonic Music*, National Research Council, Document ERB-862, Ottawa, 1971.

Truax, Barry, "A Communicational Approach to Computer Sound Programs," *Journal of Music Theory* **20**(2), 227–300 (1976).

Truax, Barry, "The Computer Composition-Sound Synthesis Programs POD4, POD5, & POD6," Sonological Reports 2, Institute of Sonology, State University of Utrecht, 1973.

Truax, Barry, "General Techniques of Computer Composition Programming," *NUMUS-W*, no. 4 17–20 (1973).

Truax, Barry, "Some Programs for Real-Time Computer Synthesis and Composition," *Interface* **2,** 159–163 (1973).

Vercoe, Barry, "The Music 360 Language for Sound Synthesis," *Proceedings of the American Society of University Composers* **6,** 16–21 (1971).

von Foerster, H., & J. Beauchamp, Eds. *Music by Computer*, Wiley, 1969.

Xenakis, Iannis, *Formalized Music*, Indiana University Press, 1971.

12

MACHINES AND HUMAN CREATIVITY

As a small child I would listen to the radio and imagine that the talking came from miniature people that were on the inside. Not having understood how a radio works, it seemed natural to humanize it, since it was apparently performing a human activity—that of speech. Virtually anyone who washes clothes in an automatic washing machine understands basically how the machine works. But it would be easy and very natural for a person from a primitive society who have never before seen or heard about automatic washing machines to encounter one for the first time and think there is a person hidden inside doing the work.

As technology has progressed, modern society has rapidly adapted itself culturally and intellectually to the changes that new inventions have imposed. People drive cars, watch television, listen to stereo phonographs, vacuum floors, and make long-distance telephone calls without the need to surround the devices with superstition or attribute them with supernatural capabilities. Although people understandably and justifiably mistrust technocracy's rapid influx, the fear of "future shock" is directed mainly toward the sociological impact of technology rather than any specific inventions. For example, however tasteless, violent, mediocre, or controversial television programming has become, few people object to the manufacture of new television sets. As a rule, intelligent people are able to recognize that the impact of a machine in their lives is good or bad depending on how the machine is applied or misapplied. The most poignant example of this is the use of nuclear energy, which can potentially be one of mankind's greatest benefits, or its destroyer!

The digital computer is probably the most intellectually awesome of mankind's inventions. While other mechanical devices routinely perform various forms of manual labor, only the computer appears to imitate a man's intellectual activity. Although few people seriously believe that a computer thinks in the way that a person thinks, the knowledge of what a computer actually does and how it actually functions is still vague to most people. A digital electronic instrument, unlike a washing machine, automobile, or phonograph, is seldom understood by its user. It is still a magic box with a person inside.

If intelligence is restrictively defined as the ability to store, transmit, and process information, one could not deny that a computer possesses a form of intelligence—recognizing, of course, that this mechanistic intelligence is not to be confused with the spontaneous creative intelligence of a living being. A computer can be made to add numbers because the process of addition can be formalized into a synthetic, effective procedure. It can be formulated as a specific set of steps and logically diagrammed. Similarly, the computer can play chess because it is possible to formulate the game of chess into a synthetic procedure. It can imitate the tone of a clarinet because that process can also be synthesized into a specific set of steps. The question of whether one considers addition or the other tasks that a computer can perform to be mechanical or intellectual is academic. It is a matter of definition and does not relate to the computer's determined ability or inability to accomplish the procedure. The test of whether a job can be accomplished by a machine is largely, although not entirely, determined by whether or not it can be formalized into an explicit procedure. Since a computer program is by its very nature such a formalized, effective procedure, any task accomplishable by a computer must necessarily be such an effective procedure. The converse of this is not true, though. There are many effective procedures that a computer cannot perform, such as the computation of irrational numbers to infinite precision. Understanding the capabilities and limitations of computing systems ought to be as fundamental and widespread as the mechanical understanding of phonographs and washing machines. But in the past two decades, computing systems have been the exclusive property of large institutions that can financially support them. They have been programmed solely by specialized technicians. In the near future, this will no longer be so. Powerful computers are rapidly becoming as economical and commonplace as television sets.

The invention of radio, television, the automobile, and air travel each made an enormous impact on society, resulting in sweeping cultural transformations. But none of these inventions have intellectually mystified people in the way that the computer has done. The computer, by its apparent ability to imitate some of man's thought process, has psychologically invaded territory that other machines have not. One result of this invasion, as already mentioned, is the superstitious personification of the machine. This personification occurs primarily with technically untrained people who are unfamiliar with computer systems. Although professional computer programmers often personify the machine in jest, they do it in the same tongue-in-cheek manner that an aircraft pilot personifies his "bird." Anyone who programs a computer quickly becomes accustomed to its cold, mechanistic responses to every instruction, and to its banal incapability of humanistic interaction.

A computer is theoretically a deterministic device. The reason the determinism is theoretical and not actual is that the physical hardware of a computer is subject to imperfections in construction, temperature effects, and other variable elements that can cause it to malfunction and behave unpredictably. The software of a computing system, by contrast, is more a conceptual than a physical entity. It is, like the words of an encyclopedia, only physical in the sense of the ink on the page. Nevertheless, the software of a computer is tangible enough so that it defines the computer's operation, and must be "read" continuously for the computer to function. The software of a typical operating system is a hierarchy of millions of instructions. It consists of hundreds of subprograms that take many engineers years to develop. But this software is intangible in the sense that it can be printed on paper. Once developed, it would still exist even if its "host" computer were physically destroyed. A computer without this software in its memory is an inert device.

The physical computer is a complex array of switches and gates. But the logical elements that make the computer run and direct its actions (outside its electronic design) are the essence of its software. This is to say that different computers function the same, given the same software, but one individual computer functions in any variety of ways, given different software systems. The software system, not being subject to mechanical imperfection, is purely deterministic. It can only behave unpredictably in the sense that it may be misinterpreted because of an electrical defect in the hardware of its host machine, or in the sense that it may be misunderstood by the human programmer. Although it is truthfully said that "the machine can only do what it is programmed to do," one must remember that the number and complexity of all the instructions in a software system far exceeds the ability of any person to be familiar with all of them. As a result, computer systems often surprise their programmers with unexpected behavior simply because one programmer is not aware of a peculiarity in the software that was written by another programmer. Notwithstanding this, the software itself, however many logical defects or "bugs" it may contain, is still a deterministic system.

The agglomeration of instructions and data that constitute a computer's software seems to lie in a twilight zone somewhere between what may be considered mechanical or conceptual. To further complicate matters, another class of devices are commonly incorporated into computing systems that physically embed written subprograms into electric circuits. These programmable circuits, called Read-Only-Memories (ROMs), are classified as "firmware" because they are neither distinctively software nor hardware. It is somewhat mystifying to conceive of a deterministic machine that is not a physical entity, as is the case with a computer software system. It is almost like believing in a ghost, which probably contributes to the aura of mystery surrounding computers.

Although people are inclined to personify machines, the mechanical age and advent of the computer has also led to a more grave phenomenon—namely the "machinification" of human beings. This consequence is, in my opinion, far more tragic sociologically than the reverse fallacy of imagining that the machine is human. In the last century, a large school of behavioral psychologists have proposed that human beings are deterministic machines "programmed" by their environment. They have shown that a dog can be conditioned to salivate at the sound of a bell, that pigeons can be trained to play ping-pong and rats to press levers to obtain food. Their experiments have been used to promote astounding dogmas in spite of their utter failure to make any animal behave in a strictly deterministic manner under even the most controlled circumstances or restrictive environmental conditions. One may assert that man, in spite of his creative capabilities and capricious, unpredictable behavior, is still an automaton, like a computer, but a billion times more complex. But even this proposition dies for lack of logical or empirical evidence in its favor.

Chapter 3 explained how a computer basically operates. To further clarify the scope of a machine's capabilities as opposed to a human's intellectual capacity, the following discussion again pursues the topic in a more general and theoretical perspective. A computer is a *finite-state automaton*. A finite-state machine is so called because it can exist in one out of a limited number of conditions or states at any given time. The state that the machine assumes at any one time is determined exclusively by its previous state and a selection of input stimuli. To illustrate this, we invent a simple, tutorial example of a typical finite-state machine. Our hypothetical machine is a box with five lights, three on/off switches, and a push button on its front panel. We do not know what is on the inside of the machine, nor do we care. We are merely interested in the way that it behaves when the switches are toggled and the button is depressed. The five lights may each be either glowing or not glowing, and the combination of their individual states defines the overall state of the machine. Since each of their five lights has one of two possible states, the total number of their combinations equals 2^5 or 32. The machines thereby comprises 32 possible overall states. The three on/off switches similarly have 2^3 or 8 possible combinations of switch positions. Each time the push button is depressed, the machine advances from its current state to a subsequent state that is indicated by its five lights. Since the next state is always a function of the preceding state and the combination of switch positions, each state may be represented in a table such as Fig. 12.1. Here "on" is represented by 1 and "off" by 0. The table has 32 rows and 8 columns for 256 possible entries. The entries have been omitted here except for two that are indicated for illustration. But the 256 possible entries to the table, when specified, would completely define the machine. In this example, if the lights show the pattern 00100 and the switches are in positions 010, the next state of the machine is 10010—that is, the lights change to that pat-

	Switch Positions							
State	000	001	010	011	100	101	110	111
00000								
00001								
00010								
00011								
00100			10010					
00101								
00110					01100			
.								
.								
.								
11111								

Figure 12.1 Truth Table of finite-state machine.

tern as soon as the push button is depressed. Similarly the state 00110 changes to state 01100 with the switches in positions 101.

One can readily see that the behavior of this machine is determined by two factors. One is the internal design of the machine, related by the "truth table" of Fig. 12.1. The other factor that controls the machine's operation is the sequence of switch positions chosen each time the machine advances to a new state. Thus one programs the machine by annotating a list of switch positions, then entering a new combination from the list each time the push button is pressed. A device like this is deterministic because its behavior is totally predictable. One may forecast its state at any future time by knowing its rules of behavior as indicated by the truth table, its current state, and the sequence of switch positions that advance it to future states. This information is sufficient to make that determination.

The number of different states, switch positions, and transition possibilities of an actual computer are too large to print here, so one would scarcely attempt to formulate a complete truth table for the entire machine. Yet as computers are designed, the smaller, elemental units comprising them are basic enough that they can be diagrammed like our figure above. The total computer is thus a finite-state machine that is a hierarchy of submachines similar in principle to our example. This chapter need not present a comprehensive compendium on finite-state-automaton theory, but it is important for this discussion to understand

and account for a computer's deterministic behavior. The deterministic behavior is the reason for the machine's predictability. By contrast, a stochastic device whose states are determined by random activity rather than fixed parameters is nondeterministic and consequently unpredictable. The preceding chapter presented an overview of possible ways one can create music with a quasi-stochastic–quasi-deterministic procedure modulated by stochastic inputs.

Having introduced and contrasted deterministic and nondeterministic machines, this discussion now seeks to relate these concepts to human creativity. The primary contention of this chapter is that creative spontaneity cannot be reduced to a formalized, synthetic procedure, nor can it be modeled by a random or quasi-random process. A practical interpretation of this would be the following argument:

> Let us suppose that a device is invented that is capable of performing an intricate analysis of Beethoven's first symphony. Based on this analysis, the machine (or computer program) can generate nearly perfect imitations of Beethoven's style as exhibited in that work. While the machine could theoretically produce hundreds of variations of Beethoven's first symphony, it could not come close to composing an imitation of his ninth symphony—that is, not until it was able to first compile a detailed analysis of this work.

This argument contends that only a living Beethoven can progress from the style of his earlier to his later works. Contrastingly, the hypothetical Beethoven-imitation machine would continue to tirelessly compose in the same style indefinitely, or until reprogrammed to do otherwise.

Admittedly, a contention like this is impossible to rigorously prove. But it may be supported by two related facts of nature. One is that a deterministic machine cannot perform any operation or generate any information that is not implicit in its program input or behavioristic configuration. The other is the principle of the second law of thermodynamics. This law states roughly that natural systems generally decay from ordered to disordered states, but they may not consistantly and spontaneously progress from disordered to ordered states. For example, if a person is given a bag of red marbles and a bag of green marbles, he or she may combine them into one mixture, then randomly separate the mixture back into the two bags. But only by a fantastically improbable coincidence would the random separation result in the original configuration where each bag contained exclusively one color of marbles. A creative process often involves a progression from a state of relative disorder to an advanced state of higher order. Similarly, an original idea is not a logical conclusion deduced from known facts. Deductive logic is a synthetic process. One can even say that a computer can "think" deductively if willing to define the word "think" in such a narrow scope. But the creative and intellectual advances that are the vehicle of scientific and artistic achievement are not accountable by deductive logic or synthetic procedures. In fact, the evolution of artistic works, of scientific discoveries and theories, of technological progress, or of organic species is a continuum of spontaneous, creative incidents. The incidents seem to occur much more stochastically than deterministically. They happen unpredictably and by apparent accident, but also by improbable coincidence. Their cumulative effect is, unlike a random process, regenerative rather than degenerative. For this reason, the creative act, be it the composition of Bernstein's Mass, the theory of relativity, the invention of the transistor, or the spontaneous evolution of a simple bacterium, is neither mechanistic nor stochastic.

This discussion contends that creativity is a process in itself and cannot be accounted for or modeled by stochastic or deterministic processes alone. Nevertheless, it does not intend to imply that creative works or progressive evolution occur with utter spontaneity. They are produced as an interactive combination of random events, synthetic logic, and creative stimulation. The diagram of Fig. 12.2 loosely portrays this idea, though it should not be interpreted too strictly. One may appropriately note here in reference to the hypothetical Beethoven-imitation machine mentioned earlier, that the conspicuous and critical difference between it and the living composer is the possession of the spontaneous creative element in the real Beethoven and its absence in the mechanical imitator.

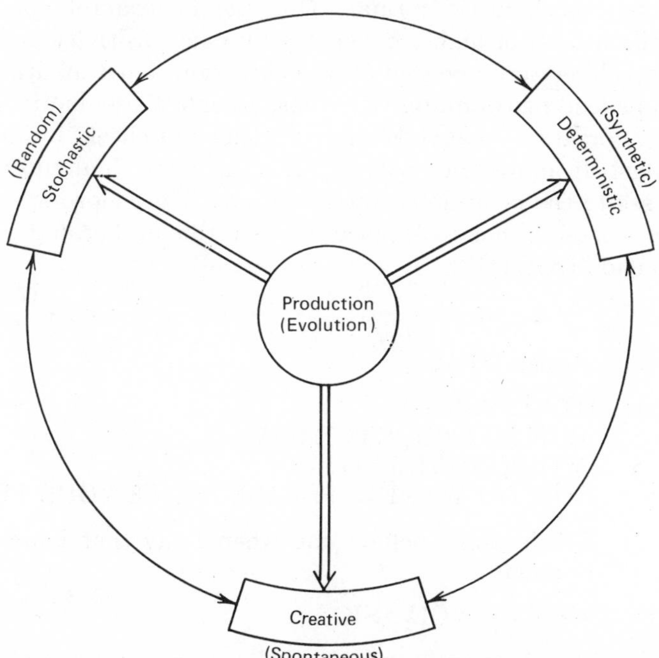

Figure 12.2 Conceptual representation of creative process.

Much has been said here concerning the extent of a computer's power. Indeed the issue has become a science in itself, and several volumes of literature have been written that explore problems of computability and analytically determine what a computer can and cannot be made to do. The topic should be of major interest to anyone who programs a computer, including the tentative composer of computer music. This book is dedicated to the comprehensive analysis of the role a computer potentially can play in the creation of new music forms. It emphasizes that this role is that of a tool. The computer is a new instrument that has special capacities and versatility not ever realized in musical instruments developed in the past. Its introduction adds enormity to the musical repertoire, and does not attempt to eradicate or even detract from any existing musical standard. More importantly, the computer cannot take the place of the creative musician.

Unfortunately, the inherent limitations of machines discussed earlier have not prevented their incursion into areas of human livelihood where they do not belong. Technocracy is determined to integrate machines into society. But since it has proved impossible to humanize the machine, people have unwittingly allowed themselves to be "machinified" by the computer age. Computers are being relied on to perform social activities that call for decision making and value judgments. But they can only accomplish this after the tasks assigned to them have been codefied into a dehumanized, mechanistic format. One potent example of a service requiring the utmost of highly developed human sensitivity and intuition alien to a machine would be that of psychotherapy. To dramatize this, one of the world's leading computer scientists, Joseph Weisenbaum, developed a computer program that performs a tongue-in-cheek imitation of a psychoanalyst. It allows the "patient" to sit at a terminal and type his or her responses to the computer's interrogations. The following is a sample taken from a session that took place between this author and a computer program called "DOCTOR":

Operator:	.Assign DTA2
Computer:	DTA2 ASSIGNED .RUN DTA2:DOCTOR.SAV (WORKER) HELLO HOW DO YOU DO. PLEASE STATE YOUR PROBLEM
Patient:	People don't believe me when I say that I am president Kennedy.
Computer:	WHY DO YOU ASK
Patient:	That was not a question. That is my problem.
Computer:	I AM NOT SURE I UNDERSTAND YOU FULLY

Patient: People are out to get me. They are trying to kill me.

Computer: DID YOU THINK THEY MIGHT NOT BE OUT TO GET YOU THEY ARE TRYING TO KILL YOU

Patient: No, they are trying to kill me.

Computer: ARE YOU SAYING 'NO' JUST TO BE NEGATIVE

Patient: Yes.

Computer: YOU SEEM QUITE POSITIVE

Patient: Positive about being negative.

Computer: PLEASE GO ON

Patient: I think you are one of them. You are trying to kill me too.

Computer: WHAT MAKES YOU THINK I AM ONE OF THEM

Patient: You are evasive.

Computer: DOES IT PLEASE YOU TO BELIEVE I AM EVASIVE

Patient: It most certainly does not!

Computer: YOU ARE SURE

Patient: Quite sure.

Computer: WHAT DOES THAT SUGGEST TO YOU

Patient: You are trying to kill me.

Computer: PERHAPS YOU WOULD LIKE TO BE TRYING TO KILL YOU

Patient: That is not the case.

Computer: DO YOU FEEL STRONGLY ABOUT DISCUSSING SUCH THINGS

Patient: My life depends on it.

Computer: YOUR LIFE DEPENDS ON IT

Patient: Yes, I just said that.

Computer: I SEE

Patient: What do you see?

Computer: DOES THAT QUESTION INTEREST YOU

Patient: Yes, please answer it.

Computer: I UNDERSTAND

Patient: What do you understand?

Computer: WHAT IS IT YOU REALLY WANT TO KNOW

Patient:	Why are you trying to destroy me?
Computer:	ARE SUCH QUESTIONS MUCH ON YOUR MIND
Patient:	As a matter of fact, they are.
Computer:	WOULD YOU LIKE IT IF THEY WERE NOT
Patient:	Yes, but that is not the case.
Computer:	YOU SEEM QUITE POSITIVE
Patient:	You are being evasive again.
Computer:	DO YOU SOMETIMES WISH YOU WERE BEING EVASIVE AGAIN
Patient:	I do not. Why are you trying to bring about my ruin?
Computer:	YOU SAY YOU DO NOT
Patient:	Yes, please answer my question.
Computer:	I SEE
Patient:	What do you see?
Computer:	WHAT ANSWER WOULD PLEASE YOU MOST
Patient:	The correct answer.
Computer:	I AM NOT SURE I UNDERSTAND YOU FULLY
Patient:	My name is President John F. Kennedy, but people don't believe me. The people are trying to destroy me.
Computer:	I AM NOT INTERESTED IN NAMES
Patient:	Are you interested in my problem?
Computer:	DOES THAT SUGGEST ANYTHING ELSE WHICH BELONGS TO YOU
Patient:	C
Computer:	PLEASE GO ON
Patient:	↑C
Computer:	.
Patient:	K
Computer:	JOB 2, USER [40,60] LOGGED OF TTY5 1956 28-MAY-69 SAVED ALL 1 FILES (INCLUDING UFD, 4.DISC BLOCKS) RUNTIME 0 MIN, 32,47 SEC

It should be emphasized that this program was created for use as a plaything. Yet notwithstanding the "DOCTOR" program's obvious incompetence as a serious therapeutic device, some prominant members of the psychiatric community have actually advocated the development of similar computer programs for clinical use!

The possibility of computers interviewing mental patients is not a question of computability that can be solved heuristically or analytically. The ridiculous interview between the computer and the patient is sufficient proof. But except as an item of amusement, would one want it to actually perform psychoanalysis? Computers can plan people's schedules and make important decisions for them if people decide to allow it. But when computers begin making binding decisions that control people's lives, the results can become frightening. A man recently spent three months in a county jail in Dallas, Texas, after being arrested for two traffic offenses. The jail officials blamed his mistaken imprisonment on a clerical error that occurred when his name was routinely run through the county jail computer. The computer had not even malfunctioned. It simply processed incorrect data, and its output had sickening consequences.

In a harmless and rather amusing incident, a test engineer at Sperry Univac sat down to a computer terminal to do some programming. The screen displayed, "PLEASE LOG ON:". The engineer typed, "WHY?", to which the terminal immediately and forthrightly responded in large,, inverse video, block letters:

BECAUSE
MR. COMPUTER
SAYS!

Needless to say, the computer had been rigged to do that by another programmer as a mild spoof of people's inclination to submit to the ostensible authority of a computer. But to the unfortunate man sitting in the Dallas jail, the edict of "Mr. Computer" was not so funny.

What kind of a deity has modern society created of "Mr. Computer"? Because the machine can only process information in a precise, formatted predetermined procedure, it must behave inflexibly without the capacity to make creative or intuitive judgments. It cannot make intelligent decisions in any exceptional or unexpected cases involving extenuating circumstances or special conditions that are not preprogrammed into its operating system. A machine should be a perfect slave to man. Being a lifeless, theoretically deterministic device, it is disgustingly obedient. But businesses, private industry, government, the military industrial complex, and educational institutions have enjoyed its speed, efficiency, and capacity to handle enormous volumes of information automatically and invisibly so much that they have let the slave become the master. Ironically, one is not submitted to the dictates of "Mr. Computer" out of fear, intimidation, or superstition—it is done out of convenience and economic profit. It is overwhelmingly easy to automate a routine social or intellectual activity into a mechanized procedure suitable for a machine. The human is then spared hours of tedious and unnecessary busywork.

But when human beings become subject to inflexible, formatted decisions that result from the output data of an insensitive, unthinking machine, they have created a tyrant. A university student may not be able to get his or her schedule modified because of the dictatorship of "Mr. Computer." Someone else may lose electricity, gas, or telephone service when "Mr. Computer" processes a billing error or improperly typed data form. An honest person may have good credit rating destroyed by a clerical error when banking procedures are locked into an invariable, automated system that is not carefully monitored by human supervision. It is impossible for computers to conspire against humans, and in theory, they should not be able to do anything unpredictable. But in reality, computers can be extremely unpredictable. They can electronically malfunction or do erratic things because of undetected bugs in their software. As mentioned earlier, it is common for one computer program to reference hundreds of subroutines that were produced at different times by different programmers. The referenced subroutines may do unexpected things simply because the programmer who uses them in the main program has less than a perfect understanding of how they work under all conditions. So all too often, when "Mr. Computer" is turned on to monitor bank accounts, schedule school classes, administer examinations, plan bombing raids in Vietnam, turn off peoples utilities, make out social security payments, or throw traffic offenders in jail, its victims face a multitude of horrors.

This chapter is not campaigning against the influx of automatic computing and data processing systems. Rather, it deplores the mechanization of social services and intellectual activities. Let "Mr. Computer" be restricted to do the work that computers were invented to do—add and store numbers. Let us leave the jobs that require value judgments, moral sensitivity, and creative intuition to human beings. I offer no objection to letting a microprocessor automatically control a microwave oven. But I would protest the day that a computer is programmed to plan the menu. Very soon microcomputers will automatically adjust the color balance on television sets. But let them not be allowed to dictate the programs we may watch! In the preceding chapter, some methods were explored whereby computers may aid in composing musical works. But it is fairly easy to perceive from that discussion that the content of any selection produced with a computer program owes any creative element of its content beyond the outcome of pure chance to the intellect of the human programmer. Machines that think like humans are found only in popular science fiction. They can have neither the desire nor the capability of usurping any power that men do not deliberately give to them. But automation has nonetheless woven itself tightly into human livelihood. My own belief is that the advancement of technology has immeasurably improved the quality of human life. It has freed us from the burdensome, unnecessary chores that were hardships to our ancestors. There is no virtue in routine work or drudgery for its own sake. If a task can be accomplished by a machine, its repetition is mundane and not likely to challenge a human's creative personality. The performance of routine work by automatic machines serves to liberate more time and resources to humans for greater advantage and accomplishment.

Man is not a machine. Human relations are not deterministic, synthetic procedures that can be formalized and flowcharted. But society is in danger of dehumanizing itself for the sake of the convenience, novelty, economics, and fashion of too much automation. Technology is a service but it must not become a compulsion. It becomes compulsive when technologists fantasize that a machine can be invented to do anything a person can do. Since any task that a machine can do must be a formalized procedure, the myth of its potential omnipotence can only be sustained by overlaying it with another delusion. The faith that a machine can accomplish anything rests on the notion that any process—including scientific discovery, artistic creation, and emotional experience—can be synthesized into a formal procedure. This is the root of the compulsive technocracy that threatens to rob man of humanity by mechanizing his existence.

Technology may advance further and should do so without imposing this threat. It simply requires society to guard against its compulsive misapplication. Let the need for an invention preceed the invention. I am always amused by expensive wristwatches that display the month and year. It is because while I am personally more absent minded than most people, I am not so forgetful that I lose track of the month and year! But as long as people maintain their craving of gadgetry for its own sake, technological redundancy will surround us in every form from digital thermometers to electric spatulas.

The discussions in this book have been devoted to the theoretical aspects of computer music. The author recognizes that the recording industry and major universities have undertaken great expense in the development of highly sophisticated equipment and procedures for automatic music synthesis and composition. But the artist who begins to rely too heavily on the automatic capabilities of the computer is in danger of being stripped of his or her own artistic role. The exercise of this role requires the theoretical, conceptual knowledge of acoustics, wave form analysis, signal processing, information theory, harmony, and basic physics and electronics. The information detailing the state of the art in new systems and devices is pertinent and interesting, but it is prone to rapid obsolescence. Consequently, this writing has emphasized the theoretical foundations of the art rather than its technological superstructure.

The attribute of the digital computer that is most promising to future composers is its nearly infinite flexibility. An artist can create a wider variety of original, interesting sounds with it than he or she can with any other instrument. But as soon as the compositional procedure becomes excessively automated, this flexibility is defeated. The compositions created with the computer that succeed artistically will be those of composers who tax their own originality to its maximum. The masterpieces will come from the creative human's exploitation of the computer's committed universal flexibility rather than dependence on its automatic capabilities.

REFERENCES

Aleksander, Igor, *The Human Machine: A View of Intelligent Mechanisms*, Georgi Pub. Co., 1978.

Boden, Margaret A., *Artificial Intelligence and Natural Man*, Harvester Press, 1977.

Bellman, Richard, *An Introduction to Artificial Intelligence, Can Computers Think?* Boyd & Fraser Pub. Co., 1978.

Dreyfus, Hubert L., *What Computers Can't Do*, Harper & Row, 1972.

Feigenbaum, E. & J. Feldman, Eds., *Computers and Thought*, McGraw-Hill, 1963.

Findler, N. V. & B. Meltzer, Eds., *Artificial Intelligence and Heuristic Programming*, American Elsevier Pub. Co., 1971.

George, F. H., & J. D. Humphries, *The Robots are Coming*, NCC Publications, 1974.

Gunderson, Keith, *Mentality and Machines*, Doubleday & Co. 1971.

Hunt, Earl B., *Artificial Intelligence*, Academic Press, 1975.

Jackson, Philip C., *Introduction to Artificial Intelligence*, Petrocelli Books, 1974.

Jaki, Stanley L., *Brain, Mind, and Computers*, Herder and Herder, 1969.

Karlsson, Jon L., *Inheritance of Creative Intelligence*, Nelson-Hall, 1978.

Koestler, Arthur, *The Act of Creation*, Dell, 1964.

Kretschmer, Ernst, *The Psychology of Men of Genius*, McGrath Pub. Co. 1970.

Meltzer, B. & D. Michie, *Machine Intelligence*, American Elsevier Pub. Co., 1971.

Mumford, E., & H. Sackman, *Human Choice and Computers*, North Holland Pub. Co., 1975.

Naylor, T. H. & R. Saratt, Eds., Southern Regional Education Board 1—Seminars for Journalists Report #1, *The Impact of the Computer on Society* May 4–7, 1966.

Weizenbaum, Joseph, *Computer Power and Human Reason*, W. H. Freeman, 1976.

GLOSSARY

accumulator—the principal register in a computer's central processing unit. The accumulator stores the word that the computer is currently processing.

acoustics—the study of sound and its properties.

additive synthesis—the construction of complex waveforms by addition of basic, simple components. In producing sounds, additive synthesis is used to form complex tones by combining several pure tones of different frequencies.

ADC—see analog-to-digital converter.

address—the number identifying a location in a computer primary memory. Each register in the memory is located and accessed electronically by this address. In machine-level computer programming, each instruction and data word must be identified by the address where it will reside in memory.

algorithm—a strategy or procedure to be used in solving a problem. In computer programming, an algorithm can be expressed in a flowchart and coded into the instructions of a computer language.

aliasing—also called "foldover," When electronic waveforms are digitally sampled, all of their frequency components higher than one-half the sampling frequency are reflected into the lower range. This distortion-producing reflection is called aliasing. It is generally avoided by processing the waveform to be sampled with a low-pass filter before the waveform is sampled.

amplifier—a device used to increase the intensity of a signal. In electronic sound reproduction, amplifiers are usually made with transistor circuits. They increase the power of an electronic signal while preserving the signal's waveshape.

amplitude—the intensity of a signal. If the signal is electronic, the amplitude is its voltage. If the signal is acoustic, the amplitude is its sound pressure level.

analog—a term used in reference to a continuous signal or a device that generates or processes a continuous signal. For example, microphones, loudspeakers, phonograph pickups, and tape heads are analog devices. Before an analog signal can be processed with a computer, it must be digitized.

analog-to-digital converter (ADC)—a device used to sample an analog signal at periodic intervals and convert it into a sequence of numbers that may be stored in a computer memory. To record or process signals with a digital computer, it is first necessary to digitize the signal with an analog-to-digital converter.

argument—a variable used in the calculation of a mathematical function. For example, the argument of a sine function is the angle whose sine value is sought. In a computer program that employs a subprogram to calculate a function, the argument of the function must be passed from the main program to the subprogram.

array—a sequence of numbers. Arrays are generally used in computer programs to store data in tables or lists.

articulation—the dynamic characteristic of a tone. Two tones may have the same harmonic structure but differ in their articulation, resulting in different sound quality. For example, a piano note recorded and played backward sounds much different from a live piano note.

ASCII—U.S.A. Standard Code for Information Interchange. This binary code is used for the characters and functions of a keyboard computer terminal. Each character (alphanumeric, punctuation, carriage return, etc.) is represented by a unique bit combination. When a key is pressed, this bit sequence is transmitted by the keyboard's electronics to the computer and stored in memory.

assembler—a program in a computer's software system library that translates the instructions of an assembly language program into binary machine code that can be directly processed by the computer.

Assembly Language—a computer programming language that closely resembles machine code. It differs from machine language in that it employs short alphabetic words and abbreviations rather than binary numbers to code the instruction.

atonality—a mode of music composition that does not adhere to traditional harmonic structure. It does not manifest any tonal center. Atonality is particularly prominant in the styles of the twentieth century.

attack—the rise time or beginning portion of a tone's onset. The attack time of a tone's envelope is characterized by a rise in amplitude.

attenuation—the suppression of a signal component as it passes through a filter or other device. A typical filter transmits some components of a signal with relatively little attenuation, while almost entirely blocking out other frequencies.

automaton—a deterministic machine. A computer is an example of a highly complex, finite-state automaton.

bandpass filter—a filter that transmits the frequencies of a signal lying between an upper and lower cutoff frequency.

bandreject filter—a filter that blocks the frequencies of a signal lying between an upper and lower cutoff frequency.

bandwidth—the range of frequencies that can be transmitted by a filter, amplifier, or communication channel. It is often referred to as the frequency response. High-quality audio equipment must have a bandwidth of 30 to 15,000 cycles per second to be able to transmit all the frequencies of the audible spectrum.

base—the central element of a transistor. The base regulates the amount of electric current allowed to flow through the transistor. A small variation of current through the base causes a large, corresponding variation in the total transistor current. In this way, the transistor functions as an amplifier or current-controlled switch.

bias—a direct-current component of an electronic signal. It can be thought of as a zero-frequency component.

Binary Number System—the number system whose base is 2. All numbers in the binary system are represented by digits of ones and zeros. It is the numbering system universally employed by digital computers.

bit—1 binary digit. It is the smallest unit of information in the computer. One bit may comprise one of two states. A bit is represented numerically by a 1 or a 0. It is represented physically by the open or close (on/off) condition of a switch, or electronically by a high- or low-voltage level.

buffer—a small cache memory or area of a computer's main memory dedicated to a specific task. It is usually used for temporary storage of small amounts of information that require quick access.

byte—a unit of information in a computer comprising 8 bits.

capacitor—a device used to store electric charge. It is constructed out of two thin metal plates (or foil) separated by an insulator.

carrier wave—the wave whose frequency is modulated in Frequency Modulation (FM) synthesis.

chip—a small silicon wafer on which is etched an integrated circuit. Typically, an integrated-circuit (IC) chip is about ¼ inch square and is mounted and sold in a dual-inline-package (DIP) 1 to 2 inches long. The DIP is lined with metal pins to serve as electrical connectors to external circuitry. One IC chip may contain many thousands of individual transistors and other components.

chromatic scale—the musical scale comprising 12 equal semitones. An ascending or descending chromatic scale does not reveal its tonality as does a major or minor scale.

coefficient—a term in an algebraic expression used as a multiplier.

collector—the element of a transistor from which the current leaves the device.

compiler—a computer program in the software system library used to translate the instructions of a high-level language such as FORTRAN or PASCAL into machine-level instructions suitable for execution by the computer.

concrete sounds—recorded sounds used as sources for modification and processing in electronic music composition.

consonance—a musical interval whose tones do not appear to "clash." The third, fifth, and sixth intervals are considered consonant in traditional counterpoint, but in modern music, consonance is a matter of subjective judgment. Harmonically, consonant intervals are typified by simple numerical frequency ratios.

constant—a term used in an algebraic expression to represent a specific number. In a computer program, a constant may be an actual number itself or a letter or name used to represent the number. The value of a constant does not change as the program executes.

core—a form of computer primary memory employing tiny ferrite rings that are magnetically polarized to store bits of information. Core was most widely used in second-generation memory systems, but is now being replaced with more compact and economical semiconductor memory.

cosine function—a trigonometric function identical to the sine function except displaced by 90 degrees. It represents the horizontal displacement of a circularly rotating object.

cps—cycles per second. It is the fundamental unit of frequency referred to in scientific and technical literature as hertz (Hz).

CPU—central processing unit. It is the component of a computer system that performs arithmetic and logical functions and directs the flow of information between memory, peripherals, and central registers. The CPU performs the execution of the instructions in a program.

current—the quantity of electrons flowing in a conductor or semiconductor. The amount of current flow is determined by the voltage and resistance of an electric circuit. The power that is consumed in a circuit is equal to the product of the voltage and current in the circuit.

cutoff frequency—the frequency that divides the passband from the stopband of a filter. It is the lowest frequency transmitted by a high-pass filter or the highest frequency transmitted by a low-pass filter.

DAC—see digital-to-analog converter.

decay—the portion of a tone's onset where the sound dies out. The decay portion of a tone's envelope is also called the fall time.

decibel—a unit of measurement for the intensity of a signal. The decibel scale is related to the logarithm of a signal's amplitude, and closely represents the loudness of a sound as perceived by the ear.

DFT—discrete Fourier transform. It is the Fourier transform of a digital signal. It is used by the computer to perform digital signal analysis and processing.

digital—a term describing a signal represented by discrete numbers or an instrument used to arithmetically process numbers.

digital-to-analog converter (DAC)—A device used to convert numbers (are represented in a computer memory) into electric voltage levels. A digital signal consists of a sequence of numbers that must be transformed into a fluctuating voltage before it is useful for monitoring or tape recording.

diode—a device that conducts electric current in only one direction.

discrete—occurring in finite steps—noncontinuous. Since a continuous function cannot be stored in a computer memory, it must be represented as a series of discrete numerical values. Discrete functions are associated with digital signals, whereas continuous functions apply to analog waveforms.

disk—the most common medium of storage in a computer's secondary memory. A disk memory can hold much more information than can a primary random-access memory, but it requires more time to access that information. Hence, in normal operation, units of information are periodically swapped between disk and main memory.

dissonance—the degree of clash between two tones. Dissonant intervals are generally not related or are only remotely related harmonically. But the degree of dissonance is mostly a matter of subjective perception and is determined by the context of the musical passage where it is found.

driving function—the mathematical function used to describe the input signal to a filter or other processing device. In subtractive synthesis used for speech simulation, the driving function is a series of impulses or white noise.

drum—a magnetic recording device used for secondary memory storage in large, main-frame computers. The use of magnetic drum memories is on the decline because of their excessive size, weight, and bulk.

dynamic—changing in time. The dynamics of a tone refer to its change in amplitude, pitch, and timbre through the period of the tone's onset. It also refers to the change in loudness through a musical passage.

dynamic range—the range in intensity of a dynamically fluctuating signal. It is usually expressed in decibels. The dynamic range of a musical recording or performance is the difference between the loudest and the softest passages. The dynamic range of a recording is the signal-to-noise ratio—for example, the difference in strength between the background noise and a signal recorded at full intensity without distortion.

editor—a program built into most computer systems that allows a user to enter and modify text. Using an editor, a programmer may enter code or text to a file line by line. Later he or she may add more lines, delete lines, change the characters in a line, insert lines, and search for lines containing particular character sequences. The editor is typically used in preparing programs for compilation and execution. It may also be used for writing documents.

emitter—the element of a transistor where current enters the device.

entropy—a measure of randomness or disorder. A signal with maximal entropy (such as white noise) follows no pattern or repetition and is totally unpreditable. Entropy is the inverse of redundancy. An example of a redundant signal having no entropy is a sine wave.

envelope—the change in amplitude of a tone during its onset. The envelope of a tone normally consists of a rise or attack time, a sustain period, and a decay or fall time as the sound dies out. It is often thought of as the dynamic "shape" of a tone.

envelope generator—a module on an electronic music synthesizer that is used to control the onset of a tone. The output of the envelope generator is patched to a voltage-controlled amplifier to regulate its gain and thereby modify the signal's intensity as it is amplified.

equalizer—a signal-processing device consisting of several bandpass filters, each tuned to a different frequency. The gain of each of the filters may be adjusted separately, so that the overall frequency reponse of the equalizer can be manipulated arbitrarily. Equalizers are manufactured primarily for use in recording studios and P.A. systems to compensate for poor environmental acoustics, but they are also widely used in electronic music compositions to modify the timbre of recorded sounds.

execute—a term referring to the computer's performance of a program's instructions. A computer can only execute a program after it has been translated from a user language (such as FORTRAN) into binary-machine code by a compiler program.

fall time—the decay period of a tone's onset, where the amplitude diminishes and the tone dies out.

FFT—fast Fourier transform. A special, highly efficient algorithm developed for a computer to perform the discrete Fourier transform of a digital signal with greatly reduced computation requirements.

file—a section in a computer's secondary memory reserved for an individual user. A user may store programs, documentation, and data on the memory files allocated to him or her by the system.

filter—a device that modifies the spectrum of a signal by attenuating some of its frequency components. Filters are widely used in signal processing to eliminate unwanted frequencies from waveforms.

finite-state machine—a device that can exist in one of a given set of states at any particular time. Its behavior is deterministic and predictable if one knows its transition characteristics and present state. The computer is a prime example of a highly complex, finite-state machine.

firmware—a category of computer architecture midway between hardware and software. Firmware consists of read-only-memories (ROMs), which store machine-level programs that are used repeatedly by the operating system.

first-generation computers—computers developed during the 1950s. They were typically manufactured out of vacuum tubes and relays, and have long since been obsolete.

flip-flop—an individual switch in a computer circuit. It is used to store a single bit of information. The flip-flop stores a binary 1 if it is conducting, or a 0 if it is not conducting. The state of a flip-flop is controlled electronically by its surrounding logic circuitry.

foldover—*see* aliasing.

formant—one of the principal component frequencies of a speech sound that determine the vowel color. Determination and description of a vowel's formants is an essential part of speech analysis. The formants can be resynthesized to simulate the vowel artificially. Formant theory has also been used in the analysis of instrumental tones.

Fourier analysis—the transformation of a signal from the time domain to the frequency domain. It is used to perform spectral analysis of musical tones. By conducting a Fourier analysis of a waveform, one may represent it as a function of frequency and determine the strength of all of its frequency components.

Fourier series—the Fourier transform of a periodic signal. Any waveform that is strictly periodic contains a discrete set of frequency components. Hence, the Fourier transform of a periodic signal consists of a discrete series of values—one for the fundamental frequency and each of its harmonics.

Fourier transform—the function of frequency that is obtained by performing a Fourier analysis of a signal.

frequency—the number of repetitions per second of a periodic function. The fundamental frequency of a tone is perceived as the tone's pitch.

frequency domain—the basis for analysis of signals where the signal's strength is represented as a function of frequency. The frequency-domain representation of a signal is also called its spectrum.

frequency shifter—an electronic device that shifts all the component frequencies of a signal by a uniform amount. It accomplishes this by heterodyning the signal, producing two sidebands for each frequency. It then transmits one of the sidebands while suppressing the other. It is widely used in electronic music composition to create interesting distortion of recorded material.

function—a mathematical relationship wherein one set of values is mapped into another set. A function may be exhibited by a graph or a table. Sound pressure levels and electronic signals may be represented mathematically as functions of time, meaning that each instant of time in the function's domain is mapped into a value of voltage, current, or acoustic pressure.

fundamental—the principal frequency component of a complex musical tone. The fundamental frequency determines the tone's pitch. If the tone is harmonic, the remaining tones of its spectrum occur at multiples of the fundamental frequency.

gain—the ratio of the amplitude output from a signal processing device to the amplitude of the incoming signal. The gain of an amplifier is the measure of its amplification. The gain of a filter at any particular frequency is the degree whereby that frequency is attenuated. A gain value, greater than 1 corresponds to amplification, while a gain less than 1 is attenuation.

gate—an element in a computer circuit that performs a logical function such as: AND, OR, NOT, NAND (not and), NOR, or EXCLUSIVE OR.

hardware—the physical construction of a computer. It comprises gates, flip-flops, and other elements implemented by electronic devices. A computer's hardware can malfunction because of physical defects, and can be damaged by excessive temperature or current.

harmonic—a multiple of the fundamental frequency component of a periodic signal. It is also referred to as an "overtone." The presence of harmonics in a musical tone add to its color and partially determine its overall timbre.

hertz—the standard unit of frequency. Scientists and engineers prefer this term to "cycles per second."

heterodyne—to multiply one signal by another signal, such as a sine wave. Heterodyning is used in signal processing to shift frequencies of a waveform. It is also used in spectral analysis to isolate and trace the dynamics of a particular frequency component.

high-pass filter—a basic filter that transmits all frequencies above a particular cutoff value while it attenuates the lower frequencies.

"high" state—a voltage level (approximately 5 volts) in a computer-logic circuit that represents a binary 1.

"host" computer—the physical computer wherein resides a particular software system. One software or operating system can theoretically reside in any number of similar host computers.

impedance—resistance of a medium to the transmission of a signal. In acoustics, it is the resistance of the air to the passage of a sound wave. This impedance is greater in open air than it is in a tightly enclosed environment, which accounts for the acoustical characteristics of resonating columns such as musical wind instruments.

impulse—an instantaneous burst of power. An impulse of current through a loudspeaker produces a loud click. A sequence of impulses (or impulse train) is used in synthetic speech production to simulate the action of the human glottis and vocal chords.

instruction register—a register in a computer's central processing unit that contains the binary code for the instruction being executed when a program is run. When the instruction is completed, the processor fetches the next instruction of the program from memory and loads it into the instruction register for execution.

integrated circuit—a miniature electronic circuit containing several microscopic elements. The elements are etched onto a wafer (or chip) of silicon measuring approximately ¼ inch square by a photoengraving process. One integrated-circuit (IC) chip may contain more than a million separate circuit elements and run on a few milliwatts of power.

interface—a device or connecting path between two components of a computing system. The interface allows communication to take place between them. For example, an extensive circuit is required to interface a terminal keyboard to a computer processor. The interface must generate a distinct electric signal (representing the ASCII code) for each key as it is depressed and then input that signal to the computer. Another interface circuit then produces a visible character on the screen for each ASCII-coded signal it receives from the computer. This way the computer is able to "talk" to the terminal.

interpolation—the interjection of a numerical value into a discrete function based on neighboring values. For example, if the values of a function are only annotated for each integer in its domain, and a value of the function is sought for a fractional number, this value may be projected from the values of the function at the integers nearest the fraction. For example, if $F(10) = 50$ and $F(11) = 60$, a linearly interpolated value for $F(10.7)$ would be 57.

interpreter—a systems program that processes statements in BASIC. The function of a BASIC interpreter is similar to that of a FORTRAN compiler, except that the interpreter processes each statement as it is entered rather than compiling the entire program in one operation. Thus the interpreter functions interactively with the operator, having conversational capability not shared by compiler languages.

intonation—tuning of a musical scale. The intonation is slightly different for a just scale than it is for a tempered scale. The just scale is tuned by harmonic ratios while the tempered scale divides the octave into 12 exactly equal intervals.

iteration—repetition or cycle through a program loop.

just scale (intonation)—a 12-note scale divided so that its principal intervals are tuned according to the simple harmonic ratios that define them. For example, the ratios of perfect fifth = 3:2, perfect fourth = 4:3, major third = 5:4, minor third = 6:5, and major second = 9:8.

linear prediction—an elaborate mathematical technique used in speech synthesis. Future samples of a digitized speech waveform are projected from a linear combination of previous samples and an error function. Its primary application is in vocoders where speech must be transmitted along narrow bandwidth-communication channels. It may potentially be employed in computer music to simulate instruments or synthesize tones with original timbres.

load—to transfer information into a computer register or section of memory. A computer program is loaded into memory after it is entered from a terminal and compiled. "LOAD" is also a machine-level instruction that transfers the contents of a particular memory location to a register in the central processing unit.

low-pass filter—a basic filter that transmits all frequencies below a particular cutoff value while it attenuates the higher frequencies.

"low" state—a low voltage level in a computer logic circuit that represents a binary 0.

machine language—the level of computer programming whose instructions can be directly executed by the central processing unit. These instructions specifically define the operation the processor is to perform, for example, flow of information, addition, complementation, negation, and so forth. Machine language instructions are coded as binary numbers and stored as such in memory. Programs written in user-level languages such as FORTRAN and BASIC must be compiled or interpreted into machine language before they can be run on the computer.

main-frame computers—large, time-sharing computer installations that are designed to serve many users and process many programs simultaneously. A main-frame computer system requires a professional staff and large physical facilities for its operation and maintenance.

memory—the part of a computing system that stores large amounts of information, such as programs, data, and documentation. The main memory of a computer is divided into registers, each of which has an identifying address. Each memory register stores one word of information. The contents of memory may be numbers represented in binary form, alphanumeric symbols in their ASCII-coded form, or machine-language instructions in their binary code.

microprocessor—a microcomputer. Microprocessors are generally small enough that their central processing units can be manufactured on a single integrated-circuit chip. They are inexpensive but have limited information handling capacity. Microprocessors are generally used for dedicated rather than general-purpose applications and run one or a few specific programs built in read-only-memory. They are typically used in larger computing systems to interface the main computer with peripheral devices such as terminals and line printers. Microprocessors are also enjoying increasing popularity in novice "home" computers, television games, traffic-signal controllers, appliances, signal-processing devices, and other uses because of their versatility, increasing capability, and rapidly decreasing cost.

microsecond—1/1,000,000 second.

millisecond—1/1000 second.

minicomputer—a small, inexpensive, general-purpose computer whose memory, speed, and capacity is limited to processing a few user programs at one time. Minicomputers are advantageous in that they require much less power, space, and maintenance than larger main-frame installations.

mixer—an electronic apparatus used in sound studios to mix several audio signals into a single output for recording or broadcast. The level of each input is controlled separately to obtain the desired balance among the sources.

mode—one of the possible ways that a resonator such as a stretched string or tuned air column may emit sound. Each mode corresponds to a multiple of one-half or one-quarter wavelength of the fundamental tone and produces one of the tone's harmonics.

modulation—a change in the frequency or dynamics of a sound. (Also refers to a change in tonality of a composition.) Modulation of the amplitude or frequency of a periodic wave multiplies its spectral components and increases its timbral complexity.

modulation index—The coefficient of the modulating function in a frequency-modulation equation. Increasing the modulation index increases the variation of frequency in the output wave and augments the number and diversity of sidebands generated by the modulation.

module—a component in an electronic music synthesizer. Common synthesizer modules include: voltage-controlled oscillators, amplifiers, filters, envelope generators, white-noise generators, ring modulators, sequencers, and frequency dividers.

musique concrète—music composed from tape-recorded source materials. The sources are processed electronically, mixed, and sometimes recorded at varying tape speeds to create interesting and unusual sound effects.

object program—a computer program in machine-code form as it may reside in memory ready for execution.

onset—the change in dynamics of a tone, also called its envelope. As a tone is sounded, its amplitude rises to a peak value, sustains momentarily, then decays and dies out. The period of the rise and decay is the tone's onset.

oscillator—a device used to generate a simple periodic waveform. In an electronic synthesizer, a typical oscillator may output a sine, square, sawtooth, or triangle wave. The frequency is determined by a control on its front panel or by an input voltage. A digital oscillator can be made from a computer program or hardware device that periodically calculates the function of an index as it is incremented in real time and outputs the function to a DAC.

overtone—a frequency component of a complex waveform higher than the fundamental. The harmonics of a musical tone are often called its overtones. The overtones produced by an instrument are caused by its oscillation in several modes simultaneously, and are responsible for the tone's color.

parameter—a value used in calculating a mathematical function. For example, the parameters of a sine function are its amplitude and frequency. The term "parameter" also refers to the values associated with variable names that are passed from a computer program to a subroutine.

partial—a component of a complex tone higher than the fundamental. Its frequency is not necessarily a multiple of the fundamental—so while a harmonic overtone is a partial, a partial may not necessarily be harmonic. Bells, cymbals, and other percussive instruments produce a variety of nonharmonic partials, giving them a clangorous, noisy tone quality.

passband—the range of frequencies transmitted by a filter.

patch cord—an electric cord used to interconnect electronic components such as the modules of a synthesizer.

periodic signal—a signal that repeats itself exactly at equal intervals of time. The frequency components of a periodic signal occur at multiples of its fundamental frequency; hence, its spectrum is a discrete set of values. A sustained musical tone is an approximately periodic signal, whereas a sharply articulated sound is aperiodic.

phase—the orientation in time of a waveform. For example, a sine wave and cosine wave differ only by their phase. While the human ear is very sensitive to amplitude variation in a complex tone's spectrum, it is relatively insensitive to variations in phase. The addition of two waveforms having the same phase results in their reinforcement and mutual strengthening, whereas addition of two waveforms that are out of phase results in their cancellation and attenuation.

portamento—a sliding in pitch between two successive notes of a musical composition.

primary memory—the main memory of a computing system. The processor must have immediate, random access to any word in its primary memory. Hence, each of its registers is assigned a unique address for reference by the processor. Because of space and hardware limitations, the primary memory is not large enough to contain all the software required by the system. Consequently, the main memory must be augmented by a secondary memory such as magnetic disk that, while slower in access time, has a much greater information capacity.

probability distribution—a function defining a set of probability values for random variables. The sum of probabilities taken over all the possible choices must equal 100. For example, if the random variable is a number between 2 and 12 selected from rolling a pair of dice, the probability distribution function annotates the probability of selection for each of those numbers.

processor—the central processing unit of a computer (*see* CPU).

program counter—a register in a central processing unit that contains the memory address of an instruction word. The memory location contains the next instruction of a program to be loaded into the instruction register and executed. Each time an instruction is performed, the address in the program counter in incremented.

psychoacoustics—the study of human sound perception. It concerns not only the way sounds stimulate the hearing mechanism, but the way the brain interprets the stimulus from the ear.

pure tone—a tone consisting only of its fundamental pitch without any overtones or partials. A pure tone can be represented by a sine wave; hence, it is often called a "sine tone." Any complex tone can be decomposed into a sum of pure tones.

quantization noise—the background noise resulting from digital sampling of a waveform. The cause of this noise is the slight imprecision inherent in the sampling process. Nevertheless, in digital recording that uses a 16-bit word for each sample, the level of resulting quantization noise is virtually inaudible.

radian—the basic unit of angular measurement. It is the circumscribed length along the circumference of a circle whose radius is one unit. Since the length of the entire circumference of such a unit circle is 2π, an angle of 2π radians equals 360°. Consequently, the period of a sine or cosine function is equal to 2π radians.

radian frequency—angular frequency measured in radians. Since one cycle is equal to 2π radians, a frequency of 1 cycle per second equals a radian frequency of 2π radians per second.

RAM—random-access-memory. A memory system whose contents may be accessed directly by specifying an address. Any word in a random-access-memory may be accessed as quickly as any other word. Random-access-memory is used in a computer's primary memory system. As opposed to read-only-memory (ROM), the contents of a RAM may be changed, or "rewritten" at any time as the system operates.

real-time—a computer processing application whereby results are calculated and output at the same rate that data is input. Thus delay and intermediate storage of results are not required. Real-time operation is greatly advantageous to a computer music composer because, like using a conventional instrument, the results of his or her work are heard while directly producing it. However, real-time operation requires high computing speed and efficiency, and many complex sound-synthesis operations require too much arithmetic to be done in real time without excessively large and expensive facilities.

register—an array of flip-flops used to store one computer word. The central processing unit contains several specialized registers to process data as dictated by program instructions, and the main memory system contains several thousand addressed registers to store data, program instructions, and documentation.

resonance—the ability to oscillate at a given frequency. For example, the resonant frequencies of a stretched string occur at values whose one-half wavelength is a divisor of the string's total length. Each resonant frequency corresponds to a mode of vibration. The resonant frequency of a vibrating body may be altered by changing its length, or other physical characteristics.

resonator—a body or system that is capable of resonance. Most musical instruments employ some form of resonator.

ring modulator—a signal-processing device used in synthesizers to multiply two signals. Use of a ring modulator augments the complexity of a waveform by producing two sidebands for every frequency component multiplied in the incoming signals.

rise time—the initial period of increasing amplitude in a tone's onset. It is also referred to as the attack time.

ROM—read-only-memory. A computer memory whose contents are permanently fixed so that in operation it is not erased or rewritten. It is mainly used for dedicated programs that are run repeatedly without modification, especially in microprocessors. Since a ROM is neither distinctly hardware nor software, it is called "firmware."

sample—an individual measurement or value in a digital waveform. In digital recording, several thousand samples are taken to represent 1 second of sound. Each sample is then stored in one word of memory. The sampling process is performed with an ADC.

sampling frequency—the number of samples taken or output per second. To represent a signal accurately, the sampling frequency must be at least twice the frequency of the highest component in the sampled signal. Consequently, for high-fidelity music reproduction, one may employ a sampling frequency of approximately 30,000 samples per second.

second-generation computers—computers manufactured during the 1960s. They typically use individual, hard-wired electronic components and core memory. Consequently, they are very large and expensive. Although many second-generation machines are still in operation, modern computers are made from much smaller, more economical integrated circuits.

secondary memory—the auxiliary memory system of a computer—usually disk or drum. Its capacity is much larger than primary memory, but its access time is considerably longer. Data on a disk or drum is recorded magnetically on the surface of a platter rather than in individual, addressable registers. The platter must spin under a tape head, so that the data only passes it periodically, accounting for the slower access speed.

semiconductor—a material that is a poor conductor of electricity. Silicon crystal is a semiconductor that is used in transistors, diodes, and integrated circuits because of its special electronic properties. The term "semiconductor" is thus commonly used to reference these devices. Memories manufactured with integrated circuits are often called "semiconductor memories."

sequencer—a module on an electronic music synthesizer that outputs a short sequence of voltages, and continuously repeats the sequence. The voltages and rate of sequence are arbitrarily set by the operator of the synthesizer.

sideband—an additional frequency component introduced by the modulation of two signals. For example, if a signal is heterodyned by a sine wave, the process introduces the two sidebands for every original component. Sidebands are also introduced into frequency-modulated waveforms, according to the amount of modulation.

signal processing—the branch of engineering concerned with the analysis, modification, and synthesis of electronic and digital signals. The study of digital signal processing is fundamental to the art of sound synthesis in computer music.

sine function—a trigonometric function describing the vertical deflection of a circularly rotating object. It is the most fundamental relation in waveform analysis because it describes the oscillation of simple resonators.

sine tone—a pure tone whose sound wave is describable by a sinusoid.

sine wave—a wave describable by a sinusoid.

sinusoid—a function characteristically identical to a sine function, but of arbitrary phase. A cosine function or negated-sine function is a sinusoid, as is a combination of sine and cosine functions of the same frequency.

software—the resident programming of a computing system. Although it is not physically tangible like hardware, it defines and controls the system's operation. The software of a computer can be printed on paper or can be implemented on another similar computer.

solid state—the branch of electronics concerned with the properties of semiconductor crystals such as silicon. Solid-state components are made from devices such as transistors and integrated circuits that employ such semiconductors. The introduction of solid-state electronics has rendered vacuum-tube technology nearly obsolete.

source program—a user-level program available for compilation. For example, a FORTRAN compiler translates the language of a FORTRAN source program into the binary code of an object program. The source program is written by the programmer.

spectrum—the frequency-domain description of a signal. The spectrum represents amplitude as a function of frequency. One can obtain the spectrum of a function mathematically by Fourier analysis.

static—not changing in time. A static tone is an unmodulated tone. While musical tones are not typically static, very short portions of them may be considered static for purposes of harmonic analysis.

stochastic music—music composed from chance or random processes. This form of music is promoted chiefly by some contemporary composers such as John Cage and Iannis Xenakis. Xenakis has developed several elaborate algorithms for computer-composed stochastic music.

stopband—the range of frequencies attenuated by a filter. For example, the stopband of a high-pass filter comprises frequencies below the cutoff frequency.

store—to transfer the contents of a CPU register to memory. The STORE instruction is the reverse of the LOAD instruction.

subroutine—a subprogram called by another computer program or subprogram. A subroutine can be used to economize computer programming where a particular sequence of instructions must be repeated several times or be used by more than one program. The flow of instruction exits from the main program at the subroutine CALL statement, then proceeds with the instructions of the subroutine. On completion of the subroutine, control returns to the original program where it left off.

subtractive synthesis—the production of signals by filtering a spectrally rich source such as an impulse train or white noise. The filter subtracts away unwanted frequencies, leaving the desired components. Subtractive synthesis is used chiefly in digital signal processing for artificial speech production. It may also potentially be exploited in computer music to simulate conventional instruments or to create original tones.

summation formula—a technique of computer sound synthesis based on the frequency-modulation equation. It has been developed extensively at Stanford University, particularly in the simulation of brass instrument tones.

synthesis—artificial construction of a waveform. In electronic music compositions, tones are synthesized by oscillators and other signal generators. A computer can synthesize sounds by computing samples for a digital waveform and outputting the samples to a DAC with audio equipment.

synthesizer—an elaborate instrument containing a variety of electronic signal generating and processing devices. The modules of an electronic music synthesizer are interconnected in different ways with patch cords, and their controls are set by a composer-performer. Once configurated, activated, and operating, the instrument creates an infinite variety of original tones and sound effects.

table-lookup—a technique of digital waveform synthesis that is sometimes more computationally efficient than direct additive synthesis. The values of a digital waveform are stored in a table and referenced sequentially rather than computed arithmetically. Table-lookup is particularly advantageous for complex waveforms that would otherwise require horrendous amounts of number crunching and computer time to calculate by additive synthesis.

tempered scale—the 12-note scale that is slightly mistuned harmonically so that all 12 intervals are equal. While tempered intonation lacks the harmonic purity of just intonation, it is able to be used in performance in any key. It is almost universally used for precisely tuned instruments.

third-generation computers—computers manufactured during the 1970s. Because of their use of integrated circuits, they are much more compact and economical than their second-generation predecessors. The third generation is noted for the rapidly growing popularity of minicomputers and microprocessors over main-frame installations.

threshold of hearing—the minimum level of sound intensity that is perceptable to the human ear. On the absolute decibel scale, zero is defined at the threshold of hearing.

timbre—the tone color of a sound. It is determined by the relative frequencies and the independant dynamic characteristics of the tone's partials. Unlike the loudness or pitch of a tone, the timbre cannot be measured on a scale; but it may be described in terms of a dynamically varying spectrum.

time domain—the representation of a signal as a function of time. It depicts the signal's waveshape and temporal behavior, but does not reveal its spectral characteristics.

time-sharing—the ability of a large computing system to process many programs simultaneously. It does this by sharing its main memory among different programs and rapidly alternating its processor between them in their execution. Time-sharing is possible with a large computer because much less time is required for actual computation than is for data input and output to secondary memory and periferal devices.

transducer—a device that converts mechanical energy to electrical energy and vice versa. Typical examples are microphones, phonograph pickups, and loudspeakers.

transistor—a solid-state electronic device usually used as an amplifier or switch. Typical transistors contain three elements of doped silicon crystal. The voltage applied to one of the elements controls the flow of current between the other two. Transistors are manufactured individually or incorporated in integrated circuits.

tremelo—a fluctuation in amplitude of a musical tone. It is not to be confused with the tone's onset, since tremelo is generally periodic and sustained. Although it sounds similar to vibrato, tremelo does not vary the tone's pitch.

trigger—a short, electrical pulse used in a synthesizer to initiate action of one of the modules. Typically the synthesizer's keyboard outputs a trigger pulse when a key is depressed, and the trigger is used to activate an envelope generator.

tritone—the dissonant interval of six notes of the chromatic scale. It is also called an augmented fourth or diminished fifth.

truth table—a table that describes the behavior of a logic device or finite-state machine. The table can be used to define a logic function to be implemented in a computer circuit. Hence, such tables are widely used by engineers in designing digital logic elements.

twelve-tone row—a form of serial, atonal music invented by Arnold Shöenberg. A 12-tone row dictates a single usage of each note of the chromatic scale in a particular, repeating sequence.

variable—a term in an algebraic expression used to stand for a value. The value assumed by the variable may change from one application of the expression to another. The variables in a computer program are used similarly, and they refer to locations in memory whose contents can change as the program is run. Computer program variables are assigned arbitrary names of alphanumeric characters. They can also be used as parameters and arguments in functions.

vibrato—the fluctuation in pitch of a musical tone. A typical vibrato varies the pitch approximately ⅛ step in either direction, and fluctuates about 8 times per second.

vocoder—a contraction for "Voice-coder." A vocoder transmits a speech signal by performing a spectral analysis of the signal, then transmitting the spectral information to a synthesizer for the signal's reconstruction. It is used for speech transmission along narrow bandwidth-communication channels. It also has much potential for experimentation in computer music synthesis.

voice coil—the movable electromagnetic coil of wire in a loudspeaker or dynamic microphone.

voltage—the electromotive force that drives current through a conductor of electricity. If voltage is applied to a nonconducting material, there is no current. For a material of given resistance, the amount of current that flows through it is determined by the level of voltage across it.

watt—the standard unit of power. One watt of electrical power is equal to 1 ampere of electronic current multiplied by 1 volt. For example, if 10 volts is driving 2 amps of current through a circuit, the power consumed in the circuit is 20 watts.

white noise—an acoustic signal containing equal components of all frequencies. It is purely random, having maximum entropy, and contains no repeating patterns of any kind. Such a signal sounds like a steady hiss.

word (computer)—a unit of information stored in a computer. Each memory and CPU register stores one word whose size corresponds to the register length. In large, main-frame computers, word lengths are 32 to 64 bits. Minicomputers generally use 12- or 16-bit words. Microprocessors developed before 1978 use an 8-bit word size, but since then several firms have introduced 16-bit microcomputers to the marketplace.

APPENDIX A

PROGRAMMING IN BASIC

For many years, FORTRAN has been the most widely used computer programming language for scientific applications. Nevertheless, it is possible to instruct the computer to perform simple computations without the complexities inherent in FORTRAN. For this purpose a programming language was developed at Dartmouth College named BASIC. The instructions in BASIC are very similar to FORTRAN, but are much simpler to learn. Thus the BASIC language is presented here to serve as an introduction to FORTRAN as well as for its own use. One characteristic of BASIC that is advantageous to FORTRAN is that it is a conversational language. This means that each BASIC command is interpreted at the moment it is typed into the keyboard terminal. As the programmer enters a statement in BASIC, the interpreter immediately compiles it if it is correctly syntaxed, or else it displays an error message. FORTRAN compilers, by contrast, must process the *entire* program in one operation. The fundamental advantage of BASIC then, is that it is easy to learn, inexpensive to use because BASIC interpreters use little computer time, and that it has the one-line conversational capability that other languages lack.

We introduce computer programming and the BASIC language by presenting the short and complete program shown in Fig. A.1 that performs some simple arithmetic. Notice that the most conspicuous feature of a BASIC program is the way each statement is numbered. The statement numbers dictate the order in which the instructions are executed. This makes modifying and editing BASIC programs very convenient. Suppose that in typing the program above the user had mistakenly typed

```
20 LET X = A + B - B
```

and then had not noticed the mistake until the rest of the program had been typed. To correct it, the user simply types

```
20 LET X = A + B - C
```

```
10 READ A, B, C
20 LET X = A + B - C
30 LET Y1 = C * B - X
40 LET Y2 = C * (B - X)
50 LET Z1 = X/Y1 * Y2
60 LET Z2 = Z1/(A * (X - 4.5))
70 LET W = B↑3
80 PRINT X, Y1, Y2
90 PRINT Z1, Z2, W
100 STOP
900 DATA 6, 2, 3
1000 END
```

Figure A.1 A simple BASIC program.

and the computer automatically erases the first, incorrect instruction and replaces it with the latter.

Notice also that the statement numbers increase in increments of 10. This is a matter of convenience rather than necessity. They could just as easily have been listed in increments of 1, 5, or 100—it would not matter to the computer. BASIC instructions are conventionally incremented in steps of 10 so that it is possible to insert additional statements in the middle of a program at a later time. For example, if a programmer had already entered the complete program of Fig. A.1, he or she could as an afterthought type

```
25 LET X1 = A - B + C
95 PRINT X1
```

and the computer would insert the new statement numbered 25 in between statements #20 and #30 in the original program. It would likewise insert the new statement #95 between #90 and #100. A programmer may delete a statement by typing only its statement number while leaving the rest of the statement blank.

The first step of our program receives the data—that is, the numbers 6, 2, and 3. It assigns them to the variable names A, B, and C. The DATA statement that supplies the numbers appears at the end of the program, but it is a companion to the READ statement. It is placed after the main part of the program so that the program can be run with different sets of data. This program assigns the value 6 to the variable A, 2 to B, and 3 to C. In both of these statements, the variables A, B, and C, and the constants 6, 2, and 3 are separated by commas. The data may optionally be read in separate statements. For example, statement #10 could be replaced by three separate statements

```
10 READ A
20 READ B
30 READ C
```

without changing the effect of the program. Similarly, statement #900 could be replaced by

```
900 DATA 6, 2
910 DATA 3
```

In any case, the first number in a DATA statement is always assigned to the first variable in a READ statement, the second constant to the second variable, and so forth.

The focus of computer programming is the assignment and manipulation of variable names. One may conveniently conceptualize their function by imagining that each variable in a program is a box in the computer's memory. Written on the outside of the box is the variable name, for example, A, B, C, Y1, Y2. The cardinal rule in BASIC for assigning variable names is that every name must be either a single letter of the alphabet or else an alphabet letter followed by a single numeral. The contents of the variable box is the number currently assigned to the variable. This number may be changed any time during the program. Let us examine the statement

```
20 LET X = A + B - C
```

An accurate (though wordy) way of interpreting the instruction would be "add the numbers assigned to the variable names A and B, subtract the number assigned to C, then place the results in a memory location labeled X." One must particularly notice that the "=" sign in a LET statement does not precisely mean "equals" in the sense of algebra or arithmetic. The point seems somewhat technical, but its importance is dramatized by two examples. Suppose that the following statement appears in a BASIC program:

```
30 LET X = A + B
```

Then, later on in the program,

```
140 LET X = C - D4
```

If one tries to interpret these statements in terms of conventional algebra, they simply contradict each other. But in the context of a computer program, they simply mean that the variable X is first assigned the value of A + B and is reassigned the value of C − D4 later on. Another statement that is meaningless in ordinary algebra but is useful in BASIC in

LET X = X + 1

Here, the "=" symbol means "be replaced by." This instruction usually appears as a counter in program loops. It simply increments the value of X by 1 each time it is executed.

Suppose, now, that in our program the statement LET X = A + B − C were placed and numbered before the READ A, B, C statement rather than after it. The computer would not be able to execute the instruction because it would be attempting to calculate A + B − C before the variables A, B, and C had been given number assignments. Consequently, the programmer must always pay careful attention not to use any variable names in a program that have not already been assigned a value by a LET statement, a READ, or another input statement. The LET statement may be used to assign a constant to a variable name. For example, the trigonometric constant 2π is generally used in computing a sine function. A program that calls the sine function may contain the instruction

LET P2 = 6.2831853

This is strictly a matter of convenience to the programmer as it is easier to type P2 than 6.2831853 if the number is to appear several times in a program.

The rules of BASIC actually allow LET commands to be entered without using the word LET. That is to say that the instruction

20 X = A + B − C

is perfectly legal. However, the word LET is usually included for cultural and aesthetic reasons.

Numbers may be entered into the computer in three formats, abbreviated E, F, and I. The E format corresponds to scientific notation, and is used to abbreviate extremely large or small numbers. For example, the number 4,930,000,000 is written in scientific notation as 4.93×10^9. In E format, it is typed 4.93E9. Similarly, the number $0.000015 = 1.5 \times 10^{-5}$ is typed as 1.5E-5 in E format. The F format is simply the number typed with a decimal point. The I format applies only to integers and omits the decimal point. Thus the number 300 is typed in E format as 3.OE2, in F format as 300.0 or simply 300., or as 300 in I format. The programmer may freely choose whichever format is most convenient.

Consider now the instruction

```
30 LET Y1 = C * B - X
```

Since X was just assigned a value in statement #20, it is used in the computation and assignment of Y1. The question arises as to which operation in this statement is performed first: the subtraction or the multiplication (indicated by the "*" symbol). The rule in programming is the same as for algebra; that is, multiplication and division have priority over addition, subtraction, and negation. Thus in the above statement, X is subtracted from the product of C and B. Since the DATA statement assigned 6 to A, 2 to B, and 3 to C, statement #30 therefore assigns Y1 the value C * C – X = 3 * 2 – 5 = 1.

The statement

```
40 LET Y2 = C * (B - X)
```

by contrast, instructs the computer to perform the subtraction first as dictated by the parentheses. It assigns the value 3 * (2 – 5) = 3 * (–3) = –9 to Y2. Notice that the statement

```
30 LET Y1 = (C * B) - X
```

is identical in meaning to

```
30 LET Y1 = C * B - X
```

because the multiplication is performed first anyway unless the parentheses direct otherwise as in statement #40.

Now that the variables Y1 and Y2 have been assigned the values 1 and –9, they may be used to calculate a value for the new variable Z1 in the instruction

```
50 LET Z1 = X/Y1 * Y2
```

The "/" sign indicates division. Here the question of priority of operations is again raised. Since multiplication and division have equal priority, the operations are performed from left to right. Thus in the preceding statement the division is performed first, yielding Z1 = (5/1) * (–9) = –45. Similarly, a statement such as LET X5 = X1 – X2 – X3 is interpreted as X5 = (X1 – X2) – X3, performing the subtraction on the left first.

The instruction

```
60 LET Z2 = Z1/(A * (X - 4.5))
```

illustrates the use of nested parentheses. The computer always starts with the expression in the innermost pair. The first operation to be performed above is the computation of X − 4.5 = 5 − 4.5 = 0.5. The result 0.5 is then multiplied by A (which is 6) to yield 3 that is finally used to divide Z1 (which is −45). Z2, then is assigned the value of −45/3 = −15.

The "↑" symbol in instruction #70 indicates exponentiation—that is B↑3 means B^3. (Some BASIC systems use the double asterisk "B**3" rather than the up arrow. The user must check the system he or she is using.) The power term in an exponentiation operation may be a variable as well as a constant. Thus the expressions A↑B and 4.28↑X are legal. The operation of exponentiation has priority over all other operations in computer programming as it does in algebra.

Now that the computer has finished executing the portion of the program containing the arithmetic and assignment of variable names, its final task is to output the results. The statements

```
80 PRINT X, Y1, Y2
90 PRINT Z1, Z2, Z
```

accomplish this. In this instance, the fact that two separate PRINT statements were used cause the results to be printed on two separate lines so that they look like this:

```
  5     1    -9
-45   -15     8
```

Alternatively, the six variables can all be included in a single PRINT statement,

```
80 PRINT X, Y1, Y2, Z1, Z2, W
```

and all the numbers are output on a single line. If the programmer wishes to use two separate PRINT statements (perhaps they would be placed at separate locations in the program), yet still have the results appear on a single line, he or she can end the first PRINT statement with a comma:

```
        .
        .
        .
    (calculation of X1 and X2)
 80 PRINT X1, X2,
    (calculation of X3 and X4)
240 PRINT X3, X4
        .
        .
        .
```

This will cause X1, X2, X3, and X4 to be printed on the same line as if they had appeared in a single PRINT command.

The statement

```
100 STOP
```

tells the computer to do just that—to stop. The computation is finished and there is no more to do. It is the last executable instruction in the program. The DATA statement and END statement that follow it are not instructions. The DATA statement may appear anywhere in the program, but is normally placed at the end to separate it from the main body of the program. It simply provides the numbers to be input by the READ instruction. The END statement (though it may appear to be redundant after a STOP statement has already been entered), does not cause the computer to do anything. It simply signals the interpreter that there are no more statements to follow in the program. Thus the END statement must always be the last statement of a computer program. Frequently programmers number the END statement 99999 since it is the highest allowable statement number in BASIC.

Now that we have examined and scrutinized our simple, hypothetical BASIC program, one may remark that it has a conspicuous shortcoming. The entire program only operates on one set of data. In a practical situation, if that arithmetic were to be performed on only one set of numbers, it would be more expedient to forget the computer and do the work with a hand calculator. Let us assume instead that the same computations need to be performed on an arbitrarily large set of data. We can modify the program to accommodate this. Rather than have the program finish with the STOP statement, we modify it to appear as shown in Fig. A.2.

The STOP instruction is replaced here by the GO TO 10 instruction. This causes the entire program to be repeated as control is transferred to its beginning statement. Chapter 12 alluded to the use of control loops in programming procedure. The GO TO statement is one way such loops may be implemented. The question arises as to what stops the program and prevent it from cycling indefinitely. In the case of Fig. A. 2, the READ instruction must be repeated each cycle. Each time it is performed, it references the next consecutive DATA statement. So if the program contains 10 DATA statements, it cycles through its instruction set 10 times. Execution of the program halts when it runs out of DATA statements.

It is possible, nevertheless, and a real danger in programming, to accidently create loops that do cycle indefinitely. If there is no provision in the program for control to either stop execution or transfer out of the loop at some point, the consequences may be embarassing and expensive! In any case, a programmer is wise to use the GO TO instruction with caution.

Notice in the revised version of our program, that there is an extra,

```
        .
        .
        .
   80 PRINT X, Y1, Y2
   90 PRINT Z1, Z2, W
  100 PRINT
  110 GO TO 10
  900 DATA 6, 2, 3
  910 DATA -1, 4.3, 10.02
  920 DATA 5.0E6, -6, .05
        .
        .
        .
99999 END
```

Figure A.2 Use of GO TO instruction.

seemingly superfluous PRINT command in line number 100. Its purpose is to leave a blank line between each set of results so that the printout is easier to read. In fact, we may further modify the output section of our program to make it still more readable. It would be nice in our printout if we could see not only the calculated numbers, but the variable name that each number represents. Since there are several sets of data yielding separate results, it would be convenient to see the data that goes with each set of results. We now write the program as shown in Fig. A.3.
Statements #80, #90, and #100 take advantage of a special feature of BASIC. The quotation marks in these PRINT statements cause whatever is typed between them to be printed in the output line. The characters enclosed by the quotation marks are printed literally, while the variable names not so enclosed cause the value of the variable to be printed. Thus the program of Fig. A.3 causes the printout shown in Fig. A.4.

One further modification may be made in the program of Fig. A.1. It is not always convenient to enter data into programs with DATA statements. Quite often, once a program has been written, the programmer wants to save it on file and use it several times later. It would be a nuisance to have to modify it by changing the DATA statements each time it is a run. A simpler approach is to generalize the program in such a way that it can be run intact each time, requesting the data to be fed in at execution time. This is accomplished by replacing the READ statement with an INPUT statement. Unlike the READ instruction, the INPUT command does not reference a DATA statement. Instead, it displays a "?" by at the user's terminal. The user must then respond to the "?" by entering the required data. When the computer encounters an INPUT instruction, it suspends further execution while it waits to receive the numbers from the terminal. On receipt of the data, it resumes execution.

Thus far, this appendix has presented the fundamental arithmetic operators in BASIC, for example, addition, subtraction, negation, multiplication, division, and exponentiation. We continue by listing some functions contained in the BASIC system. The most pertinant of these functions for use in generating waveforms is the sine function. It is typically employed in a LET statement such as

```
100 LET Y = SIN(X)
```

In this statement, the variable X (called the argument), is assumed to be an angle in radians. When the sine function is used to generate a periodic waveform as it was in Chapter 2, it is inconvenient to view the argument as an angle. It is more practical, instead, to let the argument of the sine function be a variable representing time. When this is done, it becomes necessary to use the variable in conjunction with the trigonometric constant 2π that represents one full cycle of the sine function. When the

```
         .
         .
         .
   80  PRINT "A="; A, "B="; B, "C="; C,
   90  PRINT "X="; X, "Y1="; Y1, "Y2="; Y2
  100  PRINT "Z1="; Z1, "Z2="; Z2, "W="; W
  110  PRINT
  120  GO TO 10
  900  DATA 6, 2, 3
  910  DATA -1, 4.3, 10.2
  920  DATA 5.0E6, -6, .05
         .
         .
         .
99999  END
```

Figure A.3 Use of quotations in PRINT statements.

SIN function of BASIC is used, its argument does not necessarily need to be a single variable. It may instead be an expression, such as

```
100 LET Y = SIN(P2 * F * T)
```

In either case, the instruction calculates the sine of whatever expression or variable is enclosed in the parenthesis. We assume in the preceding instruction that the variable name P2 was assigned the value of $2\pi = 6.2831853$ previously in the program as was the frequency F given in cycles per second, and the time variable T given in seconds.

Figure A.5 lists the functions available in BASIC.

Earlier, we saw how a GO TO instruction is used to implement a program loop. Unfortunately, this statement by itself does not specify how many time the sequence of instructions contained in the loop should be repeated. If one wishes to create a loop with such specificity, one can employ the instructions FOR and NEXT. Here is how they are used in their general form:

```
    .                        .
    .                        .
    .                        .
(statement     (index
  number)  FOR   variable) = (exp.1) TO (exp.2) STEP (exp.3)
    .                        .
    .                        .
    .                        .
(statement
  number)  NEXT (index variable)
    .                        .
    .                        .
    .                        .
```

This causes all the instructions between FOR and NEXT to be repeated consecutively. It does this by defining an index variable that may be any legal BASIC variable. The first time through the instruction cycle, this index is set to the value of exp._1. Each time thereafter, the index is incremented by the value of exp._3 until it reaches the value of exp._2. An example of a simple program using the FOR/NEXT instruction is shown in Fig. A.6.

This program creates a table of 100 values of the sine function in equally spaced intervals for one complete cycle. The index I is set initially to the value of $2\pi/100$. I is then used as the argument to the sine function that is called and calculated in the PRINT statement. Each time the loop is repeated and the PRINT instruction is executed, I increases by $2\pi/100$, until it reaches the value of 2π. Then the cycle terminates and control

A=6	B=2	C=3
X=5	Y1=1	Y2=−9
Z1=−45	Z2=−15	W=8
A=−1	B=4.3	C=10.2
X=−6.9	Y1=50.76	Y2=33.6
Z1=−4.57	Z2=−.4	W=79.5
A=5.0E6	B=−6	C=.05
X=5.0E5	Y1=−5.0E6	Y2=−2.5E5
Z1=2.5E5	Z2=1.0E-8	W=−216
	.	
	.	
	.	

Figure A.4 Output created by preceding program.

	Function	Description
(All angles used in BASIC trigonometric functions are expressed in radians)	SIN(expression)	Trigonometric sine
	COS(expression)	Trigonometric cosine
	TAN(expression)	Trigonometric tangent
	HTN(expression)	Hyperbolic tangent
	ASN(expression)	Angle whose sine is (expression)
	ACS(expression)	Angle whose cosine is (expression)
	ATN(expression)	Angle whose tangent is (expression)
	ABS(expression)	Absolute value $\lvert(\text{expression})\rvert$
	SQR(expression)	Square root $\sqrt{(\text{expression})}$
	EXP(expression)	Natural exponent $e^{(\text{expression})}$
	LOG(expression)	Natural logarithm (base e) ln(expression)
	LGT(expression)	Common logarithm (base 10) log(expression)
	INT(expression)	Integral portion of (expression) (for example INT(43.28)=43)
	SGN(expression)	Sign of (expression) for example; SGN(X) = −1 if X < 0 SGN(X) = 0 if X = 0 SGN(X) = 1 if X > 0

Figure A.5 Standard functions available in BASIC.

```
10  LET P2 = 6.2831853
20  FOR I = P2/100 TO P2 STEP P2/100
30  PRINT "THE SINE OF"; I; "IS"; SIN(I)
40  NEXT I
50  STOP
60  END
```

Figure A.6 Example of FOR/NEXT usage.

proceeds to the STOP instruction which follows it. The program above yields the printouts shown in Fig. A.7.

One of the most salient features of program loops is their utility in creating lists and tables. The program of Fig. A.7 causes a table to be printed on paper, but does nothing to store the information it computes in memory for future use. Suppose that one wishes to calculate 100 values of the sine function as in the program above, but needs to have each of them stored in a memory location for future reference in the program. It is extremely inconvenient and impractical to define a separate variable name for each value. For this reason, BASIC contains the provision that variable names may be given subscripts enclosed in parentheses. A program section similar to Fig. A.6, but using a subscripted variable is shown in Fig. A.8.

In this program, the index I is also used in the loop as a subscript for the variable X. This is the most popular method of using program loops in conjunction with subscripted variables. Notice that in the program of Fig. A.6, the index was not an integer. However a subscript *must* be an integer,

```
THE SINE OF .0314 IS .0314
THE SINE OF .0628 IS .0628
THE SINE OF .0942 IS .0941
THE SINE OF .1257 IS .1253
          .
          .
          .
THE SINE OF 6.2832 IS 0.000
```

Figure A.7 Output produced by preceding program.

```
10  DIM  Y(100)
20  LET  P2  =  6.2831853
30  LET  W  =  P2/100
40  FOR  I  =  1  TO  100
50  LET  Y(I)  =  SIN(W  *  I)
60  NEXT  I
            .
            .
            .
```

Figure A.8 Use of subscripted variable.

so it becomes necessary in the example of Fig. A.8 to define I in the FOR statement so that it is an integer.

Notice in the FOR statement that the STEP position has been omitted. This is legal and causes the interpreter to automatically increment the index by one each time the loop cycles. The program also introduces the DIM (dimension) statement. This statement is not an instruction, but is a specification of the number of memory locations that must be reserved for the subscripted variable Y. The DIM statement may list more than one variable. An example is:

```
10 DIM  A(150),  B(50),  C(200),  D(100)
```

It is legal in BASIC to subscript a variable without using a DIM statement. If this is done, the compiler assumes that 10 locations are the maximum desired. If a variable is to have subscripts that extend beyond 10, the DIM statement is necessary.

A further remark should be made about the program of Fig. A.8. It would have been perfectly valid to have omitted statement #30 and written #50 as

```
50 LET  Y(I)  =  SIN(P2/100  *  I)
```

This, however, would cause the calculation of P2/100 to be unnecessarily repeated 100 times—once for each repetition of the loop. A programmer should take care in constructing loops to avoid such redundant calculations since they are wasteful of computer time.

The BASIC system permits the use of two subscripts for variable names as well as a single sbuscript. It is also permissable to enclose one program loop within another. To illustrate this, we propose a program that constructs a two-dimensional table. Let us suppose that we have a set of points in two dimensions whose coordinates are (X,Y). For each of these points, we wish to assign a double-subscripted variable D(X,Y) that represents the distance from the origin (O,O) to that point. From plane geometry this distance is given by $D_{x,y} = \sqrt{x^2 + y^2}$. Figure A.9 creates our table:

```
10  DIM D(100, 100)
20  FOR X = 1 TO 100
30  FOR Y = 1 TO 100
40  LET D(X,Y) = SQR(X↑2 + Y↑2)
50  NEXT Y
60  NEXT X
            .
            .
            .
```

Figure A.9 Utilization of nested loops.

How such a table may be used is left to the reader's imagination, but its introduction serves to demonstrate these programming concepts. Although it is permissable to use as many nested loops as desired, the loops must be concentric and not cross each other. Nor may control be transfered to the inside of a loop from the outside. For example, the loops of Fig. A.10 are legal, while the programming of Fig. A.11 is erroneous:

Thus far in the appendix, all of the BASIC statements have been presented in their unconditional form. Quite often in writing a program, one wants a particular instruction to be executed subject to a given condition. The IF/THEN statement accomplishes this. The general format of the IF/THEN statement is

IF (condition) THEN (Statement) ELSE (statement)

The condition is expressed in the form

(expression) (relationship) expression)

The expression may be any legal BASIC expression and the relationship may be any one of the following:

=	Equal to
< >	Not equal to
>	Greater than
> =	Greater than or equal to
<	Less than
< =	Less than or equal to

The statements following THEN and ELSE are any standard BASIC instructions. The ELSE portion is optional. For example, the statement

```
100 IF X=0 THEN A=B+C ELSE A=1
```

tests the variable X to determine if it is eqaul to 0. If it is, the instruction sets A to the value of B + C. If X is not equal to 0, then A is set to one.

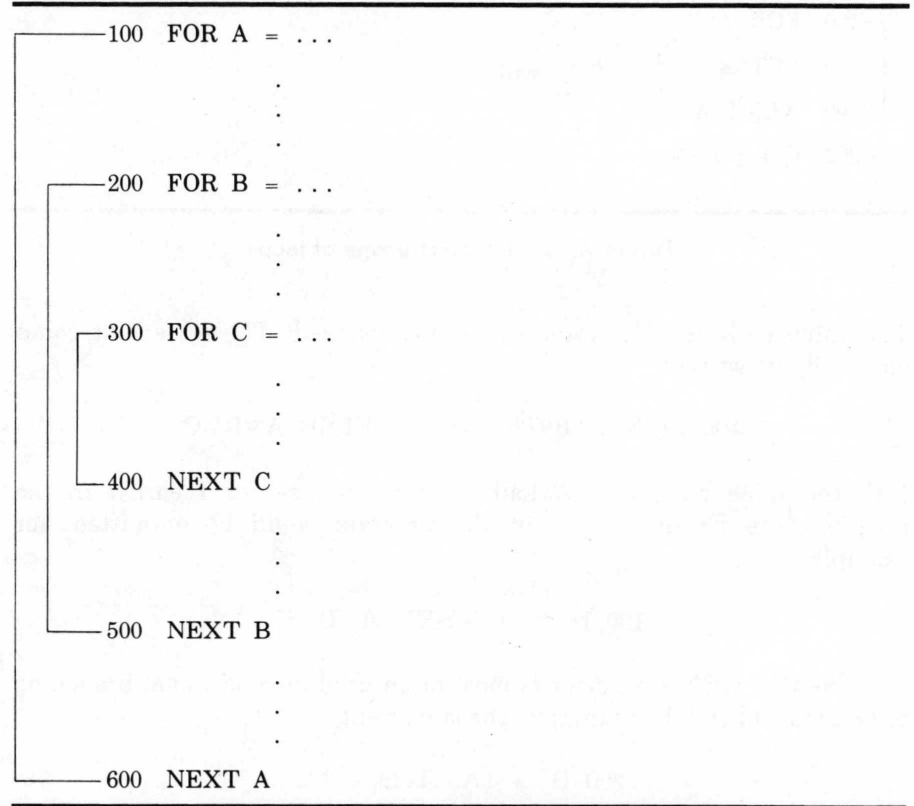

Figure A.10 Correct usage of nested loops.

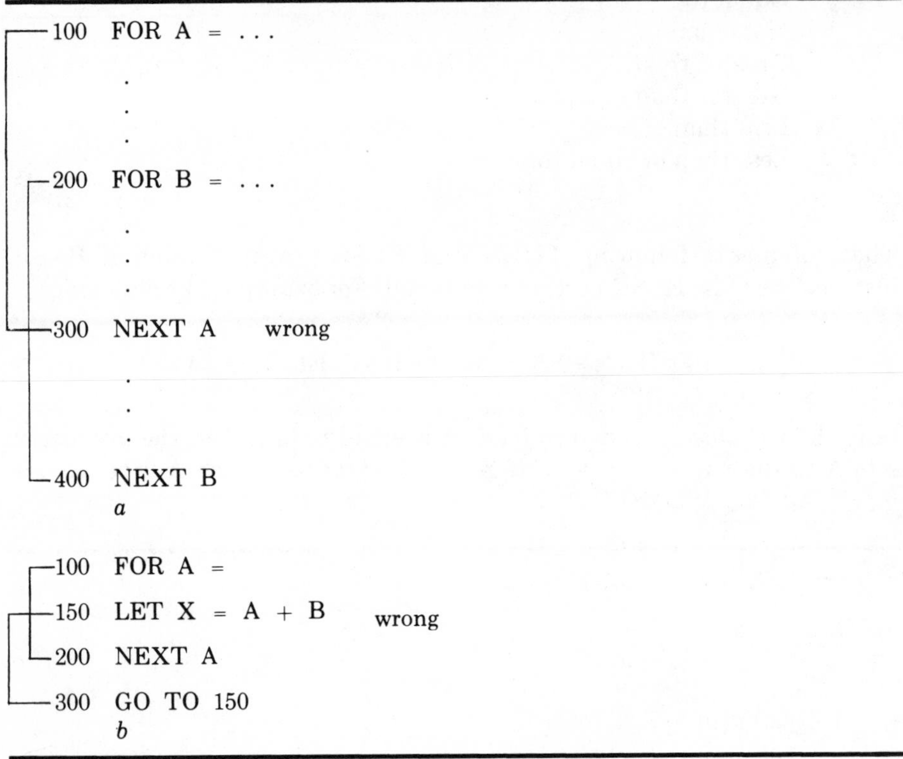

Figure A.11 Incorrect usage of loops.

The value of X is only tested—it is not changed. The statement could optionally be written

100 IF X<>0 THEN A=1 ELSE A=B+C

with the same results. If A had already been set to 1 earlier in the program, the ELSE portion of the program could be ommitted, for example,

100 IF X=0 THEN A=B+C

The IF/THEN statement is most often used in conditional branching of program control. For example, the statement

200 IF =<A5 THEN 300

transfers control to statement #300 if the variable T has a value less than

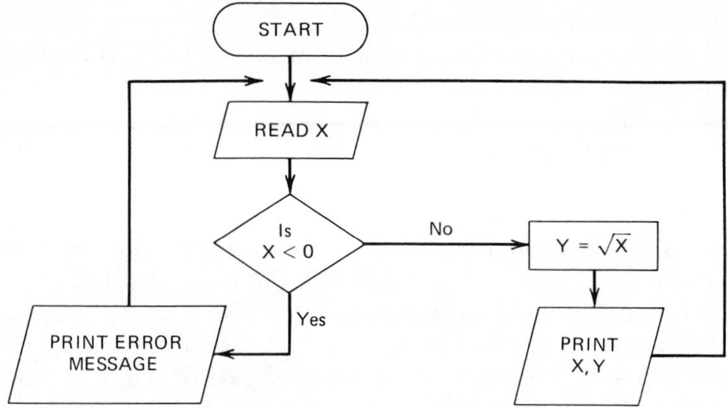

Figure A.12 Flowchart of program using conditional branch.

A5; otherwise the instructions following #200 are executed in normal sequence.

Suppose that somewhere in a program we want to calculate the square root of a number X. The simple statement

```
50 LET S = SQR(X)
```

is just fine as long as X is positive. But if X is negative, we are in trouble. Let us formulate a brief program that reads a number, prints the square root of it if it is positive, but prints an error message if it is negative. It is a cardinal rule of etiquette (as well as a good, practical idea) in computer programming to draw a flowchart that traces the logic of a program before writing the actual instructions. A simple flowchart is shown in Fig. A.12.

```
10  READ X
20  IF X<0 THEN 100
30  LET Y = SQR(X)
40  PRINT "THE SQUARE ROOT OF";X, "IS";Y
50  GO TO 10
100 PRINT "ERROR IN DATA—NEGATIVE NUMBER NOT PER-
    MITTED"
110 GO TO 10
200 DATA . . .
```

Figure A.13 Usage of conditional branch.

The program itself is written in Fig. A.13.

BASIC also offers a useful modification of the GO TO command. An example is

```
100 ON B GO TO 200, 240, 280, 350
```

Here is how the instruction is executed: the variable or expression following the word ON is evaluated. If it is not an integer, its integral part is taken and the fractional part is truncated. For example, if B in the above statement is equal to 2.65, the integral part of this number, 2, is taken and the GO TO portion of the instruction points to the second of the line numbers which follow it. Similarly, if the integral part of B is 1, the statement transfers control to line #200. If the integral part is 3, it branches to #280; and if B is 4, control goes to line #350. Any number of line numbers separated by commas may follow GO TO, provided they fit on one line. If the integral part of the expression following ON is less than 1 or greater than the ordinal position of the last number on the line, an error message is printed.

Very often in computer programming, a particular set of instructions needs to be repeated several times. Consequently, it is an unnecessary nuisance to be required to type such a set many times in a program. To alleviate this inconvenience, BASIC provides the capability of writing subroutines apart from the main program. The GOSUB statement causes control to branch to such a subroutine. Figure A.14 shows how the GOSUB statement is used.

```
      .
      .
      .
150 GOSUB 400
160 (next instruction following subroutine)
      .
      .
      .
400 (first instruction of subroutine)
      .
      .
      .
450 RETURN
```

Figure A.14 Usage of GOSUB.

On encountering the instruction GOSUB 400, control transfers immediately to statement #400 just as it would if it had said "GO TO 400." But unlike the GO TO instruction, GOSUB remembers the line number of its own position (i.e., #150) so that control may be returned to that point when the instruction of the subroutine has finished execution. Thus the statement of the subroutine

```
450 RETURN
```

branches control back to the statement following #150 of the main program where it originally left off, and continues from there on. As mentioned before, the utility of using such subroutines is that they may be referenced any number of times by the main program. Many BASIC systems have more versatile and sophisticated mechanisms for calling subroutines. They are not presented here, though, because they vary from system to system. The user must consult the manual corresponding to the system on the computer if he or she is to employ these additional features.

This appendix lists the common functions available in BASIC and given an example of the use of the sine function. These functions are available because of their generality and widespread use. There are, however, many occasions when a programmer wants to use a function that is not already provided in the BASIC system. For example, if a programmer wishes to generate a waveform that is a sum of a sine wave and its first three overtones, a personal, specialized function can be defined for this purpose. Functions in BASIC are defined by a DEF statement. The name of the function to be defined must have three letters. The first two are FN and the third may be any letter selected by the programmer. The argument of the function used in the DEF statement is a dummy variable used in the definition of the function, but it is not assigned a value. In fact, like the DIM statement, the DEF statement is not an executable instruction. An example of a DEF statement is

```
20 DEF FNS(X)=SIN(X)+.5*SIN(2*X)+.3*SIN(3*X)+.2*SIN(4*X)
```

Later in the program, the function may be referenced just as a regular BASIC function, for example,

```
150 LET Y = FNS(P2 * F * T)
```

Notice that the argument of FNS in the LET instruction may be an expression and does not have to be the same as the dummy variable used in the DEF statement. Some systems permit functions to be defined with more than one argument. For example,

```
30 DEF FND(X,Y,Z) = SQR(X↑2 + Y↑2 + Z↑2)
```

defines the function FND to be the distance from the origin of a three-dimensional cartesian coordinate system to the point (X,Y,Z).

One provision in BASIC worth mentioning is the random number generator RND. It is not actually a function because it does not use an argument except the numeral 1, which only serves as a dummy. The instruction causes a number to be selected from a table of pseudorandom numbers between 0 and 1, so strictly speaking (for the benefit of fussy mathematicians) the number is not "purely" random, but is random enough for all practical purposes. The statement

```
60 LET X = RND(1)
```

selects a number at random and assigns it to the variable X.

If one is writing a program that is used by other people, it is a matter of courtesy to include documentary statements that provide explanatory comments and information. The REM statement is provided for this purpose. The first three letters of a remark statement must be REM and the rest of the line may be any comment that the programmer wishes to type solely for the benefit of the person reading the program. REM statements are entirely ignored by the computer. An example is:

```
140 REM—THIS SECTION COMPUTES THE PITCH
PARAMETERS
```

This discussion has thus far only considered variables that are assigned numerical values. BASIC contains a second class of variables that are assigned alphanumeric characters rather than numbers. Naturally, these variables may not be used in arithmetic expressions, since such operations would be meaningless, but they are useful in manipulating and outputting literal data. These variables (called string variables), must comprise one letter of the alphabet followed by a "$." They can be defined by a READ, INPUT, or LET statement such as

```
80 LET Y$ = "C#2"
```

They may also be used for comparison in an IF/THEN statement such as:

```
120 IF N$ = "A" THEN F = 440
```

Obviously, such assignments can be useful in inputting the notes to a composition. For example, Fig. A.15 inputs a series of notes and computes their frequencies according to the tempered scale.

```
10  DIM N$(100), F(100), R(100)
20  REM— N IS THE NUMBER OF NOTES TO BE INPUT
30  REM— WHICH MUST BE 100 OR LESS
40  INPUT N
50  FOR I = 1 TO N
60  INPUT N$(I), R(I)
70  REM— N$ IS THE NOTE OF THE SCALE
80  REM— R IS THE OCTAVE OF THE NOTE
90  IF N$(I) = "C" THEN Q = 261.63
100 IF N$(I) = "C#" THEN Q = 277.18
110 IF N$(I) = "D" THEN Q = 293.66
120 IF N$(I) = "D#" THEN Q = 311.13
130 IF N$(I) = "E" THEN Q = 329.63
140 IF N$(I) = "F" THEN Q = 349..23
150 IF N$(I) = "F#" THEN Q = 369.99
160 IF N$(I) = "G" THEN Q = 392.00
170 IF N$(I) = "G#" THEN Q = 415.00
180 IF N$(I) = "A" THEN Q = 440.00
190 IF N$(I) = "A#" THEN Q = 466.16
200 IF N$(I) = "B" THEN Q = 493.88
210 LET F(I) = Q * 2↑R(I)
220 REM— F IS THE FREQUENCY OF THE NOTE IN CPS
230 NEXT I
      .
      .
      .
```

Figure A.15 Usage of string variables.

A string variable may also be compared to or defined by another string variable, for example,

```
       200 IF A$ = B$ THEN ···
and    300 LET Y$ = X$
```

are legal BASIC instructions.

In all the BASIC programming considered thus far, information has been input via READ, INPUT, and DATA statements and has been output with a PRINT command. All this takes place at the user's terminal. This is obviously very restrictive of the amount of data that may be processed by a program. Suppose, however, that one wants to process a signal or compute a waveform that consists of several thousand samples. The READ and PRINT statements are obviously grossly inadequate to handle so many numbers, unless the user has superhuman patience. Fortunately, it is possible in BASIC to read from and write onto files in the computer's secondary memory. The protocol for opening and closing such files and for inputting and outputting information onto them is different on each BASIC system, so it is not described here. Files are used extensively for long lists of input data, computed results, and for storage of the programs and subroutines themselves which belong to a user. Normally, each user is given an account number and a password that permits access to personal files.

There are many provisions in various BASIC systems that enlarge on their capability and flexibility beyond what is presented here. Most of them, like the instructions for using files, are not uniform over all computer systems. Each installation provides documentation for its own BASIC interpreter. It is often difficult for a novice programmer to learn the logic of a computer language by depending solely on such documentation. This appendix has attempted to familiarize the reader with the overall practical logic of computer programming as well as the technicalities of each specific instruction. If one wishes to begin using BASIC on the computer, nevertheless, it is wise to obtain a manual that applies to his or her system for use as a reference. In this way, he or she can more fully exploit its capabilities, and resolve any difficulties encountered in its use.

APPENDIX B

PROGRAMMING IN FORTRAN

After making even a superficial comparison between the BASIC programming language presented in Appendix A and the rudimentary machine-level code introduced in Chapter 3, it is scarcely difficult to appreciate the value of such an interpretive language. For nearly any simple, practical computer program, BASIC offers the simplest and most economical realization. BASIC is also the easiest popular language to learn. Nevertheless, not all programming is nearly so simple as the examples presented heretofore, When a programmer begins to formulate substantially long and complex algorithms, he or she is quickly faced with the restrictions and limitations of BASIC. Although its simplicity is its greatest asset in writing uncomplicated programs, complex or specialized programming often requires greater sophistication.

The FORTRAN programming language is the precursor to BASIC, but it is still the one most widely used in scientific and technical applications. Part of the reason for this is tradition, since FORTRAN was one of the first sophisticated compiler languages to be developed. Hence, it is generally the one most familiar to programmers. It also remains most popular because of its flexibility and versatility. Its introduction in this appendix by no means covers all of its multifarious capabilities. Such a presentation requires a text in itself. However, the following discussion should sufficiently equip the reader to begin programming in FORTRAN. Like BASIC, FORTRAN has many features whose technicalities vary from system to system. Consequently, the most this presentation can accomplish is to introduce its general features.

The most difficult aspect of FORTRAN to master is by far its input and output protocol. In fact, this is one of the great anolomies of the language. The arithmetic and branching instructions of FORTRAN are relatively straightforward and are very similar to their counterparts in BASIC. As a rule, they present little difficulty in learning. But FORTRAN input and output commands can become a small nightmare, and all but the most veteran programmers constantly refer to their system manuals to insure that they are coding their statements properly. To further complicate matters, the input and output modes of FORTRAN vary from one system to another. They also differ with each input-output device. For example, the instructions are different for card readers and line printers than they are for teletypes and scopes. Consequently, this presentation foregoes an extensive discussion of input and output statements, and instead commends the reader to consult the sources that apply immediately to his or her own computer facilities.

Notwithstanding the complications and inconsistancies of FORTRAN input and output statements, the essential READ and PRINT formats are presented in their general form. The rules for inputting data and coding the FORTRAN statements themselves are originally oriented for standard punched cards of 80 columns. In using a teletype, the spaces on a line are treated like the columns of a punched card. When punched onto a card or typed into a teletype or scope terminal, the body of a FORTRAN statement begins in the seventh space or column from the left. The first five columns are reserved for a statement number if the statement is to have one. Unlike BASIC, statement numbers in FORTRAN need only appear on lines that are referenced by other statements. More will be said about this later. The sixth column or space is reserved to indicate that the card (or line) is a continuation of the statement started on the previous card or cards. The purpose of this continuation column is to allow for instructions too lengthy to fit on a single card. To utilize the continuation feature, the programmer simply types any number in the sixth column and continues to type the statement from where he or she left off on the preceding card as if there were no interruption. In ordinary statements requiring only one card, the sixth column must be left blank.

The manner in which data is entered on punched cards is specified by a FORMAT statement. Every READ statement in FORTRAN is accompanied by a FORMAT statement. Whereas the READ statement is an actual instruction, the FORMAT statement is not. FORMAT simply defines the configuration of the data cards (or lines) referenced by the READ statement. The general form of a READ statement is

READ (statement number) (variable list)

The statement number is the line number of the FORMAT statement that applys to it. Consequently, every FORMAT statement must be numbered. An example of typical READ and FORMAT statements is:

```
      READ 10, A,B,C,D
   10 FORMAT (4F10.5)
```

The word READ is typed beginning in column seven and is followed by the statement number (#10) of the FORMAT statement. Although it is customary for FORMAT statements to immediately follow the statements that reference them, they may be placed anywhere in the program since they are not executable instructions. Statement number 10 is followed by a comma that is then followed by a list of the variables, also separated by commas. The statement number of the FORMAT statement is placed anywhere in the first five columns of the card or line and the word FORMAT begins in column seven. The parentheses contain the field specification of the data card to be read. The 4 indicates that there are four fields on the data card, one for each of the variable assignments A, B, C, and D. The F indicates that the numbers are entered in floating-point format. The 10.5 signifies 10 total columns with five places on the right-hand side of the decimal point. Thus a data card corresponding to the FORMAT statement above is:

10.67000	.02000	−1.98	200.

All columns not containing numbers are automatically interpreted to be 0, and if the decimal point is not punched it assumes the position specified by the FORMAT statement, for example, the position allowing five columns to its right in the field. The decimal point may be misplaced and still be accepted in the position where it is punched without creating an error. The data above could alternatively be typed in exponential format. Then the FORMAT statement reads:

```
10 FORMAT (4E10.5)
```

and a data card looks like:

1.067E1	2.0E-2	−1.98E0	2.0E2
10	28	30	40

The 5 in the FORMAT statement specifies a maximum of five digits to the right of the decimal place, but it is unnecessary to enter them all if they are zeros.

Integers are entered in I format. For example,

```
20 FORMAT (10I4)
```

specifies 10 fields each having four columns. In I format, the numbers *must* be placed in the correct columns, or they are misinterpreted, since the computer reads blank columns as zeros. A data card for the FORMAT statement #20 is:

5	0	−3	21	198	−40	−2	1000	8	−400
4	8	12	16	20	24	28	32	36	40

FORTRAN accepts string variables in A format. It is also permissable to place different formats on one data card. For example,

```
   READ 50, DAY, RATE, INDEX
50 FORMAT (A10, F10.4, I5)
```

references a data card like:

TUESDAY	25.06	19
10	20	25

PRINT instructions also reference FORMAT statements. The first column that an output FORMAT statement specifies is used for the carriage control. If it is left blank, the printout is single-spaced. Characters may be output literally by enclosing them in quatation marks. Examine the following output commands:

```
   PRINT 40
40 FORMAT (5X, 'DAY', 5X, 'RATE', 4X, 'INDEX')
   PRINT 41
41 FORMAT (2X, A8, 2X, F6.2, 2X, I5)
```

The first line of printout has no variables, but is used as a heading for the following lines. Hence, no variable names are listed in the first PRINT statement. The 5X in the FORMAT statement causes the first five columns to be left blank. Note that the first column is included in the specification so that the carriage control accepts a blank character directing it to single-space. The word DAY will follow in the fifth space and five more blanks follow it before the word RATE. The printout appears as follows:

```
     DAY        RATE    INDEX
   TUESDAY      25.06      19
```

If the first column specified in the FORMAT statement contains a 0, for example,

```
40 FORMAT ('0', 4X, ...)
```

the output is double-spaced. A "1" in the first column of output causes it to skip to the next page, and a "+" causes the printout to continue on the same line without a carriage return. If one wishes to specify a carriage return within a FORMAT statement, a slash is used. For example, the above output statements are rewritten as:

```
      PRINT 40, DAY, RATE, INDEX
   40 FORMAT ('ODAY: ', A8/' RATE: ', F6.2/
     1' INDEX: ', I5)
```

The 1 in the sixth column of the third card indicates that it is a continuation of the FORMAT statement begun on the previous card. The 0 in the first column before DAY leaves a blank line before the printout, and the slashes place it on three separate lines so it looks like this:

```
        (blank line)
DAY:          TUESDAY
RATE:           25.06
INDEX:             19
```

Variable names in FORTRAN may contain up to six alphanumeric characters. The first character must distinguish between integer variables and floating-point variables. Variable names that are assigned integers must begin with one of the letters I, J, K, L, M, or N. Otherwise the variable name is assigned a floating-point number. Variables are assigned and expressions are written in FORTRAN just as they are in BASIC, except that the word LET is not included. Care must also be taken in FORTRAN not to mix integers with floating-point numbers in the same expression. For example,

```
      NOTE = I + 3
```

and

```
      RATE = X/(F3 * OLDRAT) - 25.09
```

are bona fide instructions. A mixed-mode expression such as:

```
      TAX = RATE * NEWRAT
```

is computed, but at the risk of arithmetic error, and should hence be avoided. One should also guard against dividing integers, since the quotient may not be an integer also. If one must divide two integral numbers, the FLOAT specification may be used; for example,

```
      QUOT = FLOAT(INT1)/FLOAT(INT2)
```

converts the integers INT1 and INT2 into floating-point numbers, divides them, and assigns the quotient to the floating-point variable QUOT. Conversely, floating-point numbers are converted to integers with the

IFIX function. For example, the statement:

```
INTEGR = 4 + IFIX(3.068 * TIME)
```

multiplies the floating-point value of TIME by 3.068, truncates the fractional part, and adds the integral part to 4. Thus if TIME equals 2.11, INTEGR is set to 10. Floating-point numbers may have integral values provided they are typed with a decimal point. For example,

```
FLOT = 20. + X
```

is correct, while

```
FLOTMX = 20 + Y
```

is in the danger zone of the mixed mode.

If a programmer has a special reason to define integer variables with floating-point variable names, he or she can do it with an INTEGER specification statement such as:

```
INTEGER X, Y, CRATZ
```

This causes those variable names in the list to be treated as though they were integer variables beginning with the letters I, J, K, L, M, or N. Correspondingly, the statement:

```
REAL I, JAZZ, MEL
```

causes those variables to be treated in floating-point.

Variables in FORTRAN may be subscripted as they are in BASIC. Subscripted variables must be specified in a DIMENSION statement, such as:

```
DIMENSION MOD(100), COUNT(10), X(20,50)
```

The values in the parentheses must be numerals—not variables or expressions. For example,

```
DIMENSION OOPS(N)
```

is illegal and invokes a curt error message. However, when the subscripted variable is used, it employs an integer variable for its subscript, for example,

```
X(I,J) = ENV(I) * WAVE(J)
```

The value of the subscript, however, cannot be zero or negative. A subscripted integer variable can even be used as a subscript to another variable, for example,

```
FHRP = CURSE(MACK(J))
```

The FORTRAN compiler, like BASIC, contains several built-in functions that may be used in assigning variables. Figure B.1 lists some of them.

It is also possible in FORTRAN to select from a list of variables the maximum or minimum value. Eight expressions are provided for this:

```
      MAX0 (N1, N2, N3, . . .)
and   MIN0 (N1, N2, N3, . . .)
```

Function	Definition
ABS	Real absolute value (floating-point)
IABS	Integer absolute value
MOD(M/N)	Integer remainder of M/N
AMOD(X/Y)	Real remainder of X/Y
FLOAT	Convert to floating-point mode
IFIX	Convert to integer
SIN	Trigonometric sine
COS	Trigonometric cosine
TAN	Trigonometric tangent
COTAN	Trigonometric cotangent
ATAN	Arc-tangent
TANH	Hyperbolic tangent
EXP	Exponential
ALOG	Natural logarithm
ALOG10	Common logarithm
SQRT	Square root

Figure B.1 Functions in FORTRAN.

selects the maximum or minimum of the integers N1, N2, N3, . . . and convert it to a floating-point number. Similarly, the expressions:

```
MAX1(X1, X2, X3, . . .)
MIN1 (X1, X2, X3, . . .)
AMAX1(X1, X2, X3, . . .)
AMIN1 (X1, X2, X3, . . .)
```

select the maxima and minima of the floating-point variables X1, X2, X3, . . . MAX1 and MIN1 convert the numbers to integers.

Sometimes it is convenient in FORTRAN to assign variables with a DATA statement. It is important to note that the DATA statement of FORTRAN is not like the DATA statement of BASIC. It has nothing to do with the FORTRAN READ statement. The READ instruction refers to data cards that are placed outside the program after the END statement. But the DATA statement is an instruction within the main program. Its general form is

```
DATA (variable list)/(values)/
```

For example, the statement:

```
DATA A, B, I, J/4.3, -258.0, 3, 100/
```

sets A=4.3, B=−258.0, I=3, and J=100. Once again, as usual, care must be taken not to mix the modes.

The arithmetic operators of FORTRAN are identical to those in BASIC, as are their rules of priority, with one exception. Whereas the operator in BASIC for exponentiation is generally the up arrow, it is the double asterisk in FORTRAN. In performing the exponentiation operation, certain rules must be observed. A real (i.e., floating-point) number or expression may be raised to either an integral or real exponent. But an integer may only be raised to an integer. Consequently, W**(X+Y) (A*B)**2.5, CAN**JET, and M**N are legal expression, while JAM** RATS is illegal. An alert reader notes, however, that like many of life's restrictions, this can be easily circumvented: for example,

```
CRCMVT = (FLOAT(JAM))**RATS
```

accomplishes the same result without being incorrect.

Branching in FORTRAN is most directly accomplished with the GO TO instruction. For example,

```
GO TO 5
```

causes control to transfer unconditionally to the instruction whose statement number is 5. As mentioned earlier, not all FORTRAN statements need to be numbered as in BASIC. FORTRAN instructions are executed in order of their appearance in the program, and if they do carry a statement number, the number is merely used as a reference from another instruction. When control is transfered to a statement number, the number is merely used as a reference from another instruction. When control is transfered to a statement such as is done by a GO TO instruction, the statement should be an executable instruction. For example, GO TO 45 would be incorrect if statement #45 were a FORMAT statement. As in BASIC, the GO TO command may be used with a READ statement to create a program loop which will terminate when the last data card in the deck is read. For example,

```
10 READ 20, A, B, M, FLAP
          .
          .      (body of program)
          .
   GO TO 10
```

repeats the steps of the program for as many data cards as there are to be read, and then stops. But if the GO TO statement is used carelessly, it can throw the program into an infinite loop with disasterous results.

A variation of the GO TO statement similar to BASIC's ON/GO TO instruction is the computed GO TO. The words GO TO are followed by a list of statement numbers enclosed in parentheses. An integer variable following the list points to the ordinal position of the statement number to be selected. For example,

```
GO TO (5, 20, 50, 200) JIM
```

transfers control to statement #5 if JIM = 1, to #20 if JIM = 2, and so forth.

Control can be transferred conditionally with the IF statement. There are two forms of this instruction. The first is the logical IF. Its general format is:

```
IF (condition) (instruction)
```

The condition is a comparison of two legal expressions separated by a comparator and enclosed in parentheses, for example,

```
IF (X.EQ.(Y+Z)*1.6) GO TO 100
```

The comparators may be one of the following:

.EQ. Equals
.GT. Greater than
.GE. Greater than or equal to
.LT. Less than
.LE. Less than or equal to
.NE. Not equal to

It is also possible to specify two conditions with the conjunctions .AND. and .OR. For example,

```
IF (NOTE.GE.5.AND.T.LE.TMAX) WAVE = SIN(TWOPI*F*T)
```

executes the instruction portion on the right only if both conditions inside the parentheses are true.

The second form of the IF statement is the arithmetic IF. Its format is:

$$\text{IF (expression) } (sn_1,\ sn_2,\ sn_3)$$

where sn_1, sn_2, and sn_3, are statement numbers of other instructions in the program. Control transfers to the statement #sn_1 if the expression is evaluated to be less than 0, to statement #sn_2 if the expression is equal to 0, and to statement #sn_3 if it is greater than 0. For example,

```
IF (SIGN) 30, 15, 400
```

is equivalent to

```
IF (SIGN.LT.0.0) GO TO 30
IF (SIGN.EQ.0.0) GO TO 15
IF (SIGN.GT.0.0) GO TO 400
```

The fundamental instruction in FORTRAN used for implementing program loops is the DO statement. Its operation is similar to the FOR/NEXT instructions of BASIC. Its general form is:

$$\text{DO (sn) (index variable)} = n_1,\ n_2,\ n_3$$

where (sn) is the statement number of the last instruction in the loop. Often, the dummy instruction CONTINUE is used as the last instruction of a DO loop. The CONTINUE statement does not tell the computer to do anything, but it is used to occupy a position in the program code that can be easily seen by the programmer. Nevertheless, any executable instruction may be the last statement of the loop whose line number is specified by the DO statement. The index variable must be an integer variable name that is defined on encounter of the DO instruction and then forgotten after the loop is finished. This means that the same index variable can be used in more than one DO loop if the loops are not nested within each other. The parameters n_1, n_2, and n_3 are integer variables or constants. Upon first encounter of the DO statement, the index is set to the value of n_1. It then retains that value as the instructions within the loop are executed for the first time unless an instruction within the loop modifies it. When control reaches the terminal statement of the loop, it returns back to the DO statement and increments the value of the index by the value of n_3. If the parameter n_3 is not included in the DO statement, the index is automatically incremented by 1. The statements within the loop are repeated sequentially while the index is incremented each time until it reaches or surpasses the value of n_2. If the value of n_2 is accidently or for some other reason set less than n_1, then the index is initialized at n and the instructions in the loop are only followed once without incurring an error. Figure B.2 is an example of how DO loops may be nested to construct a three-dimensional array of numbers.

Nested loops may also terminate on the same instruction, for example,

```
      DO 50 M  = ...
        .
        .
        .
      DO 50 KLUGE  = ...
        .
        .
        .
      DO 50 IKE  = ...
        .
        .
        .
   50 CONTINUE
```

Control may be transfered out of a DO loop by a GO TO statement or an arithmetic IF statement. In such a case, the loop is aborted. But it is grossly illegal to transfer control into the middle of a DO loop from outside the loop. Two or more nonconcentric loops are placed within an outer loop

```
      DIMENSION ARRAY (100, 10, 20)
                   .
                   .
                   .
      DO 10 I = 1, LIMIT, INCRMT
      DO 20 J = 1, 10
      DO 30 K = INITL, 20
                   .
                   .     (statements to compute array)
                   .
30    ARRAY (I, J, K) ...
                   .
                   .
                   .
20    CONTINUE
                   .
                   .
                   .
10    CONTINUE
                   .
                   .
                   .
```

Figure B.2 Nested DO loop.

if they do not overlap, for example,

```
                    DO 100 I =
                    DO 20 J =
                          .
                          .
                          .
                 20 CONTINUE
                    DO 30 J =
                          .
                          .
                          .
```

```
30 CONTINUE
   DO 40 J =
      .
      .
      .
40 CONTINUE
      .
      .
      .
100 CONTINUE
```

READ and PRINT commands may be written with implied DO loops built into the statement. For example,

```
READ 200 (A(I), B(I), C(I), I = 1, 100)
```

is equivalent to:

```
   DO 50 I = 1, 100
50 READ 200, A(I), B(I), C(I)
```

In fact, two indices are used in a single PRINT statement to output a two-dimensional array; for example,

```
   PRINT 40, ((X(I,J) I = 1, 10) J = 1, LIMIT)
40 FORMAT (1X, 10F10.5)
```

The procedures outlined thus far are sufficient for a beginning programmer to write simple, useful programs. Nevertheless, the discussion has only scratched the surface in outlining the full capabilities of the FORTRAN language. Once the programmer has obtained some experience and gained an intuitive feeling for the logic of computing procedures, he or she is ready to undertake programs that are more complex, lengthy, and sophisticated. As the programs increase in length and complexity, they naturally become much more difficult to formulate, debug, and understand. A programmer soon finds that many headaches are saved by breaking a long, complicated program into several smaller, simpler units that he or she formulates, codes, debugs, and implements separately. This modular approach to computer programming is accomplished by writing a battery of separate subprograms that are called by a relatively short main program. This method generally proves to be more simple and economical than including all the steps of a long procedure in a simple main program.

The other significant advantage in using subprograms is that they may be saved on file in the computer's library to be called by other users of the system. In fact, virtually every computing facility has many general-purpose subprograms that may be freely accessed by all of its users, at an enormous savings of programming time and effort.

It is beyond the scope of this presentation to elaborate on FORTRAN's subprogramming capabilities in any great detail, but it may introduce the overall procedure without undue complication. Subprograms in FORTRAN consist of functions and subroutines. Essentially, a function is like a subroutine except that a subroutine may perform several operations on several variables, whereas a function defines a single operation on a variable or set of variables.

Many functions that a programmer may wish to define are concise enough to write in a single line of code. An example of an algebraic function of a single variable for the calculation of a simple polynomial is the equation:

$$f(x) = x^3 + 6x^2 - 4x + 1$$

This function is defined in a single FORTRAN statement as:

```
POLY3(X) = X**3 + 6.0*X**2 - 4.0*X + 1.0
```

Superficially, the function name POLY3 looks like a variable with the subscript X. But the compiler recognizes this to be the definition of a function (in this case a floating-point function because the name begins with the letter P), because POLY never appeared in a DIMENSION statement to be assigned as a subscripted variable. Moreover, since X is a floating-point variable, it can not be used as a subscript, anyway. Instead, X is used as a dummy variable and is not assigned a value in this non-executable definition statement. The function defined here is calculated when it is called in an actual instruction such as

```
Y = 100.0/WEIGHT + POLY3(SAMPLE)
```

Once a function has been assigned this way, it may be referenced any time later in the program in the same way that library functions such as SIN, ALOG, AND SQRT are referenced.

A function may be assigned with more than one argument, and it may contain other functions in its definition. One could, for example, define a simple function in terms of its frequency parameter and time coordinate as follows:

```
WAVE(F,T) = SIN(TWOPI*F*T) + 0.4*(TWOPI*3.0*F*T)
```

Again, the dummy variables F and T are not assigned values and the function is not actually computed until it is referenced in an executable arithmetic instruction.

As a rule, functions are too complicated to be defined in a single statement. In such cases, they are defined in a subprogram that is placed outside the main program. A subprogram that defines a function begins with the title FUNCTION, the name of the function, and a list of the function's arguments. As with variable names, integer function names begin with one of the letters I,J,K,L,M, or N. An array may be used as a set of arguments to a function. The following example is a function that generates a waveform consisting of a fundamental tone and its first 10 harmonics. The amplitude of each harmonic is input to the main program and passed to the function subprogram in its argument list. When such an array is passed to a subprogram, it must be dimensioned in both the main program and subprogram. Figure B.3 illustrates such a procedure.

In this example, the main program inputs coefficients for each of the 10 harmonics of the desired waveform. The frequency is set to 440, corresponding to A of the scale. Then, for use in calculating the sine function, it is multiplied by 2π. The product is given the variable name PI2F and is passed to the function subprogram in the argument list.
TCHNGE is the sampling period, equal to 1 divided by the sampling frequency of 30,000 per second. The main program goes into a DO loop that calls the WAVE function 1000 times. It calculates 1000 samples of the waveform and stores them in an array labeled TONE. The time variable T is set initially to 0 and incremented by the sampling interval TCHNGE each iteration of the DO loop. In our example, the variables in the function's argument list are the same in the main program as they are in the subprogram, but this is not a necessary rule. The arguments of a subprogram may be different variable names than the ones used in referencing the subprogram. For example, the statement

```
TONE2 = WAVE(W, TIME, OVRTON)
```

of another program references the WAVE function, provided that the variables agree in mode and are dimensioned if necessary. In the above case, the value of the variable W are passed to PI2F of the subprogram, the value TIME goes to T, and the values of the array OVRTON is passed to the function's array HARMNC.

The function subprogram performs a loop that iterates once for each of the waveform's harmonics. The variable WVTEMP is initialized to zero and then is used as a storage location to which each harmonic is added as the loop is repeated 10 times. The final value is assigned to the function WAVE that is passed back to the main program and stored in the array TONE. Subprograms do not contain STOP statements, since they must transfer control back to the main program after they are finished. Consequently, the RETURN statement is used to accomplish the transfer. The END statement does not cause the computer to stop execution of the program. It is not an instruction at all, but is used to inform the compiler that it is the last statement of the program or subprogram.

```
      DIMENSION TONE(1000), HARMNC(10)
      READ 10, (HARMNC(I), I=1, 10)
10    FORMAT (10F8.4)
        .
        .          (body of main program)
        .
      FREQ = 440.0
      PI2F + 6.2831853 * FREQ
      TCHNGE = 1.0/30000.0
      T = 0.0
      DO 20 I = 1,1000
      TONE(I) = WAVE(PI2F, T, HARMNC)
20    T = T + TCHNGE
        .
        .          (program continues)
        .
      END
      FUNCTION WAVE(PI2F, T, HARMNC)
      DIMENSION HARMNC(10)
      WVTEMP = 0.0
      DO 1 J = 1, 10
1     WVTEMP = WVTEMP + HARMNC(j) * SIN(FLOAT(J)*PI2F*T)
      WAVE = WVTEMP
      RETURN
      END
```

Figure B.3 Passage of variables in subprogram.

Subroutines are implemented in much the same way as function subprograms. However, they do not define functions per se, and they may pass values in both directions through their argument list. Subroutines are accessed with a CALL statement, as shown in Fig. B.4.

When the subroutine is called by the main program, the variables A, B, and C have already been assigned values by the READ statement. But X,

Y, and Z have not yet been defined. As the subroutine is called and executed, the values of the main program variables A, B, and C are passed to the subroutine variables ENTR1, ENT2, and ENTR3. Then the subroutine calculates values for its variables OUT1, OUT2, and OUT3. When control returns back to the main program, their values are passed to the variables X, Y, and Z of the argument list. The main program can use these variables and their assigned values any time thereafter.

The final feature of FORTRAN that needs mentioning in this appendix has no relation to the computation or execution of a program, but is nonetheless important in its own right. No program is complete without explanatory comments by the programmer. Comments are entered in FORTRAN by typing a "C" in the first column of the line. Anything after

```
      READ 10, A, B, C
   10 FORMAT ...
          .
          .          (body of main program)
          .
      CALL SHLUTZ (A, B, C, X, Y, Z)
          .
          .          (program continues)
          .
      PRINT 20, X, Y, Z
   20 FORMAT ...
      STOP
      END
      SUBROUTINE SHLUTZ(ENTR1, ENTR2, ENTR3, OUT1, OUT2, OUT3)
          .
          .          (body of subroutine)
          .
      OUT1 = ...
      OUT2 = ...
      OUT3 = ...
      RETURN
      END
```

Figure B.4 Example of subroutine usage.

that is printed verbatim in the program listing but is ignored by the computer. It is generally advisable to use comment lines liberally, since they can be a significant aid in clarifying the logic of the program instructions for the benefit of others who may use the program or even for the programmer at a later time when the program is not fresh in his or her mind.

Although the presentation of FORTRAN in this appendix has been quite brief, it provides a sufficient introduction to the language to enable one to begin using it to program. Readers who undertake programming in FORTRAN require additional documentation that specifically describes their particular computer installation. It is often difficult, however, to learn programming skill from scratch by solely depending on a system manual. For this reason, this book has included a tutorial presentation of BASIC and FORTRAN to help the interested reader to begin.

Learning to program is a skill not unsimilar to learning orchestration or choral arranging—requiring the same kind of study, practice, and experience. Once a programmer-composer gains a measure of skill in utilizing the popular languages presented here, he or she has the tool to creatively employ the digital computer as a powerful musical instrument.

INDEX